FERTILITY AND SCARCITY
IN AMERICA

Fertility and Scarcity in America

PETER H. LINDERT

PRINCETON UNIVERSITY PRESS
PRINCETON, NEW JERSEY

Copyright © 1978 by Princeton University Press
Published by Princeton University Press, Princeton, New Jersey
In the United Kingdom: Princeton University Press, Guildford, Surrey

ALL RIGHTS RESERVED

Library of Congress Cataloging in Publication Data
will be found on the last printed page of this book

This book has been composed in Linotype Times Roman

Printed in the United States of America by
Princeton University Press, Princeton, New Jersey

Contents

PREFACE ix

PART I: OVERVIEW

CHAPTER 1. THE ISSUES 3

CHAPTER 2. THE ARGUMENT IN BRIEF 14
   I. Modelling Economic Influences on Fertility 14
   II. Reinterpreting Fertility Patterns 18
      A. The Cross-sectional Pattern 18
      B. The Modernization Pattern 20
      C. Postwar Fertility Waves 21
   III. The Effect of Fertility on Income Inequality 24
      A. Sibling Position and Sibling Inequality 25
      B. Fertility and the Supply of Public Schooling 27
      C. Fertility and the Overall Trend in Inequality 29
   IV. Does Inequality Feed Itself through Fertility? 32

PART II: ECONOMIC INFLUENCES ON FERTILITY

CHAPTER 3. REMODELLING THE HOUSEHOLD FOR FERTILITY ANALYSIS 37
   I. The Starting Point 37
   II. The Family's Planning Problem 43
   III. The Optimal Number of Certain Births 57
   IV. Imperfect Contraception and Birth Probabilities 61
   V. The Formation of Family Input Preferences 66
   VI. Fertility and Modernization 74
   VII. Fertility and Socioeconomic Mobility 81

CHAPTER 4. THE RELATIVE COST OF AMERICAN CHILDREN 83
   I. What a Measure of Relative Child Cost Can Accomplish 83
   II. Defining the Relative Cost 84
   III. Bedside Calculators? 87
   IV. The Relative Cost Formula 89
   V. Building the Index Base 98
      A. Time Inputs into Children 98
      B. Commodity Inputs into Children 102
      C. The Effect of Children on Work Time 110
      D. The Effect of Children on Family Commodity Purchases 121

CONTENTS

VI. Patterns Revealed by the Index	125
A. Class Differences in Relative Child Costs	132
B. Movements in Relative Child Costs over Time	133

CHAPTER 5. AMERICAN FERTILITY PATTERNS SINCE THE CIVIL WAR   137

  I. Introduction   137
  II. The Data   141
  III. Cross-Sectional Influences on Fertility and Marriage: An Overview   145
  IV. The Postwar Baby Boom and Bust   169
  V. The Not-So-Puzzling Twenties   173
  VI. The Steady Decline, 1860–1935   174
  VII. Conclusion   176

PART III: FROM FERTILITY TO INEQUALITY

CHAPTER 6. FERTILITY AND INVESTMENTS IN CHILDREN   181

  I. What Theory Suggests   181
  II. Family Size and Sibling Achievement   184
    A. The Problem of Omitted Variables   185
    B. The New Jersey Sibling Sample   187
    C. Achievement Patterns: Regression Results   190
    D. The Link with Family Input Patterns   198
  III. Birth Control and the Schooling of Smaller Families   207
  IV. Aggregate Fertility and Public School Inputs   209
  V. Conclusion   214

CHAPTER 7. FERTILITY, LABOR SUPPLY, AND INEQUALITY: THE MACROECONOMIC EVIDENCE   216

  I. Trends in American Inequality   217
    A. The Drift to Concentrated Wealth before the Civil War   219
    B. The Antebellum Surge of Wage Inequality   232
    C. The Uneven High Plateau of Inequality, 1860–1929   233
    D. The Leveling Era, 1929–51   234
    E. Postwar Stability   234
  II. The Correlation with Labor Force Growth   235
    A. Pay Ratios and the Growth of Labor Force Size   236
    B. Labor Force Quality Growth in the Twentieth Century   236
    C. Labor Force Quality Growth in the Nineteenth Century   242

III.	Competing Explanations	244
	A. Inflation and Equity	244
	B. Unions	246
	C. The Supply of Land	248
	D. Engel's Law and the Shift out of Agriculture	248
	E. Biases in Technological Progress	250
	F. The Rate of Capital Accumulation	253
	G. The Rise of Government	256
IV.	Conclusions	257

APPENDIXES

Appendix A.	The Job-Interruption Effect on Wage Rates as a Part of Child Cost	261
Appendix B.	The Work-Time Effects of Children in the Home: Regression Results	274
Appendix C.	Time Inputs into Siblings, 1967–68: Hypotheses and Estimates	285
Appendix D.	Net Effects of Children on Family Consumption Patterns, 1960–61 and 1889–90	322
Appendix E.	Total Child Costs and Child Inputs, 1960–61	346
Appendix F.	The Index of Relative Child Costs, 1900–70	374
Appendix G.	Selected Data Used in Regressions on State Child-Woman Ratios, 1900–70	381
Index		391

Preface

Teaching often breeds research, and the present book grew out of a series of lectures in economic history in which I attempted to survey the literature linking population growth and economic growth in the past. Those lectures were breezy and ambitious at first. They noted the likely mutual interaction between modern economic growth and the demographic transition, and veered off into a theme I felt deserved more attention: the seeming tendency of fertility and income inequality to feed each other.

Lecturing on these economic-demographic interactions soon showed me some of the glaring theoretical and empirical inadequacies of the existing literature. When drawing causal arrows from population growth to the economy, most authors casually assumed one or the other labor-supply effect. Some presumed that diminishing returns and substitution effects predominated, so that extra labor supply lowered capital per worker and output per capita. Others, especially when facing the postwar growth "miracles," felt that extra labor supply bid down wage rates and shifted income toward the accumulating classes enough to raise both capital per worker and output per capita. This threw the net effect of population growth on per capita income into doubt, and in doubt it remains. At the same time I came to feel that nobody had reflected carefully enough on just how child costs, whatever that meant, evolved with economic development and differed across income classes. In the background lay the nagging suspicion that these economic-demographic interactions should also be modelled in a way that had something to do with the price of land.

These dissatisfactions led to an overambitious research grant proposal on "Fertility, Land and Income Distribution." I proposed to develop a grand computer simulation model revealing the interactions among the variables advertised in the proposal of the title. The model would be about as large as the World I model of the Club of Rome group proved to be. It would be confronted with exhaustive empirical gleanings from the whole history of the United States and modern Britain and Japan. In passing I would set straight the whole confused literature on the welfare economics of having children. The proposal succeeded, apparently on sheer *chutzpah*.

The subsequent research process was one of reverting to a careful

PREFACE

treatment of theoretical and empirical issues that the proposal had assumed were already resolved. I quickly dropped the grand simulation model, a step I have never regretted. Britain and Japan dropped by the wayside as it became clear that only the United States would easily yield the underlying empirical tests. The price of land became something to be documented and explained in its own right, and could not be pursued as a fertility determinant at any length. The work on land scarcity became a separate article in the 1974 *Journal of Economic History*, with only slight links to the rest of the research. Instead of neatly picking an influence of income inequality on aggregate fertility out of a well-established fertility literature, I found myself retreating to rethinking basic unresolved questions about how incomes and relative prices really affected fertility. At the same time, the empirical link from fertility to inequality of human capital and of income proved more fascinating at the microeconomic level than I had realized. The result was an unanticipated exploration into the interior of the household, to quantify how an extra child related to the allocation of time and goods and to subsequent child achievement.

It remains for future research to follow more leads given in my original research plan. The rethinking of the concept of relative child costs in Chapter 4 here is being extended, at last, to developing nations in a Universities-NBER paper on "Child Costs and Economic Development." The tests of the relative-income hypothesis in Chapter 5 should be extended to other countries. And the asserted link between population growth and income inequality is leading into a larger project on the macroeconomic determinants of inequality trends in several countries, to be conducted with Jeffrey G. Williamson. True to earlier form, this project has begun by answering a question I had earlier thought was answered by past literature: what really were the trends in income inequality in the U.S., Britain, and other countries?

The present book reflects generous inputs of funding and effort from others. Two agencies gambled on the proposal at the outset: The Population Council, with grant D72.64A and an earlier summer grant; and the Rockefeller Foundation, through Grant RF72017 in the Ford-Rockefeller program on Law and Population Policy. When more was needed, the Institute for Research on Poverty (backed by the Office of Economic Opportunity) and the Graduate School of the University of Wisconsin came to the rescue.

As the inquiry became more microeconomic and empirical, I was able to benefit from generous help in the acquisition and processing of survey and other data. Three scholars generously supplied computer-ready data banks. Professor Kathryn Walker of the College of Human Ecology at Cornell made available the uniquely detailed Cornell Time Use Survey data gathered in Syracuse in 1967–68, used in Chapters 4 and 6 and Appendix C. Professor Allen C. Kelley of Duke, along with his research assistant Glenn Worroch, delivered the computer tape of the 1889–90 industrial worker survey, used in Chapter 4 and Appendix B. Professor Albert I. Hermalin of Michigan supplied cards and codes for the New Jersey sample of siblings, used in Chapter 6. These data sets were processed according to my labor-intensive specifications by three expert programmers at Wisconsin: John T. Soper, Nancy Williamson, and Leo DeBever. I am deeply indebted to these people, as well as to my research assistants. Rebecca Maynard labored through the early rounds of child-cost calculations, which proved convincingly that no young couple would ever make such calculations before deciding whether or not to have a child. Patricia Lipton continued the same elaborate child-cost arithmetic, while also contributing immense labor to computer programming and the gathering of further historical data. Research help was also generously given by Moses S. Musoke, Robert Gitter, and J. Scott Winningham.

I wish also to acknowledge the helpful comments and criticisms given on earlier drafts by, among others, Duane E. Ball, James Cramer, Phillips Cutright, Richard A. Easterlin, Elizabeth Hoffman, Ronald D. Lee, Arleen Leibowitz, Warren Sanderson, Theodore W. Schultz, Julian Simon, Alan Sweezy, Boone A. Turchi, Jeffrey G. Williamson, and seminar participants at the Universities of Michigan, Pennsylvania, and Wisconsin.

Most books, I suspect, are written by families and not by individuals. This one benefited from the last-minute help in drafting figures given by my father-in-law, Frank D. White. It benefited, above all, from the support and preseverance of my wife Lin, to whom it is dedicated.

University of California, Davis
and
University of Wisconsin, Madison

Part I:

OVERVIEW

Chapter 1. The Issues

Since before Malthus, scholars have maintained a strong interest in both sides of the circle joining human fertility with the economy. The intuition persists that higher fertility, and population growth in general, must make natural resources more scarce and reduce material living standards, even though the data have not yet confirmed this pessimistic view. Scholars have also been recurrently fascinated by the possibility that economic forces may help us explain movements in fertility itself. This book takes up both kinds of issues. It seeks to redirect our concern over the economic consequences of higher fertility and population growth toward more emphasis on their tendency to heighten economic inequalities. It also seeks to improve upon our knowledge of how economic developments affect fertility.

There are reasons to be concerned about the economic implications of bringing extra babies into the world, but there is also reason to believe that the scholarship on this issue has not yet succeeded in resolving which reasons for caring are most compelling. Population growth has been suspected of (1) lowering aggregate income per capita, (2) making natural resources more scarce, (3) lowering environmental quality, and (4) making incomes more unequally distributed. The first of these concerns deserves less emphasis than it has received, while the last deserves more.

To be a proper object of social concern, extra births must have clear negative effects on the well-being of persons outside the individual family having the extra children. It must also be shown that these negative effects outweigh other positive effects that transcend the family. If the social costs of an extra child are borne only by his parents and older siblings, the extra birth is the family's business and not society's.

This simple welfare rule of thumb is one that has not been well heeded by past attempts to show that extra births reduce income per capita. An extra child may lower income per capita without harming anyone. Income per family member is almost sure to be reduced by the arrival of an extra child. The child is an extra mouth to feed, an extra "capita" in the ratio of income per capita, and this almost invariably outweighs his net contribution to family income, even in less-developed settings in which a child gives more work value to his parents' household than he detracts from the earnings of other family members. The extra child might reduce national income per capita only to the extent that he reduces income per capita within his own family. A voluntary decision to have an extra child may thus have no more serious social implications than a voluntary decision to retire from the labor force and enjoy more leisure time. Both decisions lower aggregate income per capita, yet this effect on income per capita is a weak basis for urging that society discourage such private activities.

The concern over the effects of fertility on income per capita has been misdirected for other reasons as well. Superficial looks at international cross sections have failed to reveal the expected negative relationship between the rate of population growth and the rate of growth of national product per capita.[1] It could be argued that these glances at cross sections are not a fair test of the proposition that population growth drags down the rate of growth of income per capita. It seems more useful, however, to take these simple results as another clue that to establish the economic case for restricting fertility, one must look beyond income per capita.

The absence of a simple correlation between population growth and income-per-capita growth suggests that increases in population have not pressed so relentlessly against nonrenewable natural resources as intuition and David Ricardo have said. A little reflection confirms that population growth need not constrain economic growth by making natural resources more scarce. Population growth does not affect all sectors of the economy proportionally, nor do all sectors use natural resources in the same proportion. It might be the case that population growth causes a shift in resources away from the sectors that use natural resources most heavily. This possibility deserves to be explored, the more so since there has been no long-run historical trend toward higher relative prices for most natural resource products. Such a re-examination of the link between population and natural resource scarcity would require a book in itself, and is not attempted here.

The lack of a clear effect of population growth on income per capita

---

[1] See Alfred Sauvy, "Les charges économiques et les avantages de la croissance de la population," *Population* 27 (January–February 1972), 9–26; J. C. Chesnais and Alfred Sauvy, "Progrès économique et accroissement de la population: une expérience commentée," *Population* 28 (July–October 1973), 843–857; Simon Kuznets, "Population and Economic Growth," *Proceedings of the American Philosophical Society* 3 (June 1967), 170–193; and Richard A. Easterlin, "Population," in Neil W. Chamberlain, ed., *Contemporary Economic Issues*, Homewood, Ill.: Richard D. Irwin, 1973, pp. 346–348.

also suggests other ways of redirecting the inquiry into the economic case for discouraging births. First, any further investigation of the effect on aggregate living standards ought to drop income per capita in favor of (full-time) income *per lifetime* as a welfare proxy. We care about the length of life as well as income per year. Attention should be given to the strong possibility that extra births may reduce life expectancy by spreading infectious diseases and by lowering living standards and disease resistance in poor families, thus burying those whose welfare losses are hidden from the measurement of national income per living person per year.

More important than this adjustment of the old income-per-person yardstick is the pursuit of two sets of potential "externalities," or "spillover" effects, of extra fertility that are missed by any ordinary measure of income per person. One set consists of the environmental externalities imposed on others through pollution and congestion. The other consists of externalities transmitted through the effects of extra births upon the distribution of income. Extra children may on balance raise social tensions and cries of injustice by transferring income from less fertile to more fertile households, or from poor to rich. Persons who care about such redistributions of income may bear external costs from fertility increases, or receive external benefits from fertility reduction.

Both sets of externalities deserve further exploration. In recent years the concern over population externalities has focused almost exclusively on the environmental effects. Some of the environmental externalities from population growth appear to have received more than their share of emphasis. To be sure, the average extra child would tend to pollute and crowd the world a bit if nothing were done to check this influence. But there is no reason to work on restricting fertility while leaving other things equal. As other authors have pointed out, restricting human numbers is a grossly inefficient way of combating most kinds of pollution.[2] Direct disincentives to engage in the polluting activity itself are much more efficient. The importance of emphasizing the environmental externalities is also often limited by a failure of the locus of the problem to correspond to the locus of extra population growth. Pollution, for example, seems to impose much higher psychic costs on higher-income

[2] E.g., Edmund S. Phelps, "Population Increase," *Canadian Journal of Economics* 1 (August 1968), 510–511; and Glen G. Cain, "Issues in the Economics of a Population Policy for the United States," *American Economic Review* 61 (May 1971), 410.

countries than on lower-income countries, which are not willing to give up much economic development at all to reduce pollution. The demand for clean air and clean water is highly income-sensitive. It seems, on the other hand, as though significant further reductions in the rate of population growth in higher-income countries are unlikely now that the rate has tapered off toward zero. There is reason to think that policy could make major reductions in the rate of population growth only in countries now characterized by rapid population growth, the very countries in which policy-makers place the lowest values on the quality of ambient environments.

This is not to say that all of the environmental externalities from population growth have been overemphasized. There is prima facie evidence that population growth imposes congestion costs and changes global climate in ways that are hard to offset completely without attacking population growth itself. It may be, for example, that all sorts of basic human activity, such as breathing, burning fuel, and cultivating dry lands, have the effect of shifting the monsoons dangerously toward the equator, bringing sustained drought to the populous monsoon zone stretching from Sahelian Africa through Northern India to the Philippines.[3] Such possible congestion and climatic effects may prove very serious. Not enough is yet known about such effects. They fully deserve the attention they are receiving. They cannot be pursued here, however.

The possibility that higher fertility and population growth may make incomes more unequally distributed has received relatively little attention.[4] The possibility that rapid population growth may depress wage

[3] See Reid A. Bryson, "World Food Prospects and Climatic Change," testimony before the joint meeting of the Senate Subcommittee on Foreign Agricultural Policy and Subcommittee on Agricultural Production, Marketing, and Stabilization of Prices, October 18, 1973, and the sources cited there.

[4] The most notable recent exceptions are J. E. Meade, "Population Explosion, the Standard of Living, and Social Conflict," *Economic Journal* 77 (June 1967), 233–255; Herman E. Daly, "A Marxian-Malthusian View of Population and Development," *Population Studies* 25 (March 1971), 25–37; T. Paul Schultz, "An Economic Perspective on Population Growth," in Roger Revelle, ed., *Rapid Population Growth*, Baltimore: The Johns Hopkins Press, 1971, p. 159; Neil W. Chamberlain, *Beyond Malthus: Population and Power*, New York, 1970, Chap. 7; Robert Repetto, "The Relationship of the Size Distribution of Income to Fertility and the Implications for Development Policy," Harvard University Center for Population Studies, Research Paper no. 3 (March 1974; revised, fall 1974); Hollis Chenery et al., *Redistribution with Growth*, London: Oxford University Press, 1974, Chaps. 1, 2, 11; and James Kocher, *Rural Development, Income Distribution, and Fertility Decline*, New York: Population Council, 1973.

Among the recent studies expressing concern over population growth that have

rates is frequently mentioned and then dropped. This is curious in view of the fact that concern over the income distribution remains widespread. The degree of inequality in personal purchasing power is a public good, one that different people value differently. It is an aggregate outcome, possessing the two properties that define a public good: "nonexhaustion" (my enjoyment of the degree of equality of incomes does not keep you from enjoying or disliking it) and "nonexclusion" (once it is available, it is available for us all). If population growth tends to heighten inequalities, it has a subjective cost that can be very important even if not easily measured. If there is a strong link between extra fertility and inequality, then extra fertility has an external cost which society should consider shifting to young couples with measures discouraging larger families.[5]

If there seems to be a case for worrying about a fertility-inequality link in a high-income country, there is an even stronger case in the low-income countries, which tend to have higher income inequality,[6] higher fertility, and more rapid population growth. In many such countries a link between fertility and inequality would be a link between fertility and death. It may be that the high fertility of low-income countries causes millions of deaths each year—again, without noticeably reducing in-

---

not even mentioned a link to inequality are: U.S. Commission on Population Growth and the American Future, *Population and the American Future*, New York, 1972, and the research report volumes of the same commission that deal with the economic effects of population growth; Ansley J. Coale and Edgar M. Hoover, *Population Growth and Economic Development in Low-Income Countries*, Princeton, 1958; Paul R. Erlich, *The Population Bomb*, New York, 1968; Gunnar Myrdal, *Asian Drama: An Inquiry into the Poverty of Nations*, New York, 1968; and Donella H. Meadows et al., *The Limits to Growth*, New York, 1972.

[5] Strictly speaking, a tendency of population growth to make income inequality greater than most members of society wish is not sufficient basis for policies to restrict births, since society could treat the problem of inequality directly by shifting transfers in such a way as to offset any tendencies to redistribute income away from the optimum. The process of enacting legislation to redistribute income through transfers, however, has its own social costs. Social tensions mount and large amounts of energy and funds are spent on lobbying for and against any overt redistribution. It seems likely that over the generations substantial income leveling could be achieved with antinatal policies of various types with little social cost of policy enactment.

[6] Felix Paukert, "Income Distribution at Different Levels of Development: A Survey of Evidence," *International Labour Review* 108 (August–September 1973), Table 6; and Hollis Chenery, Montek S. Ahluwalia et al., *Redistribution with Growth*, Table I.1 (1974), Table 6.

come per capita per year. The exploration of this issue in Chapters 6 and 7 below reflects and supports this very suspicion about the importance of fertility restriction in low-income countries. It just so happens that the issue is best pursued here by following the better-documented American experience, one which tells a pessimistic story about low-income countries in mirror image, by linking the decline in American population growth to the twentieth-century decline in American inequality.

There are many plausible theoretical reasons for suspecting that higher fertility will lead to greater inequality of income, and that reducing fertility will equalize incomes. Some of these are microeconomic in the sense that they are theories about how changes in fertility affect the distribution of individuals' economic endowments within a fixed set of wage rates and rates of return on property. Another relates to the supply of school support from governments and nonprofit agencies. Still others are theories about the macroeconomic effects of fertility on rates of pay. Let us review these arguments, expressing each as reasons why fertility *reduction* might *equalize* incomes.

There are, first, two relatively subtle microeconomic reasons for believing that fertility reduction would level incomes:

(1) A reduction in fertility lowers the dispersion of family sizes, since birth restriction typically reduces the number of children born into very large families by a greater percentage than it reduces the number of first-born and second-born children. Since larger family size seems like a factor that should retard the development of earning capacity in individual children, the reduction in family size differences ought to reduce later earnings inequality.

(2) Since about 1910, birth restriction in the U.S. has on balance reduced the share of children born into poor and less-educated families. The same should be true of birth restrictions from 1970 into the future, since surveys have found that in the 1960s unwanted births were still a greater share of total births among the poor. Birth restriction should thus tend to lower income inequality by cutting down on the share of children born into the extreme disadvantage of being unwanted members of large low-income families.

Both of these arguments hinge on the view that extra children strain family economic and emotional energies.

One might also suspect that reductions in fertility ease the strain on the public and philanthropic supply of resources for schools, uplifting and leveling the earning power of each generation of children:

(3) If the total amount of philanthropic and taxpayer support for schooling is characterized by inertia, then the strain on school systems should be directly related to the share of the population that is of school age. Reducing births may reduce the ratio of children to adults more than it reduces public (and philanthropic) school expenditures per adult, so that the smaller cohort of school-age children enjoys greater public educational outlays per child. To the extent that this public-support effect is more relevant below college than it is for public funding of higher education, the extra public expenditures per child should help the most disadvantaged children the most. This should reduce inequalities of schooling and income.

This presumption may not be shared by all. One could easily imagine that the effect of fertility decline is exactly the opposite. It is possible that fertility decline would actually *reduce* public support *per child* for lower-level schooling and for education in general, by reducing the share of voters directly concerned about school quality. Fertility reduction, in other words, might spark a taxpayer revolt, in which currently childless taxpayers demand so much relief that school inputs drop even faster than the number of children. This same argument about the relative voting power of parents would predict that a baby boom would subsequently raise school support per child. Probably more people share the "strain on public schools" belief [(3) above] than believe in this voting-power hypothesis. The matter of which argument makes more sense is an empirical question addressed briefly in Chapter 6 below [which finds evidence in favor of (3) and against the competing hypothesis].

There are also several macroeconomic reasons for believing in a long-run link between fertility and inequality. Since Malthus and earlier, many observers have believed that population growth depresses wage rates by supplying more workers. This belief seems to have been Malthus' main economic reason for being convinced that poor relief, which he felt would breed larger families, would create even more poverty.[7]

---

[7] Thomas Robert Malthus, *An Essay on the Principle of Population* . . . , London, 1798, Chap. 5. There is certainly reason to question whether poor relief significantly raised the fertility of the poor even in Malthus' time. See James P. Huzel, "Malthus, the Poor Law, and Population in Early Nineteenth-Century England," *Economic History Review*, 2d ser. 22 (December 1969).

Similar concern about the link between fertility and wage rates has at times been voiced by friends of labor and of business. In early nineteenth-century England, Francis Place, a birth control propagandist born into the working class, distributed handbills "To the Married of Both Sexes of the Working People," urging them to restrict births for the sake of future wages:

> By limiting the number of children, the wages both of children and of grown up persons will rise; the hours of working will be no more than they ought to be; you will have some time for recreation, some means as well as some time for your own and your children's moral and religious instruction."[8]

On the other side of the wage bargain, it was apparently business concern over the future of labor costs that recently caused Japan's former Prime Minister Eisaku Sato and Japan's Population Problems Inquiry Council to urge a crowded Japan to *raise* its fertility.[9]

A little reflection suggests that this basic argument can be divided in two:

(4) A drop in fertility would mean fewer labor-force entrants a generation later. This in turn should accelerate the rise of all employee wage rates—skilled and unskilled—relative to profit rates and to rates of return on property. Since the ownership of property is almost always distributed less equally than is human earning power, a rise in employee wage rates relative to rates of return for property holders and profit recipients makes income more equally distributed.

(5) Among employees, the reduced dispersion, and higher average level, of skills caused by the microeconomic effects of birth reduction [see (1) and (2) above] should further reduce inequality of earnings by bidding down the premia earned by higher-paid employees. That is, fertility reduction should raise the wage rates of unskilled labor more than it raises skilled wage rates. The same result is reinforced by the fact that lower fertility leads to an older, better-paid, and more experienced labor force.

---

[8] Francis Place, "To the Married of Both Sexes of the Working People," handbill, London, 1823, reprinted in Norman E. Himes, *The Medical History of Contraception*, New York, 1963, pp. 216–217. Place (earlier) fathered fifteen children, five of whom died at birth.

[9] Philip M. Boffey, "Japan: A Crowded Nation Wants To Boost Its Birthrate," *Science* 167 (February 13, 1970), 960–962.

Some other, more subtle, macroeconomic arguments relate to the presumed effect of fertility change on the demand for final products. It seems likely that lower fertility, by creating fewer mouths to feed, would reduce the relative importance of food in household budgets. This suggests that a decline in fertility should tend to have three demand side effects on overall inequality:

(6) By shifting demand away from agricultural products, reductions in fertility may lower the relative price of these products. This would tend to reduce inequalities in real purchasing power to the extent that agricultural products are a greater share of the cost of living of poor families than of rich.

(7) The same demand shift would cause a shift of labor and capital out of agriculture, in proportions that would reduce the farm sector's share of total labor employment more noticeably than its share of total capital employment would be reduced. This shift of low-paid labor out of agriculture into what will tend to be higher-paid jobs elsewhere should reduce inequality somewhat, farm labor being among the lowest paid in most countries.

(8) On the other hand, the shift in demand away from agriculture is a shift toward sectors that use low-paid labor less intensively. This might weaken the relative pay position of unskilled laborers somewhat, causing a counter-tendency toward inequality.

These three demand effects of fertility decline are each presumably of less magnitude than the two basic macroeconomic effects [(4) and (5) above], which are supposed to operate through labor supply. The net demand effect is also not likely to be large, since the last demand effect pulls in the opposite direction from the first two.

Theory thus predicts a fertility-inequality link that should be of concern to a population that cares about income inequality. If the theory is correct, there is a case for restricting fertility on income-distribution grounds. The theory needs to be tested against the facts. Chapter 6 tests the microeconomic argument about family size and inequality in detail. Chapter 7 compares the presumption of theory to the overall behavior of the American economy. This later section of the book finds ample support for the belief that fertility is a major determinant of overall inequality.

If there is good reason to go on believing that fertility reduction could enhance aggregate well-being, there is reason to want a solid basis for predicting fertility and its response to changing conditions. Such a basis is currently lacking. The study of fertility has produced many puzzles to date, and the role of economic development in determining fertility has proven particularly uncertain and controversial. On many fronts, what seem at first like clear truths about the economics of fertility turn murky upon a closer look. Take, for example, the well-known fact that as a nation modernizes its fertility undergoes a sustained decline, one that more than offsets whatever rises in fertility there may be in the early stage of modernization. We can all list the obvious sources of that fertility decline: education, urbanization, access to contraception, and "consumption aspirations" all rise with modernization, while the level of infant mortality falls. We have not yet resolved the relative importance of these factors, nor have we agreed upon a theory of why they should have affected fertility as they did. More serious, however, is another unanswered question: Why should these aspects of modernization have caused a net *decline* in fertility? Modernization brings more income along with changed attitudes. Why could not the later, more modern generations enjoy higher education, urban living, better contraceptive information, lower infant mortality, and higher consumption levels with the *same* average number of children per family as their ancestors had? There is no obvious reason why modernization should shift tastes away from childbearing more strongly than it raises the resources with which families could support children. Yet fertility declined with modernization in country after country, both under capitalism and under communism.

The same gap in our understanding arises in connection with the prevalence of a negative cross-sectional relationship between fertility and "status" or modernization variables. Within a generational cohort as well as across the generations, fertility is lower for the more educated, the more urban, the rich, and so forth. Why do the upper-status groups have fewer children on the average, instead of meeting their higher consumption standards with their higher incomes, while having the same average family size?

The economic side of fertility behavior has become even more complex as authors have tangled with some recent time-series patterns. It has seemed to some authors as though fertility responded positively to income gains in the upswing of the business cycle. The same positive relationship to income suggested itself even more strongly when the economic boom during and after World War II produced the famous baby boom in North America and to a lesser extent in other high-income countries. These patterns underlined the puzzling nature of the relationship of economic growth and modernization to fertility. If over the long haul and in cross sections modernization cuts fertility, why should the rapid rise in education, urbanization, and incomes set in motion by World War II have raised fertility? Prodded by the complexity of the income-fertility relationship, economists re-examined their own models and pointed out that the relationship should indeed be complex. Increases in income, education, and related variables affected not only family resources but also the cost of children, with no clear net outcome. To date, however, the economic side of fertility remains unresolved, the more so since nobody has yet spelled out what is meant by the "cost of children." Cost of *what kind* of child—pampered or neglected, high-income or low-income, first-born or fifth-born, male or female? And cost relative to *what alternative* to having the child?

Chapters 3 through 5 of this book re-explore the economic determinants of fertility in an attempt to clear up some of these basic uncertainties. Chapter 3 presents a theoretical model of fertility behavior designed to clarify the murky concepts of "income," "relative child costs," and "tastes" that a theory of choice brings to bear on the issue of fertility. Chapter 3 also offers a theory of taste formation which seems capable of resolving many observed fertility patterns. Chapter 4 treats the concept of relative child cost in more detail, quantifying it and examining how it has changed in America since the nineteenth century. Chapter 5 builds on this foundation and tests the reasoning of Chapter 3 against the aggregate fertility patterns of America since the Civil War.

Chapter 2. The Argument in Brief

The interactions between fertility and the economy are complex enough that any useful reinterpretation of them requires careful statements of both theory and evidence. For this reason the chapters and appendixes that follow are somewhat detailed. It is therefore helpful to survey the entire set of arguments and findings at the outset.

I. *Modelling Economic Influences on Fertility*

Used with care, a model reinterpreting the economic part of fertility behavior is capable of resolving many of the puzzles relating to past fertility patterns. Chapter 3 develops a model of couples' short-run fertility regulation. Though the model emphasizes short-run birth probabilities, it is also useful for analyzing completed cohort fertility. The model reexamines the three classic parameters of a theory of household choice: income, prices, and tastes. The income parameter needs only a slight redefinition to be used in analyzing fertility: to be a parameter, income must refer to a couple's lifetime purchasing power for given numbers and ages of their children. More extensive work needs to be done on the price and taste parameters.

The concept of the price, or the relative cost, of having another child is familiar yet undefined. It is "well known" that children "cost more" in higher-status families or in more modern societies, yet it is hard to see a correspondence between what is meant by cost here and what theories of household choice usually mean by relative cost or relative price. Is the cost of an extra child the value of time and commodity inputs devoted to that child, or the value of the time and commodities the couple would devote to other activities if they did not have the child? The two magnitudes are not the same, since having the child affects the family's earning power and the amount of taxes it pays. Two other unanswered questions are even more bothersome: To what kind of child does the "cost" refer? And cost relative to what? To say that a child "costs" more in one setting than in another is to say that a *given set of child inputs*, a given way of raising a child, costs more in the first setting. The fact that higher-status families devote more commodities to a child does not mean that a given way of rearing a child costs them more, any more than their higher grocery bills mean that they pay higher prices for food. It may mean only that they choose a different *kind* of child. Further, child cost can be analogous to the relative prices used in theories of household

[14]

choice only if it is indeed an index of relative cost rather than an absolute cost. The dollar magnitude of the cost of child inputs by itself mixes quality with unit price. Yet if we are to compare the cost of a given set of child inputs to the cost of some other bundle of commodities and time, what is this other bundle? How do we know what goes into the alternative to having another child?

These problems of defining and measuring relative child cost are briefly introduced in Chapter 3 and treated at length in Chapter 4. They are not insoluble. The average inputs of both time and commodities that go into a child can be roughly measured for a given income class and birth order. Chapter 4 and Appendixes A through E tote up the absolute dollar costs of first-born and third-born children in certain "low-income" and "high-income" urban families in 1960. The estimates come from regressions on (a) the commodity consumption patterns in the 1960–61 Survey of Consumer Expenditures and (b) the patterns of family time use in the Cornell time use survey of 1,296 families in Syracuse in 1967–68. It is even possible to estimate what commodities and time would go into the extra life activities a family would enjoy without the extra child. Once one has already estimated what inputs seemed to go into the child, the trick is to use cross-sectional regressions to determine how the child affects total family time and commodity expenditures. By subtracting the amount of time that the child seems to make other family members spend at home from the estimated total time spent on the child, one gets a rough idea of what time inputs would have gone into other activities without the child. Similarly, one can add the inputs of a commodity such as food consumed by the child to the net change in family food consumption caused by the child to arrive at an estimate of the total extra food other family members would have consumed without the child. The estimation procedure is of course rough, but it is put to use in a way that leans only on its firmer numbers, the estimates of the net effects of an extra child on total family outlays. The procedure yields two bundles of time and commodity inputs, those going into the child and those going into the activities with which the child competes. By following the ratio of the prices of these two bundles across time and classes, one gains insights into how relative child costs have been changing.

In the process of quantifying relative child costs, Chapter 4 documents a number of patterns in the economic role of children since the late nineteenth century. Some of these roles have been changing, while others have remained the same.

The effect of an extra child on family time use and paid work has been

OVERVIEW

changing in a way relevant to fertility behavior. In the late nineteenth century both urban and farm children, especially those who were not first-borns, gave the family a greater value of work time, both at home and for pay outside the home, than their rearing took from the paid work of parents and older brothers and sisters. This was especially true on farms, where children contributed heavily to housework and farm work, while having little effect on the ability of others to do their work. As incomes and education rose, children performed less and less work while living in their parents' household. With rising skill requirements, the economy found less use for relatively unskilled child labor. Parents also demanded more and more schooling for their children, a demand reflected in laws compelling schooling and limiting child labor. Meanwhile wives came to work more for pay outside the home. Since work outside the home conflicts more seriously with childrearing than work at home or around the farm, the impact of an extra child on the mother's paid work has grown considerably between the first decade of this century and the Korean War. By World War II, an extra urban child had clearly become "time-intensive" in the sense that he raised the total amount of time that other family members spent at home, by supplying less value of help with chores and paid work than he took away from others' paid work. Now that urban children have become time-intensive, increases in wage rates raise the relative cost of urban children. That is, increases in wage rates now raise the cost of a given set of urban child inputs by a greater percentage than they raise the cost of the apparent alternatives to a child. Before World War I, by contrast, wage rate increases may have lowered the relative cost of urban children, who then supplied more work than they cost other family members. As for farm children, their transition to time-intensive status was still incomplete by the mid-1960s. There is no great difference between the value of time an extra farm child contributes and the time he takes from the paid work of others.

The net impact of an extra child on family consumption patterns has changed little, despite obvious changes in what families buy for children or for other things. As incomes have risen, both the inputs into an extra child and the inputs into other things have conformed to the classic shift away from staples and toward luxuries. Families have shifted from cheaper to more expensive foods, and away from all foods to such income-elastic demands as recreation, education, and consumer durables. Yet a host of cross-sectional household surveys from the late-nineteenth and twentieth centuries reveal no change in the *net* percentage impacts of an extra child. An extra child, like a drop in family income, causes a shift in family expenditures back toward staples and away from luxuries. Children have apparently always been "food-intensive" in the sense that they raise the share of food in family budgets. The estimates suggest that this effect is a strong one. This means that fertility effects the relative demand for agricultural products, a point to which we return below. It also means that whatever raises the price of food products relative to the prices of luxury commodities raises the relative cost of children.

Taxes, like wage rates and food prices, are capable of shifting the relative cost of children. There is one episode in which changes in taxation have noticeably affected relative child costs. The prosperity and inflation of World War II brought over half of the families in the United States into the ranks of income-tax payers for the first time. Before 1941 the share of the population covered by returns paying income tax had never reached 10 percent. During and after the war a majority of families were subject not only to income taxes but also to the annual exemption per dependent. The calculations reported in Appendix F and Chapter 4 reveal that the onset of the exemption per dependent actually lowered relative child costs quite significantly between 1940 and 1945. In no other period have changes in taxes had any apparent effect on child costs.

The measurement of relative child costs is one contribution offered by the present study for the analysis of the economics of fertility. How important the index of relative child costs is in determining fertility behavior is an empirical question on which some initial light is shed in Chapter 5. Its relevance cannot be dismissed on the prejudice that a measurement so complicated and unfamiliar could not affect the behavior of young couples. As is argued in Chapter 4, it is not implausible to believe that couples could respond to the child cost implications of wage rates, tax rates, food prices, and the like, even though they are almost never aware of these implications. Young couples and those whose actions and opinions affect them are at least dimly aware of what they can afford. This simple fact means that whatever affects the actual relative cost of an extra child has a good chance of affecting the perceived cost as well. To repeat, the relevance of the relative cost measure is an empirical question.

The other restructuring of the basis theory of household choice for fertility analysis consists of a simple and incomplete yet powerful theory of taste formation. To understand fertility patterns it seems important to attribute a strong influence to the history of inputs per person in the families in which each generation of young couples was raised. It is hypothesized (in Chapter 3, Section V) that young couples retain a tendency to pattern their choices of life activities after the experiences of their original families, even in mid–twentieth century, when life styles seemed to contrast sharply across the generations. In deciding how to divide their time, energy, and funds among life activities, couples cannot reason out solutions from abstract principles and current stimuli alone. Typically, and often unconsciously, they economize on information costs by reverting to familiar paths. In patterning their lives in ways tied to (but not identical to) family history, they retain, I shall argue, a stronger sense of life styles per family member, and inputs of time and commodities per family member, than of how large a family should be. What they retain, furthermore, is a pattern of preferences, the roots of which extend further back than their personal memory. The advice and examples to which young couples respond are conditioned by their parents' views and their parents' choices of residence and social contacts. In this way, young couples' impressions about what they and their children should have or do or expect are based in part on a generation or more of family experience.

The impressions that young couples retain from past experiences are not impressions measured in dollars and cents or in hours spent. The impressions are rather a vast array of qualitative "needs" and rules of thumb for running a happy family. These impressions nonetheless carry real resource costs in time and money, so much so that it is hypothesized that they behave as if a major influence on their current family plans is the constant-dollar value of prior inputs per family member in their parents' households. The higher this value of prior inputs per person, other things equal, the more the young couple will feel pressure to limit family size to allow themselves the adult enjoyments and each child the inputs they feel necessary.

II. *Reinterpreting Fertility Patterns*

This hypothesis about prior inputs, along with the information about patterns of relative child cost, allows one to link up parts of the puzzle of modern fertility patterns.

A. THE CROSS-SECTIONAL PATTERN

One pattern that can now be made less puzzling is the generality of the negative fertility-status relationship in cross sections. The prior inputs hypothesis contains what seems to be the best single explanation (though not the only one) of why such a negative relationship should prevail in modern times. Part of this explanation is an argument about diminishing human returns. There seem to be diminishing cross-sectional economic returns to inputs into human enjoyment and development. That is, persons who have received twice as great a value of time and commodity inputs as another group of persons will *not* have incomes twice as high on the average. This seems to follow from the fact that extra time and commodity inputs into the personal development of a child must be combined with a "fixed" input: the child's own physical makeup and life expectancy. Beyond some point extra inputs into a child begin to raise his economic potential by smaller and smaller percentages, because both his life expectancy and his ability to absorb extra skills are limited. In cross sections life expectancy, and the adult period over which one receives earnings from any extra training, is not enough greater for higher-status individuals than for lower-status individuals to offset this tendency for the rate of return to drop with extra training. The diminishing-returns tendency is likely to be characteristic of modern societies, in which the input advantage of high-status individuals consists more of extra human earning power than of extra nonhuman property income. This tendency implies smaller family size for higher-status couples. Having experienced prior inputs per person that are higher by a greater percentage than their current family income advantage, they feel pressure to have smaller families to guarantee the life styles they want.

The prevalence of a negative fertility-status relationship is further explained by another link between prior inputs, income, and tastes. There is a social selectivity mechanism that sorts families somewhat on the basis of their individual tastes regarding mobility and family size. Tastes are partly random, and some people will have stronger preferences for high inputs per person and smaller family size than others raised similarly. Part of their higher inputs per person will tend to be higher investments in their own careers (especially that of the wife), raising their relative status while they have fewer children. Thus there would always be some vague tendency for families choosing to have fewer children to rise in status over others with similar upbringing, even if there were not diminishing private economic returns to investments in humans.

These effects operating through differences in personal inputs and incomes seem more basic to the prevalence of the negative fertility-status profile than some other arguments that one might think of more readily. The argument that higher-status couples have fewer children in modern societies because they have better access to the means of birth prevention seems to account for little. Their better access, and their better contraceptive efficiency, seem to be not independent explanations but rather symptoms of their greater motivation to restrict births. Feeling the pressures just described, they invest more in finding out about, and in practicing, birth control. The relative cost argument also seems to play less role in explaining cross-sectional fertility differences than does the above argument about prior inputs. The negative fertility-status relationship shows up in many contexts in which it is doubtful whether the relative cost of a particular set of child inputs is higher for higher-status couples. In nineteenth-century urban America, for example, the relative cost of any "kind" of child probably did not differ across classes. As already noted, urban children were not time-intensive then, so that the higher wage rates of higher-status husbands and wives did not raise the relative cost of a given way of raising a child. While the relative cost argument would seem to account for some of the class fertility differential in the postwar period, and for part of the rural-urban differential, it cannot do so in many cases in which higher-status couples had a much lower average fertility than lower-status couples.

B. THE MODERNIZATION PATTERN

The fact that aggregate fertility declines as a nation modernizes also is more easily explained with the help of the arguments presented here than without them. For the modernization trend, however, more emphasis should be placed on the movement of relative child costs than on the dynamics of prior inputs and current income. With modernization, the luxury goods with which extra children compete become cheaper relative to food. This is true even though historical price series fail to confirm that food rises much in relative price. The historical price series measure prices at fixed locations and for fixed states of consumer information. Modernization, however, brings people from remote areas to urban centers, and urban information to remote areas. For the urbanizing families the absolute price of food rises. For all families the true price of luxury goods and services, adjusted for improvements in access to information about such commodities, drops relative to food prices. Since the arrival of an extra child brings pressure to consume more goods and fewer luxuries, modernization shifts commodity price ratios in a direction discouraging family expansion somewhat.

Modernization may also raise the relative price of a child through its effect on wage rates. In the earlier phases of modernization, as represented by the nineteenth and earlier centuries in America, the net wage effect on relative child costs is uncertain. On the one hand, the rise in child wage rates reported by historical series would have made children seem less burdensome, since they supplied a greater value of labor at any given wage rates than they took away from others' earnings. Other wage developments are also relevant, however. It is likely that modernization brought a drop in the ratio of children's wage rates to those facing adults, especially highly schooled adults. This development is what one would expect from the observed rise in average schooling and skills, and also from the shift from frontier agriculture to settled agriculture to nonagriculture. The relative value of a child's labor time was probably highest in agriculture, and especially in the relatively unimproved land on the frontier. With modernization this ratio dropped. Dropping even faster would have been the ratio of a child's wage to the present value of the extra wages he could expect by staying in school. By raising the value of child labor more slowly than the values of adult male and female labor, modernization would have tended to keep up the relative cost of a child.

In the later stages of modernization, represented in the United States by the period since World War I, the relative cost of a child would definitely tend to be bid up by wage developments. It is in this period that child labor most clearly lost earning power relative to adult labor. At the same time, the tendency of wives to be pulled into the labor force and of children to be taken out raised the time-intensity of childrearing and made further rises in wage rates raise child costs even more.

It is possible that the same diminishing-returns explanation proposed for the cross-sectional fertility pattern has some bearing on the tendency of modernization to cut fertility over time. It probably is less relevant here, however. There is no evidence that rates of economic return to human investments secularly decline with modernization. Human life expectancy has improved so dramatically in modern times that extra training in an advanced setting may raise later personal income by as great a percentage as it did at the start of modernization. For this reason there has apparently been less downward pressure on the ratio of current family income to prior inputs per person, and less pressure to limit family size on *these* grounds, over time than in the cross section.

C. POSTWAR FERTILITY WAVES

The same framework helps to account for the postwar U.S. baby boom and bust, as shown in Chapter 5. The pronounced swings in recent

OVERVIEW

American fertility seem largely, but not entirely, explained by the equally pronounced swings in the ratio of current income per adult to prior inputs per person. On this issue the findings of the tests of Chapter 5 correspond closely to the earlier findings of Richard Easterlin. To make this point Chapter 5 takes current income as a reflection of young couples' income prospects, and a mixture of current income and income per person twenty years back as a proxy for the prior inputs that are a taste parameter. Young couples in the era from World War II to the early 1960s experienced a better improvement in income prospects over past inputs per person than did any other generation of young adults. Impressions of what it took to raise children properly were still colored by the deprivation of the Great Depression, yet unemployment was low and current income high. In this setting, young couples received few signals that extra children made it harder to make ends meet. In the late 1960s and early 1970s, by contrast, young couples found their incomes lower in relation to the inputs into them than had the previous generation. This difficulty was made more acute by the earlier baby boom itself, which flooded job markets with new career entrants after the late 1960s. In this setting, the prevailing opinion shifted to the view that children damage a woman's career, restrict couples' recreational mobility, crowd the earth, and deplete nonrenewable natural resources.

The relationship of current income to prior inputs per person thus seems central to an understanding of recent fertility swings. It does not completely account for them by itself, however. Other economic and noneconomic developments have also been relevant. The movement of relative child costs, while not conforming perfectly to the swings in fertility, appears to have played a part. As mentioned, the relative cost of an extra child suddenly dropped during World War II as most couples entered the income tax system and began to claim child exemptions for the first time. Thereafter, relative child costs drifted upward with the secular rise in real wage rates, here representing the real cost of a mother's time. It was thus the case that a drop in relative child cost preceded the early postwar jump in fertility and a slight upward drift accompanied the decline in fertility since the 1960s. In the 1950s, on the other hand, relative costs rose while fertility also rose. The movement of relative child costs, then, plays a role, but apparently not so central a role as the dynamics of current income and prior inputs per person.

These economic factors do not completely explain the postwar baby boom and bust. Their influence has *not* sufficed to explain all of what was special about the later baby boom of the 1950s and early 1960s, or about the decline in fertility thereafter. Regressions reported in Chapter 5 found fertility still significantly higher in the late 1950s, and significantly lower in the late 1960s, than the arguments above would predict. Other forces appear to have been at work as well. In the case of the 1960s fertility decline, at least, it is easy to conjecture what else was happening. The contraceptive revolution ushered in by the pill, the IUD, and the shift in lay Catholic attitudes around the time of Vatican II seem to have been significant independent influences and not just endogenous responses to economic motivations to cut births. Though the tests in Chapter 5 did not permit giving the economic variables every conceivable chance to explain things, it does appear that they account for only a large part of, and not all of, recent fertility movements.

One other recent pattern is not explained by the model introduced above until it is given an additional working part. The baby boom saw a greater rise in fertility among more-educated couples than among less-educated. This is not directly explained by the arguments about prior inputs or relative child costs. The 1940s saw the incomes of the poor and less-educated rise faster than those of the more-educated, basically because the elimination of unemployment had more effect on poor incomes than on high incomes. By itself, this would lead to the prediction that fertility should have jumped faster among the poor, whose current incomes were much higher in relation to prior inputs. Yet the class differentials in fertility dropped in those periods.

This tendency of the baby boom to be more pronounced among those with more schooling (and status) seems best explained by noting that those couples with more schooling and higher prior inputs per person are likely to be more firmly in control of their birth probabilities precisely because they have previously had more reason to restrict births, and have invested more energy in finding out about birth control options. They are thus more sensitive in their birth responses to changing conditions. When economic prospects improved across the 1940s, more-educated couples could respond by raising births faster and more effectively despite a lower percentage improvement in incomes by shifting away from relatively effective means of birth control. This extra argument is consistent with the empirical results reported in Chapter 5. However, other special explanations of the class pattern in the baby boom could also fit the same results, and the issue is unresolved. With qualifications like this one, though, the arguments introduced above seem capable of improving considerably on our understanding of fertility behavior.

III. *The Effect of Fertility on Income Inequality*

A list of theoretical reasons for thinking that higher fertility should heighten economic inequalities was given in Chapter 1. Higher fertility might raise inequality at the "microeconomic" level by making family sizes and family inputs per child more unequal. A further microeconomic effect is imparted by any tendency of higher fertility to be concentrated in lower-income families. If the class fertility differentials widen, the disadvantage of being born into a larger family will become more correlated with the disadvantage of being born to poor parents. Conversely, if fertility reduction were greater among lower-income groups, as seems likely of future birth reductions, then declining fertility would be accompanied by declining inequality in children's economic endowments. Another argument linking fertility with inequality was the belief that higher fertility might put a strain on precollege public school budgets, thus causing a widening of inequalities in schooling. The remaining supposed links between fertility and inequality were macroeconomic: higher fertility should raise the quantity, and lower average quality, of manhours of labor supplied, thereby bidding down unskilled wage rates relative to skilled rates, and bidding down all wage rates relative to rates of profit and of return on property.

Do these theories fit the facts? The bulk of Chapter 7 is devoted to showing that movements of income and wealth inequality in America are strikingly consistent with the overall hypothesis that fertility and any other source of population growth is a major determinant of the degree of aggregate inequality. Such a show of aggregate evidence does not tell us which of the supposed links actually transmits the effects of fertility to the distribution of income. Is it the microeconomic argument that fertility affects the inequality of family-formed human capital? Is it the strain on the supply of public schools? Is it the macroeconomic tendency of extra supply to bid down unskilled wage rates while enhancing the returns to property and entrepreneurship? *All* of these influences appear to be important. I shall summarize below first the evidence of Chapter 6 in favor of the microeconomic family-input effect and the strain-on-public-schools effect. The remaining point to review is the basic finding of Chapter 7 that aggregate movements in inequality conform so well to the apparent movements in inequality that it would be hard to explain them without accepting the importance of all of the fertility-inequality links mentioned above.

THE ARGUMENT

A. SIBLING POSITION AND SIBLING INEQUALITY

The view that higher family size raises the inequality and lowers the average level of schooling and other personal economic endowments has been advanced before. Most authors have been sympathetic to the view that being born into a larger family is a net economic disadvantage, whatever its effects on emotional happiness. A related literature has addressed the similar argument that being a middle sibling, like being one of many siblings, is a disadvantage for socioeconomic achievement. Several authors have claimed such an effect, which some have extended to asserting a disadvantage for last-borns as well. The argument has thus built up that any aspect of sibling position that strains parental energies and budgets, as larger family size and middle-born birth order would seem to do, is an economic disadvantage.

All of the evidence previously presented in support of this argument has been vulnerable to the charge that the importance of family size and birth order has been overstated by the omission of other variables correlated with both the numbers and the later achievements of children. It may be that unmeasured attributes of the parents of the children surveyed in past studies have fostered higher achievements in the children of those parents who also chose smaller family sizes than for other parents with the same age, schooling, race, and so forth. This omitted-variable criticism needs to be addressed if we are to believe firmly in the disadvantage of being from a larger family.

Chapter 6 retests the arguments linking sibling position with later schooling and career attainments, using as direct a test as one could ask. Use is made of a sample of over a thousand siblings, most of whom were over forty when a male sibling in each family was interviewed in New Jersey in 1963. This sample, previously analyzed by Professor Albert I. Hermalin, contains data on the age, schooling, and latest occupation not only of the interview respondents but also of their siblings living and dead. It is thus possible to test arguments about the effects of sibling position by examining differences in achievements of siblings within families as well as between families. In this way the argument that the effects of sibling position have been overestimated by omitting unmeasured parental differences can be essentially met.

The tests in Chapter 6 find that the importance of family size and birth order have not been overestimated, and may have been underestimated, by past research. Having more brothers and sisters, especially younger ones, is a significant net drag on schooling and career attainments. Being a middle-born is a disadvantage relative to being a first-born, according to intrafamily tests as well as interfamily tests. Being a last-born may be a slight disadvantage relative to being a first-born. The last-born's disadvantage, which other studies have found significant for I.Q., is not significant for schooling attainment and also probably not significant for early career attainment.

Chapter 6 also investigates the issue of *why* family size and birth order should affect schooling and careers. Considerable support is found for the view that sibling position matters because it affects inputs of time and commodities into each child. This point can be made by constructing indices of predicted time inputs and commodity inputs into a child in each sibling position and comparing these with the observed relationships between sibling position and achievement. Chapter 6 constructs such indices for time inputs, based on the Cornell time use survey of 1967–68, and discusses the apparent parallelism between the distributions of time inputs and of commodity inputs across sibling positions.

Sibling position does seem to make quite a difference in the hours of parents' and others' time a child receives. The larger the family size, the fewer hours of attention, and presumably the lower the "quality" of attention, each child receives. The same regression-based estimates that yield this finding (in Appendix C) also show that a middle-born receives much less attention than either a first-born or a last-born. Last-borns receive about as much care time as first-borns, the important difference being that first-borns have a monopoly on parent-child interactions in their infancy, while the last-borns receive extra attention primarily in their later childhood. The last-borns also seem to receive better commodity, or financial, support than the others, especially when in their teens. It is perhaps because of these input patterns that last-borns tend to stay in school about as long as first-borns, despite having significantly lower I.Q. scores.

Sibling position not only matters to child care time—it is about the only thing that matters. Detailed regression estimates in Appendix C show that the parents' education and occupation do not significantly affect child care time inputs when the ages and numbers of children are properly held constant. That is, more-educated couples do not spend significantly more time in child care than less-educated couples having children of the same ages and number. It is only by having fewer children on the average that higher-status couples devote more time to each child. In this respect patterns of time inputs differ from patterns of commodity inputs or of likely parental "productivity" in producing achievement in children. Parents with more income and education definitely provide more commodities, and may well provide more achievement-producing attention per hour, but they do not provide significantly more hours of attention to their children except by having fewer of them on the average.

Family size and birth order also outweigh mothers' labor force participation as a determinant of the time inputs received by a child. Calculations in Appendix C suggest that children of working mothers receive more total care time, though less of mothers' care time, than do children of mothers not working for pay outside the home, even when family composition is held constant. That is, for a given number and ages of children, a mother's working for pay reduces her own hours of contact with her children less than it raises the amount of extra time that others, including her husband, devote to caring for her children. It may be, of course, that child development is less enriched by an hour of extra care by others than it would be by an hour of her attention. But the ratio of the unit effects of her care time to that of others would have to be high to offset the fact that some of her time is being replaced by *more* of others' time when she takes a job. And when it is remembered that working mothers have fewer children on the average, it becomes clear that being a child of a working mother matters much less to the time inputs one receives as a child than does the number of one's siblings.

B. FERTILITY AND THE SUPPLY OF PUBLIC SCHOOLING

Like the microeconomic argument that larger families feed inequality through their effects on family inputs, the argument that larger families tend to strain public schools also receives some support from the data. The evidence in this case is aggregate.

Since the early nineteenth century, educational expenditures have taken a steadily higher and higher share of Gross National Product. One can gain considerable insight into the effects of fertility on the support for schooling by following when the rise of educational expenditures seemed most impressive. One must take care, however, to measure the right variables. At issue are the determinants of (a) total educational expenditures per child of school age and (b) public expenditures on primary and secondary schooling per child of school age. The first is relevant as a measure of direct inputs into raising the average earning power of labor force entrants. The higher it is, the less unequal will be the wage rates for different "skill" levels, because a more-educated labor force will tend to compete more sharply for the higher-skilled (that is, more highly paid) positions. The second measure has a separate importance because it is related not only to the average level, but also to the dispersion, of schooling. Should public primary and secondary expenditures become less generous per child relative to total expenditures, schooling is likely to become more unequal.

To sort out the effects of cohort fertility on educational support, one must at least separate out the effects of incomes per adult. The demand for schooling is strongly income-elastic, and only when the effects of income have been sorted out can one begin to discern the effects of fertility. Chapter 6 compares the growth of educational expenditures per child to the growth of adult incomes, and finds a surprising twist in the long-run time trend between educational support and income. From 1840 to 1950, the long-run income-elasticity of educational expenditures remained fairly steady and high. From 1950 to 1968, however, this elasticity was distinctly lower. The trend in expenditures per child since 1968 has thus far been steeper, and resembles the pre-1950 relationship to income growth. The 1950–68 drop in the response of educational expenditures per child to growth in income was especially pronounced for public primary and secondary expenditures.

Why should the income elasticity of school spending per child have dropped off for the period 1950–68? The timing of this drop is somewhat surprising, since the decade 1958–68 brought a post-Sputnik educational boom, a "teacher shortage" that is dearly missed by academic job-hunters in the 1970s. The best explanation for the sag in support per child by a newly prospering postwar generation of adults is that educational expenditures have too much inertia to keep a baby boom from dragging down school resources per child of school age. The period 1950–68 is the period in which the baby-boom cohort of 1944–62 entered the public school system. It is precisely the one period in which the share of the population that was of school age (five to nineteen) was rising rather than declining. This coincidence, plus similar evidence from a recent cross-sectional study, suggests that extra fertility does indeed strain the support for schooling per child, especially the taxpayer support for primary and secondary schooling per child. This is the opposite of what one might have thought from the fact that parents' share of voting power, backed by the cry for more schooling to catch up with the Russians after Sputnik, hit its peak in the decade 1958–68 and then gave way to a publicized "taxpayer revolt" against higher school budgets. Despite such waves, inertia in total spending seems to have been sufficient to make

THE ARGUMENT

support per child drop when the baby boom passed through the school system.

C. FERTILITY AND THE OVERALL TREND IN INEQUALITY

To test the macroeconomic part of the argument linking fertility and inequality, or to appraise the entire set of arguments, one must repair to aggregate data. What the aggregate data for the United States suggest is that the movements in inequality fit the present arguments extremely well, though other hypotheses could also fit the same aggregate data. Chapter 7 brings out this conformity of trends in inequality to trends in labor force quantity and quality, and argues that it is difficult to build an explanation for the movements in inequality without assigning a significant role to the labor supply variables that fertility effects.

The degree of income and wealth inequality in America, measured in any of several conventional ways, has not remained constant. In recent years our evidence of both current and past movements in the overall income and wealth distributions has grown greatly. Economic inequality now appears to have risen persistently from the early colonial period to World War I, followed by a well-known leveling of income and wealth between 1916 and sometime around the Korean War, and by stability in the overall distribution since the Korean War. The most recent movements are the best documented. Postwar series on income inequality before taxes show either stability or a slight rise toward inequality, depending on the measure chosen and on whether and how one adjusts for age, family size, fringe pay, and other considerations. None of the series indicates a very dramatic change. By contrast, all available series show a dramatic leveling of incomes between World War I and the Korean War. This drop in inequality is unmistakable from 1929 to Korea. There is some vague indication that incomes were more equally distributed in 1929 than in 1913 or 1916, though the difference between these peaks of inequality was not great. For the period before World War I, we have some data on wealth inequality but essentially nothing on incomes. The inequality of wealth-holding appears to have risen persistently from the late seventeenth century to World War I.

Explaining these movements in inequality is easier when we note their correspondence with trends in pay ratios, that is, in ratios of the rates of pay for highly paid to those of lower-paid groups. Changes in inequality can be decomposed into changes in these pay ratios, changes in the shares of the population represented by each group rate of pay, and changes in the inequality of income within each group. There is no law dictating that trends in overall inequality must follow trends in pay ratios. Yet it has worked out that way. The ratio of skilled to unskilled wage rates, like the overall degree of income inequality, fell in World War I, rebounded to something near its prewar level by 1929, dropped precipitously from 1929 through the Korean War, and then changed little. It is possible that this same correspondence held before World War I, though the data are much shakier for that era. The ratio of skilled to unskilled wage rates appears to have risen greatly over the century from the 1810s to World War I, with intermediate peaks coming around 1845–55 and the 1870s. The coincidence of this long rise with that of wealth inequality over the same hundred years suggests that a trend toward income inequality may have held up and down the income spectrum then, even though the skilled wage ratio did not rise as wealth inequality did before the 1810s. The behavior of pay ratios is a useful clue to the sources of inequality: whatever hypotheses one uses to account for the movements in overall inequality must also be consistent with the behavior of pay ratios.

One hypothesis that fits all of these aggregate data is the one featured in Chapters 6 and 7: income inequality responds strongly to movements in the "quality" and quantity of labor supply, which are in turn affected by fertility as well as by immigration of relatively unskilled laborers. As shown in Chapter 7, there is a close conformity between the labor supply indicators and income inequality. Before World War I the labor force grew rapidly in size but apparently not in average "quality" or "skill" per worker. Immigration was a strong influence on labor force growth then; and it was during the surges of immigration from lower-income countries (1845–55 and 1904–14) that labor supply growth most emphasized quantity over quality and the wage premia earned by skilled workers rose fastest. From World War I to the 1950s the labor force grew much more slowly in man-hours, while average labor force quality appears to have accelerated. As the present hypothesis would predict, income inequality dropped, and the wage rates of unskilled workers gained on those of all skilled occupations (except physicians). In the 1960s, the size of the labor force grew faster once again. There are also recent signs that the growth of the average schooling of the labor force has decelerated. Certainly the labor force has become younger, as baby-boom children have been finishing school. These indications would lead one to expect less leveling of incomes across the 1960s than between World War I and the Korean War. That was the case, as we have seen.

THE ARGUMENT

The evidence is thus consistent with the view that although income inequality is obviously the result of many forces, it so happens that the forces whose intensity has varied greatly over American experience have been those relating to labor force quantity and quality, and behind these lie movements in fertility as well as mortality and immigration. These demographic forces, whose considerable potential impact on income inequality might have been masked, happen to have been revealed by the major impact of such events as the shutting off of history's largest flow of immigration in the 1920s and the postwar baby boom and bust. Even though there are other major determinants of income inequality besides these, the American experiment happens to have revealed their importance.

One need not be convinced by this explanation of the aggregate inequality trends. There are two other hypotheses that are also consistent with the data, as noted in Chapter 7. One is that inequality has been responding mainly to changes in the sectoral locus of technological productivity advances. Technological progress has been concentrated in sectors using unskilled labor the least intensively at times when income inequalities have risen. The twenties was one such period. The nineteenth century as a whole may have been another. Conversely, during the two World Wars and even the Great Depression, our crude measures of technological progress show more balanced improvements across sectors. It may be that shifts in the locus of technological progress among sectors differing in their use of unskilled labor account for the patterns of inequality, while the demographic variables matter little. What can be argued about technological progress can also be argued about exogenous influences on the rate of nonhuman capital accumulation per worker. Capital accumulation per worker was apparently faster between the Civil War and World War I than thereafter. This too might feed inequality before World War I more than later by bidding up the returns to skilled occupations, which tend to be complementary in use with nonhuman capital.

While these other hypotheses are also consistent with the data, one must stretch them unreasonably to account for the movements in aggregate inequality without assigning any role at all to the straightforward argument that labor supply matters. And other competing explanations of the movements of inequality—explanations featuring inflation, unions, and the rise of government—do not even fit all the available evidence, as shown in Chapter 7.

IV. *Does Inequality Feed Itself through Fertility?*

If fertility and population growth thus appear to have a significant tendency to raise inequalities, does income inequality itself tend to raise fertility through population growth? If so, then whatever breaks the cycle of population growth and rising inequality does so with an impact that becomes cumulative over the generations.

This sort of mutual interaction between inequality and population is a possibility to be taken seriously, even though the effects of inequality on population growth are complex. To make headway on this potential feedback, future research should begin on re-examining the apparent effect of inequality on aggregate mortality. As a rough working hypothesis, it can be argued that inequality of income, whatever its source, is likely to raise mortality in low-income countries but is likely to have no net effect on mortality in higher-income countries. At least as interesting, however, is the effect of income inequality on fertility.

There is vague evidence that greater inequality of income can raise both the dispersion and the average level of fertility, two outcomes that in turn spell heightened inequalities a generation later. Any model of fertility showing a negative overall relationship of fertility to income predicts that greater inequality yields more concentration of children into poor families. The model offered in Chapters 3 and 5 is one saying that greater income inequalities mean greater class differences in fertility—in the long run. In the short run, the model predicts, greater inequality would reduce fertility differentials by cutting low incomes and padding high ones. Once this first-generation effect has passed, prolonged greater inequality would raise the dispersion of family sizes and concentrate children into lower-income groups.

The view that average fertility would also be raised by inequality has some empirical basis, though it is important not to count on this tendency too heavily. Most research on fertility patterns has favored a nonlinear relationship of fertility to income and status variables, one that suggests greater fertility differences for a given absolute difference in incomes at low income ranges than at high income ranges. The regression form used in Chapter 5 conforms to this nonlinearity by fitting fertility levels to the logarithms of income variables rather than to absolute incomes. If this preference for a nonlinear relationship is supported by future research, greater inequality does indeed raise aggregate fertility, since an extra thousand dollars a year over the generations cuts higher-class fertility less than the loss of an extra thousand dollars a year over the generations would raise lower-class fertility. If this nonlinearity holds, inequality and fertility would indeed feed each other over the generations.

The conclusion that greater inequality raises average fertility is not yet secure, however. To my knowledge there is no study clearly establishing the superiority of nonlinear over linear fertility relationships. At the same time the inequality-to-fertility link must surely depend on what causes the inequality. If inequality is great because the returns to extra schooling and training are truly great for all of society, then this method of making incomes differ widely would act to *restrict* fertility, by giving parents strong incentives to raise smaller numbers of more highly schooled and trained children. Conversely, if income inequality is propped up by social barriers that depress adult lower-class wage rates more than child wage rates, or if inequality is the result of a system that makes children the main form of saving for one's old age among unpropertied masses, then inequality is part of a system that encourages lower-class fertility.

It thus appears that higher fertility raises the income inequality of each generation of children, and that higher income inequality *may* in turn feed itself through fertility. Inequality seems to feed itself over the long run by concentrating children into poorer families, and possibly also by an effect on aggregate fertility.

This possible feedback from inequality to fertility underscores the importance for inequality of certain historical developments already emphasized in separate discussions of the determinants of inequality and fertility. One key development, it appears, has been U.S. economic development itself, which over the generations helped facilitate the twentieth-century leveling of incomes by cutting fertility. Another was the drastic cutbacks in immigration in the 1920s. These restricted the growth of the U.S. labor force and raised its average "quality," thereby allowing unskilled wage rates to gain relative to skilled wage rates and to property returns. The relative rise in unskilled wage rates came in a twentieth-century setting in which schooling demand was already so great that the extra low-skilled labor that U.S. families would supply in response to the rising wage rates was more the labor of wives than of children. The rise in unskilled wage rates thus had no tendency to lower the relative cost of a child and encourage fertility. In this way the shutting off of immigration has been a major force leveling incomes in the United States—at the expense of those who wanted to come here and could not. The leveling of incomes has thus far been concentrated into the years between 1929 and the Korean War. Once the baby boom has stopped propping up the rate of growth of the young labor force, around 1980, pressure toward more pretax income equality may resume.

This reading of American experience relating to fertility and inequality underlies the importance of limiting desired fertility through economic incentives in countries having rapid population growth and a desire to level incomes. Limiting fertility, to be sure, is a rather indirect way of equalizing incomes, since its effects are felt only a generation later. Taxing the rich and giving to the poor is surely a more direct and immediate way of attacking inequality. Yet there are political barriers to overt redistribution of income and wealth, not the least of which is the lobbying power of the rich. Society can invest in future equalization by pushing antinatal measures where these already have some political support. Furthermore, if further research suggests that inequality can be reduced in a way which also gives incentives to restrict births, then any legislation that levels incomes somewhat now may also have a cumulative equalizing effect in later generations, through fertility levels and class fertility differentials.

Part II:

ECONOMIC INFLUENCES ON FERTILITY

CHAPTER 3. Remodelling the Household for Fertility Analysis

I. *The Starting Point*

The circle linking fertility and the economy is best grasped at the point of household decision-making. It is here that both the effects of family size on the economy and the influences of economic variables on fertility are revealed most clearly. To judge the economic consequences of family size we need a framework for describing how couples adjust their consumption, saving, work, and child care to shifts in parameters relating to childbearing. To follow the other side of the circle from wage rates, property rents, and other relative prices to fertility, we must again begin with a sound model of family planning. An ample supply of conflicting models has been offered by past empirical studies of fertility patterns, which have shown fairly good results by putting almost any combination of education, earnings, rural-urban, and religious variables into aggregate family-size regressions. If we care about knowing what accounts for past patterns and about forecasting future trends, we cannot be satisfied with the fact that very different models all seem able to pick up a moderate share of fertility variance. To make believable causal inferences, we need more careful reasoning about family decision-making as well as partial empirical success.

The kind of model sketched here views married couples as planners who are constantly making and altering decisions that jointly determine their childbirths, child care, labor supply, consumption, and saving. The family is faced with a system of prices, wages, past births, and past accumulation of family property and skills that it cannot change. Of the joint decisions to be modelled, the one that will occupy center stage in this and the next two chapters is the choice of fertility regulation strategy. My main objective is to erect and test a fertility model that gives reliable predictions of the ways in which growth and inequality affect fertility. More specifically, I seek a basis for projecting the effects of growth and inequality on three fertility variables that in turn help to govern later trends in growth and inequality: aggregate fertility, dispersion in family size, and the differentials in family size between rich and poor families.

A theory of birth probabilities will be developed in this chapter in four stages: Section II presents a dry and formal model of desired lifetime family allocation of time and commodities for given family size, to clarify the income and relative cost variables; Section III gives a brief formal treatment of how family size targets are chosen at any one time; Section IV converts the model of desired family size into a model of birth probabilities over a period of five years or less; Section V advances a theory of how couples' tastes are formed regarding family size and inputs per family member, a theory that applies both to short-run birth probabilities and to completed cohort fertility. Two final sections (VI and VII) discuss the ability of this theory of taste formation to explain much, though not all, of the relationship of fertility to modernization and to mobility.

A number of intellectual debts will be incurred along the way. The initial model of family resource allocation is but another in a growing list of variations on Becker's theory of the allocation of time.[1] Part of the theory of taste formation builds on the relative-income and relative-status hypotheses of Easterlin and others.[2] The transition from the theory of desired size to a theory of birth probabilities has benefitted from guidelines laid down by Namboodiri.[3] In weaving together these and other strands of theorizing, I shall make it a point to reduce elegance of mathematical solution as much as possible in order to keep restrictive assumptions at a minimum.

The point of departure for this chapter is a puzzle that I choose to see in a well-known modern pattern. The puzzle happens to relate to class fertility differentials, although its resolution also serves as a theory of aggregate fertility levels and dispersion in family size. The more highly educated tend to have fewer children, even though they have more resources. This aggregate pattern is typical of the industrialized nations, both on cross sections and over time. It holds within urban samples and within rural samples, as well as in samples combining both residential groups. It tends to hold whether or not income is held constant. The puzzle is the fact that the more-educated do not use their extra resources

---

[1] See, for example, Gary S. Becker, "A Theory of the Allocation of Time," *Economic Journal* 75 (September 1965), 493–517; and Gary S. Becker, "The Allocation of Time and Goods Over Time," unpublished manuscript, June 1967.

[2] See, for example, J. A. Banks, *Prosperity and Parenthood*, London: Routledge and Kegan Paul, 1954; Richard A. Easterlin, *Population, Labor Force, and Long Swings in Economic Growth: The American Experience*, New York: Columbia University Press, 1968; Richard A. Easterlin, "Relative Economic Status and the American Fertility Swing," in Eleanor B. Sheldon, ed., *Economics and Family Behavior*, Philadelphia: J. B. Lippincott, 1973; and Julian Simon, "The Effect of Income on Fertility," *Population Studies* 23 (November 1969), 327–342.

[3] See, for example, N. K. Namboodiri, "Some Observations on the Economic Framework for Fertility Analysis," *Population Studies* 26 (July 1972), 185–206.

to enjoy all life pursuits, including child-rearing, more intensively with the same number of children.

To say that the negative education-fertility relationship is typical is not to say that it shows up in all cases. One can find several subsamples that show a positive relationship, especially if the couples in the sample differ more in their recent fortunes than in their mode of upbringing. Some studies have found, for example, that among U.S. Catholics and Jews those with a college education clearly wanted and had more children in the postwar baby boom than those with less schooling.[4] This pattern is noteworthy, even though a dramatic fall in births among college-educated Catholics in the late 1960s restored the usual negative profile relating education to fertility.[5] Those women who marry late are another sample for which the college-educated want and have more children, the apparent reasons being that the late-marrying women with lower schooling are a special group characterized by some subfecundity and by higher tastes for, and seniority at, careers.[6] Both the religious-group and the late-marrying sample patterns are consistent with the model developed below. Despite such cases of a positive education-fertility profile, the prevailing aggregate pattern turns out negative.

The puzzle posed here may seem easily explained in terms of three factors: access to the means of preventing births, tastes, and relative child costs. Couples with more education presumably know more about contraceptive methods, have developed greater tastes for alternatives to children, and find a given set of child-rearing commitments more costly relative to other things. Each of these three arguments turns out to have its own internal problems. Only when these problems are ironed out can the combination of all three factors plus additional taste factors provide a satisfactory model of fertility behavior. Once these three arguments are revised, they will point the way to clearer perspectives on how fertility relates to mobility and modernization.

The argument that fertility differentials by education stem from dif-

[4] See, for example, Charles F. Westoff, Robert G. Potter, and Philip C. Sagi, Jr., *The Third Child*, Princeton: Princeton University Press, 1963, Chapter 9; Larry L. Bumpass and Charles F. Westoff, *The Later Years of Childbearing*, Princeton: Princeton University Press, 1970, p. 78; and Norman B. Ryder and Charles F. Westoff, *Reproduction in the United States 1965*, Princeton: Princeton University Press, 1971, Chapter 4.

[5] See, for example, Charles F. Westoff and Larry Bumpass, "The Revolution in Birth Control Practices of U.S. Roman Catholics," *Science* 179, no. 4068 (January 5, 1973), 41–44.

[6] See, for example, Larry L. Bumpass, "Age of Marriage as a Variable in Socioeconomic Differentials in Fertility," *Demography* 6 (February 1969), 45–54.

ferences in access to the means of birth prevention is less powerful than it might at first seem. Couples with very little education do tend to have poorer contraceptive knowledge, but this fact falls far short of explaining the fertility differentials we observe. This would be true even if differences in access were responsible for all unwanted births. Survey results have shown that the less-educated would want more children than would the more-educated even if contraception were perfect.[7] Even in the samples showing a positive education-fertility profile, differences in unwanted fertility failed to reverse the sign: the highly educated Catholics and Jews that had more children wanted more.[8] The survey data also show that contraceptive efficiency rises sharply as the "desired" number of children is approached and met, so that the contraceptive failure rate depends primarily on family-size desires.

A more important failing of the access-to-birth-prevention argument is the fact that even the incidence of unwanted births is more strongly tied to differences in motivation than to differences in access. The choice of whether or how to regulate fertility is a gamble which, like any other gamble, responds sensitively to the expected psychic gains or losses from any given outcome of the gamble. The same is true of the prior decision to search for means to prevent births. Couples with less schooling have, and even expect in advance to have (see surveys just cited), more unwanted births, apparently because the overall consequences of each extra unwanted birth weigh less heavily in their minds. As soon as the motivational factors governing fertility regulation are listed and explored, it turns out that exactly the same observable variables determine the incidence of unwanted as of wanted children—for the simple reason that both kinds of birth are the outcomes of gambles tied to perceived costs and benefits that differ according to the educational and economic characteristics of the parents. To account for differentials in fertility, wanted or unwanted, we must get into a theory of the stakes involved in fertility

[7] See, for example, Larry L. Bumpass and Charles F. Westoff, "The Perfect Contraceptive' Population," *Science* 169 (September 18, 1970), 1177–1182; U.S. Presidential Commission on Population Growth and the American Future, *Population Growth and the American Future*, New York: Signet, 1972, p. 164; Judith Blake, "Income and Reproductive Motivation," *Population Studies* 21 (November 1967), 181–206; and Judith Blake, "Reproductive Ideals and Educational Attainment Among White Americans, 1943–1960," *Population Studies* 21 (September 1967), 159–174.

[8] See, for example, Westoff, Potter, and Sagi, *Third Child*; Bumpass and Westoff, *Later Years of Childbearing*; and Ryder and Westoff, *Reproduction in the United States 1965*.

regulation—that is, into a discussion that owes almost nothing to differences in access to contraceptive access.[9]

The taste argument explains that educated parents have greater aspirations for their children and greater "goods aspirations" for themselves. The latter aspirations are supposed to be unrelated to, and therefore competitive with, the existence of children in the family. Examples might be the entertainment and durables usually associated with urban comfort—movies, concerts, foreign travel, fine furniture. This argument is surely correct as far as it goes, but it ventures very little. What is there in the argument that assures that the aspirations bred by education cannot simply be met by putting more into the enjoyments of each individual family member and having the same number of children as a less-educated couple? Why don't couples with twice as much resources (and more education) tend to put twice as much into each child, put twice as much into their own child-unrelated activities, and have the same number of children? The puzzle is made more complicated if one believes that education raises one's efficiency at home production and child-rearing apart from its effect on measured income. To reply that education just has such a strong effect on people's values that they must have fewer children to do the things they want to do is to abandon explanation by saying, in effect, things are that way because things are that way. The negative education-fertility pattern is consistent enough among the more industrialized nations to require a fuller explanation. The same is true of the negative pattern relating fertility decline with urbanization, which like education is associated with gains in human earning power. The taste argument needs more working parts. These are provided in Section V of this chapter, which introduces a hypothesis linking married couples' tastes to the history of their upbringing.

The argument about relative prices or costs holds that children cost more in more-educated families, and that this price effect outweighs the income effect associated with the parents' extra schooling. To be a cost argument this line of thinking must define cost as the cost of a *given set of child inputs*: to refer to the fact that more-educated parents put more real inputs into each child is to return to the previous taste-difference

---

[9] The argument of this paragraph refers only to cross sections by education attainment, and not to time trends. The independent importance of advances in contraceptive technology over time is in no way denied here. I am only asserting that education-group differences in adopting contraception, and in fertility, are tied much more closely to differences in motivation than to differences in knowledge or access.

approach, since the higher real inputs amount to a qualitative difference in the type of child-rearing experience being purchased. Mindful of this distinction, several authors have gone on to argue that any common set of child inputs is indeed more costly for the more-educated because children are "time-intensive" (or "labor-intensive"), and time is more expensive to parents whose greater education allows them higher market wage rates.

This intuition, like that relating to tastes, is sound but inadequate. Price and cost are comparative concepts. To know that children are labor-intensive and more costly for higher-wage parents, we must know with what alternatives parents compare an extra child. Children take up some of Mother's time, but they spend time helping out as well, and ground rules are needed for deciding how the net time (and commodity) inputs into children compare to those into the activities with which they compete. An extra child is labor-intensive only if he makes other family members spend a greater value of time at home instead of working for pay than would the life course without the extra child.

When the concept of relative child costs has been refined in this and the following chapter, we shall still find the cost argument incapable of resolving the empirical puzzle by itself. Rising education and earnings seem to have been associated with declining American fertility since the early nineteenth century or earlier. Yet it turns out that urban children did not become labor-intensive until sometime between the start of World War I and World War II, and farm children are only just becoming labor-intensive. The data presented in Chapter 4 suggest that in the nineteenth century children on balance raised the family's paid work by supplying a greater value of work as minors than they took away from the earnings of parents and older siblings. As a result, the upward trend in wage rates apparently slightly *lowered* the relative cost of child inputs across the nineteenth century. Wives, with or without children, did not work outside the home enough before World War I to make the conflict between child and job a major relative-cost consideration. The widespread belief that the time-intensity of children has reduced fertility by conflicting with the improving career opportunities of wives can only be valid for the years since World War I.[10] Even in the interwar period,

[10] The relative time-cost argument cannot be resurrected for the prewar years by relating it to the timing of marriage. True, single girls worked for pay much more than did wives, and one might be tempted to think that improving wage rates would be a factor postponing marriage, since marriage was likely to bring children. The fact remains, however, that marriage ages have not risen with wage rates and schooling, so that the secular fertility decline is indeed a decline in marital fertility.

movements in relative child cost can explain very little of the observed fluctuations in fertility. It is only since World War II that the time-cost argument has assumed great importance, though its importance is likely to continue in the future.

Thus the contraceptive-knowledge explanation, the taste explanation, and the cost explanation all suffer from logical incompleteness and empirical limitations, and need some repairs. The first task of reconstruction is to lay out the basic optimization model that defines relative child cost, lifetime full income, and other key variables in the family decision-making process.

II. *The Family's Planning Problem*

Couples are viewed as deciding on life courses that maximize the expected present utility[11] of their psychic activities. Their decisions and their utilities are assumed to be joint, on the argument that marriage implies tentative solution of the problem of internal allocation and interdependence of enjoyment. They reappraise their situation every year, mindful of their own past decisions and their environment. All utility is experienced as of the moment of planning, even though the activities and their actual psychic rewards or disappointments are spread out over the rest of the couple's lives. It is hardly necessary to stress that the psychic outcomes are highly uncertain. In the case of having a child, the variance of outcomes is tremendous. Some will have their lives ruined by their children. Others will be gratified by their children beyond their highest initial hopes.

---

[11] To keep the analysis manageable, one simplifying assumption must be made about the role of uncertainty in the couple's utility maximization. The correct approach is to model the couple as maximizing the expected value of the utility of their lifetime activities, where the enjoyment of activities, the production of the activities with time and commodity inputs, and the future course of prices and health are all stochastic variables. Such multi-tiered uncertainty, however, makes the algebra of expectations unmanageable unless one assumes very special functional forms.

It is not necessary, on the other hand, to assume certainty and perfect foresight. All that is required to permit the suppression of random-variable algebra here is to replace the maximizing of expected utility with maximizing a linear function of the utility of expected values. It would be unrealistic, of course, just to equate the utility of the expected values of lifetime activities with their expected utility. The former will be less than the latter as long as people are risk-averse. So instead I assume that the utility of the expected value of any activity equals a fixed fraction of the expected utility of that same activity. In other words, a bird in the hand is worth two in the bush times an unspecified constant. This assumption allows me to use a model that looks as though couples dealt only with expected values.

The activities that produce enjoyment are potentially infinite in number, their only common denominators being that they are internally experienced, they are not marketed, and they require inputs of family resources. The following might serve as examples: enjoying one's job, getting to work on time, enjoying one's second-born child, getting revenge, keeping warm, avoiding accidents, going on a camping trip, escaping guilt, helping somebody in need. Since a couple is incapable of considering an infinite number of activities, however, no generality is lost by simply stating that utility is a function of a finite number of life activities (the Z's):[12]

$$(1) \qquad U = U(Z^1, \ldots, Z^j, \ldots, Z^J)$$

Couples are likely to make their choices over a range of activity levels for which all first derivatives are positive, all second derivatives with respect to one Z are negative, and second-order cross-derivatives are of any sign. That is, the marginal returns from any activity are apt to be positive but diminishing, and different activities can be substitutes or complements.

Each activity is produced by combining the time of family members with purchased (or inherited) commodities. Anything purchased from outside the family is a commodity, even if it consists of somebody's time, as in the case of a baby-sitter. All inputs used on an activity at the expense of others are treated similarly, even though some of them are associated in our minds with the drudgery and others with the joys of the activity. The time inputs into one's own wedding are reckoned by adding together hours of such different time as the honeymoon and the writing of thank-you notes. The time inputs into raising a child include both the hours spent wiping his nose and bottom or bailing him out of jail and the hours spent watching him succeed or care for others.

Both the time and the commodity inputs are dated and typed. The couple has in mind activities whose inputs extend over time periods (say, years) running from the present to a planning horizon that I shall assume slightly exceeds the female life expectancy given the wife's present age. The subscripts for time periods shall run from the present to

---

[12] The Z's correspond to Becker's "basic commodities" (Becker, "Theory of the Allocation of Time"). I prefer the term "activities" only to avoid a semantic logjam. If the Z's were called commodities, one would have to follow Becker in defining the inputs into them other than family time as "goods." But families purchase both goods and services, or "commodities" in common parlance, from the outside world. So to free myself to equate commodities with purchased goods and services, I refer to psychic activities.

the planning horizon as follows: $1, \ldots, t, \ldots, T$. The time inputs of each family member are, of course, different in nature. Time inputs are therefore also classified by family-member subscripts (n), running from the husband (1) and wife (2) through the youngest existing child (N). Commodity inputs, besides being dated, are typed by the subscript sequence: $1, \ldots, m, \ldots, M$.

The maximum output of any j^{th} activity is related to the inputs into that activity by the production function:

(2) $$Z^j = Z^j(L_{nt}^j\text{'s}, C_{mt}^j\text{'s}), \quad \begin{array}{l} (j = 1, \ldots, J) \\ (n = 1, \ldots, N) \\ (m = 1, \ldots, M) \\ (t = 1, \ldots, T) \end{array}$$

where the L^j's are the family time inputs and the C^j's are the commodity inputs into the jth activity. I shall assume that the production functions, like the utility function, are characterized by positive but diminishing returns to any one input, and different inputs can be substitutes or complements. The production and utility functions are also assumed to be twice differentiable. No further assumptions will be made about the form of these relationships. The outputs of home activities, like utility, are so hard to measure accurately that there is no point in getting committed to assumptions about homogeneity, returns to scale, or constancy of substitution elasticities. This agnosticism about functional form will be discussed again in other contexts below.

The production function has been introduced in a way that implies separability of the inputs into different activities. One can easily think of cases in which inputs into one activity are also put to use in others. For example, a mother can spend time ironing while taking care of two (well-behaved) children. By keeping family members alive, food purchases could be thought of as inputs into all home activities, and not just dining itself. The examples of sharing overhead inputs are endless. The straightforward way of recognizing this fact is simply to allow the inputs into any one activity, Z^j, to be potential inputs into another, Z^k, as well. Doing so, however, would clutter up the symbolic presentation of the model without adding any insight that cannot be gained by the model as it is. It seems sufficient and more convenient simply to note that this jointness of inputs reinforces the case for being flexible by allowing activities to be complements as well as substitutes. When input jointness complicates specific conclusions, as in Chapters 4 and 6 below, its relevance will be re-examined.

Couples' enjoyment of life activities is constrained by the extent of their time and commodity resources. A young couple has a limited property inheritance, limited life expectancies, an 8,766-hour year, and a limited power to sell part of each family member's lifetime for commodities by working for pay. In any year t the nth family member must allocate his full time $(\bar{L}_{nt})$ between market work and home activities as follows:

$$(3) \qquad \bar{L}_{nt} = L_{nt} + \sum_{j=1}^{J} L_{nt}^{j}$$

where the L_{nt} without superscript is the time spent at work, and the sum of the L^j's, here *excluding* market work as an activity,[13] is the nth family member's time input into home activities. The family is also forced to keep its lifetime commodity expenditures within the family's property income plus earnings. This budget constraint is represented symbolically as:

$$(4) \qquad V + \sum_{n=1}^{N} \sum_{t=1}^{T} \left[\frac{w_{nt} L_{nt}}{(1+r)^t} \right] \geq \sum_{j=1}^{J} \sum_{t=1}^{T} \sum_{m=1}^{M} \left[\frac{p_{mt} C_{mt}^{j}}{(1+r)^t} \right]$$

where V is the present value of property wealth plus expected future inheritances and transfers to the couple's household (pensions, support from grown children);[14] w_{nt} is the after-tax money wage rate for the nth family member in the Year t; P_{mt} is the after-tax money price of the mth commodity in the Year t; and r is the marginal rate of interest at which the couple trades between inputs in different years by adjusting its accumulation of human and nonhuman wealth. The inequality in (4) can be restated as an equation by defining the couple's expected end-of-

---

[13] For the next few paragraphs the text ignores the enjoyability of work and proceeds as if only nonwork activities brought utility. Later I shall treat the issue of work enjoyment explicitly.

[14] A word of clarification is in order regarding the role assigned to grown children in the present model. For as long as a child is expected to remain within the parents' household, both his support and his earnings are viewed by the parents as internal to the family. After he has left the household, his net transfers to his parents, which may be positive or negative or zero, are entered as a commodity input into their family. Nothing in this procedure conflicts with the fact that psychic parental returns from the child can be experienced any time from before his birth to the parents' deaths. In fact, the division of the parent-child economic input flows into two periods, one before and one after the child sets up a separate household, does not change the analysis at all. It only simplifies the accounting of Chapter 4 by making the model's arrangement of economic flows correspond to that of the sources of data on household expenditures and gifts.

life bequest as a (residual) commodity input into a worthwhile activity called "providing for our heirs."

The budget constraint can be converted into an equivalent *lifetime wealth constraint*, which states that the total expected value of all time plus commodity inputs into home activities cannot exceed the expected value of all of the family's full time plus nonhuman wealth. The lifetime wealth constraint is derived by adding the value of home time inputs to both sides of (4):

$$(5) \quad \text{Lifetime wealth } (Y_f) = V + \sum_{n=1}^{N} \sum_{t=1}^{T} \left[\frac{w_{nt} \bar{L}_{nt}}{(1+r)^t} \right]$$

$$\geq \sum_{j=1}^{J} \sum_{t=1}^{T} \sum_{m=1}^{M} \left[\frac{p_{mt} C_{mt}^j}{(1+r)^t} \right] + \sum_{j=1}^{J} \sum_{t=1}^{T} \sum_{n=1}^{N} \left[\frac{w_{nt} L_{nt}^j}{(1+r)^t} \right]$$

The nature of the unit time values (w's) depends on whether or not the family member in question works during part of the relevant time period. If he or she does work for pay, w is his or her market wage rate, since the optimization sketched below will show that the wage rate equals the shadow price of time in this case. If he or she does not work, then w represents a shadow price of time that equals or exceeds the market wage rate the family member could get. The implications of a family member's not working at all will be discussed below.

For the lifetime wealth to be truly a parameter, it must refer to the total value of family resources for a *given* choice of life activities. Lifetime earning potential is itself affected by the choice of home activity. Having an extra child, for example, lowers the market earning potential of the wife by causing her to lose chances to develop skills through job experience. On the other hand, the extra child himself is an addition to family resources. Watching a late movie on TV is likely to enhance one's overall productivity less than learning to sew or to make plumbing repairs. Since we are constantly faced with choices between inputs into current enjoyment and investing in our ability to command future inputs, it must be recognized that lifetime resources depend on future as well as past personal development. Lifetime wealth should thus be defined as the family's potential resources given current family size and some typical choice of activities.

Subject to its time and budget constraints, the couple chooses the set of current home inputs that maximizes its utility. The pivotal words here are "current" and "home." By choosing a set of home inputs, the household simultaneously chooses an amount of market work for each family member, since work time must equal total time minus home time. The couple also chooses only a set of current-year inputs, since conditions change each year and the couple remakes its plans. The couple, in other words, commits itself to a course of action this year and at the same time makes a tentative and alterable plan covering its entire lifetime. In making its current decisions, it will naturally place some value on keeping open its options for revising plans later. The correct formal procedure for handling this desire to ensure against irreversible mistakes, or "option demand," is to work within a model of expected utility maximization in which future conditions, like current enjoyment, are represented by stochastic variables. But as explained in an earlier footnote, it is much more convenient simply to posit that activities involving less irreversible commitment give a higher utility for this reason, and to continue working with a framework that leaves uncertainty hidden from the algebra.

To show what the constrained utility maximization implies about measures of family wealth and child cost and about couples' behavior, I shall first treat the case in which wage rates are unaffected by the couple's current decisions, each family works for pay to some extent in each time period, and family size is given. Each of these assumptions will be relaxed in turn.

The optimal plan will be one satisfying the usual first-order conditions for constrained utility maximization: lifetime wealth and each family member's time are fully utilized, and the price ratio between any two inputs equals the ratio of the marginal utilities of those two inputs in any home activity. To express these conditions algebraically, let the subscripts of U and the Z's represent partial derivatives, so that $U_j = \delta U/\delta Z^j$, $Z^j_{nt} = \delta Z_j/\delta L^j_{ntj}$, and so forth. The conditions can be outlined by stating four types of marginal equalities. The first is that the ratio of the same-year marginal utilities associated with extra time units for any two family members (n_1 and n_2) equals the ratio of their wage rates for any activity in which they both take part:

$$(6) \qquad \frac{U_j Z^j_{n_1 t}}{U_j Z^j_{n_2 t}} = \frac{w_{n_1 t}}{w_{n_2 t}}$$

Second, the ratio of the marginal utilities from extra inputs of any family member's time in any two years (t_1 and t_2) equals the ratio of the wage rates in the two years discounted to a common point in time:

$$(7) \qquad \frac{U_j Z^j_{nt_1}}{U_j Z^j_{nt_2}} = \frac{w_{nt_1}}{w_{nt_2}} \cdot (1+r)^{t_2 - t_1}$$

The same holds for a commodity input in any two years. A third equality is between the marginal utilities associated with the same input in the same year for any two activities (j and k):

$$\frac{U_j Z_{nt}^j}{U_k Z_{nt}^k} = 1 \tag{8}$$

Finally, the ratio of marginal utilities for a time and a commodity input in the same time period equals the corresponding wage-price ratio for any activity in which both are involved:

$$\frac{U_j Z_{nt}^j}{U_j Z_{mt}^j} = \frac{w_{nt}}{p_{mt}} \tag{9}$$

All of the remaining first-order conditions, aside from the lifetime wealth constraint, follow these in form.

If the forms of the utility and production functions were known and workable, one could solve these equations for all of the time and commodity input levels (the L's and C's), of which only those for Year 1 represent actual commitments. The same equations and the exhaustion-of-time constraints for each family member would also yield the labor supply of each member and the family's saving for the year. But since I wish to avoid specifying particular functional forms here, no attempt will be made to derive a specific solution, and I shall turn instead to the basic cost and living-standard measurements that follow from this framework.

The usual textbook treatment of prices and costs has to be modified to fit the present framework and objectives. The usual treatment turns at this point to the task of discussing and estimating the properties of the demand curves just derived from the first-order conditions. As far as the abstract theory is concerned, the relevant price variable for any one commodity is the vector of the price ratios involving this commodity's price and those of all the others. When it comes to statistical testing, the vector of all relative prices is typically compressed down to one or two price ratios that should act to pick up all of the really important influences of price on the quantity of this good demanded. This is done in one of two ways. One way is to pick out a couple of presumed substitute or complement goods and put the price ratios involving these and the first good into a demand regression to sort out price effects. The other way is cruder: just divide the price of the good in question by a general cost-of-living index, and enter this price ratio into a demand regression. Both procedures seek to economize on the number of variables that have to be plugged into the final regression, by compressing all relative price ratios into a single ratio between the price of the good in question and the price of "other" goods.

Even in the usual model of consumer demand, though, one is engaged in the task of developing a proxy for a price index for "other" goods without specifying which set of weights for the other-good index is most relevant for the price responsiveness of the consumer. Intuition suggests that the best "other goods" price index is one assigning to individual goods the quantity of each that would be given up if one were to choose an extra unit of the good in question. In other words, the other goods are the bundle of things that the consumer would choose to give up if he were constrained to increase his consumption of the good in question, given income and the set of prices for individual goods.[15] It is the relative price of this marginal bundle of other goods that would, if we knew the bundle contents, be the one to which the consumer would show the greatest price responsiveness. If one must condense the whole set of price ratios into one, the usual demand-theory framework would want this marginal-bundle price ratio.

The present, more complicated, framework also needs a way of condensing an endless set of relative price ratios into the most relevant ratio

[15] The more precise way of defining the "other goods" bundle at the theoretical level is to perform a hypothetical rationing experiment. Solve the first-order optimization conditions in the usual way. Then fix the quantity of the good in question, X_i, as a parameter, and differentiate the first-order conditions with respect to X_i, still using the same income and price constraints. Solve for all of the dX_j/dX_i's. These make up the bundle of goods that the consumer would give up at the margin if he were constrained to raise his consumption of X_i (still paying the market price for X_i). The other-goods price index is then the sum of the $p_j(dX_j/dX_i)$'s.

This procedure is a proxy for another that might seem more logical. The more logical approach might seem to be a direct price-response experiment. One could simply differentiate the first-order conditions with respect to p_i, holding all other prices and money income constant, and then solve the differentiated equations for the bundle of dX_j/dp_i's. This is indeed the most logical approach where it proves practicable. I have chosen the parametric-X_i approach because it happens to correspond to the form in which data on home activities are available. As the text will stress, one cannot differentiate with respect to p_i in the present family model because the price p_i is itself unobservable. In order to determine the relative input cost of a home activity (the nearest measurable thing to its psychic price), one must turn to data that estimate the input effects of having an extra unit of that home activity. This is analogous to the parametric-X_i approach being described here to set the stage for the more complicated family-model discussion of relative cost. Chapter 4 will show how the estimation is done for one particular home activity, having an extra child. Chapter 4 will also identify the special assumption that should be made in order to utilize data from cross sections in which tastes are varied.

or two in order to facilitate estimating the effects of market prices on family planning. The task of sorting out price effects must therefore begin with a procedure for defining price in this framework. The immediate problem is, though, that we seek relative-price measures for home activities, whose price in terms of other enjoyable activities is extremely difficult to measure. Many individual home activities are hard to quantify. Much harder to obtain are complete sets of all of the activity enjoyed by families, and these complete sets are what are needed to reveal psychic trade-offs. Suppose, for example, that we could observe the number of children in each family and could ask the husband and wife to quantify their activity level. ("In the last year, how many weekend outings did you take as a couple? Individually? As a family?" "How many rooms did you redecorate?" "How many flowers did you plant?") To reveal trade-offs, the investigator would have to take one of two treacherous additional steps. He (and an army of interviewers) could ask each couple a lot of what-ifs. ("What is the greatest number of weekend outings you would be willing to give up to redecorate each room of your house the way you wish?") The cost of such a procedure would be enormous and skeptics could easily reject all of the findings that emerged. The second approach is even worse. One might run cross-sectional regressions on the activity levels to see how much each unit of one activity seemed to affect the levels of others. It would be impossible to tell what the regressions would be picking up. The problem is not just that tastes may differ with each observation, as in any cross-section of households. Worse is the difficulty of separating taste differences (differences in utility functions) from home productivity differences (differences in the production functions) without massive data on both the complete sets of activity levels and all of the time and commodity inputs classified by each activity. The cost of pursuing measures of the psychic trade-offs among the Z^j's seems prohibitive.

The difficulty of directly observing trade-offs among home activities means that a different research strategy must be adopted if fertility behavior and other family behavior are to be related to observable parameters. First, the notion of relative psychic price must be replaced with the more measurable concept of the relative cost of the *inputs* into any home activity, to investigate the effects of price and wage movements on family behavior. This leaves the utility and production functions unseparated and unrevealed. The next step is to advance hypotheses about how observable variables might affect family plans through *either* tastes *or* home efficiency. For example, there is evidence that extra schooling,

[51]

holding full-time incomes constant, causes wives to shift their resources toward market work and away from food preparation at home.[16] Is this because more schooling makes food preparation less enjoyable relative to a job? Or is it because more schooling reduces efficiency at food preparation? One could perhaps resolve the issue with attitudinal survey questions or with questions about inputs and outputs in food preparation. Such survey procedures can be justified if one seeks insights into measures of family well-being or into technological change in the home. But if the focus is on explaining family behavior, as in this study, it is better to construct one's hypotheses in a way that does not hinge critically on assertions about psychic trade-off ratios or home productivity. Thus, in the example just given, it might be preferable simply to observe that schooling raises market work and lowers *inputs into* food preparation at home.

The strategy adopted here is thus to move the discussion of relative prices down to the more observable level of input costs, and to stake little on a separation of influences on tastes from influences on home productivity.[17] The immediate task, then, is to develop the relative input cost formula that will serve as the analog to the above ratio of the price of one good to the price of the marginal bundle of all other goods.

The relative input cost formula for any activity hinges critically on the choice of quantity weights that go into the bundles of inputs for the activity and the things it replaces at the margin. The importance of the choice of weights is especially clear for major lifetime commitments, such as migrating or having another child. The list of inputs into such major commitments is the same as that for the alternative activities: the time of each family member and the full range of commodity input categories. In these cases the relative cost ratio depends entirely on the differences in the proportions that various inputs represent in the two life courses.

---

[16] In some studies the wage rates are in fact held constant, as in the illustration here, but in some cases they are not. Some recent evidence on the effects of parental schooling can be found in Arleen Leibowitz's doctoral dissertation (1972) and in Robert T. Michael, "Education in Nonmarket Production," *Journal of Political Economy* 81, no. 2, pt. 1 (March/April 1973), 306–327. Both authors are aware of the difficulty of separating taste from efficiency effects. Leibowitz's chapter on home time use includes separate attitudinal ratings of the enjoyability of various home tasks.

[17] Accordingly, the theory of "taste formation" presented in Section V below is one that does not require separability of taste differences from differences in personal productivities. The role of tastes there could as easily be played by productivity. The simpler term "tastes" is used because its present meaning is more familiar to most readers.

To reveal how the inputs into the jth activity differ in their proportions from those into the alternatives with which the jth activity competes, the following marginalist procedure is adopted: Begin with the optimum position sketched in Equations (6)–(9) above. Fix Z^j as a parameter and differentiate the first-order conditions with respect to Z^j. Solve for the dC^j/dZ^j's and the dL^j/dZ^j's. These represent the bundle of commodity and time inputs into an extra unit of the jth activity. Multiplying each of them by its discounted price yields the marginal cost of the jth activity (in dollars):

$$(10) \quad \text{COST}_j = \sum_n \sum_t \frac{w_{nt} dL_{nt}^j/dZ^j}{(1+r)^t} + \sum_m \sum_t \frac{p_{mt} dC_{mt}^j/dZ^j}{(1+r)^t}$$

for cases in which wages, prices, and interest rates are exogenous. Empirical estimates can be made on the basis of studies estimating the year-by-year input bill for extra units of the activity in question. Figures might be available, for example, on the time and commodity costs of taking a family fishing trip or adding a room to the house in "spare time."

The marginal input cost formula takes on a slightly different form if the wage rates and prices are themselves affected by the family's choices. This possibility is most likely to arise in connection with the effects of self-training or work leave on one's subsequent wage rates. In the case in which wage rates respond to the level of activity j, the marginal cost formula becomes:

$$(11) \quad \text{COST}_j = \sum_n \sum_t \frac{w_{nt} dL_{nt}^j/dZ^j}{(1+r)^t} + \sum_m \sum_t \frac{p_{mt} dC_{mt}^j/dZ^j}{(1+r)^t}$$

$$+ \sum_n \sum_t \frac{L_{nt} dw_{nt}/dZ^j}{(1+r)^t}$$

Such an expanded formula might apply, for example, to the family fishing trip. If the trip is essential to the father's ability to cope with his work when he returns, his subsequent wage rates will be raised by the vacation. If, on the other hand, he is taking an unpaid leave at short notice, his employer may be unfavorably impressed, and his future earning power may be reduced.

The formula for the marginal input cost of an activity must next be compared to the cost of the inputs taken away from all other activities at the margin. For any other activity, the effect of shifting to another unit of Z^j on that activity's inputs can be derived by differentiating the first-order conditions in the manner just described. To estimate the input effects for each activity that is affected by the shift toward Z^j is not necessary, however. All that is needed is to reveal the bundle of inputs taken from *all* other activities combined. This can be done by combining direct estimates of the inputs into an extra unit of Z^j with estimates of the effect of an extra unit of Z^j on the family's total use of each input. Taking the example of the family fishing trip, the amount of gasoline expenditures the trip took away from other home activities is the amount directly used up on the trip minus the effect of the trip on the family's total gasoline consumption. Similarly, the number of hours of the father's time the trip took away from other home activities is the time he spent on the trip minus the decrease in his paid working hours resulting from the trip. In this way the set of inputs into competing activities can be revealed by subtraction. In the algebra of the present optimization model, the input cost of the activities that would be foregone for an extra unit of Z^j is:

$$(12) \quad \text{COST}_{-j} = \sum_n \sum_t \frac{w_{nt} dL_{nt}^{-j}/dZ^j}{(1+r)^t} + \sum_m \sum_t \frac{p_{mt} dC_{mt}^{-j}/dZ^j}{(1+r)^t}$$

where each $dL_{nt}^{-j} = -\sum_{k=1}^{J} dL_{nt}^{k}$ and each $dC_{mt}^{-j} = -\sum_{k=1}^{J} dC_{mt}^{k}$ for $k \neq j$.

As long as wage rates and prices are unaffected by the level of Z_j, the two bundles of inputs would have the same dollar value: $\text{COST}_{-j} = \text{COST}_j$.

The marginal inputs into the jth activity and of the activities against which it competes define the weights that go into the index of the relative input cost of any home activity. The relative cost of any activity (P_j) is the ratio of the cost of its inputs[18] to the cost of the inputs into the ac-

---

[18] At this point the text proceeds to gloss over the fact that the total dollar cost of the two bundles would not be equal if the couple's own choices affected wage rates (or prices, or the interest rate). It will sound as though the index is a ratio of the expression in Equation (10) to that in Equation (12), rather than (11) over (12). This means that in cases where COST_j does not equal COST_{-j} the ratio is between indices that are both set at unity for a common base period, even though their dollar magnitudes are not the same in that base period. Even in such cases, this procedure seems best. To try to make COST_j equal COST_{-j} when the choice shifts wage rates would require assigning the effect of the choice on earning potential to some time or commodity category as an "input" into the jth activity. This is a reasonable procedure, yet I have chosen to let the comparison

tivities with which it competed in the base period. That is, the relative cost of an activity is a ratio of index numbers derived by applying fixed base-period input share weights to varying input price indices. For any i^{th} input (now either time or commodity), let c_i represent its share of the present discounted value $COST^0{}_j$ in the base period, let d_i represent the same for $COST^0{}_{-j}$ and let p_i be the input's price or wage index (in the base period, $p^0{}_i$ equals unity). Then the relative input cost of the jth activity in any setting is:

$$(13) \quad P_j = \frac{COST_j/COST_j^0}{COST_{-j}/COST_{-j}^0} = \frac{\sum_{i=1}^{N+M} c_i p_i}{\sum_{i=1}^{N+M} d_i p_i} \quad (\Sigma c_i = \Sigma d_i = 1)$$

where the null superscripts refer to the base period. This formula makes it clear that the relative cost of any activity will tend to move with the prices of the inputs it uses intensively, and against the prices of the inputs it uses less than do the activities which it would replace. Thus, for example, a rise in real wage rates will raise the relative cost of activities that are time-intensive and lower the relative cost of commodity-intensive activities.

It might seem that the procedure just described would give input weights that are inappropriate for measuring movements in relative costs, since the inputs into $COST_j$ and $COST_{-j}$ were derived for a given initial set of wages and prices. It can be argued that as soon as relative wages and prices start moving, families will start choosing between other alternatives than those represented here. If wage rates rise, for example, both Z_j and the alternatives to it may become more commodity-intensive as people seek to substitute commodities for time. There is indeed a familiar index number problem here: any change can make the weights inappropriate for measuring the change. Yet the relative cost index is one that is likely to remain appropriate even in the face of changing input prices, since only the differences in input shares (the c_i's minus the d_i's) matter. As long as the input-share differences change little, the fact that the input shares in both bundles are changing will not make the index less applicable. The algebraic conditions sufficient to make the index

---

be between unequally valued bundles when wage rates are not exogenous. My treatment of this measurement issue is shown in more detail in Appendixes A through F.

exactly correct despite changing conditions are not very strict,[19] and the conditions that would make it approximately correct are broader still.

Thus far the framework has sidestepped two issues relating to the value of time: how to deal with the fact that work itself brings pleasure and pain aside from pay, and how to value the time of a family member who does not work for pay. Both call for a brief clarification.

By discussing optimization with respect to inputs *other* than work, or "home" activity inputs, the framework has derived the marginal conditions that are relevant to the trade-off between paid work and home time. The marginal utility of any home time use is its marginal utility over the enjoyment that would be experienced if the same time were spent at the job of one's choosing. If one wishes to imagine a shift in the enjoyability of work, one can simply hypothesize a downward shift in the marginal utility of each home use of time. Marginal utility must be relative to some *numeraire*, and time on the job is used as the *numeraire* activity here. It can be argued that treating the enjoyability of work as something strictly relative fails to distinguish extra enjoyability of work from extra displeasure in being at home. True, we all see a difference between having a job become less boring and having one's home life become more so. But to make this distinction operational, one would need some way of tracking the trade-off between any life activity (e.g., the job) and living in a coma or not at all. This way of letting the enjoyability of work be explicit raises some nasty "value of life" issues that cannot be tackled here.

---

[19] To derive the sufficient conditions, change the symbols in a way that expresses input shares as price levels times quantities rather than as price indices times input shares. For the base period

$$c_i = \frac{p_i X_{ji}}{\text{COST}_j} \quad \text{and} \quad d_i = \frac{p_i X_{-ji}}{\text{COST}_{-j}},$$

where the X's are now real input quantities (present discounted values divided by present input prices). Let the COST values be so defined that their movements reflect changes in quantities as well as changes in price levels. It can be shown by differentiating that the input share difference $c_i - d_i$ is unaffected by any one price movement ($\overset{*}{p}_k$) as long as

$$c_i(1 - c_i)(\overset{*}{p}_k + \overset{*}{X}_{ji}) = d_i(1 - d_i)(\overset{*}{p}_k + \overset{*}{X}_{-ji}),$$

where the asterisks denote percentage rates of change and k might or might not be the same as i. For any c_i and d_i, there is an infinite number of pairs of X's in response to $\overset{*}{p}_k$ (along a straight line) that satisfy the equation. In general, the greater the inequality in the shares of any input in the two bundles initially, the greater the difference between the two input-quantity responses that would be sufficient.

The fact that most family members will end up not working in any given year requires an alteration in the way of valuing time. If it turns out that the family finds it nonoptimal for, say, the wife to work, the optimization exercise must be performed anew with her paid work time constrained to be zero. In this second round of optimization the shadow price of her time is determined from the first-order conditions along with the allocation of all time and commodities across home activities. Since the wife is passing up the option to work, the shadow price of her home time (in terms of commodities) will be somewhat above her would-be market wage, though the magnitude of this discrepancy will be limited by substitution in the home between the use of her time and the use of such marketed inputs as her husband's time and commodities.

The discrepancy between the shadow price of a nonworking wife's time and her would-be wage rate poses some problem for the measurement of relative costs and lifetime wealth, but the difficulty is not too serious. Using her market wage rate in measures of lifetime wealth would bias the latter measures downward a bit. The measurement of movements in the relative cost of any home activity, on the other hand, is little affected if the wage rate misrepresents the shadow price of a family member's time. The value of a family member's time has a significant effect on the relative price of a home activity only if that activity affects the total amount of time that family member devotes to home activities. This is not true for a nonworker whose shadow price is well above the market wage rate. The relative cost index as constructed above succeeds in reflecting the irrelevance of wage rate movements by entering the same amount of the nonworker's time in the numerator ($COST_j$) and the denominator ($COST_{-j}$). Any bias in the choice of a time price for the nonworker thus affects numerator and denominator equally, therefore making no difference to the behavior of the relative cost index.

III. *The Optimal Number of Certain Births*

The optimization model can now be extended to encompass decisions regarding family expansion. The extension must be made in stages. I shall first proceed as though the couple were planning its completed family size in the face of uncertainty over the psychic returns to be gained from the child and the input costs of the child. Next the choice of timing of births will be briefly discussed, still assuming that births are certain though their consequences are not. The treatment of timing will convert a theory of completed family size into a sketch of a theory that recognizes the sequential nature of family growth decisions. In the next section, I shall shift to a theory of birth probabilities to incorporate the obvious fact that couples choose not birth outcomes but strategies of fertility regulation. Only in the final section shall I develop the model of tastes that is a crucial supplement to this formal discussion of how incomes, costs, and psychic benefits are linked by optimization.

The optimal completed family size is not a number that falls out of the first-order conditions above, since the number of children is not a continuous variable. Couples can only consider integral numbers of children. The optimal family size can therefore be determined only by scanning separate optima for each family size and choosing the best of these. For each family size the planning couple considers what its life would be like if it chose the best course it could, given that family size. This best course would reflect the couple's preferences for work, for home activities, and in particular for the levels of inputs into each child. In choosing between the optima for different family sizes, the couple does not find a tangency point but rather finds the family size for which the discrete changes in utility of switching to any other size would be negative.

The choice of family size will, as in the continuous-variable case, depend on tastes, home technology, lifetime wealth, and relative costs. Most of the taste considerations are obvious enough. Most people want to "be parents" to at least two children strongly enough to rule out the childless and one-child alternatives. Others cannot conceive or raise additional children for medical or emotional reasons. People also have strong preferences for the amount of inputs to be devoted to each child, and choose a family size that makes this input level feasible. At the present formal level of discussion, no more need be said about taste factors. As for lifetime wealth, its definition and relevance are the same for family-size decisions as for other choices. We need only bear in mind that it must be defined and measured for a given family growth course, since the number and timing of births affects the parents' pay scales and, of course, the earnings of children within the parents' household. The other measurable economic variable, the relative cost of children, can also be easily derived from the model of the last section. Only two changes are needed to convert the formula for the relative cost of any activity into a relative child cost formula. First, for convenience, replace the symbols $COST_j$ and $COST_{-j}$ with the new labels $COST_N$ and $COST_H$ as mnemonics for the input cost of adding the Nth family member and the cost of the input cost of the *home* activities he or she would replace.

Second, use discrete changes in place of the partial derivatives above. The resulting formula identifies the index weights and input price movements to which numbers will be attached in Chapter 4.

Little would be gained at this point by trying to specify a functional form for the relationship between optimal family size and the wealth, taste, and cost variables. Even with the present assumption that conception and nonconception are perfectly controlled, the optimal family size is an awkward bracketed function of lifetime wealth and relative costs, taking integral jumps whenever threshold wealth and cost levels are crossed. By the time the full model is sketched for an individual family and then aggregated over families, it is hard to sustain any presumption about what the final form of the fertility function should be. It is best to concentrate on correctly specifying the variables on which fertility should depend and the signs of first derivatives, leaving the choice of functional form to be determined by apparent goodness of fit.

The theory of family size just sketched, like many theories of completed family size, has a logical flaw. It admits that uncertainty about future benefits and costs is fundamental, yet argues as though the couple commits itself to a single plan. Clearly family planning is sequential, with the couple standing ready to revise plans along the way as they get further information about economic conditions, about the children already born, and about their own feelings. They remake their plans every year, or at least every time they have another child. One familiar pattern of family planning that is clearly sequential is that which is based on a preference regarding the sex of children. A couple determined to have two sons and indifferent to daughters will quit if the first two children are healthy boys, but will continue to shake the dice if they turn out to be girls. Other couples revise their family size "targets" up or down after finding out the initial physical and emotional effects of having their early children. What is needed then is not a theory of desired final family size so much as a theory of the number of births desired over the next few months or years. This requires that the influences on projected family size already alluded to be supplemented by a theory of the timing of births, or a theory of what factors govern the share of total desired births to which couples actually commit themselves over some shorter period of time.

There are many factors governing the timing of births. All of the influences on desired completed family size are also relevant to timing. So are some other factors, some tending to make births more widely spaced and some tending to push them closer together. Births will tend to be more widely spaced (1) the more the mother needs to recuperate and adjust after each birth, (2) the more worried the husband and wife are about giving enough time to each of two or more very small (time-consuming) infants, and (3) the more uncertain the couple is about changing economic conditions. This last is an "option demand" argument for birth postponement. Having a child is an irreversibility, like leveling Redwood National Forest or having a vasectomy. Since couples are not free to kill off or sell off children who don't turn out as hoped, the couple has an incentive to hold out for better information before getting committed to any extra child. The couple places some value on keeping its options open by limiting fertility when in doubt about the advisability of expanding the family. In general, the greater the uncertainty that can be resolved by holding out for better information, the greater the option demand for postponing births, and therefore the lower the optimal birth rate for any time period. The option demand factor, unlike the other two, is a factor tending to postpone *first* births as well as later births.

A corresponding list of factors promotes the earlier birth and closer spacing of each child after the first. Couples are often concerned about the possibility of later subfecundity and damage to maternal health caused by late-age childbirth. Often they also wish to provide the existing children with brothers and sisters near them in age. There is also an option demand for accelerating births caused by fear of infant mortality: a couple having a target number of surviving children in mind will want to retain the option of having extra childbirths should older children die or be at high mortality risk.

There is another timing factor, one that is economic and tends to push the timing of births in both directions. Childbearing conflicts with the mother's schooling and work, especially in the twentieth century. Taking time out for maternity not only reduces a woman's earnings by reducing her work hours, but it also lowers her lifetime wage rate since being at home cuts back her formation of human capital at school or on the job. The stronger this effect, and its magnitude is growing, the stronger her incentive to minimize the loss of training and earning time. Women with more schooling and higher potential wage rates will tend to postpone their first births[20] but tend to accelerate subsequent births

---

[20] The incentive to postpone a first birth is tied to the importance of training and earning power only after an additional consideration is introduced: percentage increases in earning potential, and the rate of return to human capital formation, tend to decline with each additional year of schooling or job experience. The years of human capital formation that matter most are the earlier years, and for this reason wives with more training and higher training potential

to hasten the day of re-entry into the labor force.[21] Which of the two effects is more important for the total fertility rate is an empirical issue, the outcome depending on whether later changes in plans for completed family size respond more sensitively to postponement of a first birth or to acceleration of subsequent births.

IV. *Imperfect Contraception and Birth Probabilities*

What has been sketched thus far is a theory of age-specific planned fertility. It can be applied to time periods of commitment of any length, though periods of five years or less would seem most appropriate in view of the emphasis on the couple's tendency to revise its plans after the period in question. The theory must now be converted, however, from a theory of planned and certain births to a theory of birth probabilities.[22] Couples typically choose among fertility regulation strategies having different birth probabilities. Of these only abortion, sterilization, and complete abstinence from coition offer certainty (at a cost in each case).

The married couple must gamble. They must choose a fertility regulation strategy the outcome of which is uncertain. Even a strategy guaranteeing nonconception, like sterilization, is risky in that it may later prove to lead to great unhappiness or great happiness, since its psychic

---

have an incentive to postpone first births. I shall return to the relationship between the rate of return on extra human investments and their level and timing in the section of this chapter on input norms.

[21] For some evidence that higher education reduces the spacing of births for a given completed parity and age of mother, see Sue Goetz Ross, "Timing and Spacing of Births," ms., NBER, 1972; Robert T. Michael, "Education and the Derived Demand for Children," *Journal of Political Economy* 81, no. 2, pt. 2 (March/April 1973), S161–162; Bumpass and Westoff, *Later Years of Childbearing*, pp. 34–36; and U.S. Bureau of Census, *Childspacing . . . 1960* (1968). The evidence relates to actual births, while the current text draws implications relating to intended births. Still, the following section of this chapter will make clear my reasons for assuming that patterns holding for actual births hold for intended births and unintended births alike.

[22] In what follows no mention will be made of the case in which couples desire more children than the "natural" rate dictated by social practices and biological constraints, since such cases are rare in America since the mid–nineteenth century. For a larger framework incorporating both regulated and natural fertility, see Richard A. Easterlin, "The Economics and Sociology of Fertility: A Synthesis," ms., April 1973.

The necessity of shifting attention from a theory of completed family size to a theory of birth probabilities over a shorter period of time has already been stressed by Namboodiri ("Economic Framework," p. 198) and by the sources by Goldberg and by Mishler and Westoff cited there.

effects cannot be perfectly foreseen. The couple thus maximizes expected utility by choosing a strategy of fertility regulation from among a finite number of strategies, each of which yields a level of expected utility. The range of strategies considered consists of variations on those regulation techniques known to the couple. The expected utility of each strategy is the product of the probability of conception within the period of commitment times the expected utility of conception, plus the probability of nonconception times the expected utility of not conceiving. The expected utility of each outcome—conception and nonconception—depends on the psychic cost and input cost of adopting the contraception strategy. The expected utility of conception depends on the psychic cost of taking inputs ($COST_H$) away from other activities and on the psychic benefits from raising the child, which in turn are a weighted average of the utilities of such outcomes as the sex of the child, the health of child and mother, and so forth. If conception occurs, the couple reappraises its plans given the existence of another child. If not, the couple reappraises its plans as soon as it feels the need to reappraise.

The process of choosing a birth control strategy can be illustrated with the help of Figure 3–1. The situation portrayed there might be that of a young non-Catholic couple in the 1950s having two children and not planning a third within this planning period (say, a year). The assumption that the third child would be unplanned is reflected in the downward slope of each strategy line: the outcome of not conceiving this year is preferred to conceiving, all things considered. This comparison of outcomes reflects all of the considerations introduced in Sections II and III above. The couple also has its own feelings about different methods of birth control. They find abstinence and rhythm highly undesirable, and the diaphragm involves some inconvenience and a slight economic cost. These feelings about methods are reflected in the vertical ranking of the four alternative strategies for any given probability of birth outcome. The strategies also differ, of course, in their birth probabilities. Sensing all these things, the couple selects the strategy—again, not the outcome—with the highest expected utility. In Figure 3–1, using a diaphragm is optimal. If wage and price movements were to raise the relative cost of a third child, the strategy lines would tilt counterclockwise somewhat, possibly making it optimal to abandon contraception. This sort of diagram illustrates the interplay of the utility of outcomes, the utility of birth control methods, and per-

Figure 3-1. A Hypothetical Choice of Birth Control Strategy.

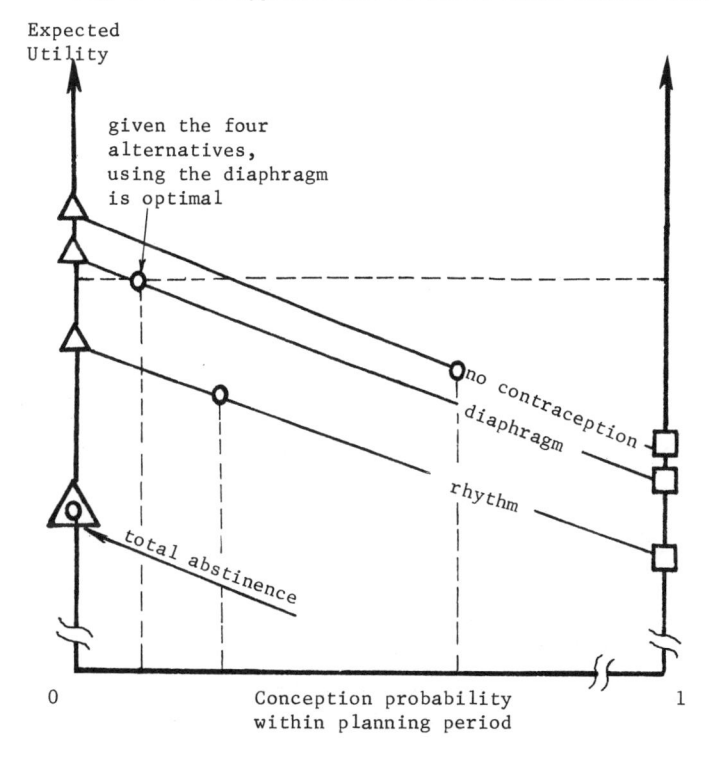

[Figure: Graph with Expected Utility on vertical axis and Conception probability within planning period on horizontal axis (0 to 1). Four downward-sloping lines labeled "no contraception", "diaphragm", "rhythm", and "total abstinence". Annotation: "given the four alternatives, using the diaphragm is optimal."]

Key: □ = maximum utility of conceiving a child within this planning period, with use of the strategy in question.

△ = ditto, not conceiving.

○ = expected utility (vertical axis) and conception probability (horizontal axis) of each birth control strategy.

ceived method effectiveness through which the couple chooses its best gamble.

This probabilistic structure points the way to a reordering of the tasks of fertility analysis. It suggests that the theories of planned and of unplanned births are one and the same. The best theory is a unified theory of gambling with coition and conception. The easiest way to see this is to consider how the concepts of "unwanted" and "unplanned" births could be made operational within this framework. When asked whether an existing or possible child is "unwanted," couples are being asked about an *outcome* of their best fertility regulation strategy, not about the desirability of the strategy itself. An unwanted child is one for whom the expected utility of conception[23] at any time in the parents' lives is less than the utility of not conceiving. An unplanned child is one for whom the utility of conception within this time period, say five years, is less than the utility of not conceiving within this time period. Yet both unwanted and unplanned births can result from optimal family planning, since the couple typically chooses among regulation strategies and not among outcomes. The concepts of planned and unplanned children, like the concepts of lifetime wealth and relative child cost, are specific to the outcomes of fertility regulation strategies, and are thus merely different aspects of the same optimization problem.[24]

How do socioeconomic factors impinge on the choice of fertility regulation strategy? Socioeconomic variables affect the range of strategies known to the couple, their perceived and true probabilities of conception, and their perceived and ultimate utilities of each outcome. For reasons already mentioned (pages 40 and 41 above), I think more emphasis should be placed on the link between socioeconomic variables and the utilities of the outcome than on class differences in access to contraceptive knowledge or in the efficiency of using any one strategy. The argument against stressing differences in contraceptive knowledge and skill deserves elaboration here.

It is clear that improvements such as the pill have become more accessible as the nation has become wealthier and more educated. The corresponding pattern also holds somewhat for recent cross sections: those few Americans who do not know about some major technique of birth restriction are poor and uneducated. Yet the number who have not heard about, say, the pill is too small for differences in education to explain differences in fertility through differences in contraceptive knowledge. Nor did the large differentials in fertility in the nineteenth century seem to reflect a link between education and

[23] Couples may in practice confuse a question about the desirability of the conception outcome with the desirability of the birth outcome. They may call a planned conception unplanned, for example, if the birth resulted in twins or in a boy when a girl was preferred.

[24] Strictly speaking, the concept of relative child cost should be specific to a given fertility regulation strategy. The data used to measure relative child cost in Chapter 4 may not exactly coincide with this definition, since the parameters are estimated from cross sections over which strategies presumably differed. No significant bias should result, however, since the market cost of fertility-regulating inputs is so low that the work and expenditure patterns associated with the conception outcome of one strategy will be practically identical with those for another strategy.

knowledge of techniques, since the main techniques of that time were known to all classes. While the data do suggest that the supply of the means to regulate fertility is an important parameter, the data also suggest that the socioeconomic patterns we observe in the use, acceptability, and even the knowledge of fertility control methods relate at least as strongly to motivation as to access. As noted above, surveys show that the groups that end up having more children want more in advance and even expect in advance to have a greater number of unwanted children. The tendency of planned, unplanned, and actual births to share similar correlations with socioeconomic (and religious) variables suggests a serious identification problem. We cannot separate out the effect of a socioeconomic variable, such as schooling, on knowledge of contraceptive techniques (given the desirability of each contraception outcome) from its effect on the motivation to restrict births (given a degree of contraceptive knowledge). It can always be argued that knowledge differs across groups primarily because those who care more invest more in acquiring knowledge about fertility control. The issue is difficult to resolve empirically. I nonetheless choose to pursue the motivational argument here, in order to explore a set of hypotheses that have not been given due emphasis to date.

The present argument is that low-fertility groups, such as the more-educated groups in most cross sections, are groups that have fewer unwanted births (as well as fewer wanted births) primarily because they have more at stake in birth probabilities. The rationale for this argument might seem at first glance to lie in the fact that the optimal input level for an extra child will be much higher for the more highly educated couple, whereas the market cost of inputs into fertility-reducing strategies is not higher (and is often lower) for them. An extra child would cost them more, so they might seem to have a greater incentive to avoid an extra unwanted birth. This does not follow, however, and a more careful argument must be made. Each child indeed takes more inputs in the more-educated family, but up to some point the amount of inputs the more-educated couple would *want* to devote to an extra child is also greater.

To argue that the incentive to prevent each unwanted birth is stronger for the more-educated couple, we must more carefully specify how the *net* gain or loss in utility is likely to relate to birth order and to parents' education.[25] The comparison must be between the first un-

[25] The difficulty of inferring strong motivation to control births from the level of child cost alone has already been noted by Michael ("Derived Demand," p. S160n).

wanted or unplanned birth in each context. If the more-educated couple wanted two children and the less-educated couple wanted four, the relevant question is whether the arrival of a third child, the first one for which the utility of conception fell short of the utility of nonconception, would cause a greater net loss of utility to the more-educated parents than the fifth would cause for the less-educated parents. Phrased this way, the question seeks to compare utilities across families, which is treacherous. More tractable is a variation on the same theme: if both couples were equally skilled at using any fertility regulation method, would we expect the demand curve for any more restrictive method to be higher for the more-educated couple? It would seem very plausible to suppose that they had a greater demand for such insurance. As Chapter 4 will confirm, the inputs into the first unwanted child represent a greater share of total lifetime wealth for the more-educated couple, primarily because the first unwanted child occurs at an earlier birth order. Since the first unwanted child forces a greater percentage reallocation of inputs in the more-educated family, it disrupts their lives more. It seems reasonable to infer that the absolute amount of inputs into other activities they would forego in order to purchase birth prevention insurance is much greater. Restated in this way, the argument is valid that the higher input norms attached to each child by the more-educated couple gives them a greater stake in preventing unwanted births.

V. *The Formation of Family Input Preferences*

The model of fertility, and the explanation for the education-fertility pattern, remain incomplete. The last section argued that whatever made couples want fewer children also tended to make them have fewer unwanted births. The issue remains: what makes the more-educated want fewer children, both over time and in cross sections? Of the variables treated so far, only the relative cost of a given set of child inputs can contribute to an explanation of why those with more resources choose fewer children rather than the same number of children on the average. As already mentioned, the relative cost variable, even combined with the contraceptive-knowledge argument, seems incapable of explaining the socioeconomic patterns fully. Fertility has declined with education (and related modernization variables) even in settings in which the relative cost of a given set of child inputs has not been rising. To complete the explanation, we must re-examine the effects of education and related variables on tastes.

All of the modernization variables, I shall argue, transmit their effects on tastes primarily through a single intermediate variable: the prior inputs into members of the families in which the current generation of young adults grew up. These prior inputs are a prime determinant of young couples' views toward birth outcomes. Their influence spans all of the couples' adult lifetime. In what follows, it is convenient to describe prior inputs as an influence on completed cohort fertility, even though this chapter incorporates them into a theory of shorter-run birth probabilities.

To want fewer children is to want more time and commodity inputs per family member. Tastes for family size are thus tied to tastes for inputs per person. This link is assured by the budget constraint:

$$(14) \quad \begin{pmatrix} \text{Lifetime} \\ \text{wealth} \end{pmatrix} = \begin{pmatrix} \text{value of inputs} \\ \text{into child-unre-} \\ \text{lated activities} \end{pmatrix} + \begin{bmatrix} \text{inputs per} \\ \text{child, into} \\ \text{child-related} \\ \text{activities} \end{bmatrix} \times \begin{pmatrix} \text{number of} \\ \text{children} \end{pmatrix}$$

which is a simplification of Equation (5) above. Since the net effect of changes in family size on lifetime (potential, full-time) wealth is slight, a choice of family size or of birth probabilities is a choice of inputs per family member. A theory of input preferences can thus serve as a theory of family size preferences. I shall sketch such a theory here in three stages. First I shall present and briefly defend my choice of taste parameters. Next I shall argue that the parameter emphasized most, prior inputs per person in the two families that raised the young couple currently making its family decisions, has similar percentage taste effects on inputs into adult activities and on inputs per child. I shall then return to the task of showing that the model can explain the prevalence of a negative relationship between fertility and modernization variables. The theory sketched here is applicable to both cross-sectional and time-series patterns of behavior.

Young couples' tastes are clearly affected by a whole host of environmental conditions. Some of these are so specific to the individual couple that they must be treated as random noise in regressions. Others are more systematic and involve a trade-off between child-related activities and child-unrelated activities. For example, devout Catholicism—at least from 1930 to 1964—has been a taste variable making devout U.S.

Catholics desire both more children and a higher ratio of inputs per child to strictly adult-activity inputs than others prefer. The same trade-off is involved in any other religious or cultural variable that defines woman's achievement in terms of children. More common, however, are taste influences that entail shifts between family size on the one hand and inputs per family member—adult or child—on the other. Five influences that seem to have this property are:

1. The pattern of family time and commodity inputs into the couple as they were growing up
2. The child-unrelated activities enjoyed by the parents of the young couple
3. The social inputs into them (such as public educational expenditures)
4. The pattern of current family expenditures and time use in the group with which the young couple compares itself
5. The number of the couple's siblings

Though all of these parameters influence couples' tastes, my hunch is that they rank as durable influences in the order in which they have been listed here. The first two are viewed as the key parameters in the forming of tastes for both inputs per child and inputs into the couple's child-unrelated activities.

Before describing the mechanism through which prior inputs into the young couple and their parents affect their tastes, I should briefly give my reasons for thinking that the other three parameters listed above are likely to have less systematic relevance. The apparent importance of these variables stems largely from the fact that they are correlates of prior inputs into the young couple. Even when education is publicly financed, for example, the educational attainment of young adults is governed largely by the levels of family inputs,[26] including the amount

[26] Studies of educational attainment usually reveal the importance of "family background" variables that reflect more than the levels of family inputs per child. The background variables can be viewed as symptoms of three components of a comprehensive family background variable: heredity, the levels of family time and commodity inputs, and the efficiency with which the parents produce educational attainment and other achievements with given inputs. The present text proceeds as though the input levels and their economic value were a good proxy for the overall influence of family background. Chapter 6 will defend my belief in a strong correlation between the input value and such outcomes as educational attainment.

My subordination of the educational experience to home background as a fertility factor is also supported by data showing that college seniors' expecta-

of the child's time unavailable for immediate home use because the child is in school. This is especially true where, as in America, higher-income families can purchase public-school quality by buying a residence in a richer school district. The behavior of the young couple's comparison group, while another proximate influence on their tastes, seems better viewed as the result of other taste and income variables. A couple's comparison group will tend to be selected, either by the couple or by the actions of their parents, so as to match the couple's own prior input levels, current income, and independent idiosyncrasies of tastes. The parents' choice of residence and social groupings makes the comparison group of the young couple partly the result of a history of family inputs extending back even beyond the couple's memory. Finally, the number of the young couple's siblings seems inappropriate as an independent variable in fertility analysis for a number of reasons.[27]

The prior inputs into the couple's development are viewed as influence on both their tastes for child-unrelated activities and their tastes for inputs into each child, as well as influences on their income. The case for assuming that these prior inputs affect the levels of child-unrelated activities is fairly straightforward. The argument has already been made by others, using education in place of child inputs. The more a child receives extra inputs in the home or in public facilities, the greater his or her familiarity with less traditional and less essential goods and services

---

tions and preferences about family size are formed before they come to college (Charles F. Westoff and Raymond H. Potvin, *College Women and Fertility Values*, Princeton: Princeton University Press, 1967).

[27] Specifically, I have three objections to the use of the number of couples' siblings as an independent variable in explaining current fertility. First, my theoretical prejudice is that young couples learn to be more rigid in the choice of inputs into each child (how each should be raised) than in the choice of family size. Interview data and casual observation suggest that people are more tolerant of great differences in family size than they are deviations from input norms "appropriate to one's position." (See, for example, the sort of responses about family size quoted at length by Lee Rainwater, *And the Poor Get Children*, Chicago, 1960, and his *Family Design*, Chicago, 1965.) Second, using the number of siblings can give misleading results. Since the number of siblings amounts to a lagged value of the dependent variable (current fertility), it can display significant influence in a regression even if the true relationship gave no independent role to the number of parents' siblings. The sibling term could be capturing parts of all sorts of influences that affected succeeding generations similarly. Finally, despite this likely statistical bias in favor of a sibling variable, it seems unable to follow correctly the fertility impact of wars, the Depression, and educational advance in American history. The young couples of the decade 1965–74, for example, grew up with more siblings than did the young couples of the 1950s, yet they had much lower fertility.

—the sorts of inputs already spent on him or her. It is natural for a person to expect the establishment of a separate household to be accompanied by a steady expansion of the sorts of home inputs into personal recreation and skills enjoyed during childhood.

The influence of prior inputs on tastes regarding inputs into one's own children is as natural as, and if anything more rigid than, the effect of prior inputs on tastes regarding current adult-activity inputs. The mode of child-rearing is the part of the previous family life that young couples experienced most directly. It is also the part of our family past on which we depend most heavily for guidance, because we perceive that the child-rearing process is complex and that learning by trial and error without reference to past experience is risky. The pull of the familiar is strong when a young parent is faced with the infinite range of uncertain considerations in child-rearing. Few of us can optimize by the light of pure reason in such matters without falling back, often unconsciously, on the only child-rearing pattern we had studied firsthand before marriage. Couples thus tend to provide the sorts of inputs of time, energy, and commodities that promise to raise the kind of child they feel capable of enjoying, guiding, and understanding—one that receives inputs like those they received.

People's perceptions of their own upbringing are not, of course, perceptions of the economic value of the family inputs into them. Nobody knows the input magnitudes put into him. What we remember and adhere to are notions of what a child should and should not have. These "needs" come in many dimensions. We have views on discipline, allowances, diet, smoking, religious instruction, living space, child work, and so on—views rooted mainly in family history. Yet the dollar values of the inputs these preferences tend to reflect and produce is an important magnitude. Couples' family size preferences are governed by a vague sense of how much of the things they and each of their children "need" can be afforded on their income. They will accordingly behave as though they were aware of the dollar magnitude put into each child and the dollar magnitude of prior inputs into themselves, even though in fact they never tote up the child input bill.

The effect of the prior-inputs parameter on current inputs per family member is not absolutely rigid. As prices, income, and birth outcomes progress over the years, couples do alter the input levels per family member. It seems likely that couples' price and income elasticities of inputs per family member rise as income rises in relation to prior inputs. When income falls, couples tend to cling fairly closely to the input standards they feel they need, and to cut family size if possible. Their unwillingness to cut inputs per child greatly stems from the desire to ensure against failure as parents by giving each child something like (though not exactly) the inputs they received. They will also tend to keep down the responsiveness of both adult and child activity inputs to income increases ("Sure, we could afford to send her to camp again, but she doesn't need it and it's high time she learned the value of the dollar. Why, when I was her age. . . ."), but the line is held less firmly when incomes are rising than when they are falling.

By itself, this asymmetry implies that fertility should drop more severely in response to income cuts than it should rise when prospects improve. The asymmetry in fertility response need not show up clearly in the data, however, since in the short run fertility declines are limited by the inability of parents to have negative births when incomes fall.

The emphasis on the absolute levels of prior inputs as a taste parameter is quite consistent with other authors' stress on the importance of the incomes and customary expenditure levels of a couple's comparison group. It has been argued that couples' family size preferences are governed largely by the ratio they perceive between their current income and the levels of living expected of someone in their position. The comparison-group yardstick is variously interpreted as the couple's perceived income adequacy,[28] the expenditures or incomes of friends or others with the same education and occupation,[29] or the level of investments per child that will preserve the differential between the family's status and income and the social average.[30] As mentioned above, this comparison norm is largely governed by the couple's own style of upbringing and individual tastes. Young couples and their parents tend to select an external yardstick that makes them feel capable of measuring up, as adults and as parents. Just as they would feel deprived if their inputs per family member fell below the expectations generated by their own upbringing, they also feel uncomfortable and threatened by com-

[28] See, for example, Ronald Freedman and Lolagene Coombs, "Economic Considerations in Family Growth Decisions," *Population Studies* 20 (November 1966), 210.

[29] See, for example, ibid., p. 212; and Deborah Freedman, "The Relation of Economic Status to Fertility," *American Economic Review* 53 (June 1963), 415.

[30] This last form of the relative-status hypothesis was perhaps most clearly advanced by Banks' study of Victorian fertility:

> At bottom the desire for education [of one's own children] sprang from the fundamental aim of preserving the social differential, in income as well as in status. (Banks, *Prosperity and Parenthood*, p. 164)

parison and contact with a group to whose tastes and achievements they would have a hard time adjusting. Couples thus seek out associations with people having similar prior inputs, just as they did in seeking a partner in marriage, and they tend to raise their own children in a way that is familiar and promises a good chance of successful replication of their own capabilities and tastes.[31] In other words, the status and living standards of the comparison group are largely a symptom of a couple's own upbringing.

Not all of the influence associated with couples' comparison group norms, however, should be assigned to the prior inputs into a couple. Current movements in class tastes still have an effect on inputs and fertility apart from the history of the couple. Any current force that gives couples the impression that the returns from, or necessity of, extra inputs per person are rising will reduce the number of their likely childbirths. Examples would be events that promised reductions in discrimination and improvements in socioeconomic mobility. Whenever possible, such events should be introduced as independent variables, and the influence attributed to comparison-group norms should be divided up between these current forces and family-history variables such as prior child inputs.

The argument thus far can be summarized schematically with the help of Figure 3–2. Any young couple, like that represented as Generation one at the right of the diagram, reaches a family size and set of input levels under present and past influences. Most of the relative cost influences, such as the relative cost of another child, remain parameters of the present state of the economy. Income prospects are also largely a function of the current state of demand for labor and property. Some of the

[31] The argument that couples try to prepare children for lives like their own by providing inputs like those they received is at least consistent with the literature on class differences in modes of childbearing. (See for example, Robert R. Sears, Eleanor E. Maccoby, and Harry Levin, *Patterns of Child Rearing*, Evanston, Ill., 1957, Chap. 12; Urie Bronfenbrenner, "Socialization and Social Class through Time and Space," in W. Warren Kallenbach and Harold M. Hodges, eds., *Education and Society*, Columbus, Ohio, 1963, pp. 171–177; Catherine S. Chilson, *Growing up Poor*, Washington, 1967; Melvin L. Kohn, *Class and Conformity: A Study in Values*, Homewood, Ill., 1969.) In fact, this argument is even consistent, perhaps by chance, with the observation of Bronfenbrenner that class differences in attitudes toward child discipline seemed to lessen between the late 1920s and the 1950s. This was a period over which the distribution of income also became much more equal. It may be that the economic forces that caused the prior inputs experienced by young adults to converge also fostered a convergence in the degrees of parental emphasis on child obedience and child independence.

REMODELLING THE HOUSEHOLD

Figure 3-2. Some Intergenerational Influences on Family Behavior.

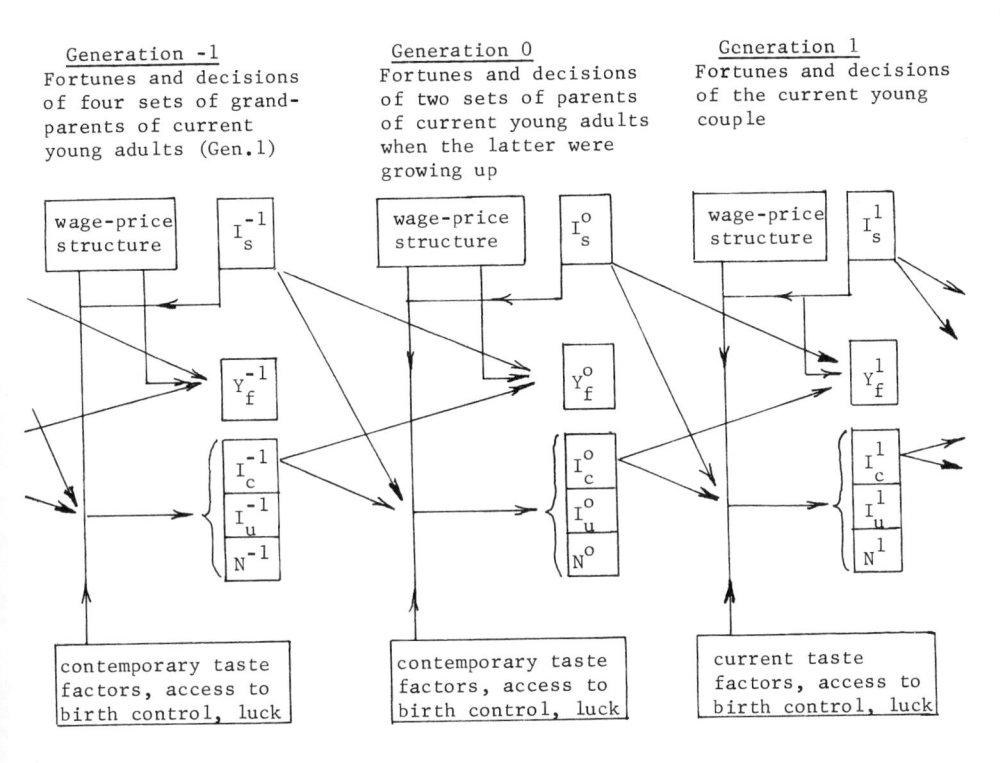

Generation -1	Generation 0	Generation 1
Fortunes and decisions of four sets of grandparents of current young adults (Gen.1)	Fortunes and decisions of two sets of parents of current young adults when the latter were growing up	Fortunes and decisions of the current young couple

[Diagram with boxes for each generation showing: wage-price structure, I_s^{-1}, I_s^0, I_s^1; Y_f^{-1}, Y_f^0, Y_f^1; I_c^{-1}, I_u^{-1}, N^{-1}; I_c^0, I_u^0, N^0; I_c^1, I_u^1, N^1; with arrows connecting them. Below each column: "contemporary taste factors, access to birth control, luck" (for Gen -1 and Gen 0); "current taste factors, access to birth control, luck" (for Gen 1).]

Key: Y_f = family lifetime expected wealth, for a given family composition.

I_s^0 = society's inputs into the children of Generation 0 (the young adults of Generation 1).

I_c^0 = the family's childrearing inputs per child, same generation.

I_u = inputs into child-unrelated activities.

N = completed family size (i.e. the birth outcomes of a whole generation of shorter-run fertility regulation strategies like those modelled in Section IV above).

influence of income on the couple's behavior, on the other hand, stems from the inputs of the previous generation into the couple's child development and nonhuman wealth. As for tastes, the influence usually attributed to educational attainment, peer-group pressure, and occupation has been transferred to the family's past, and in particular to the pattern and levels of prior inputs into the young couple by their parents (I^0_c) and by society (I^0_s). Other taste variables, such as religion, can be left in the present.

[73]

What has been gained by pushing most of taste influences and maybe half of the determination of income back a generation? First, a basis has been established for better separating income and taste correlates from each other. The taste variables rooted in past magnitudes are less closely tied to current income than are occupation and socioeconomic status, enabling sharper testing of this and other models in samples where people's past histories are quite different from their current fortunes. For example, the identification of past influences helps to sort out the determinants of aggregate fertility in the wake of wars and swings in economic conditions. Samples characterized by a high degree of personal mobility can also yield better descriptions of fertility patterns when data on past inputs are applied. This gain seems real enough, since Chapter 5 will argue that the prior inputs into a current generation of adults can in fact be measured fairly reliably at the aggregate level. A second gain is that one can proceed from this model to link current fertility behavior to the past economic and social parameters that lie behind the family's pattern of upbringing. That is, current fertility can be linked not only to current movements in job prospects, attitudes toward women, and so forth, but to the movements of these parameters over several generations, data permitting. The prior-inputs variable highlighted here, in other words, can be used as a mechanism for tying current fertility behavior to more remote historical forces.

VI. *Fertility and Modernization*

Used carefully, the model can also explain why a negative relationship should prevail between fertility and modernization variables (education, urbanization, high incomes) both in trends and in cross sections. I shall first consider and reject one hypothesis that might seem to account for the negative profiles, and then advance two other arguments that seem more satisfactory.

Discussions of the transition to low fertility often seem to imply an "adult-bias" argument, to the effect that modernization variables have stronger effects on tastes for child-unrelated activities and inputs than they have on inputs per child or income. Modernization creates aspirations for new goods that are predominantly child-unrelated, and the fact that this taste effect is stronger than the income effect of modernization presses such couples to restrict family size in order to satisfy their child-unrelated aspirations.

The adult-bias argument finds little empirical support. To understand why, one must keep in mind the distinction between the inputs required by an extra child and the inputs that would typically go into raising child-rearing inputs for a given number of children. The inputs into an extra child are predominantly traditional inputs with low income elasticities of home demand: food, clothing, shelter, and mother's time. The inputs that would be used to raise inputs per child, however, are just as new, as modern, as income-elastic a bundle as those into the sorts of child-unrelated activities promoted by education, urbanization, and so forth. To raise inputs per child, one consumes more education, recreation, housing space, toys, and transportation.

Whether one argues from the rise of certain groups of goods with modernization or from rough estimates on how modernization affects the total value of inputs per child, one fails to find that modernization raises adult-activity inputs more than it raises inputs per child. Indeed, I shall advance the null hypothesis that increases in prior inputs into a couple (here playing the role of modernization) would have the same percentage effect on child-unrelated inputs as on child-rearing inputs per child if income and relative prices were held constant.

This null hypothesis about tastes received support from what little evidence we have. First, a listing of the "new goods" most associated with modernization in U.S. trends and cross sections fails to establish any bias between adult activities and inputs per child. The outstanding "new goods" categories are transportation, medical care, recreation, and education. Private expenditures on these categories seem as related to increases in child-related inputs per child as to adult inputs. There is little reason for concluding that foreign travel outweighs travel with children to parks and Disneyland, or that increases in using cars to commute outweigh increases in chauffeuring children, and so forth. Second, recent cross-sectional regressions have found that higher education tends to shift household demand for goods and time as much toward child-related inputs (education, time spent on child care) as toward child-unrelated inputs.[32] Finally, the USDA estimates of child commodity costs in 1960–61 imply that neither increases in income nor movement from

[32] On commodities, see Michael, "Derived Demand," pp. S128–164. On time use, see Appendix C below. Holding family size constant, Michael found a shift toward higher budget shares for private education, recreation, toys, medical care, and insurance, and toward lower budget shares for alcohol, tobacco, furniture and appliances, TV, and cars. Appendix C below finds that an increase in parental education has an insignificantly positive effect on the amount of time spent on child care if family composition is held constant, and a significantly positive effect per child if family size is not held constant.

farm to city raises child-unrelated commodity inputs more than these changes raise child-bearing inputs per child, whether or not one holds family size constant.[33] It seems advisable to assume that education, urbanization, and higher income raise tastes for inputs per child as strongly as they raise tastes for inputs into child-unrelated activities.

What then is the mechanism making those with more education, income, urban residence tend to have fewer children? Aside from the higher relative cost of given child inputs, which explains part of this pattern in some settings, two mechanisms can be identified. The first operates through the effect of prior inputs on tastes plus the tendency for extra investments in human capabilities to yield diminishing returns; the second works through the social selectivity of individual tastes regarding family size.

The argument has been advanced above that prior inputs into the young couple are a strong force governing tastes regarding inputs per family member. To help the following argument, I shall make a more restrictive assumption that is plausible but not strictly necessary: I shall assume that a percentage increase in prior inputs would cause the *same* percentage increase in inputs per family member for given income and relative costs.[34] Thus a couple raised on inputs whose economic value was twice the social average would tend to put twice as much as the average family into each child. The difficulty is, however, that differentials in income will fail to match differentials in prior inputs. Couples want-

---

[33] USDA, Agricultural Research Service, *Cost of Raising a Child*, CFE(Adm.)-318, Hyattsville, Md., 1971, esp. Table 6. The figures actually tend to imply that the ratio of adult inputs per child *declines* with urbanization and rising incomes when family size varies with these variables as in the 1960 census. This tendency, however, would be offset to an unknown degree by the tendency of the higher-parity estimates (farm, lower incomes) to involve more sharing of the same inputs by more than one child. For a description of the estimating method used by the USDA, see Jean Pennock, "Cost of Raising a Child," paper delivered at the 47th annual Agricultural Outlook Conference, Washington, D.C., February 1970.

[34] The assumption that is strictly necessary for the following argument about diminishing returns is that

$$\frac{\partial(Y_f^1/I_c^0)}{\partial I_c^0} < \frac{\partial(I^1/I_c^0)}{\partial I_c^0}$$

where I^1 is average current inputs per family member for all home activities, and the other two variables are as defined in Figure 3-2. This condition would be likely to hold even if the right-hand term were slightly negative. The text assumed that the right-hand term is zero only in order to allow me to speak of "diminishing returns" rather than of "returns that diminish faster than input preferences diminish with rising prior inputs," a cumbersome phrase.

ing to give each child a set of inputs that would cost twice as much as the average value of inputs, because they themselves were raised that way, will tend not to have twice as much family wealth; the doubling of the inputs into them will typically fail to double their purchasing power. The reason for this is that the rate of economic return to investments in a child declines as the level of investment rises—or so I assume. The theoretical basis for this assumption is that returns to scale and rates of return should decline over the relevant range of investments as long as there is at least one fixed input. The fixed input is the child himself, whose capacity to absorb skills (or to live and work longer) has limits. Thus parents who received inputs having twice the average value will tend to have *less* than twice the average family resources, and will therefore tend to have fewer children to make it possible for each of their children to receive inputs having twice the average value.

This diminishing returns mechanism can operate even though couples are unaware of the total cost of the inputs into themselves or each of their children, and unaware of the same magnitudes for other families. All that is required is that they wish to raise children in a way resembling their own upbringing, and that they develop a sense of what they can afford. Under these conditions the higher prior input levels associated with such variables as the parents' level of schooling will be accompanied by lower preferred family sizes.

The hypothesis of diminishing returns to investments in child development should not seem surprising. We might have inferred as much from the fact that the unadjusted cross-sectional rates of economic return on schooling seem to decline with the level of schooling.[35] These unadjusted rates tend to reflect the returns to the entire package of investments in an individual in the home, at school, and in the early years of his or her career.[36] The same pattern of declining returns is shown by

---

[35] See, for example, W. Lee Hansen, "Total and Private Rates of Return to Investment in Schooling," *Journal of Political Economy* 71, no. 2 (April 1963), 128–141; Giora Hanoch, "Personal Earnings and Investment in Schooling," unpublished doctoral dissertation, University of Chicago, 1965; and Fred Hines, Luther Tweeten, and Martin Redfern, "Social and Private Rates of Return to Investment in Schooling, by Race-Sex Groups and Regions," *Journal of Human Resources* 5, no. 3 (Summer 1970), 318–340.

[36] This assumes that home inputs vary cross-sectionally in roughly constant proportion with inputs into schooling and job training.

Some readers may question the use of the cross-sectional rates of return as evidence of diminishing rates of return for an individual. It might be pointed out that the tendency of the marginal rates of return to diminish reflects capital market imperfections and differences in time preferences leading to underinvestment in human capital. This is true, but not damaging to the present argument. To explain

estimates of the value of additional job experience, and of extra schooling for given family background and job experience. However, these more refined measures hold some inputs constant in each case, and are less telling than the tendency of the unadjusted cross-sectional rates of return to decline as more and more resources are invested in an individual.

The second mechanism tending to promote a negative fertility-modernization profile is the social selectivity of individual tastes relating to mobility and family size. Among any sample of couples raised similarly, some will prefer smaller families and more inputs per family member than others. Part of their higher inputs per person will tend to be higher investments in their own career advancement (especially that of the wife), raising their relative status while they have fewer children. Thus there would always be some tendency for families choosing to have fewer children to rise in relative status and income over others with similar upbringing, even if there were not diminishing private economic returns to investments in humans.

These two mechanisms, buttressed by relative child cost effects and postwar improvements in contraception, help to explain both the long-run downward trend in fertility with modernization and the prevalence of the negative fertility-modernization pattern in cross sections. At the same time, these forces do not operate so rigidly and tightly that the negative relationship must be expected in every sample or subsample.

The model predicts the same downward trend in aggregate future fertility that it has been designed to help explain in the past. As inputs per person rise over the generations, fertility should go on falling. In this

---

how inputs per person, incomes, and fertility vary cross-sectionally, one should use the cross-sectional rates of return as they stand, since they reflect the differences faced by different people. Yet the diminishing returns argument, referring as it does to the returns to an investment in an individual person, is also valid and relevant here. If we agree that the educational system shifts people on the basis of "ability," part of which is innate and not the result of even home inputs, then one would conclude that those who in fact finished college would have commanded higher pay than those with less ability even if both groups had stopped their schooling and training at the same early level. Thus the returns facing an individual of given ability would decline even more sharply at the relevant later stages of human investment than the cross-sectional data suggest.

We do not know whether rates of return to schooling and other human investments have diminished over time, as they seem to do in cross sections. Weak indirect evidence surveyed by Gary S. Becker (*Human Capital*, New York: Columbia University Press, 1964, pp. 127–134) suggests that the rate of return on a college education declined considerably from 1900 to 1939 and changed little from the latter date to 1961.

respect, the current model differs from the recent "relative status" hypothesis of Easterlin, which implies that fertility will remain constant for constant growth in income, per worker or per capita, over the generations.[37] The implication that fertility goes on declining with modernization fits past trends comfortably enough. It does clash, however, with the intuition that further declines in fertility far below zero population growth (ZPG) rates will be checked by the presumed desire of most couples to have at least two children. It does seem plausible that there may be a floor on family size not predicted by the model. It would be unwise to insist that no such additional taste factor would limit the further decline in fertility. The model should thus be interpreted as asserting here only that fertility is unlikely to rise over the long run in modernized countries, and not that it must go on declining.

An interesting question that follows on this discussion is what the model implies about trends in the cross-sectional fertility differential as a country modernizes. There is a tradition of concern over the dyseugenic specter of having all the children born to poor parents, and it is natural to ask if either the model or the facts imply a widening of class differentials in fertility over time.

Both the model and the facts remain agnostic about a simple overall trend in fertility differentials, though both give some vague arguments in favor of an early widening and a later narrowing. Two arguments suggest an early widening of fertility differentials. First, the model suggests that for any given state of access to birth control, differentials should widen with the historic rise in the share of human investments in the extra legacy that each generation of upper-income parents leaves to its children. This prediction stems from the fact that the diminishing returns argument is assumed to apply only to investments in human development and not to investments in property bequests, which yield steadier and lower inframarginal returns. Second, one could add to the model the conjecture that in certain earlier phases of modernization health improvements might reduce subfecundity primarily among the poor, again widening class differentials in average family size.

In later phases of modernization, three considerations suggest a trend toward smaller class differences in fertility. First, major improvements in contraception, though first adopted by the more-educated, would on balance bring a greater percentage reduction in family size among the poor and less-educated, since unwanted births seem to be a greater

[37] See, for example, Easterlin, "Relative Economic Status and the American Fertility Swing."

share of the total in these groups. This development would tend to compress the differentials. More generally, any force tending to reduce aggregate marital fertility is likely to compress the differentials by pushing the lower-fertility groups down against the two-child minimum that seems necessary to the role of "being a parent." Finally, in most economies, the later stages of modernization have been accompanied by declining income differentials, as will be shown in Chapter 7. Over time this means that inputs per person will also converge. The present model would predict a convergence in class fertility rates after incomes have become more equally distributed. Thus the model plus outside theoretical presumptions suggests an early widening followed by a later compression of class fertility differentials.

Do the facts agree with this vague prediction of theory? We have very few hard historical data on trends in class differentials. Data are particularly scarce for premodern settings. For medieval and early modern Europe and for today's less-developed countries, some samples show a positive fertility-class profile, while others show the reverse, and still others show mixed patterns or no pattern.[38] Family reconstitution studies may soon shed new light on this issue for early modern England and Tokugawa Japan. By the later half of the nineteenth century, the profile had become negatively sloped for Britain and America, and was apparently widening, up to 1910 in the American case.[39] Between 1910

[38] A positive wealth-fertility profile was found in the 1427 cadastral survey of Tuscany by Klapisch (in Peter Laslett, ed., *Household and Family in Past Time*, Cambridge, 1972, p. 274), and in Chinese peasant samples for the 1930s (for sources, see Dennis Wrong, "Class Fertility Differentials Before 1850," *Social Research* 25 [Spring 1958], 72n). A mixed pattern was reported for early modern England by Laslett, op. cit., pp. 153–155.

[39] N. E. Himes, *The Medical History of Contraception*, New York, 1963; Wrong, "Class Fertility Differentials"; Clyde V. Kiser, "Differential Fertility in the United States," in Ansley Coale, ed., *Demographic and Economic Change in Developed Countries*, Princeton: Princeton University Press, 1960, pp. 77–112, and the sources cited there. Despite his evidence of a widening of American class differentials in the period 1885–1910, Kiser refers to a "trend toward contraction" (p. 91) of differentials from 1800 to 1940, citing Jaffe's 1940 conjecture (p. 411 of Jaffe) that "it is likely that fertility differentials were as large at the beginning of the nineteenth century as they are today." But an examination of Jaffe's basis for this statement removes any confidence in it. He attaches fertility levels to local "planes of living" that are defined in a way that defies any meaningful comparisons with the status, occupational, or income groupings of the 1940 census. Jaffe's study can be cited as a vague indication of a negative fertility-wealth relationship for the early nineteenth century, but it cannot be contrasted with 1940 patterns. A more recent review of the evidence by Kiser ("Educational Differentials in Fertility in Relation to the Demographic Transition," in International Union for the Scientific Study of Population, *International Population*

and 1940 the American data show no clear change in the differential. Since 1940 the differential has been greatly reduced. In the baby boom the increases in fertility were greatest among more highly educated groups.[40] Since the mid-1960s the most dramatic declines in fertility (except among Catholics) have been among lower-education and lower-income groups, who have apparently shifted considerably toward more effective contraception. What data we have do suggest an early widening and a later compression of class fertility differentials, though hard conclusions must wait upon better historical data.

VII. Fertility and Socioeconomic Mobility

The prior-inputs hypothesis of taste formation, when combined with the rest of the present model, offers some suggestions for reinterpreting the relationship of fertility to mobility as well as to modernization. It suggests that three variations on the relationship between mobility and fertility should be re-examined on the basis of a more careful comparison of the prior inputs into young couples with their current fortunes. One variation is the issue of whether household cross sections should show a negative relationship of fertility to social and economic mobility. Recent studies suggest that the relationship might be positive, negative, or nonexistent.[41] The present model suggests that this issue cannot be resolved until the variables are respecified in a number of ways. First, the fertility variable must be an age-specific rate for a period of five years or less, and not children ever born, since conditions and plans are constantly changing. Second, the occupation and full-time (not actual) earnings of husband and wife must be standardized for family composition since there is good evidence that the presence of children not only takes the wife out of work and lowers her wage rate but does the reverse to the husband. Finally, the measure of inputs into the couple should be developed as carefully as possible from background variables. It should work out that the ratio of prior inputs to current income is a significant negative influence on fertility for couples changing status as well as for

---

Conference, London, 1969, Liège, 1971, vol. III, pp. 1926–1935) concurs with the chronology outlined here.

[40] See, for example, Clyde V. Kiser, Wilson H. Grabill, and Arthur A. Campbell, *Trends and Variations in Fertility in the United States*, Cambridge: Harvard University Press, 1968, Chap. 9.

[41] See for example, David Featherman, in Bumpass and Westoff, *Later Years of Childbearing*; P. M. Blau and Otis Dudley Duncan, *The American Occupational Structure*, New York: Wiley, 1967; and Westoff, Potter, and Sagi, *Third Child*.

others. Couples on the rise, for example, should have lower fertility the more their increases in income and status are the result of their upbringing rather than recent fortunes.

A second mobility issue for which the framework of this chapter can be helpful is the fertility patterns of migrants. Migrants are a population for whom present fortunes and mode of upbringing differ greatly, and their fertility should be explainable largely in terms of the input norm hypothesis plus a relative cost argument. For example, international migrants should exhibit high fertility relative to comparable families in both the country of origin and the country of destination as long as the rise in income (relative to prior inputs) outweighs a rise in the relative child cost index. One-way migrants to a frontier area should have very large families, both because their income prospects improve and because the relative cost of child inputs drops with the ratio of food prices to the wage rate for child labor. Migrants from farms to the city should have their family size fall between the farm and city patterns, since the relative cost of a given set of child inputs rises with the move, while the family's input norms remain below those of urban-origin couples in the same economic position. This pattern, however, need not hold for college-educated couples of farm origin, since they have been raised in a manner nearly as expensive as that of their urban counterparts. The substitutability of high education for urban origins as a fertility-reducing factor has already been documented.[42]

Finally, the framework should be helpful in analyzing cases of aggregate mobility. Wars and the Great Depression have greatly shaken up the usual tight correlation between incomes and past child input norms, creating baby booms in some settings and baby busts in others. These experiences should lend themselves to the sort of model sketched here. Chapter 5 will deal with American fertility reactions to the Civil War, the Depression, and the two World Wars, advancing arguments already introduced in a different form by Easterlin's work on the postwar baby boom.

[42] See, for example, Otis Dudley Duncan, "Farm Background and Differential Fertility," *Demography* 2 (1965), 240–249.

Chapter 4. The Relative Cost of American Children

I. *What a Measure of Relative Child Cost Can Accomplish*

One of the main hindrances to the development of a satisfactory economics of fertility has been the difficulty of defining and measuring a simple concept—the relative cost of a child. The problem is worth trying to solve. All of the issues regarding the effects of relative market prices on fertility center around this concept. To prepare the way for testing hypotheses about child costs and other fertility influences in Chapter 5, this chapter expands upon the theoretical introduction of the relative-cost concept of Chapter 3, and supplies measures of the variation in the cost of American children, over time and across groups.

While the measurement of relative child cost does encounter some technical problems discussed below, it turns out that the estimates depend on fewer considerations than one might at first think. The concept, though hard to quantify with precision, is indeed straightforward and readily usable. It helps us understand the limitations and the power of past arguments about child costs and fertility by making these arguments more testable. It is subtle enough to take account of the fact that some cost elements, such as the price of parents' time, are more relevant in some settings than in others.

It is surprising that the present exercise has not been attempted before.[1] Many previous authors concerned with economic influences on fertility have assumed that the concept of relative child cost could be measured. They have further assumed that married couples are aware of how much children cost when making decisions about family size. In many instances, child cost has been explicitly mentioned in discussions of how

---

[1] The closest approach to the measure being developed here is an exercise recently performed by my colleague Glen G. Cain in some unpublished appendices (Appendix C of "Appendices to 'Income Maintenance Laws and Fertility in the United States,'" Institute for Research on Poverty, University of Wisconsin, Discussion Paper 118–72, April 1972; and the appendix attached to "Issues in the Economics of a Population Policy for the United States," Institute for Research on Poverty, University of Wisconsin, Discussion Paper 88–71, 1971). Cain's estimates are derived in the same way as the measures of absolute child cost presented midway through the present chapter. (Similar estimates have been made by Reed and McIntosh, in Volume II of the *Research Papers* of the President's Commission on Population Growth and the American Future, 1972.) For his purposes, however, it was not necessary to pursue the further task of attaching a cost to the alternative to another child and setting up an index of *relative* child cost.

selected forces would change that cost. One example is the frequent explanation of rural-urban fertility differentials with the argument that children cost less on a farm. Children are thought to be more economical on a farm partly because they need things thought by some to be cheaper on the farm (e.g., food and space) and partly because they supply labor to the family farm before maturing. Clearly, the importance of these considerations depends on how large are the weights of food, space rent, and labor time in the appropriate index of relative cost. Some observers assume that rearing children is relatively labor-intensive, so that higher wage rates mean children are more costly.[2] One also often hears that the cost of having an extra child depends on child parity (rank) and on child spacing. The phrase "cheaper by the dozen" is common shorthand for the hypothesis that there are economies of scale in raising children. It is equally common to hear that having children close together, whatever its other disadvantages, economizes by spreading out the use of durables ("hand-me-downs") and by shortening the mother's absence from the labor force. In each case, the existence and measurability of the relative cost of a child is presumed, but the measurement is not attempted.

A useful by-product of the exercise of calculating the relative cost of an extra child is a new historical perspective on how the effects of children on the economics of the family have been evolving. In the process of revealing what commodity and time inputs are more closely tied to child cost than the costs of other things, this chapter will present cross-sectional estimates of how the presence of children has affected the expenditures and employment of family members at various times since the late nineteenth century. The estimates of commodity-demand and labor-supply effects will be of further use in Chapters 6 and 7, which trace the effects of extra children on the economy.

II. *Defining the Relative Cost*

The basic concept of relative child cost is one step removed from the clear but nonoperational idea of the relative *price* of an extra child. The relative child price, in the jargon of the model of Chapter 3, is the marginal trade-off between the psychic enjoyment of the extra child and the

[2] See, for example, Glen G. Cain, "Issues in the Economics of a Population Policy for the United States," *American Economic Review* 61 (May 1971), 413; Jacob Mincer, "Market Prices, Opportunity Costs, and Income Effects," in Carl Christ, ed., *Measurement in Economics*, Stanford, Calif., 1963, pp. 76–78; and Glen G. Cain and Adriana Weininger, "Economic Determinants of Fertility: Results from Cross-Sectional Aggregate Data," *Demography* 10 (1973), 206–207.

enjoyment of the other activities that would have to be curtailed in order to enjoy the extra child. The price of enjoying an extra child is the psychic value of the units of adult peace and quiet, facial smoothness, sleep continuity, personal mobility, and so forth that are foregone when the child is born and raised. The relative price, in other words, derives from the marginal rates of substitution between enjoying another child and the other home activities with which the enjoyment of the child competes. This notion of a psychic price is obviously relevant to family size decisions. It is also obviously of little practical use, since we cannot measure such trade-offs. There is no marketplace in which people swap children for other psychic satisfaction. We can observe only the prices of the time and commodity inputs into psychic activities, and not the trade-offs among the activities themselves. And since interview questions about attitudes can provide only crude data on people's trade-offs, we must abandon the concept of child *price* at this point.

The relative *cost* of *inputs* into child-related activities, however, is more observable. The relative cost of an extra child is simply the ratio of two price indices: the price of all inputs of other family members' home time and of commodities (purchased goods and services) into the extra activities that would have been enjoyed in the absence of the extra child. This ratio of input costs will also serve as a proxy for the underlying relative price of children as long as the rates of productivity improvement in raising children and in other home activities do not differ. Unfortunately, the impossibility of measuring unmarketed psychic outputs precludes our knowing just how closely movements in relative input prices parallel the price ratios among psychic activities. Thus if a productivity improvement makes interaction with children more enjoyable without affecting the time or commodity inputs into children, this effect on the relative price of a child will be missed by measuring the relative input cost. With this limitation, nonetheless, a measure of the relative (input) cost of children is still capable of focusing on much of the alleged influence of the system of market prices on fertility incentives.

If the relevant concept is one of *relative* cost, careful attention must be given to the question: relative to what? The alternative to having an extra child should be whatever couples themselves would choose if they chose not to have the extra child. For couples that do decide to have, say, a third child, the alternative bundle of inputs is that stream of extra home time and commodity purchases for the previous four family members that would have been enjoyed had the third child not arrived. For couples that consider but reject the thought of having a third child, the same sort of calculation applies: we seek measures of the inputs they retain for other use by not having another child in the family and the inputs that would have gone into the extra child if it were conceived shortly—we will say three months—after the time at which the option of expanding the family was most seriously weighed.

Whether a given family decides to have the extra child or not, one of the two bundles is unavoidably counterfactual and not directly observable. It is impossible to observe directly, even after their decision, what time and commodity commitments would have accompanied the course of action *not* taken by any given family. We cannot observe how a family with a third child would have spent its time and money without that child, nor can we develop a factual measure of the resources that a family with two children would have spent on the third child that does not and will not exist. The problem here is the familiar point that all causal inferences necessarily involve exercise in fiction: we can never discern the effect or impact of anything without comparing two sets of events, of which at least one is contrary to fact.

The problem of inferring what alternatives couples are comparing when contemplating expanding their families is not insoluble. It seems reasonable to use controlled proxies for the alternatives considered but not taken by turning to cross-sectional data. In what follows it will be assumed that a couple that has a third child would, without that child, have followed the average course of lifetime commodity expenditures and time allocation displayed by couples of the same age cohort who had only two children but who had the same full lifetime potential income, the same amount of education, and the same area of residence. Similarly a couple ending up with two children in its family will be assumed to have contemplated but declined the life course followed by the average family having the same attributes as they, except for having had a third child.

The concept of relative child costs developed here makes two further basic assumptions designed to deal with the obvious uncertainties surrounding the conception and survival of the extra child. First, the concept takes conception or its absence as already given. The two alternatives being compared are the enjoyment of life with the nonexistence of the extra child a certainty and the enjoyment of life *given* the extra child. As already noted in Chapter 3, the relative-cost concept does not weigh the psychic and economic costs of purchasing different conception probabilities. No measurement will be made of such broader probabilistic concepts as "the relative cost of using withdrawal instead of the pill" or "the relative cost of abstinence by married couples." Such concepts clearly have more direct relevance to the explanation of family-size outcomes, but they pose measurement problems that seem insoluble. I shall opt instead for the somewhat narrower measure of the cost of having and raising a child relative to the costs of following a course of life in which the child is assured not to exist.

The other assumption relating to uncertainty concerns the chances of survival of family members. I shall simply assume that the relative cost being considered is that based on the assumption that each family member will have a slightly larger life expectancy than the average for people in his or her cohort with his or her full lifetime potential income, education, and location.

III. *Bedside Calculators?*

Discussing the assumptions about uncertainties raises a more basic issue on which some disclaimers from Chapter 3 need to be repeated and expanded: What is to be assumed about people's perceptions of the relative costs being quantified here? People may speak prose without knowing what prose is, but is their family size really tied to an abstract concept over which Ph.D.'s—and only Ph.D.'s—will argue? The best assumption about people's cost awareness seems to lie somewhere between two extreme views—the view that people's reactions to the relative cost of children explain nearly all of fertility differentials, and the view that their total ignorance of or indifference to the relative cost magnitude makes it irrelevant to their fertility behavior.

People unquestionably react to a wider variety of forces than are channeled through the measure of relative child cost. The relative-cost measure cannot capture even all of the economic determinants of fertility, let alone all fertility determinants. The highly uncertain returns from raising a given child completely escape measurement here. The important economic concept of lifetime income, allegedly one of the main economic determinants of family size, is also bypassed here. As has been mentioned, no attempt is made to discern what conception probabilities and psychic costs people associate with different modes of contraception. More broadly, none of the influences on family values coming from social pressures, educational experience, and other forces are caught here. People unquestionably react to a wider variety of forces than are channeled through the measure of relative child cost, and the present measure seeks only to improve on part of the economic side of explaining fertility patterns.

It would be a serious mistake to argue that people do not respond at all to changes in the relative cost of extra children. It is true that most of us perceive the costs of having or not having children only dimly. We do not quantify the alternative costs before jumping into bed. Still, both our actions and our folklore betray an awareness of the alternative costs facing us.[3] Few are not aware that having more children raises the importance of food in the family budget. As wage rates rise, we emphasize more and more the cost of interrupting careers to raise children, sensing that children are labor-intensive. Peasants the world over sense that family formation and expansion has a capital cost because the costs of raising children come sooner than the marginal time and commodity expenditures of the smaller-family alternative, and they accordingly time marriages and births in ways related to the scarcity of wealth as directed by recent harvests. The mere fact that young couples, and those who advise them, have a sense of what they can afford is evidence enough that whatever influences the cost of children has a good chance of affecting perceived costs and desired fertility in the aggregate. This presumption is safe as long as *some* people, some of the important ones near the margin of having extra children or not, react to some notion of how much time and commodity inputs they can afford to put into another child.

The uncertainty and incompleteness of people's awareness of child costs poses a delicate strategic problem for the researcher interested in estimates of relative child cost. If people only dimly perceive a few main elements of this measure, should we not restrict the calculation of relative cost to those few elements they notice? The better answer seems to be negative. We have no way of being sure just which of the underlying subtle cost differences occur to young couples or to those who advise them, and so any limitation of the relative cost calculation to, say, just food effects could be inappropriate for a large part of the fecund population. The only sound strategy here seems to be to tote up all the conceivably relevant cost elements that can be quantified. Some elements make a great difference to the outcome, and some do not. Any reader wishing to restrict his view to a cruder measure of relative cost, on the argument that the families being studied did the same, can decompose the present laborious calculations by consulting Appendix E.

---

[3] Interview data can also capture the dependence of desired family size on income and child costs. See, for example, the data reported in Ronald Freedman and Lolagene Coombs, "Economic Considerations in Family Growth Decisions," *Population Studies* 20, pt. 2 (November 1966), Table 9.

To avoid introducing errors that can be avoided at low personal cost, however, I shall present the fullest possible calculations of relative costs. That is, I shall proceed with the kind of elaborate calculation that conjures up the extreme image of a married couple's consulting market statistics and a bedside electronic calculator before jumping into bed.

IV. *The Relative Cost Formula*

To establish the formula to be used to measure the relative cost of a child, we must begin with a formula for the absolute cost of an extra child. This will be followed by an expression for the cost of the alternative to having an extra child. The relative cost formula is an index of the ratio of these two costs.

The absolute cost of adding an Nth family member is the present discounted value of all of the time and commodities put into that child at the expense of other home activities. Some of the terms in this definition will require clarification. The rate of discount to be used will be discussed presently. The reference to "present" value indicates that all values are to be discounted back to the imagined date of decision on whether or not to have another child. Such decisions are made repeatedly, of course. The assumption will be made, nonetheless, that people who in fact had the extra child in question decided to do so one year before its birth. (For those families declining to have another child, the assumption will be made that the time at which they most strongly considered the matter was such that the extra child, if born a year later, would have arrived according to the median spacing between its parity and the previous parity, for families like the ones being considered.) As for "value," each commodity receives its market price, and each family member's time inputs are valued at his market wage rate.[4] To simplify,

---

[4] The wage rate may be below the true shadow price of a family member's time if that person stays out of the job market and specializes in home activities. This might seem to be a crucial point, since most housewives are not working for pay at any given time. It is not crucial to the results below, however, for three reasons. First, specialization is less widespread than the data on recorded work for pay would suggest. Women work to produce commodities for sale both at home and on farms without their work's being recorded officially. Second, the shadow wage of a truly specialized wife is likely to be kept near the market wage rate by substitution between her time and both commodity inputs and the time of other family members, as mentioned in Chapter 3.

The most important argument in favor of focusing on the market wage, however, is that the choice of time value matters only for those persons for whom the wage rate is indeed the appropriate value. The index of relative child cost being developed in this chapter is an average index for a large group of families. These

I shall assume that the family views present commodity price ratios as an accurate reflection of future ratios, and expects real wages to move according to the usual life-cycle pattern. A final simplification is the restriction of commodity detail to just a few commodity classes: food, clothing, rent, health care, and a few others.

With these explanations, the formula for the absolute cost of the Nth family member, discounted to one year before his or her birth becomes:

$$\text{COST}_N = \sum_{t=0}^{T} \frac{\left[\sum_{n=1}^{N} w_{nt} L_{nt}^{N} + \sum_{j=1}^{J} p_j C_{jt}^{N} \right]}{(1+r)^{t+1}}$$

where T is the number of years until the couple's lifetime planning horizon; w_n is the after-tax dollar wage rate of the Nth family member, valued at the rate being earned by workers with that member's attributes at the time of decision; L^N_{nt} is the Nth family member's time input into the extra child in the tth year, for $n = 0, \ldots, N-1$; for $n = N$, L^N equals *minus* the work time contributed by the Nth family member while still within the household, either at paid work or at household chores that would have to have been performed whether or not this extra child existed; C^N_{jt} is the input of the jth commodity into the extra child in the tth year—for the years after the child has left the home, this set of variables reflects the net flow of transfers from parents to child (parents' gifts and bequests minus support by children); P_j is its price, at the decision time one year before birth of the Nth family member; and r is the rate of discount, discussed below. Special treatment is given here to the extra child's own economic contribution to the household. While he is still a member of the parents' household, his contributions of time for paid work and for unavoidable household chores are to be subtracted from the time devoted to him by other family members, in order to ar-

---

families can be divided into (1) those for which the wife (and other family members) is near the margin of working for a market wage, and (2) those with wives who definitely prefer to stay at home, where the shadow price of their time is above the market wage. The wage rate is a good reflection of the value of wives' time in the first group, and it is for this group that children are relatively labor-intensive and take the mother out of work to a great extent. Wives in the second group, on the other hand, would put the same total time into home activities with or without an extra child. Since the same real time inputs are involved on both sides of the choice, the wife's shadow wage rate affects the total dollar values of both sets of inputs, but not the differences between these dollar values. For this reason noticeable deviations of the shadow wage from the market wage would have little bearing on the indices developed in this chapter.

rive at an estimate for the net time input into him. His earnings at paid work must also be included in the income of the expanded family when deducing the effect of the extra child on the family's commodity consumption. His earnings are implicitly viewed as a substitute for the same value of earnings on the part of other family members, as though they are permitted to work less for the same total commodity consumption if he exists.

In what follows we shall not be interested in the dollar value of the absolute cost. Only an index of this cost is important, since we are interested in comparing costs across time and region. Accordingly, let us define a cost index which is simply the value of $COST_N$ divided by its value in a base period. Keeping the rate of discount fixed for now, we can represent this cost index with the formula:

$$P_N = \sum_{i=1}^{N+J} c_i p_i \quad (\Sigma c_i = 1.00)$$

where P_N is the index of absolute child cost, p_i is the price index for the ith child input, whether the time of a family member or one of the J commodity classes, and c_i is the share of the ith input in total cost in the base period.

The next task is to set up a similar price index, P_H, for all the inputs going into the "alternative bundle," the extra enjoyment of various activities without the extra child. It is here that a crucial use is made of cross-sectional studies. As noted above, we cannot observe what a family does with the "extra" resources it would have spent on a child that does not exist. We can, however, use cross-sectional data to show us the *differences* in total home inputs that accompany differences in family size, with other things as equal as possible. These differences are revealed by examining the effect of the extra child on the pattern of the family's external trade—its exports of labor time in exchange for commodity imports into the home.

An extra child will raise some commodity imports into the home and lower others. Those goods for which imports are raised are those used more in child-raising than in other home activities. As we can see below, rearing an extra child raises food imports considerably, has a smaller effect on imports of clothing and shelter, and greatly reduces imports of other commodities. Knowing these import effects allows us to reveal the commodity inputs into the "alternative bundle," or "H bundle." Using the superscript H for the whole set of activities that are the alternative to having the extra child, we can express the following identity for each year t:

Value of the ith input taken away from other home activities by having the extra child $\equiv$ Value of the ith input devoted to raising the child $-$ Increase in imports of the ith input caused by having the extra child

or, in terms of symbols, as follows:

$$-C_i^H \equiv C_i^N - (C_i^H + C_i^N)$$

The term on the left side can be revealed by estimating the items on the right. The C_i^N values are estimated by studies trying to quantify the commodity inputs into individual children. The net import effects can be derived from household expenditure surveys showing the variation of family expenditures with the number of children for comparable income and age classes. The resulting figures for the C_i^H's can be cross-checked for plausibility against independent estimates of income elasticities of expenditure.

When one is calculating the effects of a child on the family's commodity imports, considerable care must be taken to specify correctly the income that the family would have without the child. One cannot simply compare consumption patterns of families with the same income and different family size, since family size affects income, both through hours worked and through wage rates. The arrival of an extra child is often accompanied by an immediate reduction in family income, since the wife often drops out of the labor force. This effect of income must be recognized when calculating the net effect of conceiving the extra child on family consumption patterns. Family income, and therefore family consumption of each kind of commodity, is also affected in another important way. The fact that the wife's job is interrupted when the baby arrives means that for the rest of her life she will have less job experience and will tend to receive a lower wage each hour than if she had not had the child. This *job-interruption* effect on her wage rate, like the loss of work hours, lowers the family's income. Thus in order correctly to calculate the income the family would be able to spend over the parents' lives without the child, I shall add the extra wages without the child to family income in order to estimate the consumption expenditures foregone by having the child. This sort of adjustment for lost pay increases is discussed in more detail in Appendix A, on "The Job-Interruption Effect."

The time taken away from other home activities each year by an extra child can be estimated by using another identity. For any n^{th} family member other than the extra child, the fact that total living hours per year are fixed means:

$$L_{nt}^N + L_{nt}^H + \Delta L_{nt} = \Delta \bar{L}_{nt} = 0$$

where the N superscript is for inputs of time into the Nth family member, the H is for activities that are alternatives to having another child, the L's without superscripts are time spent working for pay in the labor force, and the bar is for total available time. The value of home time taken from other home activities during the year t $(-L_{nt}^H)$ can be derived by subtracting any reduction in labor exports from the estimate of the time put into the extra child (L_{nt}^N). The reduction in labor time exports can be estimated from studies of labor force participation, while the time spent on an extra child can be estimated from time-budget studies.

In this way figures can be derived for all of the inputs, both time and commodity, into the alternative activities. The absolute cost of the alternative bundle of inputs can then be measured by the formula:

$$\text{COST}_H = \sum_{t=0}^{T} \frac{\left[\sum_{n=1}^{N-1} w_{nt}L_{nt}^H + \sum_{j=1}^{J} p_j c_{jt}^H\right]}{(1+r)^{t+1}}$$

Assumptions about saving will be shortly introduced which make the difference between the total input costs ($\text{COST}_H - \text{COST}_N$) in a base period equal to the effect of job interruption on the wife's lifetime earning power minus the value of the income tax reductions (and transfer payment rights) tied to the extra child. A distinction is thus being made between the total value of inputs taken away from other activities and the value put into the child.

If one wishes a dollar value on the cost of a child, then the total value taken away from other activities, or COST_H, is the relevant measure. Yet in what follows I shall pay no attention to this magnitude and shall instead pursue a relative price index. This choice needs brief justification here. The main task to be performed by a measure of child cost is to quantify the effects of changes in prices and wages on the relative cost of a given set of child inputs. Changes in the levels and proportions of inputs are definitely not to be viewed as changes in cost. Shifts in input quantities for a given set of prices and wages reflect either shifts in income or shifts in tastes. To mix these factors into a single measure along with movements in the costs of given inputs is to invite needless confusion. The mere fact that rich people choose to spend more on their children than do the poor does not mean that a given set of inputs into an extra child is necessarily more costly in a rich family than in a poor one. Rather, it means that the rich and poor rear different kinds of children. The level of inputs must be held constant if we are to keep differences in relative cost separate from difference in kinds of child-rearing.

This statement of the necessity of focusing on the relative costs of a given set of child inputs implies that the best cost measure is an index number with fixed base-period weights. I shall in fact follow this route, but with one modification. If input *proportions* are changing significantly over time, the fixed-weight index, while analytically clear, may not be the best one to relate to the family size decisions of families outside of the base period. In order to develop a cost index that continues to reflect the costs being compared by large numbers of families over generations, it is advisable to use different weights for different stretches of years if the typical input proportions are changing. An adjustment of this sort will be made below, to allow for the fact that the relative labor-intensity of children has risen across the twentieth century. It will turn out, however, that this is the only adjustment needed in the weights for the key urban series, which can otherwise make use of fixed weights throughout. To show why no other adjustments need to be made in the weights, I must first complete the development of the index formula and bring out a key point about differences in cost shares.

The next step in developing the relative cost index formula is to introduce the index-number counterpart to $COST_H$, the total cost of the inputs into the activities with which an extra child competes at the margin. The cost index for the alternative life activities (the H bundle of inputs) is:

$$P_H = \sum_{i=1.00}^{N+J} d_i p_i \left(\sum_{i=1}^{N+J} d_i = 1.00 \right)$$

where P_H is the index of absolute cost of the alternative to having another child, p_i is defined as before, and d_i is the share of the ith input in the total cost of the H bundle in the base period.

Now that we have defined indices for the input costs of the two alternatives to be compared, the definition of the relative cost index for an extra child is simply:

$$P_C = P_N/P_H$$

Since P_c is a *relative* price index, we need to be concerned only with the *differences* in the shares of each input in the two component indices. It can be shown that the effect of a given percentage movement in the price (or wage) of one home input yields a percentage change in the relative cost of an extra child governed only by the difference in the shares of that input in the numerator and denominator bundles of inputs:

$$\left(\frac{\Delta P_c}{P_c}\right) \approx \sum_{i=1}^{N+J} \left(\frac{\Delta P_i}{P_i}\right) \times (c_i - d_i)$$

This is an important and useful result. It suggests that the task of applying the same base-period input weights across very different contexts might not be so inappropriate as the heterogeneity of children would at first suggest. The fact that the total cost of an individual child differs sharply across income classes and over time can now be seen to be irrelevant for the *relative* cost of a child. Even the input proportions within the N bundle can vary without changing the movements in relative cost. The fact that families with higher incomes make luxury commodities (commodity expenditures other than food, clothing, and shelter) a much higher share of their total child inputs than do poor families is of questionable relevance. It might turn out that their alternative bundles, the inputs into activities in lieu of the extra child, also use these commodities heavily. The kind of family that can and will pay a lot for a child's recreation is the sort of family that will also pay a lot for recreation if it decides not to have the extra child. When we restrict our attention to those ways in which the input shares for an extra child differ from the shares at stake in the alternative life activities, it turns out that movements in relative child cost are governed by just a few common differences between having a child and not. One is that children, like poverty, raise the share of food in total commodity expenditures, so that food prices matter. A second is that rearing children is labor-intensive relative to the alternative life course in those settings in which the alternative involves work outside of the home by mothers; in other settings, such as family farms, this labor-intensity of children is reduced or reversed. Finally, having children commits a family to more immediate expenditures, so that rates of interest and rates of return on such assets as family grain reserves assume a great importance to the relative cost of a child. Other differences in the ways in which families with different incomes and residences rear children prove to have little effect on movements in the relative cost of children.

Before we can turn to the task of building up indices from U.S. data, two other basic points about the formula must be treated, one relating to savings effects and the other to the discount rate. Our calculations will virtually assume that lifetime differences in savings caused by an extra child are zero. That is, we will give no separate discussion to the possible but unknown effects of having another child on the size of bequest that a couple expects to leave to heirs forty or fifty years later. Any actual or perceived effects of another child on total bequests will be treated implicitly as equivalent to the consumption of some extra commodities forty or fifty years from the time of decision regarding family expansion. Savings effects are more noticeable and deserve more explicit treatment, however, over *parts* of a couple's adult lifetime. The one division that will be important here is the break between the first nineteen years (from decision date to the eighteenth birthday of the child if it exists) and later years. Virtually all of the studies relating children to the family's economic behavior concern themselves only with children under eighteen present in the household. This is true whether the study relates to the allocation of time or to expenditures on commodities. It will turn out (in the estimates in Appendix E below) that having an extra child cuts family savings over the eighteen years of the child's presence at home. The extra savings accumulated over these eighteen years by the families that do *not* have the extra children must somehow be allocated to the inputs on which they will be spent in later years (relative to the expenditures of the families with the extra children). The procedure adopted here is to allocate them across commodities and time according to information on marginal propensities to consume and on the labor force behavior of older parents whose children have left the home.

The other remaining issue is more troublesome: what discount rate is appropriate for child and other costs that are spread over an entire lifetime? When making family size decisions how sharply do people really discount effects that are far in the future? The ordinary folklore about family decision-making is of little help here. Some will argue that couples don't look into the future at all, and are thinking only of the first few years with the extra child. This view implies that the rate of discount is very high and that only short-run pleasures, obstetrical costs, and the heavy short-run time demands of a child matter much. Yet others are equally convinced that some people have children to provide for themselves in their old age and that middle-class couples limit family size because of the costs of providing a college education. Such views reflect the assumption that people discount future costs and benefits at low discount rates or even at a zero discount rate. The issue is a serious one, since the level of discount rate does affect the base-period weights to be developed below.

Theory usually argues that the appropriate rate of discount is the rate of return on courses of action involving a similar degree of riskiness in trading between present and future purchasing. What kinds of investments with observable rates of return compare in risk to the commitment of conceiving an extra child? One rate that may seem comparable is the rate of return on extra human capital. This choice is at least reasonable, since couples choosing to have a child often forego investments in extra schooling or job experience, especially for the wife. The marginal private rate of return on schooling will be used below at a "preferred" discount rate estimate. In addition, calculations will also be shown for discount rates that are 5 percent higher than the preferred rates. These "high" discount rates are intended as upper bound estimates of the unknown "true" discount rate. For example, the following rates of discount will be used in the detailed cost estimates below:[5]

	Low discount rate, %	*Preferred discount rate, %*	*High discount rate, %*
Low- and middle-income couples, high school grads	0	13	18
Higher-income couples, college grads	0	8	13

Readers feeling that different rates are appropriate may interpolate or extrapolate on the basis of Tables 4–6 through 4–9 below.

[5] The preferred rates are approximate marginal rates of return for extra schooling for males, based on the rates calculated by Giora Hanoch ("Personal Earnings and Investment in Schooling," unpublished doctoral dissertation, University of Chicago, 1965, Tables 6 and 7) for 1959. For persons finishing high school, the marginal rate was set between the rates on all levels of schooling completed (twelve grades) and the rate on the college education foregone. Similarly, the preferred rate for college graduates was set between the rate earned on college and the rate on advanced study. (The rates for females are more widely spread between high school and college, to judge from rates for 1959 calculated by F. Hines, L. Tweeten, and M. Redfern, "Social and Private Rates of Return to Investment in Schooling, by Race-Sex Groups and Regions," *Journal of Human Resources*, 5, no. 3, Summer 1970, 318–340.)

The preferred rate turns out to be higher at the margin for the less-educated, lower-income family, as one would expect. The same inequality in private discount rates between rich and poor shows up in the rates of interest they experience on financial assets and borrowings, though the real rates are lower for financial instruments than for education.

V. Building the Index Base

Armed with the relative-cost formula and the assumptions just discussed, one can proceed to put together estimates of absolute and relative child cost from a variety of sources. Each of these sources produces estimates of only part of the parameters sought here, and considerable calculating effort is required to weave these disparate estimates into a final index. As we shall soon see, however, the way in which the relative cost index will behave for America since the nineteenth century can be discovered just by noting a few basic patterns revealed by past studies. To see the overall outlines of movements in relative child cost one needs less information than is buried in the tables and appendixes of this chapter. The indices for urban child cost embody detailed calculations that are warranted only because this is the first empirical study of this sort. Most of the key properties of the relative cost index should be evident by the end of this section, even before the indices themselves are presented.

A. TIME INPUTS INTO CHILDREN

Only in this century have serious attempts been made to figure out how much time family members spend on rearing an individual child. In the United States such estimates began to emerge as by-products of larger time-budget studies after World War I.[6] The 1920s saw a wave of studies of how women spent their time, the wave apparently having been set off by women's wartime work contribution and the extension of suffrage. The Bureau of Home Economics supervised a series of time-budget studies administered through agricultural experiment stations in the late 1920s. The most careful of these studies was Maud Wilson's analysis of time used by Oregon wives, which set a pattern followed by subsequent time-budget studies.

Table 4–1 displays some of the firmer estimates of time spent on children. It is not necessary to dwell at length on the fact that such figures are of limited reliability. A few words of caution will suffice. Much of home time is spent on several tasks at once, and any allocation of such joint time to individual chores must be arbitrary. Survey respondents are often hard-pressed to recall how they spent the day to which the interview questions relate. In addition, the data in Rows (1)–(5) are

[6] For a bibliography of the early attempts at time-budget studies in the United States, see Benjamin R. Andrews, *The Economics of the Household*, New York, 1935, pp. 441–443.

gathered in a form that masks some of the allocation of time between a given child and other family activities. These survey results are displayed only in two- or three-dimensional means. Only with the Syracuse sample for 1967–68 used in deriving Rows (6) and (7) was regression analysis possible.

For all the difficulties surrounding the time-use figures, they do reveal certain patterns clearly enough. First, the time cost of a child is highest at the outset, declines rapidly across the preschool years, and settles at a low level throughout the school years. The time demands of the later years cannot compare to those of a nonverbal infant prior to toilet training. Second, the wife's time takes up the lion's share. In 1926 or in 1968, in urban or in farm homes, her time burden dwarfs the contributions of the husband, the rest of the family, and any hired help. The clarity of these two patterns helps to explain why most time-budget studies have focused on the housewife and have grouped the data according to the age of the youngest child.

An important issue is the way in which time inputs into children seem to vary historically in response to urbanization, income growth, and advancing education. It is hard to reach firm conclusions on this issue by comparing studies like those in Table 4–1, since no two time-use studies were conducted in the same way. When comparing families from different areas in a single set of surveys in the late 1920s, the Bureau of Home Economics thought it detected a greater commitment to child care among urban and more-educated wives:[7]

	Care of family (hours/week)	*Persons per household*
559 farm wives	3.9	4.3
249 rural nonfarm wives	4.7	4.0
178 small-city wives	9.8	4.0
222 big-city wives	9.3	3.9

[7] The pattern for family care time runs counter to the pattern for total work time in the home and in production of commodities for the market. Farm women work most, both in the home and in producing for the market (on the farm), followed by rural nonfarm wives. This implies a familiar pattern: women enjoy more of the activities that such studies define as "leisure" rather than work as they move to the cities and experience higher incomes and education (Ibid., p. 442). The results of this sample of rural and urban families for the 1920s are discussed at greater length in U.S. Department of Agriculture, Bureau of Human Nutrition and Home Economics, "The Time Cost of Homemaking; A Study of 1,500 Rural and Urban Households," mimeographed memorandum, 1944.

Table 4-1. Selected Estimates of Time Costs of a Child by Age of Child, 1926-1968.
(Average hours per week)

	Age of child, in years:																		
	Under 1	1	2	3	4	5	6	7	8	9	10	11	12	13	14	15	16	17
(1) 1926-27, first child, Oregon farms, mother's time on physical care only:	15.9	5.4				5.4	1.4	←――――――――――――――――――→							1.4	1.1	1.1	1.1
effect on father's chores:	1.8					1.8	0	←――――――――――――――――――→							0	0	0	0
child's chores:	0	0	0	0	0	0	-3.3	←――――――――――――――――――→							-3.3	-5.0	-5.0	-5.0
(2) 1936, N.Y. farms, first child, child care:	23.2	17.3	13.7	10.5	7.5	5.4	3.8	2.8	2.1	1.5	1.2	0.9	0.7	0.7	0.5	0.4	0	0
change in other chores, whole family:	5.3	5.3	5.3	3.3	3.3	3.3	4.1	←――――――――――――――――――――――――――――――→										4.1
(3) 1943, Vermont farms, first child, child care:	24.8	17.0	13.5	13.5	12.0	12.0	3.0	3.0	2.8	←―――――――――――――――→								2.8
change in other chores, whole family:	14.0	14.0	14.0	12.8	12.8	12.8	12.8	12.8	←――――――――――――――――→									10.8
(4) 1952, rural-urban NY state, first child, physical care by mother:	18.9	19.6	9.1	9.1	7.7	8.4	4.2	5.6	4.2	←―――――――――――――――→								4.2
effect on meal preparation:	2.6	←―――――――――――――→																2.6
(5) 1967, Indiana, first child, phys. care by whole family:	10.6	10.6	7.0	←――――――→		7.0	3.5	←――――――→			3.5	1.8	←―――――――――→					1.8
some chore effects:	5.4	←――――――――――――――→																5.4
(6) 1967-68, Syracuse, first child, all care by all persons:	29.3	19.8	13.3	←――――――→		13.3	6.8	←――――――→			6.8	2.4	←―――――――――→					2.4
effect on others' chores:	2.1	3.4	2.6	←――――――→		2.6	1.8	←――――――→			1.8	0.6	←―――――――――→					0.6
child's help with chores:	0	←―――――――――→				0	-2.1	←――――――→			-2.1	-6.4	←―――――――――→					-6.4
(7) 1967-68, Syracuse, third child, all care by all persons:	16.2	10.5	4.1	3.6	3.6	3.6	1.7	1.7	1.7	2.6	2.6	2.6	1.9	1.9	1.9	2.4	2.4	2.4
effect on others' chores:	2.1	3.4	2.6	←――――――→		2.6	1.8	←――――――→			1.8	0.6	←―――――――――→					0.6
child's help with chores:	0	←―――――――――→				0	-2.1	←――――――→			-2.1	-6.4	←―――――――――→					-6.4

RELATIVE COST OF AMERICAN CHILDREN

Notes to Table 4–1

The estimates for the time costs of each child are calculated on the assumption that he or she remains the youngest child in the home until he or she leaves at age eighteen. This assumption is made because the marginal cost of a child is that increment to cost caused by the extra child given the children and events that have preceded his birth. Thus the estimates for a first child are most appropriate to an only child, and those for a third child refer to the last-born of three children. This procedure fits the concept of marginal cost, even though subsequent births would reduce the time inputs received by any one child. For a more detailed treatment of the effects of sibling position on time inputs into an individual child, see Appendix C.

The entries for the child contributions to household chores are given a negative sign to reflect their being time contributions to tasks that others would have performed without the child. They represent, in other words, negative time costs caused by the existence of the child.

Row (1). Calculated from Maud Wilson, *Use of Time by Oregon Farm Homemakers*, Corvallis, Ore., 1929, Corvallis Agricultural Experiment Station Bulletin 256, pp. 26–27. Physical care excludes reading, playing, and teaching activities shared by parents and child. The data were gathered by asking 288 farm wives about family time use over a "typical" week.

Row (2). Calculated from Jean Warren, *Use of Time in Its Relation to Home Management*, Ithaca, N.Y., 1940, Cornell Agricultural Experiment Station Bulletin 734, passim. Definition of child care is not given explicitly, and may or may not include play, reading, and teaching activities. The net effect on chore time (other than child care) is the sum of calculated net effects on washing, mending, bedmaking, lunchpail-packing, dishwashing, routine care of house, and food preparation. The sample consisted of 497 farm homemakers in Genesee County, N.Y., interviewed in the spring of 1936.

Row (3). Calculated from Marianne Muse, *Time Expenditures on Homemaking Activities in 183 Vermont Farm Homes*, Burlington, Vt., 1946, Vermont Agricultural Experiment Station Bulletin 530. Interviews were spread over three summer weeks in 1943. The estimates for child care apparently include entertainment care and personal interaction time as well as physical care. Data are also given on the contribution of daughters and sons to household and farm work. These are not displayed here, however, since the wartime labor shortage was stated as a factor in significantly raising children's workloads above normal levels.

Row (4). Calculated from Elizabeth Wiegand, *Use of Time by Full-Time and Part-Time Homemakers in Relation to Home Management*, Ithaca, N.Y., 1954, Cornell Agricultural Experiment Station Memoir 330. The measure of physical child care explicitly excludes such activities as play and teaching. The effect on meal preparation is the sum of effects of an extra child of any age on food preparation time plus dishwashing time. Ninety-five farm families in Genesee County and 155 families in the city of Auburn were interviewed in the spring of 1952.

Row (5). Calculated from Sarah L. Manning, *Time Use in Household Tasks by Indiana Families*, Lafayette, Ind., 1968, Purdue Agricultural Experiment Station, Research Bulletin No. 837. The measure of physical child care excluded reading, playing, and general supervising activities. The chore effects estimate the net effects of children on the time spent at meal preparation, dishwashing, washing time, ironing, sewing, and mending. The sample consisted of 4 weekly records from each of 111 families, of which 41 were farm families.

Rows (6) and (7). Calculated from regressions reported in Table C–1 of Ap-

[101]

Similarly, two recent regression analyses have concluded that more-educated wives devote more time to each child than do less-educated wives.[8]

Each of these results, however, is partly misleading, for reasons elaborated in Appendix C below. The comparisons made by the Bureau of Home Economics seem to reflect only differences in the way in which similar activities are reported by rural and urban wives when interviewed. Appendix C also argues, contrary to the regression results just cited, that more-educated wives do not spend significantly more time in child care when one has correctly adjusted for the numbers and ages of children. More-educated wives spend more time on each child only to the extent that they have fewer children on the average. It seems safe, however, to conclude that higher education and urbanization *do not reduce* time inputs *per child*.

B. COMMODITY INPUTS INTO CHILDREN

There is a long tradition of estimating the commodity inputs into rearing a child. The exercise is at least as old as the work of Ernst Engel published in 1883.[9] Most of the literature on the cost of a child, in fact, has

---

pendix C, except for the net chore effects, which were calculated from unreported regressions using the same data source. For a discussion of the method of estimation, see the text of Appendix C. The third child represented in Row (7) was assumed to have been born three years after the second and six years after the first. The child care time is the sum of separate estimates of the time given by all persons to physical care and to other care of children in three parts of the year (nonsummer weekdays, summer weekdays, and weekend days). The net effect of the child on chores is his impact on the time spent at meal preparation, meal cleanup, and washing by all persons. The time he spent helping out is a measure of his contribution to all household chores. The time he spent performing chores that needed doing only because he existed, which should net out to a zero impact on time cost, were thus implicitly included in the net chore effect and then resubtracted out as part of his chore contribution.

---

[8] C. Russell Hill and Frank P. Stafford, "Allocation of Time to Preschool Children and Educational Opportunity," unpublished manuscript, Ann Arbor, Mich., February 1972; Arleen Leibowitz, "Women's Allocation of Time to Market and Non-Market Activities," Ph.D. dissertation, Columbia University, 1972; Arleen Leibowitz, "Education and Home Production," *American Economic Review* 64 (May 1974), 243–250.

[9] *Der Werth des Menschen*, Part 1: Der Kostenwerth des Menschen, Berlin, 1883. Several earlier studies toted up the cost of giving whole families a decent living, but none spelled out the commodity inputs into an individual child by specific social class. For a bibliography of early budget studies giving some detail on child commodity inputs, see Faith M. Williams and Carle C. Zimmerman, *Studies of Family Living in the United States and Other Countries*, Washington, 1935, USDA Miscellaneous Publication No. 223. For a review of the methodo-

been confined to commodity cost, with almost complete silence on time costs. Estimating the value of the commodities devoted to an individual child is not difficult for such commodities as food, clothing, and private education. For these goods what is consumed by one family member is fairly distinguishable from the consumption of others. It is otherwise for overhead items like rent and utilities, and one must be arbitrary. Lacking good data on the living area and other overhead taken away from other family members by an extra child, past studies have usually assigned shares of overhead among family by an arbitrary formula—often an equal share for each family member. This is probably the best one can do.

Commodity cost estimates like those shown in Table 4-2 almost always find that total commodity costs are closely tied to the child's age, sex, and parity, and to family income. The level of outlays steadily grows with the age of the child until he leaves home around age eighteen. This contrasts sharply with the rapid dropoff in time expenditures revealed in Table 4-1 above. The one clear difference by sex is that teenage boys consume more food and less clothing than teenage girls (only boy-girl averages are used here). Another pattern revealed by nearly all relevant studies is that children of later birth order involve less commodity (and time) cost. These studies, however, have not separated the effects of spacing from the effects of family size. There is good reason to believe that a fourth child following the third by six years or more entails just as great a commodity cost as a first child. Finally, all studies confirm that commodity expenditures, unlike hours of time inputs, rise sharply with family income. The underlying income elasticity of commodity expenditures per child may be about unity.

The outstanding pattern regarding the shares of individual commodities in the total expenditures on an individual child is a familiar income effect: as income rises, the share of sundries (the "other" category in Table 4-2) rises while the share of food falls.

The data and patterns just mentioned, however, relate only to the period in which the child is present in the household of his or her parents. A correct accounting of the commodity inputs into a child (the C^N's) should include the effects of a child on the net commodity outlays of the parents after the child has grown up and left home. These effects are of two types: those set in motion by the saving and work effects of

---

logical problems involved, see Thomas J. Espenshade, "The Price of Children and Socio-Economic Theories of Fertility," *Population Studies* 26 (July 1972), 207–221.

Table 4-2. Selected Estimates of Commodity Inputs into U.S. Children, by Age of Child, 1889-1961.
(Current dollars)

Age of child, years	(1) 1889, Pennsylvania workers' third children, food only	(2) 1919, Chicago poor, third or fourth child. food	clothing	rent	health	other	total	(3) 1922-23, Iowa farm, third child. food	clothing	rent	health	other	total
<1	$10.9	83.3	27.0	20.0	36.0	4.5	170.8	41	26	28	51	25	171
1	10.9	← →	27.0	←	←	← →	137.8	41	←	←	18	← →	138
2	10.9		27.0				137.8	52			← →		149
3	10.9		33.0				143.8	← →			→		149
4	29.0		33.0				143.8						149
5	29.0	83.3	33.0			4.5	143.8		26		18	25	149
6	29.0	96.2	45.0			7.5	171.7		38		6	32	156
7	54.5	← →	← →			← →	—		← →		←	←	← →
8	54.5												
9	54.5	96.2	45.0			7.5	171.7						
10	54.5	109.2	54.0			9.3	195.5	52	38				156
11	65.3	109.2	54.0			← →	195.5	72	64	→	→		202
12	← →	109.2	54.0				195.5	72	64	28		32	202
13		120.9	60.0			9.3	213.2	72	64	30		63	202
14		120.9	60.0			9.3	213.2	114	83	30			296
15		140.4	90.0			17.5	270.9	114	83	30			296
16		140.4	90.0			17.5	270.9	114	83	30	6	63	296
17	65.3	140.4	90.0	20.0	3.0	17.5	270.9	114	83	30	6	63	296
Undiscounted total	805.7	1875.2	912	360	87	156	3390.2	1160	825	510	213	627	3335

Table 4-2 (continued). Selected Estimates of Commodity Inputs into U.S. Children, by Age of Child, 1889-1961. (Current dollars)

Age of child, years	(4) 1927-30, Vermont farm, third child.						(5) 1935-36, white urban working family, $2500, third child.						(6) 1960-61, North Central farm family, $4380, third child.					
	food	clothing	rent	health	other	total	food	clothing	rent	health	other	total	food	clothing	rent	health	other	total
1	76.3	14.8	59.2	54.0	30.6	234.9	82	14	78	319	150	643	107	29	48	437	254	875
1	↔	↔	↔	10.9	↔	191.8	82	14	↔	16	↔	340	130	29	↔	37	254	498
2	↔	14.8	↔	↔	↔	191.8	88	26	↔	14	↔	356	↔	47	↔	↔	253	515
3	76.3	21.0	↔	↔	↔	198.0	88	↔	↔	20	↔	362	130	↔	↔	↔	↔	515
4	95.3	21.0	↔	↔	↔	217.0	100	↔	↔	24	↔	378	163	↔	↔	↔	↔	548
5	↔	21.0	↔	10.9	30.6	217.0	100	26	↔	24	150	378	163	47	48	37	253	548
6	↔	26.3	59.2	3.6	35.7	222.7	100	34	↔	20	157	382	164	70	47	36	257	574
7	95.3	26.3	61.8	↔	↔	222.7	116	35	↔	14	↔	400	195	↔	↔	↔	↔	605
8	133.4	29.3	61.8	↔	↔	263.8	131	35	↔	13	↔	414	195	↔	↔	↔	↔	605
9	133.4	29.3	74.1	↔	↔	276.1	137	39	↔	13	↔	424	195	↔	↔	↔	↔	605
10	133.4	29.3	↔	↔	↔	276.1	138	39	↔	13	↔	425	227	70	47	36	257	637
11	133.4	29.3	↔	↔	35.7	335.8	149	39	↔	14	↔	437	227	98	48	34	270	678
12	171.6	50.8	↔	↔	↔	335.8	150	51	↔	14	↔	450	228	↔	↔	↔	↔	699
13	↔	50.8	↔	↔	↔	335.8	158	51	↔	14	↔	458	249	↔	↔	↔	↔	699
14	↔	50.8	74.1	↔	35.7	335.8	163	51	↔	15	↔	464	249	98	↔	↔	↔	699
15	171.6	61.5	98.2	↔	45.8	380.7	164	69	↔	16	↔	484	249	↔	↔	↔	270	699
16	181.1	61.5	98.2	↔	45.8	390.2	165	69	↔	18	↔	487	276	112	↔	↔	269	739
17	181.1	61.5	98.2	3.6	45.8	390.2	165	69	78	18	157	487	276	112	48	34	269	739
Un-disc. total	2230.5	611.1	1267.5	151.7	642.3	4903.1	2276	713	1404	599	2777		3553	1282	858	1042	4680	11415

Table 4-2 (continued). Selected Estimates of Commodity Inputs into U.S. Children, by Age of Child, 1889-1961. (Current dollars)

Age of child, years	(7) 1960-61, "low-income" urban family, third child food	clothing	rent	health	other	total	(8) 1960-61, "high-income" urban family, third child food	clothing	rent	health	other	total
<1	122		122	434	69	780	173	61	155	458	110	957
1	150	33	126	34	75	418	214	61	162	58	138	633
2	150	42	130	←	77	433	214	98	167	59	147	685
3	150	↔	131		80	437	214	←	170	↔	152	693
4	187	↔	133		81	477	273		174		158	762
5	187	42	129		83	475	273	98	170	59	159	759
6	187	70	124		84	499	274	144	164	61	187	830
7	222	←	125		86	537	325	→	167	←	177	874
8	222		125		85	536	325		169		180	879
9	222	→	125		85	536	325		170		181	881
10	258		124		83	569	390		172		185	952
11	258	70	126		83	571	390	144	173		186	954
12	258	101	144		120	657	391	210	198		232	1092
13	282	←	144		120	681	436	↔	199		263	1169
14	282	↔	148		129	694	436		205		276	1188
15	282	101	192		141	750	436	210	268		430	1405
16	314	121	192		141	802	482	281	269		396	1489
17	314	121	192	34	141	802	482	281	271	61	6900	7995
Undisc. total	4047	1300	2532	1012	1766	10,657	6053	2780	3423	1084	16,017	29,357

RELATIVE COST OF AMERICAN CHILDREN

NOTES AND SOURCES FOR TABLE 4-2

Where the commodity inputs differ by sex for a given age and parity, a simple average of the figures for a boy and a girl was taken. The inputs differ by sex only for food, clothing, and personal expenditures for certain ages.

Col. (1). U.S., Congress, House, *Sixth Annual Report of the Commissioner of Labor,* 1890, H. Exec. Doc. No. 265, 2867, Part 3, pp. 621, 664. Scales are presented expressing the ratio of each child's food bill to that of a working middle-age adult male. For Pennsylvania, the latter is $72.60 a year. Scales were not worked out for commodities other than food.

Cols. (2). Distilled from Florence Nesbitt, *The Chicago Standard Budget for Dependent Families,* Chicago, 1919, by S. P. Breckinridge, "Family Budgets," in U.S. Dept. of Labor, Children's Bureau, *Standards of Child Welfare,* 1919, Bureau publication no. 60, p. 35. Although the budget is advanced as a *norm* for use by welfare agencies, its commodity amounts are based on actual household expenditures in Chicago. The figure for rent is one-sixth the average rent of a family of five or six on the Chicago poverty line. On the Chicago poor, see also Leila Houghteling, *The Income and Standard of Living of Unskilled Laborers in Chicago,* Chicago: University of Chicago Press, 1927. A figure for obstetrical costs of $33, taken from the work by T. M. Adams cited for Cols. (4) below, was added to health costs for the year beginning with birth.

Cols. (3). Calculated from J. F. Thaden, *Standard of Living on Iowa Farms,* rev. ed., Ames, Iowa, 1928, Iowa State Agricultural Experiment Station Bulletin No. 237, rev. Thaden estimates the *net* effect of the third child on the family's total housing rent. I have derived a gross figure for the rental value taken from other family use by the third child by dividing his cumulative index for the rent expenditures of a family of five by five. An obstetrical bill of $33 has been added to the first year's health bill, based on figures from the study by T. M. Adams cited in the next note.

Cols. (4). Calculated from Marianne Muse, *The Standard of Living on Specific Owner-Operated Vermont Farms* (Burlington, Vt.: Free Press Printing, 1932), Vermont Agricultural Experiment Station Bulletin no. 340. Estimates were made of the rental value of the space taken by a third child by dividing the author's estimates of the rent for a five-person family by five. An obstetrical bill of $43.10 was added in, based on the 1927-30 cost of a delivery, four office calls, and two five mile house calls by physician, as priced in T. M. Adams, *Prices Paid by Vermont Farmers . . . 1790–1940* (Burlington, Vt.: Free Press Printing, 1944), Vermont Agricultural Experiment Station Bulletin no. 507, p. 60. Both Muse and Thaden were influenced in their choices of age-weight for rent and other expenditures by the study by Kirkpatrick cited below.

Cols. (5). Calculated from Louis Dublin and Alfred J. Lotka, *The Money Value of a Man,* New York: Ronald Press 1946, revised edition, Chap. 4. The earnings for this family exceed the median income of $1524 for the families covered in the 1934–36 Bureau of Labor Statistics survey on which these estimates were based. The figures are based on averages from cities all over the country. The child does not work. His or her college education is not financed by the parents. For commodities other than food, clothing, and health care, the child is simply assigned one-fifth the cost of the family's expenditures. The obstetrical cost estimates of the authors apparently come from New York city. These, like others cited by the Metropolitan Life Insurance Company, are much higher than the birth costs given for rural Vermont.

Col. (6). U.S. Department of Agriculture, Agricultural Research Service, Consumer and Food Economics Research Division, "Cost of Raising a Child,"

[107]

memorandum CFE (Adm.)-318, September 1971, Table 3. The obstetrical cost estimate was derived by deflating the estimate used by Sohn, Cain, and others for 1970 by the price index for medical care.

Cols. (7) and (8). Calculated in Appendix E, Tables E-2 and E-4, below. Four years of college, priced at $6500, were added to the cost of the higher-income child in Col. (8). This cost was not weighted by the probability of that child's going to college. Thus it was assumed that the child in Col. (8) was perfectly certain of attending college at his or her parents' expense. Similarly, it was assumed to be perfectly certain that the children in Cols. (1)–(7) would not attend college at their parents' expense.

For a definition of the family income streams used in the "low income" and the "high income" estimates, see Appendix A.

Other potentially useful estimates of this type are given in: (a) U.S. Department of Labor, Bureau of Labor Statistics, *Cost of Living in the United States*, Washington: GPO, 1924, Bulletin no. 357, especially detailed for clothing; (b) Ellis L. Kirkpatrick, *Family Living in Farm Homes: An Economic Study of 402 Farm Families in Livingston County, New York*, Washington; GPO, 1924, USDA Bulletin 1214, presenting 1920–21 data; (c) Metropolitan Life Insurance Company, *Statistical Bulletin*, various articles, December 1925–mid-1926 on the cost of a child in an urban family earning $2500 a year; (d) Community Council of Greater New York, *Annual Price Survey: Family Budget Costs, October 1968*, New York, 1969; (e) Sara Sohn, "The Cost of Raising a Child," manuscript, Institute of Life Insurance, Division of Research and Statistics, 1970; (f) Glen G. Cain, "Issues in the Economics of a Population Policy for the United States," University of Wisconsin, Institute for Research on Poverty, Discussion Paper 88–71, 1971, appendix; and (g) Ritchie Reed and Susan McIntosh, "Costs of Children," in U.S. Commission on Population Growth and the American Future, *Economic Aspects of Population Change*, Washington: GPO, 1972, vol. II of the Commission Research Reports. The estimates by Sohn, Cain, and Reed and McIntosh were based on the studies by the USDA and the Community Council of Greater New York cited above.

Rougher impressions for a much earlier era can be gained from Jackson Turner Main, *The Social Structure of Revolutionary America*, Princeton: Princeton University Press, 1965, Chap. IV.

the previous process of raising the child, and the net transfers between grown-up children and their parents. The first type will be discussed later in this chapter and measured en route to the 1960 relative-cost weights in Appendixes A, D, and E below. The second category, the net transfers between grown-up children and their parents, is one on which the existing literature has produced more assertions than data. Some have argued that young couples expect to leave certain levels of bequest to each child they raise, and that they take this into account when thinking about family size. Others, at least when discussing settings without Social Security, argue that couples desire extra children in order to assure support for themselves in their old age. We know that the prevailing level of net transfers between adult children and their parents is very low in the postwar world of Social Security, nuclear families, and high education. The bequests that parents leave in non-human form are not great, especially when discounted back to dates of decision-making about family size. Offsetting these bequests somewhat is the lower level of likely transfers from adult children for the support of their parents.[10] It seems safe to ignore the net transfers between adult children and their parents when computing the relative child cost weights for the postwar urban U.S., especially since we shall be concerned only with input proportions and not with total dollar costs.

It is likely that parents counted much more on old-age support from their children before World War II than they have done since then. This dependence on children in old age was probably greater among lower-income families, both urban and rural. Indigence among the elderly varied inversely with the number of their children,[11] and a large share of the elderly lived with their children. We lack reliable evidence on the dollar magnitudes of support received, however, and it is difficult to be certain that these magnitudes loomed larger in couples' expectations than did the likely bequests they would leave to their children. Presumably, poorer elderly persons were not recipients from their

---

[10] There is abundant evidence that since World War II very few retired persons live or expect to live with their children, and that the degree of economic support for parents by adult children is low whether or not the generations live together. See David Stern, Sandy Smith, and Fred Doolittle, "How Children Used To Work," *Law and Contemporary Problems*, 1975; John C. Beresford and Alice M. Rivlin, "Privacy, Poverty, and Old Age," *Demography* 3 (1960), 247–258; Irene B. Taeuber and Conrad Taeuber, *People of the United States in the 20th Century*, Washington, 1971, Table VI–7; and Edward Pryor's estimates from Rhode Island census data in Peter Laslett, ed., *Household and Family in Past Time*, Cambridge, 1972.

[11] Stern, Smith, and Doolittle, "How Children Used To Work."

children, while the wealthier were net donors to their children in their old age and their wills. Lacking numbers, these considerations must be omitted from any quantitative estimates of the costs of children before the age of Social Security.

For the postwar urban setting, at any rate, sufficient data are available to put together estimates of the total time and commodity cost of a first or third child for 1960. Tables 4–1 and 4–2 give the necessary data for urban families at two income levels (using the 1968 Syracuse time inputs for 1960). The steps involved are to value time at prevailing wage rates, to discount values at the discount rates given above, and to sum up the total values. This exercise is essentially identical to that performed recently by Cain and by Reed and McIntosh. This step has been taken, but the absolute dollar magnitudes are of secondary interest and are displayed only in passing in Tables 4–6 through 4–9 and Appendix E below. The *relative* cost of a child is more closely tied, as explained above, to the differences between the shares of individual inputs in this overall bundle and the shares in the bundle of inputs that would go into the activities with which an extra child competes. To discover those key differences we must turn to the effects of an extra child on the family's net exports of labor and its net imports of commodities. These trade effects are what govern movements in child costs most directly.

C. THE EFFECT OF CHILDREN ON WORK TIME

As with the time inputs into children, the effects on time spent at work producing commodities for the market are again dominated by the effects on the wife's time allocation. After a brief word about effects on husband's time at paid work, I shall focus on the wife's labor force participation, and then finish this section with a few comments on children's work time.

Even without concrete regression results, we can see that having an extra child could hardly reduce the husband's labor force participation. True, infants apparently are labor-intensive enough to raise the shadow price of time in the home, and that might have caused some husbands to work less in order to help out. But the overwhelming evidence of the time-budget studies is that husbands spend very little time taking care of the children in any case. What time they do contribute comes on Sundays and at odd hours. The Syracuse data also suggest that the time they spend with the children is also spent at care other than physical care—i.e., at the enjoyable part of interacting with children, which can be viewed as quasi leisure of a sort that husbands (or their employers) will not let impinge much on their work week. If the presence of infants drives up the physical care demands, it is the wife's time that is affected.

The available regression estimates of the effect of a child on a father's yearly hours of paid work vary considerably. Some studies find no effect; some find an implausibly large tendency for fathers to work extra hours. These estimates are discussed in Appendix B. As a best guess, I shall assume that the presence of one or more children in the home raises the father's paid work time by 50 hours per year.

Information is more plentiful on the most important work-effect parameter: the effect of children on the labor force participation of wives. I shall begin with the fairly clear picture that other authors have provided for urban families in 1960, and then expand the discussion to earlier periods and to farms.

After adjustments for the effects of parents' ages, schooling, color, nonwife family income, and employment status of the husband, the regressions by Bowen and Finegan imply the effects of children on the wife's 1960 working hours shown in Table 4–3. These figures are shifts in averages that reflect both changes in the share of wives working and changes in average weekly hours of those working. The most common shift due to an extra child, of course, is zero, since most wives are not working anyway. For those who are working, the reduction in work caused by an extra child is greater than is shown in these overall averages.[12]

Two basic patterns stand out in the figures in Table 4–3. First, the effect on hours of paid work relates to the age of a first child in the same way as do total time inputs into the child. Both series start at high levels and drop off quickly to age six. Second, a comparison of the columns reveals the great importance of child spacing. A third child born six years or more after the second would have at least half as much effect on wives' paid work as would an only child, since in the absence of the third child the wife would have almost as great a likelihood of working

[12] The reduction in work time for women who would hold jobs without the extra child is apparently greater even than the time they put into the extra child. This conclusion, at least, is implied by the Bowen-Finegan data for work in 1960 and the time budget data on the time cost of children. This means that women who would have been working without an extra child are forced to quit work to such an extent when having the child that their time inputs into home activities other than the extra child are actually raised by having the child. For these women the net time input into the alternatives to a child $(-L^H)$ is actually negative. This pattern does not prevail in the overall averages, however. The fact that most mothers are not working anyway keeps the average effect on hours worked below the hours of time input into the extra child, so that $(-L^H) > 0$ overall.

ECONOMIC INFLUENCES ON FERTILITY

Table 4-3. Effects of Children in the Home on Paid Working Hours by Wives in Census Week, 1960

(Hours per Week)

Age of (youngest) Child	A First Child	A Third Child, Born 3 Years after the Second and 6 Years after the First
under 1	17.43	4.30
1	14.68	2.89
2	13.75	2.27
3	13.15	4.61
4	11.79	3.27
5	11.48	2.96
6	8.52	0
7	8.52	0
8	8.52	0
9	8.52	0
10	8.52	0
11	8.52	6.60 - (2nd child enters 14-17
12	8.52	6.60 age bracket)
13	8.52	6.60
14	1.92	0
15	1.92	1.34 - (2nd child leaves home)
16	1.92	1.34
17	1.92	1.34

Source: William Bowen and T. Aldrich Finegan, *The Economics of Labor Force Participation* (Princeton: Princeton University Press, 1969), pp. 101-102.

Note: One minor anomaly in the results on p. 101 of Bowen-Finegan is interpreted as irrlevant here. They find that wives with grade-school children as well as preschool children work 0.4 hours a week more than wives with preschool children only. This is apparently due to the ability of the very oldest grade schoolers to help out at home, and to their higher commodity demands. The estimates support the assumption that this stimulus to labor force re-entry by some mothers is adequately explained by putting 13-year-olds in with the 14-17 group rather than lumping them in with the 6-12 group, as in the regressions reported. This makes the extra 0.4 hours irrelevant here, because by assumption the third child enters grade school just as the first reaches 13.

as a childless wife. Yet in the case of the third child lagged by three years, the effect is greatly reduced. This means that a closely spaced extra child is much less labor-intensive than is a first-born or a child born long after its older siblings. Comparing these figures with the time spent on children by Syracuse mothers in Table 4–1 suggests that a closely-spaced later child, while taking much less time off the mother's paid work than would a first child, takes somewhat more time away from her other home activities than a first child. The more important point, though, is that the relative labor-intensity of a child, and the sensitivity of its relative cost to wage movements, varies positively with the length of the birth interval. In what follows I shall use the terms "first child" and "third child" to refer to the two types represented in Table 4–3. It should be remembered that the assumption about spacing is more important to the results below than is the parity of the child.

The effects of an extra child on the wife's hours of paid work are not confined to the period in which the child is growing up in the home. Her career is also affected during the pregnancy and after the child has grown up and left the home. Fortunately there are reasonable estimates of the strength of these effects on urban wives in the early 1960s. The magnitude of a typical work loss during pregnancy can be judged from a survey taken in 1963 by the Public Health Service.[13] The average work loss is around 2.93 months, or 488 hours a full-time work year, for women who had jobs at the time of conception. Weighting this figure by the average weekly hours and the likelihood that the wife was in the labor force at the start of pregnancy yields an average work loss of 220 hours for mothers of first children and 46.4 hours for mothers of third children of the assumed (three year) spacing.[14] These figures are to be added into estimates of how the child inputs (N bundle) differ from the inputs into other activities (the H bundle).

After the child has grown up and left the home, it continues to keep down labor force participation by the mother. The mother, having stayed out of the labor force for so long, commands a lower wage and therefore has a greater tendency to remain out of the labor force (see Appendix A regarding the job-interruption effect on the wage rate).

[13] U.S. Department of Health, Education and Welfare, National Center for Health Statistics, *Employment during Pregnancy: United States—1963*, Vital and Health Statistics, Series 22, No. 7, Washington, 1966, Table 1.

[14] The average work loss during pregnancy was calculated in the following manner. The 1963 survey showed that 15.1 percent of those indicating when they stopped work stopped in the first trimester of pregnancy, 34.1 percent in the second trimester, and the remaining 50.8 percent in the third. Assuming seven months of work loss for the first group, four months for the second, and one month for the third yields an average work loss of 2.93 months for those who had been working at the start of pregnancy. To translate this into an average over working and nonworking women, I used the labor force participation rates and average weekly hours given in Bowen and Finegan (pp. 101, 102). The resulting estimates are consistent with results for 1967–69 subsequently reported by James A. Sweet, "Employment during Pregnancy," University of Wisconsin, Center for Demography and Ecology, Working Paper 74-16 (October 1974).

Fortunately, this effect of grown-up children on the wife's working hours has been quantified by James Sweet[15] on the basis of 1960 census data. This "Sweet old mother effect" comes to 0.86 hour per week for the first child ever born and 0.79 hour per week for the third. It lasts from the end of child raising to age sixty.[16] This effect represents an addition of commodities (earn more, buy more) and a subtraction from the home time in the H bundle (since working more means less home time).

For urban wives in 1960, then, we have fairly good estimates of four effects of extra children on a wife's pay: (1) she loses hours of work during pregnancy, (2) she loses work time while raising the child, (3) she tends to work less after the child has left the home, and (4) her wage rate is depressed by job interruption and loss of experience.

How would the parameters for other settings compare to those just presented? When one moves away from the postwar urban setting, one finds that only the second and largest of the four effects has been at all quantified by past studies. There are some survey data on how women's paid work time is affected by the presence of children in the home. The magnitudes of the other three effects must be assumed without direct information. It is reasonable to suppose that the average work loss during pregnancy was about three months for nonfarm wives working at the time of conception before World War II as well as since then. The work loss during pregnancy has probably been smaller for farm wives. As for the Sweet old mother effect and the job-interruption effect on wage rates, these are arbitrarily assumed to be postwar nonfarm phenomena. These effects are presumably significant only for more skilled occupations, in which accumulated experience matters a lot. I suspect that only in the years since World War II did enough nonfarm wives move into such jobs to make past experience an important determinant of the yearly earnings.

The effect of children in the home on the labor force participation of nonfarm wives has apparently been rising across the twentieth century. The data seem to conform to a simple pattern: whatever raises the percentage of married women working outside the home raises, to a lesser

[15] James A. Sweet, "Family Composition and the Labor Force Activity of Married Women in the United States," Ph.D. dissertation, University of Michigan, 1968, Table 4–9.

[16] The effect on a mother's work when she is in her sixties is less certain and probably less pronounced. Sweet's regressions refer only to wives over 44 and under 60. The continuation of the same effect into the later age range would probably be offset by a tendency of the wife with fewer children to retire earlier and enjoy her greater prior accumulation of Social Security benefits.

extent, the effect of children in the home on the percentage of wives working. This observation seems valid both for trends and for cross-sections. To demonstrate this tendency, however, requires examination of trends in some data that are rather rough and not exactly comparable over time. The indicators given in Table 4–4 are slightly inappropriate in a number of ways. First, they often refer to total nonfarm "gainful employment" rather than to work by urban wives. Second, they lump together children of very different ages, clouding the year-by-year effects of the presence of infants. Finally, the various data sources adopt differing definitions of labor force participation.

The figures in Table 4–4 do manage, nonetheless, to reveal a rise across this century, both in the share of married women working and in the effects of children on wives' employment. What information we have suggests that in the late nineteenth century very few wives worked outside the home, with or without children. There were several reasons for this. First, the wage rates facing wives in the marketplace were not high relative to those of their husbands because women, as potential workers with less skills and job experience, faced stiff competition from immigrants and teen-agers. Second, wives were told both by social attitudes and by the burdensome labor-intensity of washing by hand, cooking from raw materials, and tending fires that their place was definitely in the home. To be sure, they could take in sewing, laundry, boarders, and lodgers. The data show that these practices were indeed quite common. Such work in the home, however, was less affected by the presence of children than was work at a regular job outside the home.[17] Work in the home could be combined with supervision of children or could be shifted to hours when the children were at school or asleep. This is obviously not true of a job outside the home, where discipline and punctuality were more important.

The fact that the presence of children had little apparent effect on nonfarm wives' paid work before World War I has an important implication for the role of movements in relative child cost in explaining the

[17] In the 1889 household survey, for example, the percentage of households having income from boarders and lodgers was actually higher for families with children than for families without:

	Families with children	Without children
With income from boarders, etc.	593	40
Without boarders	1,505	354

It would appear that having children makes a wife *more* willing, if anything, to give up time to the earning of income from boarders and lodgers, so that the effect of children on her total paid work may have been slightly positive.

ECONOMIC INFLUENCES ON FERTILITY

Table 4-4. Rough Indicators of Trends in the Effects of Children in the Home on Employment of Married Women, 1875-1970.

	Year	Percent of married women, husband present, working outside the home	Effect of children under indicated ages on the percentage of wives at work (the no. of wives affected, as a % of all wives, husband present) under 6	under 10	under 18
Nonfarm Massachusetts,	1875	2.3			
Nonfarm Illinois,	1884	7.0			
9 industries,	1889-90	6.9	1.7	1.7	2.1
	1890	4.6		2.6	
	1900	5.6			
25,021 workers' wives,	1901	8.7			
	1910	10.7			
Philadelphia	1918-19	20.0			10.4
Rochester,	1920	8.8	10.1 (ch<5)		7.4
	1920	9.0			
Chicago,	1928	17.2*	13.3*		10.7*
	1930	12.0			
	1940	14.7	20.4**	11.1	
	1944	21.7			
	1947	20.0	18.3		
	1948	22.0	20.6		
	1949	22.5	21.2		
	1950	23.8	21.9	17.7	
	1955	27.7	21.4		
	1960	30.5	22.6		12.3
	1965	34.7	22.5		
	1970	42.3	21.0		11.3

*Includes women taking in boarders and lodgers. This practice accounted for over half the employment of the sampled Chicago wives.

**For 1940, the comparison is between women in families with children under 5 and those without children under 5. The latter group will include some families with older children, and not just childless families.

Sources for Table 4-4

(1) *For 1875*: Massachusetts Bureau of Labor Statistics, *Sixth Annual Report*, in Public Documents of Massachusetts, 1874, vol. V, nos. 30–32. Note: the survey was one of families where the husband did work, and thus slightly underestimated wives' average labor force participation.

(2) *For 1884*: Illinois Bureau of Labor Statistics, *Third Biennial Report*, Springfield; H. W. Rokker, 1884, p. 274. Out of 1,597 husband-wife families, 111 wives had income.

(3) *For 1889–90*: 473 wives out of 6,809 worked outside the home. Among wives of husbands associated with the cotton and woolen industries, about 13% worked outside the home. Working wives were less than 1.5% of wives in the other seven industries. Source for six industries, 1889: U.S. 51st Congress,

decline in nonfarm marital fertility. Even without constructing the complete index of child costs, one can see that if an extra child had little effect on paid work, the extra child must not have used the mother's home time much more intensively than did the alternatives to the child. With or without the child, the wife was confined to the home. This means that the upward trend in women's wage rates failed to raise the relative cost of children to nonfarm married couples across the nineteenth century. The impressive reductions in nonfarm marital fertility before World War I were apparently not linked to wage increases through movements in relative child costs. If the rise in wage rates did play a role in marital fertility decline, that role must have related to wages as income or as correlates of parental tastes and norms, and not to wage rates as the cost of a mother's time. This point will be reinforced by the data presented below on the contribution of urban children's earnings to family incomes in the late nineteenth century.

Farm wives, like their prewar urban counterparts, have worked primarily in or near the home on family farms. The extent of their work and of the influence of children on it is harder to judge than for urban wives. We know that a farm wife's farm work (as opposed to her production within the home) is a part-time operation not subject to any standard number of weekly hours. Data on her "labor force participa-

---

1890–91, House Executive Documents, No. 265, Part 2. For three industries, 1890: U.S. 52nd Congress, 1891–92, House Executive Documents, No. 232, Part 2. The effects of children were estimated from the regressions on wives' out-of-home work reported in Appendix B below.

(4) *For 1901 workers' wives*: U.S. Commissioner of Labor, *Eighteenth Annual Report*, Washington: GPO, 1903, p. 28. Figure is the percentage of wives earning income outside of the home during 1901.

(5) *For Philadelphia, 1918–19*: Gwendolyn S. Hughes, *Mothers in Industry*, New York, 1925, p. 96. The taking-in of boarders and lodgers is reflected in these figures to an unknown extent.

(6) *For Rochester, 1920*: U.S. Bureau of the Census, *The Woman Homemaker in the City*, Washington: GPO, 1923, pp. 24–26.

(7) *For Chicago, 1928*: Day Monroe, *Chicago Families*, Chicago: Chicago University Press, 1932, pp. 147, 212–225.

(8) *For the effects of children under 10*: Clarence D. Long, *The Labor Force under Changing Income and Employment*, Princeton, 1958, p. 115.

(9) *For census years, 1890–1930*: U.S. Women's Bureau, 1925, p. 34; idem, 1953, p. 9.

(10) *1970*: U.S. Bureau of the Census, *1970 Census of Population*, vol. 1, pt. 1, sec. 2, Table 216. Figures refer to married women, husband present, ages 16–64.

(11) *For all other*: Bowen and Finegan, p. 97, 585, 586. Unadjusted figures for married women, 14–64.

tion" are therefore especially treacherous, because such data depend critically on just how many hours of work makes one a worker in the eyes of those gathering the figures. For this reason, and because of the seasonality of farm work, the census returns on the farm employment of women are of little help. Between 1910 and 1920, for example, a subtle change in the wording of the census questions about farm work threw thousands of farm wives out of the labor force.[18]

We must turn to sample surveys of farm families for estimates of the hours worked in farm production and off-the-farm jobs by farm wives. The only clustering of such data that I am aware of is the set of time-budget studies of farm households since the 1920s. The overall extent of farm work and outside work by farm wives is suggested by the following averages across seasons:[19]

		farm work	*average hours per week of paid work off the farm*
49	Idaho farm wives, 1926	9.7	n.a.
92	*rural* Montana wives, 1929–31	9.2	n.a.
288	Oregon farm wives, 1926–27	11.3	2.7
102	*rural* Rhode Island wives, 1926–29	3.3	4.5
100	South Dakota farm wives, late 1920s	11.5	n.a.
137	Washington farm wives, 1928	9.9	n.a.
497	New York farm wives, 1936	6.8	2.0
183	Vermont wives, 1943 (wartime)	10.1	n.a.
95	New York farm wives, 1952	7.0	under 0.6
85	Wisconsin farm wives, 1953	8.0	n.a.
	U.S. farm wives, 1965–66	7.1	5.2

Comparing these averages with census data on paid work by nonfarm wives suggests two patterns. First, farm wives worked more total hours outside of the *house* than did nonfarm wives before World War II, and

[18] Joseph A. Hill, *Women in Gainful Occupations, 1870 to 1920*, reprint of 1929 edition, New York, 1972, Chap. 3.

[19] The sources for data relating to the 1920s are the studies by I. Z. Crawford, Richardson, Wilson, Whittemore and Neil, Wasson, and Arnquist and Roberts cited in Andrews, *Economics of the Household*, p. 443n. The later studies are those by Warren, Muse, and Wiegand cited in the notes to Table 4–1 above; M. L. Cowles and R. P. Dietz, "Time Spent in Homemaking Activities . . . ," *Journal of Home Economics*, No. 48 (January, 1956), p. 30; and U.S. Bureau of the Census, *1964 Census of Agriculture*, vol. 3, pt. 2, Washington, 1968, p. 58 and Table 8.

about the same amount as nonfarm wives since then. Second, farm wives have never worked as much outside the home (off the farm, in their case) as have nonfarm wives. This latter pattern suggests that having an extra child should have less impact on the paid work of farm wives than of other wives.

Additional scraps of information seem to confirm that having a child reduces the work of farm wives less than it reduces work by urban wives. This, at least, is the impression given by two Northwest farm surveys in the late 1920s and by the 1/1000 sample from the 1960 census. Maud Wilson's survey of Oregon farms in 1926–27 derived the following reductions in a farm wife's work time caused by a first child (p. 16):

    child under 1: 6.2 hrs./wk.
       1–5: 4.5
      6–14: 3.3
      15–up: zero, apparently

These magnitudes are supported by a survey of Washington farms in 1928, which showed an average cut in the mother's work of 3.4 hours per week over all ages of the child.[20] This effect appears somewhat smaller than the effect for urban wives in the late 1920s. A similar tale is told by 1960 census data on the effects of farm and urban children on their mothers' work. Regressions run for 1960 by James Sweet find that for each age range of the youngest child, the presence of children has about two-thirds as much effect on the labor force participation rate of farm wives as it has for urban wives.[21]

There is good theoretical reason to believe that the presence of children does have less impact on the work of farm wives, as these data suggest. The task of supervising children conflicts less with work, since the wife and other family members can more easily arrange to be in or near the house than can their urban counterparts. It is also easier for farm children to accompany their parents into barnyards or fields than it is for urban children to tag along with mother to the factory or store. Thus

---

[20] Inez Arnquist and Evelyn Roberts, *The Present Use of Work Time of Farm Homemakers*, Washington State Agricultural Experiment Station, Bulletin 234, Pullman, Washington, 1929, p. 17.

[21] James A. Sweet, "The Employment of Rural Farm Wives," Institute for Research on Poverty, University of Wisconsin, Discussion Paper 124–72, April, 1972, p. 46. The comparison is between the effects of children in the home on the total (farm plus nonfarm) labor force participation rate of farm wives and the rate for urban wives, both sets of effects being derived from regressions run on the 1/1000 census sample for 1960. No allowance could be made for the effect of farm children on the average hours of those wives who did work.

farm children, like urban children before World War I, are apparently not very wife's-labor-intensive relative to the family activities they replace. This hypothesis seems especially plausible in settings in which farm or peasant families are extended beyond the nuclear two-adult unit.

The earnings contributed by children to their parents' households have been largely unmeasured, especially for farm families. Ideally measurements should be made of both the work contribution of the children while in the parents' home and their transfers to the parents after they leave. The latter transfers were discussed in the previous section. We have few prewar data on the ages of leaving home, as well as on the extent of support for parents thereafter. The age of eighteen seems to be the most common (modal) one for leaving home, according to surveys extending back into the last century. Median and mean ages have always been a year or two higher, apparently, but surveys of family income and work seem to fix on the age-eighteen threshold. The choice of an age for typical home-leaving is not critical for present calculations, as long as the age of assumed departure is roughly the age at which the child's own income just about matches his or her consumption expenditures.

Data exist on the earnings of children while still in their parents' homes. Table 4–5 and Figure 4–1 outline the trend over the last hundred years. With economic growth has come an increasing emphasis on skill and work experience, depressing the ratio of wage rates for nonfarm children to those for nonfarm adults. The rise in parents' demand for extra schooling for their children, accompanied with a lag by compulsory schooling and child labor laws, has also dramatically reduced labor-force participation rates and average yearly hours for minors. As a result, both farm and nonfarm children today generate much lower earnings in relation to those of an adult male than they earned in the late nineteenth century (Figure 4–1).

This change is of fundamental importance for trends in child cost. In the last hundred years urban America has moved from a situation in which minors apparently gave more labor earnings to the household than they took away from the mother's earnings (especially in textile-producing areas) to a situation in which their net effect on family labor supply is negative. The implications of wage rate increases for movements in relative child cost have thus been reversed. Before the late nineteenth century, the nature of child costs in urban America was consistent with (though not necessarily responsible for) the classic pessimistic view that wage rises would only encourage the masses to have extra children until wage rates were bid back down by the extra supply of laborers. Since

World War II or a bit earlier, however, rising real wages have brought increases in the relative cost of children.[22] Even though Chapter 5 will argue that movements in incomes and tastes are at least as important to America's fertility trend as movements in the cost variable, the reversal in the implications of wage rates for child costs is at least part of the explanation of this trend.

There has been a similar drift away from labor-supplying status for children in the farm sector. It is clear that any generation of farm children growing up before World War II contributed a much greater value of labor time to farm and household work than they made their mothers take away from work outside the house. To be sure, the farm child's work contribution was not great enough to match the total time-plus-commodity cost of his rearing. Yet it does appear that any rise in real farm wage rates would have lowered rather than raised the perceived relative cost of a farm child, even a first-born. The same may still be true today, though only barely so at most. Since World War II the farm work contribution of farm children has continued to drift downward while farm wives have come to work more and more off the farm. In all likelihood there is no strong relationship today between farm wage rates and the relative cost of farm children.

D. THE EFFECT OF CHILDREN ON FAMILY COMMODITY PURCHASES

The final step before calculating the weights that go into the cost indices of a child and the alternative to the child is to examine the available evidence on how a child affects the family's total purchases of each commodity. The ultimate purpose of such an examination, as was explained earlier in this chapter, is to set up estimates of the amounts of commodity inputs ($-C^H$'s) implicitly involved in the activities that the extra child would replace. It will turn out, as with the work effects just reviewed, that one can reach some basic results along the way, even before the relative cost index is set up below.

To pursue concrete numbers, one can use regression results to quantify how the consumption effects of a child vary with the child's age and spacing behind the previous child, adjusting for the income and age of the parents. From such regressions one can compute both the direct

---

[22] Whether or not the net effect of urban minors in family labor supply in the period 1917–45 was positive or negative depends on the choice of discount rate.

Strictly speaking, the value of the child's work contribution must include the value of his chore contribution at home. Adding the value of such home chore time makes World War II the most likely threshold between labor-supplying and labor-intensive children.

ECONOMIC INFLUENCES ON FERTILITY

Table 4-5. Work and Earnings of Children Living with Parents, Various Surveys, 1875-1965.

(averages of rates for boys and girls, unless sex is indicated)

	Age of Child								Prime-age adult male earnings
	10	11	12	13	14	15	16	17	
1875, eldest children of Massachusetts workers									
% with some income	7.7	12.5	65.7	81.3	83.3	98.0	90.8	90.8	
average income/yr.	$12	16	96	130	167	233	258	281	$572
1889-90, New York industrial workers' children									
% with some income	5.2%	←	→	5.2%	44.2	44.2	48.3	48.3	
average income/yr.	$10	←	→	10	127	127	148	148	$442
1889-90, Georgia industrial workers' children									
% with some income	20.7%	←	→	20.7	29.9	29.9	67.8	67.8	
average income/yr.	$36	←	→	36	71	71	169	169	$323
1901, workers' children, South Atlantic Region									
% with some income		←—————	24.6	—————→			71.9	to (20) →		
average income/yr.		←—————	$37.6	—————→			109.8	→		$558
1901, workers' children, North Atlantic Region									
% with some income		←—————	9.4	—————→			70.9	→		
average income/yr.		←—————	$19.3	—————→			$145.6	→		$618
1929-30, Northeast dairy farm boys attending school and living at home (underestimates)									
% working on farms	9.0%	←	→	9.0	22.5	31.7	52.4	65.9	
hrs./wk., those working	18.1	←	→	18.1	22.0	29.7	33.0	46.2	
average income/yr.	$11	←	→	$11	43	66	122	214	$705
April 1960 census, urban children									
% with some income	|←	(negligible)	→|	8.4	12.1	20.7	22.4	
hrs./wk., those working	"	"	"	"	9.2	10.8	13.1	13.3	
average income/yr.	"	"	"	"	$41.6	101.7	214.5	330.6	$4,000
1965, farm children									
hrs./wk. at farm work	6.4	←	→	6.4	9.3	9.3	10.4	10.4	
hrs./wk. nonfarm work	|←	(negligible)	→|	0.9	0.9	3.4	3.4	
average income/yr.	$211	←	→	$211	336	336	445	455	$1,902

RELATIVE COST OF AMERICAN CHILDREN

SOURCES AND NOTES TO TABLE 4–5

Figures for average income per year are ratios of total income to the number in the age-group, whether working or not.

1875: Massachusetts Bureau of Labor Statistics, *Sixth Annual Report*, Boston, 1875, vol. V, nos. 30–32. The survey covered 396 male workers' families, of which all but four had children. The adult male average is that for the household heads surveyed.

When conducting a similar survey in 1884, the Illinois Bureau of Labor Statistics (*Third Biennial Report*, p. 270) noted the peculiarity of the Massachusetts pattern: "In Massachusetts, whose extensive mills afford unusual opportunities for the employment of women and children, the percentage of families (with earnings by wives and children) is 64+, affording a very wide contrast with our 24+ percent (in Illinois, where most of the wife-and-child earnings were from children over 16)."

1889–90: New York and Georgia: calculated from regressions reported in Appendix B below.

1901: U.S. Commissioner of Labor, *Eighteenth Annual Report*, Washington: GPO, 1903, Tables I–I, I–G, III–I. Again, the adult male figure is an average for household heads (all husbands). The rates for children are averages for the age groups 10–15 and 16–20.

1929–30: my own calculations. The labor force participation rates are from the 1930 census of population, and the hours worked for those doing farm work are from Howard W. Beers, *The Money Income of Farm Boys in a Southern New York Dairy Region* (Ithaca, N.Y.: Cornell University, 1930), Cornell University Agricultural Experiment Station Bulletin no. 512, pp. 23–26. The boys were assumed to be paid at 60 percent of the 1930 New York farm wage rate, which the USDA estimated at 22.6¢/hr.

These estimates *underestimate* the average farm work of boys in dairy farm families, for two main reasons: (1) The labor force participation rates from the census refer to a very narrow definition of what constitutes being employed. (2) The sample used by Beers consisted only of farm boys who were in school, lived with their parents, and did at least half of their recorded farm work on their parents' farm. A broader sample would have given a considerably higher estimate of average hours worked.

1960: Bowen and Finegan, *Economics of Labor Force Participation*, p. 385. The 1960 census, like each census beginning with 1940, did not ask about employment or earnings for children under fourteen because the magnitudes were known to be negligible. The earnings in the table assume a wage rate of $1.00 an hour for the child and $2.00 an hour for the adult male.

1965: U.S. Bureau of the Census, *1964 Census of Agriculture*, Washington: GPO, 1964, vol. 3, pt. 2, Chap. 2. Weekly hours are averaged over boys and girls, over all children whether working or not, and over the 52 weeks of a year from March 1965 to March 1966. The adult male in this case was assumed to work 2,000 hours a year at the 1964 U.S. average hired farm worker's wage rate of 95.1¢/hr. The child was assumed to earn two-thirds of this hourly rate.

[123]

ECONOMIC INFLUENCES ON FERTILITY

Figure 4-1. Average Earnings of Children Living with Their Parents, By Age, As a Share of Those for an Adult Male, 1875, 1889-90, 1960, and 1965.

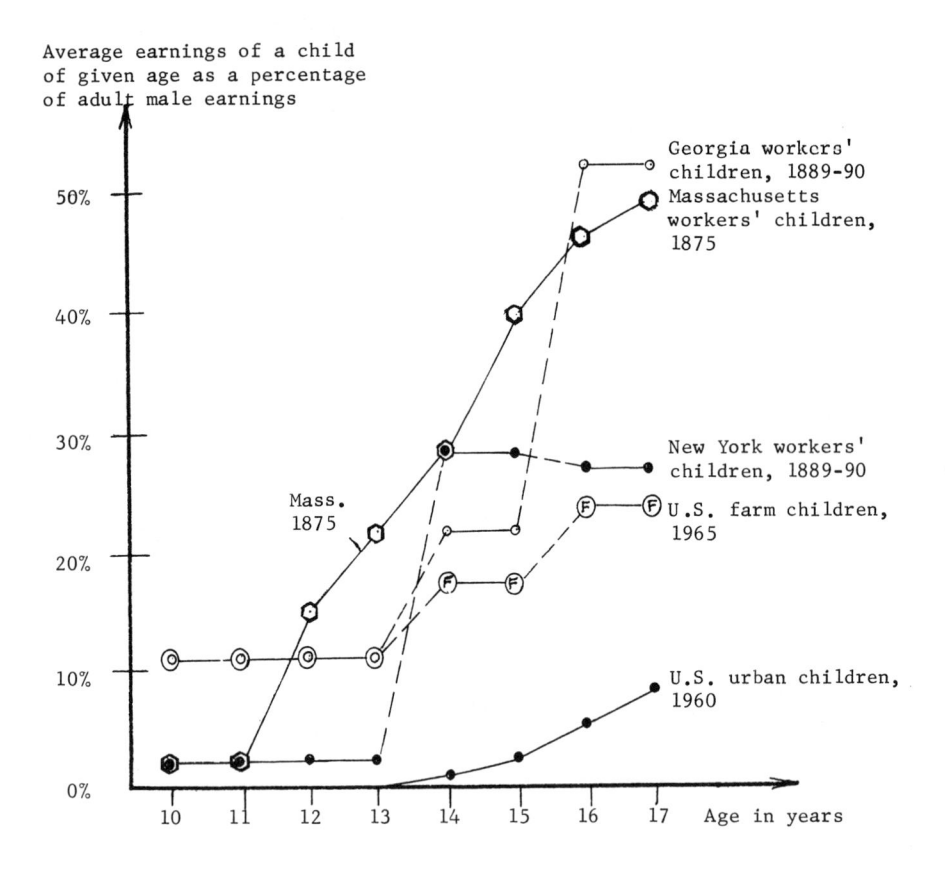

[Chart showing average earnings of a child of given age as a percentage of adult male earnings, by age in years (10-17), with series:
- Georgia workers' children, 1889-90
- Massachusetts workers' children, 1875
- New York workers' children, 1889-90
- U.S. farm children, 1965
- Mass. 1875
- U.S. urban children, 1960]

(Sources and notes: same as for Table 4-5.)

effects of an extra child for given parental income and the indirect effects on consumption via induced changes in family income. The negative effects of the child on savings over the first eighteen years can also be translated into consumption cuts in the years after the child has left the home. All this has been done for 1960 urban families in Appendixes D and E below.

Such an elaborate reckoning is not needed, however, if one seeks only the broad outlines of how children affect the shares of each commodity group in family budgets. Some simple patterns can be identified with the help of existing consumer budget studies. Drawing on a host of budget studies conducted in several countries over the last hundred years, Figure 4–2 displays some key elasticities of household expenditures with respect to family size as well as to total expenditures.

One broad pattern revealed by the data plotted in Figure 4–2 is that there is a good analogy between extra children and poverty: an extra child does to the levels of spending on food and on "all other" commodities what poverty does to the budget shares of these commodity groups. An extra child, like a cut in income, consistently raises the importance of food expenditures. Extra children are definitely "food-intensive." An extra child cuts family spending on the "all other" category, just as a cut in income cuts both the level and the budget share of this type of consumption. Within the broad "all other" group, of course, different commodities relate to family size in quite different ways. Children do cut into family spending on automobiles,[23] for example, but they have the opposite effect on the demand for day care, which is also buried in the "all other" category.

Of particular interest is the negative impact of children on expenditures for rent. Most studies have found that parents, to make ends meet, actually tend to reduce their outlays on shelter when having another child. It would be premature, however, to conclude that greater family size paradoxically reduces the demand for living space and land. House rent is not the same thing as space rent. Extra children presumably raise the demand for rooms, floor space, and lot acreage, yet at the same time reduce the demand for housing value per room or per acre so much that total rent demand is cut. For the moment, it can simply be noted that a rise in house rents in general will not raise the relative cost of a child.

VI. *Patterns Revealed by the Index*

Now that all of the elements of the calculation of a relative child cost index have been introduced, the index itself can be examined. The weights in the index and the movements of prices since the nineteenth century reconfirm the various patterns in cost movements already deduced by examining the historical record of work and consumption effects.

Tables 4–6 through 4–9 show the input proportions (index weights) for first and third children in urban families in 1960. For any one birth order and family income level, some conclusions already reached stand out clearly once again. Additional children, especially first-borns, are

[23] Martin H. David, *Family Composition and Consumption*, Amsterdam, 1962.

Figure 4-2. Family-Size Elasticities and Total-Expenditure Elasticities of Consumption, a Potpourri of Survey Samples, 17 Countries, 1875-1955.

(Sources: H.S. Houthakker, in Oct. 1957 *Econometrica*; J.G. Williamson, in 1967 *Explorations in Economic History*; similar results are reported for 1889-90 and 1960-61 U.S. surveys in Appendix D below.)

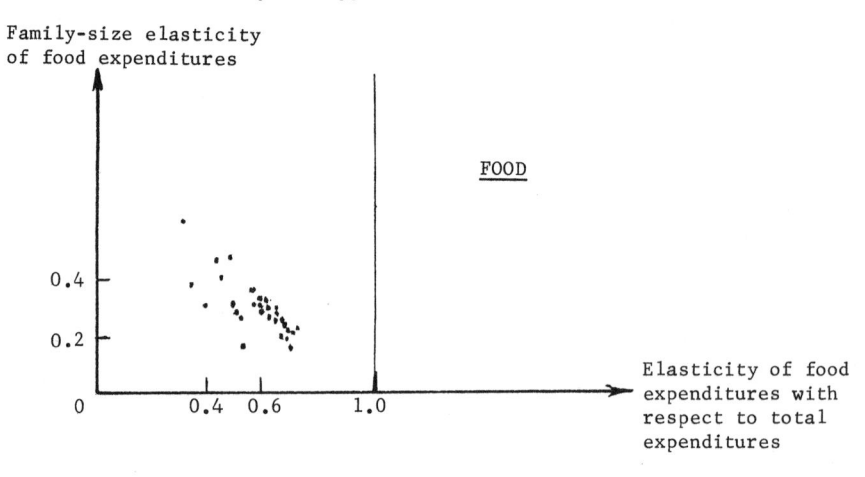

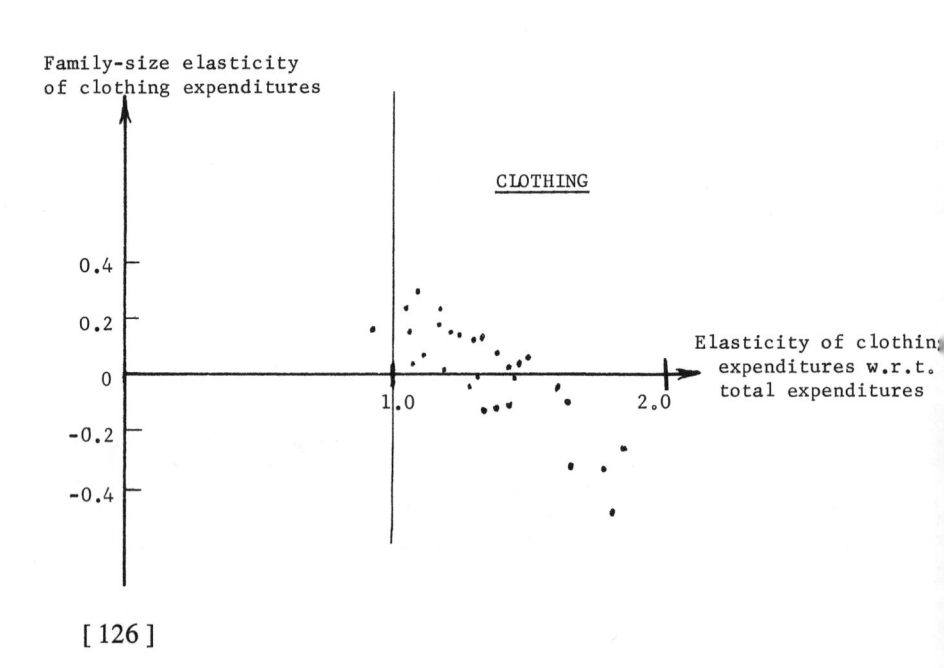

Figure 4-2. Family-Size and Total-Expenditure Elasticities of Consumption, a Potpourri of Survey Samples, 17 Countries, 1875-1955 (continued).

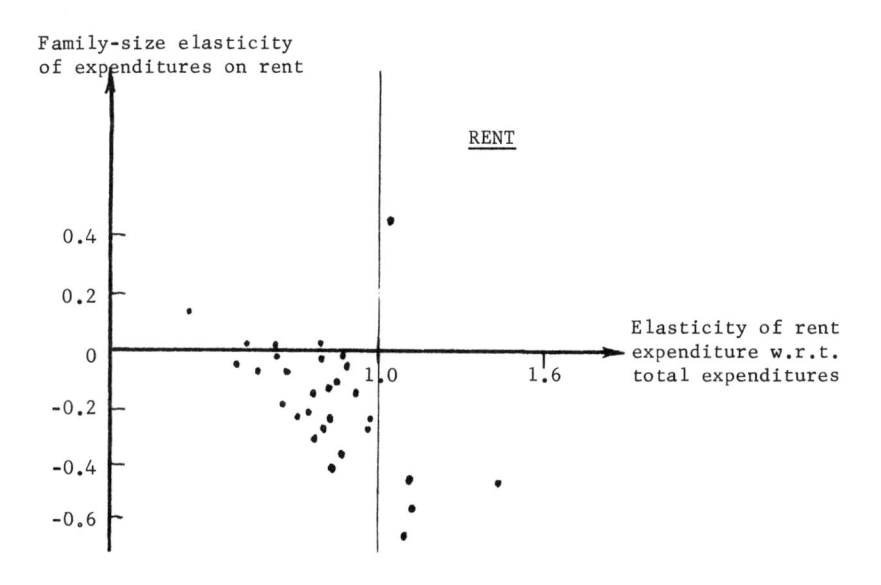

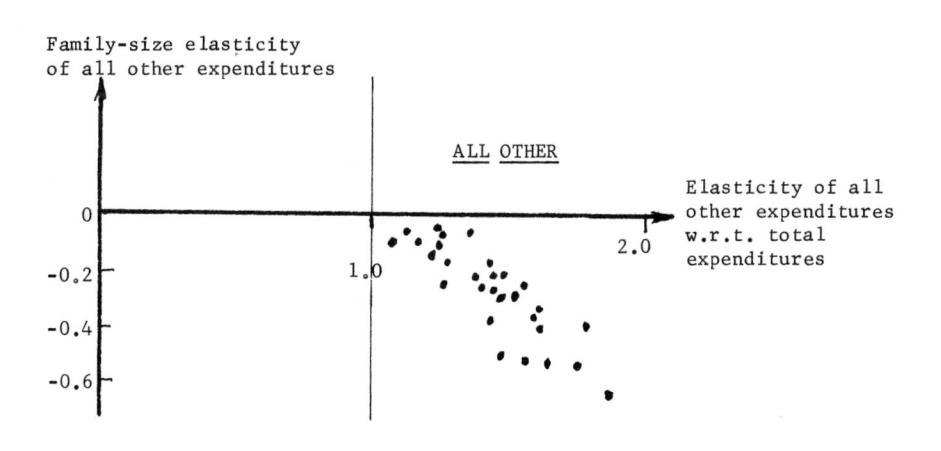

Table 4-6. Cost Shares, "Low-Income" Couple's First Child and Alternative Activities, Based on 1960 Urban Cross-sectional Data.

		Child Inputs (N bundle)			Alternative-activity Inputs (H bundle)			Differences in Shares (%) (N-H)		
discount rate	=	0%	13%	18%	0%	13%	18%	0%	13%	18%
Total amount, all inputs	$	21102	9069	7365	28138	8135	6417			
	%	100	100	100	100	100	100	--	--	--
Adult Time Inputs	$	8569	4591	3970	2603	1644	1493			
	%	40.6	50.6	53.9	9.3	20.2	23.3	31.3	30.4	30.6
Child's chore and paid work contribution (-)	$	-1849	-333	-188	--	--	--			
	%	-8.8	-3.7	-2.6	--	--	--	-8.8	-3.7	-2.6
Net Time Inputs	$	6720	4258	3782	2603	1644	1493			
	%	31.8	47.0	51.4	9.3	20.2	23.3	22.5	26.8	28.1
Food	$	4267	1378	1008	4630	930	706			
	%	20.2	15.2	13.7	16.5	11.4	11.0	3.7	3.8	2.7
Shelter	$	3562	1304	990	4604	1144	858			
	%	16.9	14.4	13.4	16.4	14.1	13.4	0.5	0.3	0.0
Medical Care	$	1107	618	544	1182	281	189			
	%	5.2	6.8	7.4	4.2	3.5	2.9	1.0	3.3	4.5
All other commodities	$	5446	1511	1041	15119	4136	3171			
	%	25.8	16.6	14.1	53.7	50.8	49.4	-27.9	-34.2	-35.3
Child Clothing	$	3043	nc	nc	--	--	--			
	%	14.4	nc	nc	--	--	--	14.4	nc	nc
Utilities	$	1649	nc	nc	2514	nc	nc			
	%	7.8	nc	nc	8.9	nc	nc	-1.1	nc	nc
Transportation	$	0	0	0	2475	nc	nc			
	%	0	0	0	8.8	nc	nc	-8.8	nc	nc
Recreation	$	628	nc	nc	383	nc	nc			
	%	3.0	nc	nc	1.4	nc	nc	1.6	nc	nc
Education	$	126	nc	nc	00	00	00			
	%	0.6	nc	nc	00	00	00	0.6	nc	nc
Total Commodity Inputs	$	14382	4811	3583	25535	6491	4924			
	%	68.2	53.0	48.6	90.7	79.8	76.7	-22.5	-26.8	-28.1
Difference in Total Bundle Values*	$	7036	-934	-948						

* = (a) the reduction in the mother's rate of pay as a result of the child times the hours she would have worked without the child, minus (b) the value of the income-tax exemption per child.

nc = not calculated.
-- = zero by definition.
0 = zero by assumption.
00 = zero by estimation.

Table 4-7. Cost Shares, "Low-Income" Couple's Third Child and Alternative Activities, Based on 1960 Urban Cross-Sectional Data (three-year child spacing).

		Child Inputs (N bundle)			Alternative-Activity Inputs (H bundle)			Differences in Shares (%) (N-H)		
discount rate	=	0%	13%	18%	0%	13%	18%	0%	13%	18%
Total amount,	$	15050	6801	5533	16059	6721	5556			
all inputs	%	100	100	100	100	100	100	--	--	--
Time Inputs by adults and	$	6043	3331	2842	4195	2534	2280			
older siblings	%	40.1	49.0	51.4	26.1	37.7	41.0	14.0	11.3	10.4
Child's chore &	$	-1650	-297	-168	--	--	--			
paid work contr.	%	-11.0	-4.4	-3.0	--	--	--	-11.0	-4.4	-3.0
Net Time Inputs	$	4393	3034	2674	4195	2534	2280			
	%	29.2	44.6	48.3	26.1	37.7	41.0	3.1	6.9	7.3
Food	$	4047	1304	954	2079	670	536			
	%	26.9	19.2	17.2	12.9	10.0	9.6	14.0	9.2	7.6
Shelter	$	2532	902	686	2907	1172	888			
	%	16.8	13.3	12.4	18.1	17.4	16.0	-1.3	-4.1	-3.6
Medical Care	$	1012	586	507	757	272	189			
	%	6.7	8.6	9.2	4.7	4.0	3.4	2.0	4.6	5.8
All other	$	3066	975	712	6121	2073	1663			
	%	20.4	14.3	12.9	38.1	30.9	29.9	-17.7	-16.5	-17.0
of which: Child clothing	$	1300	nc	nc	567	nc	nc			
	%	8.6	nc	nc	3.5	nc	nc	5.1	nc	nc
Utilities	$	1413	nc	nc	1562	nc	nc			
	%	9.4	nc	nc	9.7	nc	nc	-0.3	nc	nc
Transportation	$	0	0	0	583	nc	nc			
	%	0	0	0	3.6	nc	nc	-3.6	nc	nc
Recreation	$	271	nc	nc	299	nc	nc			
	%	1.8	nc	nc	1.9	nc	nc	-0.1	nc	nc
Education	$	82	nc	nc	97	nc	nc			
	%	0.5	nc	nc	0.6	nc	nc	-0.1	nc	nc
Total Commodity	$	10657	3767	2859	11864	4187	3276			
Inputs	%	70.8	55.4	51.7	73.9	62.3	59.0	-3.1	-6.9	-7.3

Difference in total
bundle values* $ +1009   -80   +23

* = (a) the reduction in the mother's rate of pay as a result of the child times the hours she would have worked without the child, minus (b) the value of the income-tax exemption per child.

nc = not calculated
-- = zero by definition
0 = zero by assumption

Table 4-8. Cost Shares, "High-Income" Couple's First Child and Alternative Activities, Based on 1960 Urban Cross-Sectional Data.

	Child Inputs (N bundle)			Alternative-Activity Inputs (H bundle)			Differences in Shares (%) (N-H)		
discount rate =	0%	8%	13%	0%	8%	13%	0%	8%	13%
Total amount, all inputs $	41520	21402	15890	68658	18873	13121	--	--	--
%	100	100	100	100	100	100			
Adult Time Inputs $	16131	10523	8647	4898	3682	3357			
%	38.9	49.2	54.4	7.1	19.5	25.5	31.8	29.7	28.9
Child's chore and paid work contri. $	-3684	-1229	-661	--	--	--			
%	-8.9	-5.7	-4.2	--	--	--	-8.9	-5.7	-4.2
Net Time Inputs $	12446	9294	7986	4898	3682	3357			
%	29.9	43.4	50.3	7.1	19.5	25.5	22.8	23.9	24.8
Food $	6423	2969	2027	11614	2460	1553			
%	15.4	13.9	12.8	16.9	13.0	11.8	-1.5	0.9	1.0
Shelter $	4630	2325	1657	8765	2315	1492			
%	11.1	10.9	10.4	12.8	12.3	11.4	-1.7	-1.4	-1.0
Medical Care $	1563	976	794	3969	776	489			
%	3.8	4.6	5.0	5.8	4.1	3.7	-2.0	0.5	-1.3
All other commodities of which: $	16458	5838	3426	39412	9640	6230			
%	39.5	27.3	21.6	57.4	51.1	47.6	-17.9	-23.8	-26.0
Child clothing $	4891	nc	nc	--	--	--			
%	11.7	nc	nc	--	--	--	11.7	nc	nc
Utilities $	3223	nc	nc	3408	nc	nc			
%	7.8	nc	nc	5.0	nc	nc	2.8	nc	nc
Transportation $	0	0	0	4334	nc	nc			
%	0	0	0	6.3	nc	nc	-6.3	nc	nc
Recreation $	1498	nc	nc	432	nc	nc			
%	3.6	nc	nc	0.6	nc	nc	3.0	nc	nc
Education $	6846	nc	nc	3	nc	nc			
%	16.4	nc	nc	0.0	nc	nc	16.4	nc	nc
Total Commodity Inputs $	29074	12108	7904	63760	15191	9764			
%	70.1	56.6	49.7	92.9	80.5	74.5	-22.8	-23.9	-24.8
Difference in Total Bundle Values* $	27138	-2529	-2769						

* = (a) the reduction in the mother's rate of pay as a result of the child time the hours she would have worked without the child, <u>minus</u> (b) the value of t income-tax exemption per child.

nc = not calculated.
-- = zero by definition.
0 = zero by assumption.

Table 4-9. Cost Shares, "High-Income" Couple's Third Child and Alternative Activiti Based on 1960 Urban Cross-Sectional Data (three-year child spacing).

		Child Inputs (N bundle)			Alternative-Activity Inputs (H bundle)			Differences in Shares (%) (N-H)		
discount rate	=	0%	8%	13%	0%	8%	13%	0%	8%	13%
Total amount,	$	32108	16628	12341	36650	14748	11560			
all inputs	%	100	100	100	100	100	100	--	--	--
Time Inputs by										
adults and	$	11324	7583	6268	8022	5717	4789			
older siblings	%	35.3	45.6	50.1	21.9	38.8	41.4	13.4	6.8	8.7
Child's chore &	$	-3013	-1011	-546	--	--	--			
paid work contr.	%	-9.4	-6.1	-4.4				-9.4	-6.1	-4.4
Net Time Inputs	$	8311	6572	5722	8022	5717	4789			
	%	25.9	39.5	45.7	21.9	38.8	41.4	4.0	0.7	4.3
Food	$	6053	2806	1917	5214	1607	1136			
	%	19.0	16.9	15.5	14.2	10.9	9.8	4.8	6.0	5.7
Shelter	$	3423	1684	1195	5357	2089	1499			
	%	10.7	10.1	9.7	14.6	14.2	13.0	-3.9	-4.1	-3.3
Medical Care	$	1084	930	761	1798	833	616			
	%	3.4	5.6	6.2	4.9	5.6	5.3	-1.5	0.0	0.9
All other	$	13237	4636	2746	16259	4502	3520			
	%	41.3	27.9	22.2	44.4	30.5	30.4	-3.1	-2.6	-8.2
of which:										
Child clothing	$	2780	nc	nc	1088	nc	nc			
	%	8.7	nc	nc	3.0	nc	nc	5.7	nc	nc
Utilities	$	2837	nc	nc	4190	nc	nc			
	%	8.8	nc	nc	11.4	nc	nc	-2.7	nc	nc
Transportation	$	0	0	0	1859	nc	nc			
	%	0	0	0	5.1	nc	nc	-5.1	nc	nc
Recreation	$	885	nc	nc	1221	nc	nc			
	%	2.8	nc	nc	3.3	nc	nc	-0.5	nc	nc
Education	$	6735	nc	nc	259	nc	nc			
	%	21.0	nc	nc	0.7	nc	nc	-20.3	nc	nc
Total Commodity	$	23797	10056	6619	28628	9031	6771			
Inputs	%	74.1	60.5	54.3	78.1	61.2	58.6	-4.0	-0.7	-4.3

Difference in total
bundle values* $ 4542 -1880 -781

* = (a) the reduction in the mother's rate of pay as a result of the child times the hours she would have worked without the child, <u>minus</u> (b) the value of the income-tax exemption per child.

nc = not calculated
-- = zero by definition
0 = zero by assumption

labor-intensive relative to the life activities with which they compete. For either birth order, the net addition to family home time caused by the child is a similar proportion of total child cost for the low-income and high-income families, suggesting that the time-intensity of a given child varies little across income classes, as was conjectured in Section IV of this chapter.[24] Additional children also use much less of commodities other than food, clothing, and shelter than do the alternative activities. A third child, spaced three years after the second, costs somewhere around 80 percent as much as a first child.[25] A little under half of the value of inputs into a child is the value of time inputs, whatever the income level and birth order.

A. CLASS DIFFERENCES IN RELATIVE CHILD COSTS

The input patterns described above and summarized in Tables 4–6 through 4–9 allow one to reinterpret some common statements about class differences in relative child costs. One common assertion is that nonfarm children are more costly in higher-income families than in low-income families. Another is that children are more expensive in the city than on the farm. Both statements are intended to help explain fertility differentials. Yet they cannot be made testable until one has again answered those two key questions: Cost of *what kind* of child? Cost *relative to what?* For relative cost to have its price-inspired meaning, it must measure the ratio of the costs of two *fixed bundles,* evaluated at the prices prevailing in different settings.

The relative cost of a nonfarm child is indeed higher at the wage rates

[24] This sentence may seem to clash with one result reported for third-borns in Tables 4–7 and 4–9. There the net difference in time's shares of bundles, as shown in the right-hand columns, appears to be 6.9 percent for the low-income third child (at 13 percent discount rate), yet only 0.7 percent for the high-income third child (at 8 percent). The difference, however, is due almost entirely to discrepancies between the total sizes of the N-bundles and H-bundles. When both the time inputs into the child and the time inputs into the alternative life activities are expressed as fractions of the *same* total bundle (either N or H) and not as fractions of the *respective* bundles, it turns out that the net change in time inputs is about the same fraction of total cost for the two income classes, as asserted in the text.

[25] It should be repeated that the inputs were calculated on the assumption that each additional child being considered is a prospective last-born. That is, the costs of the child are those incurred by adding the child to the family consisting of everyone older than him or her. No calculation was made of the costs of a middle child, one for whom it is given that later children will come along with or without him.

facing higher-income families, whether the bundles being compared are (1) low-income families' child inputs vs. low-income families' alternative-course inputs, or (2) high-income families' child inputs vs. high-income families' alternative-course inputs. This is true for the postwar U.S. because an extra nonfarm child is relatively time-intensive at any income level. Notice, however, that the fact that the relative cost is higher for higher-income families is *not* due to the separate fact that more real inputs go into a higher-income child. The latter is a difference in type of child, not a difference in relative cost rooted in price differences facing couples.

The differences in child costs between farm and city are subtler when relative cost is given its present definition than in conventional discussions of this issue. *What kind* of child is relatively more expensive with urban than with farm wage rates and prices? An extra urban child, relative to the urban alternatives to that child, is definitely more expensive in the city, where (a) real wages are higher, (b) food is more expensive relative to luxuries, and (c) land-intensive, child-oriented living space is more expensive. An extra farm child is probably more expensive than farm alternatives in the urban setting, though probably only because of (b) and (c) above. The wage effect (a) probably has little impact for couples who compare farm-type children with farm-type alternatives. In the city, a child who worked as much for pay as a farm child would earn higher pay. This child-wage effect would tend to offset the higher price of the mother's time in the cities.

If this seems too subtle an approach to the "obvious fact" that children cost more in the city than on the farm, it is only because what is obvious is not a difference in relative costs so much as a difference in types of children preferred in the two settings. Urban couples choose to raise each child on more real inputs than do farm couples. Nor is their choice simply a response to differences in relative prices, since *both* the inputs into a child *and* the inputs into the alternatives to that child cost more overall in the city. To explain why urban couples choose to have fewer children, one must supplement arguments about differences in relative costs with a hypothesis designed to explain why their tastes (or personal productivities) are more biased toward high-input children.

B. MOVEMENTS IN RELATIVE CHILD COSTS OVER TIME

Movements in relative child cost can be followed over time by plugging data on wage rates, tax exemptions, and commodity prices into sets of

ECONOMIC INFLUENCES ON FERTILITY

weights like those in Tables 4–6 and 4–7.[26] Appendix F lays out the steps that intervene between the weights and the final index, which is plotted for the twentieth century in Figure 4–3.

The movements of the index shown in Figure 4–3 stem mainly from changes in taxation and in real wage rates. Changes in taxation have been important to child costs only for one five-year period, but in that period their influence was dramatic. Between 1940 and 1945 the income tax system suddenly became relevant to middle- and lower-income families. In 1940 less than 10 percent of the population had high enough incomes to be covered by taxable returns. In 1945, after five years of

Figure 4-3. Relative Cost Indices for a First-Born and a Third-Born Child, Urban U.S., 1900-1970.

(1960 = 100)

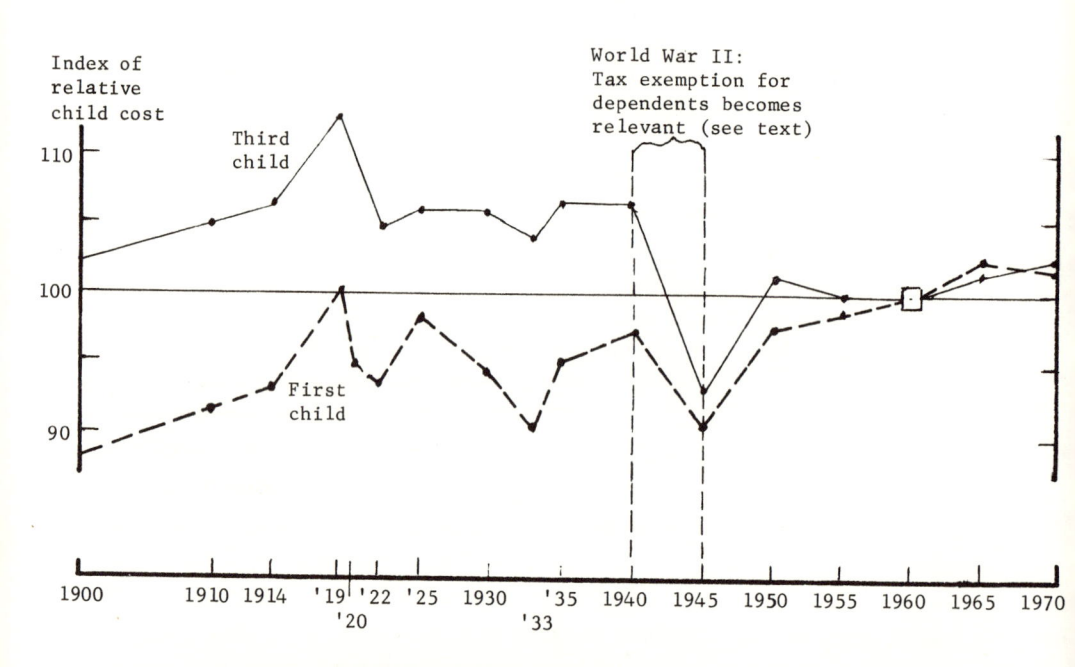

(Source: Appendix F, Table F-4.)

[26] The low-income weights from Tables 4–6 and 4–7 have been chosen over the high-income weights in Tables 4–8 and 4–9 on the grounds that the former income level was more representative of urban families both in 1960 and for other dates.

prosperity and inflation, fully three-fourths of the population was involved in paying income taxes. Entering the ranks of taxpayers for the first time brought the average household into contact with the yearly tax exemption of $500 per dependent. The tax reduction thus brought by each child added up to 9 percent of the cost of a first child and 16 percent of the cost of a third. These cost reductions more than outweighed the effect of rising real wage rates on child costs, with the result that the cost index dropped 7 percent for a first child and 13 percent for a third between 1940 and 1945.

It is not implausible that such a drop in child costs could have played a role in the early postwar surge of births. To be sure, few couples explicitly decided to have extra children because they were thinking about income-tax exemptions. But the exemption probably made it a lot easier for couples to perceive that other couples who had extra children after the war were managing to make ends meet. By lowering the actual economic burden of an extra child, the new relevance of the tax exemption probably lowered the perceived burden as well. Were it not for the income tax exemption, the upward drift in the cost of time (real wage rates) and the rise in the price of food relative to luxuries in the 1940s would have retarded the baby boom more than actually happened. This conjecture is supported by regression results in Chapter 5 (Table 5–1) below.

Aside from the World War II experience, the general drift of the indices is upward, especially for the more time-intensive first-born child. The upward drift is somewhat overstated for the years up to World War I, however. As already stressed, children were less time-intensive in that era than the 1960 weights would imply. Thus the prewar rise in real wage rates would not have raised the index quite as much as is shown in Figure 4–3. Only a rise in the relative price of food caused a true increase in the relative price of children between the turn of the century and World War I. Between the wars the indices, like real wages, showed no clear trend. Since World War II the indices have risen once again. Their sharp rise in the late 1940s was the result of increases in both real wage rates and the relative price of food. The more gentle rise since 1950 has been the result of rising real wage rates. This postwar drift failed to prevent a further rise in fertility across the 1950s, though it did coincide with a decline in fertility across the 1960s. The overall simple correlation between rising relative child costs and declining fertility across this century has not, on balance, been very impressive. Relative costs may still have played the role predicted for them by theory. Regression results in

Chapter 5 suggest as much. It is clear, though, that movements in these relative costs by themselves cannot explain the course of American fertility across this century.

The 1960-based index constructed here will continue to be applicable for at least the next decade or two. The weights derived in Tables 4–6 and 4–7 are not likely to become rapidly obsolete. Throughout the postwar period the net effect of an extra child on work time by mothers appears to have changed little (Table 4–4 above). As long as the net work effect continues to be stable, any given percentage increase in real wage rates should have a similar impact on relative child costs to that which it had in the 1950s and 1960s.

The trend in relative child costs, like the validity of the 1960 weights, is not likely to change greatly in the 1970s and 1980s. Over these two decades, neither real wage rates nor the relative price of food seems likely to fall. If this forecast on wages and prices is correct, then relative child costs will not fall and will probably rise gently, as they did in the 1950s and 1960s. This does not mean, however, that fertility will show a similar gentle drift. Indeed, one prediction of the next chapter is that fertility could exhibit wide swings *if* the economy did the same. To make or judge that prediction, however, one must look beyond relative child costs to the entire set of fertility determinants.

CHAPTER 5. American Fertility Patterns Since the Civil War

I. *Introduction*

The theory of fertility outlined in Chapter 3 and extended in Chapter 4 can be tested against American fertility patterns in recent decades. It turns out that the model is capable of explaining much, though not all, of the intriguing temporal and cross-sectional patterns of fertility in the United States.

The same fascinating set of puzzles confronting the social scientist interested in the link between fertility and modernization in general reappears in the history of American fertility. There is, first, the long and fairly steady decline in the birth rate, by 60 percent or more, from 1800 or earlier to the middle of the 1930s. The initial level was extraordinarily high, a fact plausibly attributed to the availability of land in a frontier nation. Part of the puzzle is how so great a decline in birth rates was achieved. There was no trend toward postponement of marriage. The median age of marriage for women, and the share of them never marrying, could not have risen enough before 1890 to account for the extent of observed birth reduction. Since 1890, when national census data on marriage began, marriage has become slightly more prevalent and has occurred at earlier median ages for women. We can only speculate from what little we know of the vast prehistory of contraception that couples turned mainly to withdrawal and abstinence until the use of condoms became widespread in the late nineteenth and early twentieth centuries.[1]

The question of why birth restriction came to be practiced more and more has seemed less troubling at first glance. We have come to expect declining birth rates as the land fills up and as modernization brings a shift from agriculture toward the cities, declining infant mortality rates, rising incomes, more schooling, and advances in technology of contraception. It seems natural enough that couples in more modern settings have higher goods aspirations and better information about known contraceptive techniques. It is interesting to note the similarity in the long-run trends in birth rates for all major classes of American society. To be sure, some classes at times reduced their fertility faster or slower than the rest of the nation. Southern white fertility, for example, dropped less

[1] Norman E. Himes, *The Medical History of Contraception*, New York, 1936, Chaps. VIII, XIII.

than that of other regions between 1870 and 1900, and the birth rate of native-born New England women failed to drop at all between the 1860s and the 1920s.[2] The black birth rate dropped somewhat faster than the white rate between 1880 and 1920, and since 1960, but rose relative to the white rate between 1920 and 1960. Yet the overall record shows an impressive similarity in the extent of the great decline up to the 1930s. The ratio of rural to urban fertility, the ratio of black to white fertility, and the rankings of different regions by fertility changed little.

The same negative relationship between fertility and modernization prevails, of course, in modern cross sections as well as for the trends: fertility is lower among more-educated, urban, affluent, and better-informed couples. One can still wonder why such couples do not manage to gratify their modern consumption desires out of their higher incomes while having the same average number of children as others have, rather than fewer children on the average. In general, though, this question has not been posed, the implicit answer being that tastes and relative child costs must somehow differ so strongly in the cross section that having fewer children is the average outcome for higher-status couples.

The inverse relationship between fertility and modernization variables has not carried over into recent time-series patterns. Birth rates vary positively with income over the business cycle. This potential contradiction might be resolved in either of two ways. First, it could be argued that the positive cyclical pattern is but an adjustment in the timing of births (and marriages) with no implications about family sizes over the longer run. The other possible resolution is to strike income from the list of modernization variables that reduce fertility. Income, perhaps, encourages births, while everything else that grows with income in the long run and in the cross section—education, urban residence, and so forth—reduces births.

This entire line of reasoning seemed to receive a setback from the long baby boom extending from the end of World War II into the early 1960s. Fifteen years or more was a long time for temporary catching-up by returning soldiers and their wives. The tactic of again distinguishing between income and contemporaneous modernization variables might have seemed attractive were the facts less unkind. The baby boom was not just a national response to improvements in income combined with little change in the usual correlates of income. The exodus from agriculture and the rise of young adults' education, for example, proceeded

[2] Joseph J. Spengler, *The Fecundity of Native and Foreign-Born Women in New England*, Washington, 1930, Table XIX.

faster than ever. To make matters worse, fertility rose fastest among the urban and the most-educated.

A new set of fertility patterns seemed to take over around 1965. Incomes continued to grow as rapidly as they had from the late 1940s to the late 1950s, while the growth in the schooling of young adults decelerated. Fertility fell off sharply, matching the mid-Depression lows in the early 1970s. The fertility differentials by race, income, and religion narrowed. The differentials by education converged by some measures of period fertility but not by others.

Of all these patterns the one that has seemed most difficult to fit into a single model has been the postwar baby boom, and on this front an attractive explanation has been offered by Richard Easterlin.[3] The swings in national fertility between the Depression and the present seem to fit neatly into a model of tastes that gives a central role to the consumption standards inculcated in young adults from the households in which they were raised. Armed with this hypothesis, one can explain the postwar baby boom by noting that the young couples of that era found their income prospects much brighter than the hardships they had experienced, or their parents had talked about, in the Depression. Given a tendency to raise children in a manner affected by their own upbringing, they felt they could afford several. The couples of prime childbearing age after 1965 felt the opposite: raised in postwar prosperity and then faced with a job market flooded with young applicants, they felt pressure to postpone or prevent childbearing.

The reconciliation hinging on the relationship of prior consumption standards to current prospects for young couples has not yet met all potential criticisms. In particular, there remains an objection to the role it gives to current income, voiced earlier by Ansley Coale. Coale doubted that income-related explanations of the postwar baby boom could explain why no such boom occurred in the 1920s:

> ... the interpretation of the baby boom as the natural consequence of prolonged prosperity is hardly more tenable than the earlier interpretation of the [slight revival of the birth rate in the later] 1930's as momentary. The next earlier period of notable prosperity in the United States—the 1920's—was a period of sharply falling fertility.

---

[3] Richard A. Easterlin, *Population, Labor Force, and Long Swings in Economic Growth: The American Experience*, New York: Columbia University Press, 1968, Chaps. 4, 5, and "Relative Economic Status and the American Fertility Swing," in Eleanor B. Sheldon, ed., *Economics and Family Behavior*, Philadelphia: J. B. Lippincott, 1973.

In fact, as Dudley Kirk points out, the depressed 1930's produced *more* births by far than one would expect on the basis of an extrapolation of the prosperous 1920's.[4]

Easterlin shared Coale's concern about the 1920s, and endeavored to reconcile that experience with his model of postwar behavior with several references to special influences on rural, native urban, and foreign-born urban fertility.[5] His reconciliation failed to convince Alan Sweezy, who criticized it and renewed Coale's scepticism.[6] Sweezy also found the Easterlin model incapable of explaining the striking tendency of fertility to rise more among couples with more education and higher husband's job status during the baby boom.[7] World War II and the subsequent prosperity were accompanied by a dramatic reduction in income inequalities, with those in the bottom income and educational classes gaining considerable ground. If prosperity relative to past family incomes set off the baby boom, why was not the boom more characteristic of less-educated couples than of the more-educated?

To the historian accustomed to savoring history's infinite variety, the problem of reconciling these patterns may seem artificial. The social scientist who tries to fit a wide range of experiences to a single theory is off on the wrong quest, he may argue. The simplest way out of the seeming contradictions is to recognize that there may be no unifying theme to it all. Fertility is a complex matter, so why not just offer different careful explanations for different episodes? The supply of plausibly relevant variables will always exceed the number of patterns to be explained, and the task of the demographic historian might rightly be to decide which of several long listings of influences best fits each unique experience.

The subject matter of human fertility is such that this stress on historical uniqueness will always command respect. Yet it is important to avoid giving up on the generalizing hypotheses. There are indeed common themes, common models, that fit broad ranges of the history of fertility. By identifying the explanatory power as well as the limits of these generalizations, the demographic historian can offer a considerable

---

[4] Ansley J. Coale, "Introduction," in Ansley J. Coale, ed., *Demographic and Economic Change in Developed Countries*, Princeton, 1960, pp. 5–6.

[5] Richard A. Easterlin, *Population, Labor Force, and Long Swings,* pp. 82, 89, 92, 99–100.

[6] Alan Sweezy, "The Economic Explanation of Fertility Changes in the United States," *Population Studies* 25 (July 1971), 258–260.

[7] Ibid., pp. 260–262.

service to others who think they care little about history. A wider public has come to realize that population growth has profound long-run effects on the social positions of age groups, on the level and the distribution of income, and on the position of natural resources in the economy. Interest in the future of fertility is thus widely shared. By separating generalizable from unique influences in the past, the demographic historian can offer a set of conditional predictions about the future course of fertility.

The variables we have usually used to sort out past fertility patterns are not likely to be of much help in analyzing or predicting future American fertility patterns. The share of population in agriculture, the share in cities, levels of education, rates of infant mortality, rates of immigration, racial shares—none of these traditional variables is likely to shift dramatically in the future. Nor do these variables vary so widely across the national population as they used to. There is the danger that the history of fertility will seem to offer no predictive power for the United States. That danger can be avoided if an effort is made to measure and apply the general variables that do underlie much of the seeming disunity in American fertility history and will continue to do so.

II. *The Data*

Only aggregate data can test the ability of the hypotheses above to account for the intriguing fertility patterns observed for the United States. In part this is so because some of the more challenging tasks of explanation relate to the behavior of aggregate time series. The use of aggregate data is also dictated by the nature of the prior family inputs variable that has been placed at the center of a model of taste formation. To measure these prior family inputs at the level of individual young adults requires, if not direct data on the time and commodities they received, at least data on income per family member in their parents' household over the years since their earlier childhood memories. Interviews cannot generate reliable data on the incomes of parents of young adult interviewees except for the current period. Little faith can be had in the answers to, say, 1970 interview questions asking, "How much did your father earn in 1960?" Approximations can be had by finding out the father's occupational history and the respondent's schooling, but these are certainly imperfect substitutes.

What is hard even to approximate at the individual level can be tracked somewhat more accurately at the state level for the United States since the Civil War. Since 1870 the decennial census has recorded the state or country of birth of persons residing in each state. These place-of-birth data give a fair indication of where the young adults in each state were raised, even though the data are not broken down by age groups. If we know the levels of real income per capita in the various places of birth, these can be combined with the shares coming from each place of birth to produce a rough measure of the earlier income per capita enjoyed by the current generation of young adults as they grew up. The prior family inputs variable introduced in the hypotheses above can then be represented by such measures of past income per capita in places of birth, plus current levels of income per person at work, which represent not only income prospects but also the more recent influences on the material standards felt by young couples.

Estimates of state personal incomes per capita are available for the United States for 1840, 1880, 1900, 1919–21, and annually from 1929.[8] For the fraction of each state's population born abroad, the background income per capita has been estimated on the basis of economic historians' guesses as to the ratios of foreign countries' GNP per capita to U.S. GNP per capita. These and the data on places of birth will be put to use in estimating background incomes per capita for dates twenty years before each of several censuses.[9] This procedure yields estimates

---

[8] For estimates of state income per capita in 1840, see Richard A. Easterlin, "International Differences in Per Capita Income, Population, and Total Income," in National Bureau of Economic Research, *Trends in the American Economy in the Nineteenth Century*, Princeton, 1960, Table A–1; for 1880, 1900, and 1919–21, see Easterlin, "State Income Estimates," in Simon Kuznets, Dorothy Swaine Thomas et al., *Population Redistribution and Economic Growth*, Philadelphia: American Philosophical Society, 1957, vol. I, Table Y–1; for 1929–55, see Charles F. Schwartz and Robert E. Graham, *Personal Income by States since 1929*, Washington, GPO, 1956, Table 2; and for years since 1955, see various issues of U.S. Department of Commerce, *Survey of Current Business*.

[9] The choice of twenty years as the lead time for the prior income experience variable is, of course, arbitrary, and other lengths of time between past experience and current fertility could have been chosen. It was felt that the combination of a long lead like twenty years plus the implicit taste component of current income per worker would succeed in encompassing the full range of relevant family income experience. With additional time and research funding, one could derive the background incomes per capita for only ten years earlier (than each census for which fertility is being observed), and for the period from the 1930s on, even annual background incomes could be worked up. These might be employed in a large pooled sample covering the states for census years to determine more finely the relative importance of the most recent, vis-à-vis more distant past income experience in affecting desired fertility.

Aside from refining the choice of time leads for the income experience variable, it would also be desirable to have measures more specific to the recent income experience of *young adults* than the measures used here. For the present it must

of a background income, or prior income, variable that represents part of the material standards felt by different cohorts of young couples whose fertility is measured in the censuses of 1900 and 1920–70.[10]

Using state aggregates has another advantage besides allowing us to trace past income experience through place-of-birth data. State aggregates have been presented consistently in each decennial census, with reasonably comparable definitions of demographic and socioeconomic variables for different censuses. With samples of states it is thus possible to investigate historic changes in the importance of each of several fertility influences. Survey data based on observations from individual families, by contrast, are seldom so comparable over long periods of time. Since it is likely that the parameters of fertility behavior change over time, the opportunity to identify these structural changes is an important advantage of the use of census aggregates.

The use of aggregates also has its dangers. In particular, there is the danger of attributing the behavior of one group within a state to another group. This is due in part to the necessity of investigating the fertility and marriage patterns of all groups added together. It has not proved possible to develop complete state-by-state data sets on the fertility and other attributes of nonwhites versus whites, or Catholics versus others, or foreign-born residents versus natives, or farm families versus others. Some of the key variables, especially the income estimates, are not broken down by such groupings at the state level. Only the demographic variables have some of these breakdowns for states. In what follows it is necessary to proceed with considerable caution in making any inferences about *whose* fertility and marriages are being explained by movements in state incomes and other all-state variables.[11]

---

be assumed that current personal income per worker for all age groups (adjusted for taxes and the cost of living, but *not* for hours worked) is a fair reflection of both the recent experience and the income prospects of young adults.

[10] The procedure for calculating this background income per capita, along with the estimates for each state in each census, is described in Appendix G.

[11] An additional problem that could arise with aggregate data has proved to cause little difficulty in the present inquiry. Whenever testing a model of individual behavior from grouped data, one must worry about the fact that the cells—in this case, the states—are of different size. The differences in their sizes threaten to invalidate the assumption of homoskedasticity on which least-squares regression analysis leans. For a uniform variance among individual behavioral units (households) larger states will tend to have lower variance than smaller states. A means of restoring homoskedasticity to the state residuals is to multiply all variables for a state by the square root of the number of units (here the number of females 15–49) and run a regression on such weighted variables without

With this warning observed, considerable insight into fertility patterns can be derived from the available data. With some investment in time, it has proved possible to draw up a sample of state data covering seven censuses: 1900 and 1920–70. For the censuses of 1900, 1920, and 1930 there is a set of data for each of thirty-seven states east of the Rockies (not including the District of Columbia), and for 1940–70 all forty-eight contiguous states plus the District of Columbia are represented.

From this overall data base it proves possible to vary the type of statistical regression in three ways. First, the dependent variable can be either a fertility measure or a measure of shares of young women who are married, since the additional information on shares married was an inexpensive by-product of gathering data needed for fertility analysis. The fertility measure used is, of necessity, simply the ratio of living children 0–4 to females 15–49 after adjustment for estimated under-enumeration. This child-woman ratio is not as desirable for some purposes as an age-specific fertility rate or a total fertility rate, but these rates are not available. Nevertheless, child-woman ratios have been shown to be reasonable proxies for fertility rates,[12] especially when, as below, the age distribution of females is included in the list of independent variables. The main difficulty with the child-woman ratio is that it mixes together the direct effects of other variables on fertility, the effects of these same variables on infant mortality, and the effect of infant mortality on fertility. In what follows it must be assumed that the overall influences of other variables on fertility are proportional to their influences on the child-woman ratio.

The second variation in type of test made possible by the available census data is alternation between cross sections of states within a single census and pooled samples of states over several censuses. The use of

---

a constant term. This weighted regression technique produced results very similar to the unweighted regression estimates for the postwar period (the only sample for which both techniques were tried). There being little difference, only one of the weighted regressions has been reported below, on the grounds that the unweighted regressions are easier to interpret.

[12] For a discussion of the conditions under which the child-woman ratio is a reasonable proxy for fertility rates, see Donald J. Bogue and James A. Palmore, "Some Empirical and Analytical Relations among Demographic Fertility Measures with Regression Models for Fertility Estimation," *Demography* 1 (1964), 316–338; Wilson Grabill and Lee Jay Cho, "Methodology for the Measurement of Current Fertility from Population Data on Young Children," *Demography* 2 (1965), 50–73; and Barry S. Tuchfeld et al., "The Bogue-Palmore Technique for Estimating Direct Fertility Measures from Indirect Indicators as Applied to Tennessee Counties, 1960 and 1970," *Demography* 11 (May 1974), 195–206.

pooled samples—one for the three postwar censuses and one for all seven censuses—has the advantage of enlarging the sample so as to permit sharper significance tests where independent variables are somewhat correlated. The use of pooled samples is often suspected of misestimating significance statistics because errors in measurement or specification that are specific to certain time periods or states might give too much show of significance to variables associated with those periods or states. This problem is dealt with in two ways below. One is to use dummy variables specific to regions or to certain census years as competing independent variables in the pooled regressions. Any error specific to these regions or censuses should be absorbed by the dummy variable.

Another way of dealing with possible biases in significance tests for the pooled samples is to employ the third variation in type of regression allowed by the data. Having data for consecutive censuses, it is possible to run regressions in which the variables are decadal rates of change rather than levels. This redefinition of the variables makes each observation consist of differences between magnitudes observed for a given state and the corresponding magnitudes for the same state ten years earlier. Any errors that are constant for the same state for consecutive censuses will be netted out, providing another means of checking the robustness of the conclusions reached from straightforward cross-sectional regressions using levels rather than rates of change.

III. *Cross-Sectional Influences on Fertility and Marriage: An Overview*

Using the data and the types of regressions just described, it is possible to follow over time the changes in the roles of different variables in explaining how fertility and marriage vary across the country. Tables 5–1 through 5–4 present selected regressions relating child-woman ratios, shares of females ever-married or single, and their rates of change between censuses to a host of explanatory variables. These regression results will be examined in this section to identify structural changes in the determinants of cross-sectional fertility and marriage patterns. The remaining sections will use the same information plus the results of other studies to reinterpret several larger patterns in the course of American fertility.

The most consistent influence on fertility differences among states over this century appears to have been the *prior income experience* of young couples. This conclusion comes from the behavior of the present

DEFINITIONS OF VARIABLES USED IN REGRESSIONS IN TABLES 5-1 THROUGH 5-4

Dependent Variables

CW = child-woman ratio = the ratio of children 0–4 to women 15–49, all races. The census data were adjusted for underenumeration, using the underenumeration estimates of Coale and Zelnik for whites and those of Coale and Rives for all nonwhites.*

DCW = decadal change in the child-woman ratio = CW for the state in a given census minus CW for the previous census.

WED1529 = the share of women 15–29 who are ever-married. (WED1529 was computed by taking the simple average of the percent shares married in each five-year age interval.)

LNSPINST = the natural logarithm of the share of never-marrieds (spinsters) among women 30–44 (= 1 − .01WED3044). (This variable was put into natural log form to conform to a clear nonlinearity in the relationship of the share married in the 30–44 age group to the independent variables.)

DWED1529 = decadal change in the share of women 15–29 ever-married.

Independent Variables

DEMOGRAPHIC VARIABLES

WED1529 = the share of women 15–29 who are ever-married (as above).

WED 3044 = the share of women 30–44 who are ever-married. (WED3044 was computed by taking the simple average of the shares married in each five-year age interval.)

PRIMAGE = the share of women 15–49 who are 20–34 (prime childbearing age), after adjusting the underlying figures for whites and nonwhites for estimated census underenumeration.

SEXWH = a measure of the excess of white males 15–49 over white females 15–49 = the natural log of the ratio of white males 15–49 to white females 15–49 (both adjusted for estimated underenumeration), times the share of females 15–49 who are white (i.e., times 1 − NONWHITE).

SEXNW = a measure of the excess of nonwhite males 15–49 over nonwhite females 15–49 = the natural log of the ratio of nonwhite males 15–49 to nonwhite females 15–49 (both adjusted for estimated underenumeration), times the share of females 15–49 who are nonwhite.

SEXGAP = the average imbalance of males 15–49 over females 15–49, all races together = SEXWH + SEXNW.

DWED1529 = decadal change in the share of women 15–29 ever-married.

DPRIMAGE = decadal change in the share of women 15–49 who are 20–34.

DSEXWH = decadal change in SEXWH, a measure of the excess of white males 15–49 over white females 15–49.

DSEXNW = decadal change in SEXNW, a measure of the excess of nonwhite males 15–49 over nonwhite females 15–49.

DSEXGAP = decadal change in SEXGAP, the average imbalance of males 15–49 over females 15–49.

PRIOR INCOME, CURRENT INCOME, AND RELATIVE CHILD COSTS

YCAPORIG = prior income per capita = the natural log of personal income per capita, adjusted for income taxes and the cost of living, in "places of origin" twenty years earlier. For further details on its calculation, see Appendix G.

* Ansley J. Coale and Melvin Zelnik, *New Estimates of Fertility and Population in the United States*, Princeton, 1963; and Ansley J. Coale and Norfleet W. Rives, Jr., in Jan. 1973 *Population Index*, pp. 3–36.

YWORKER = current income per person in the labor force = the natural log of personal income, adjusted for income taxes and the cost of living, per person in the labor force, 1940–70, and per person gainfully employed, 1900–30.

RELCOST = an index of the relative cost of a nonfarm third child, 1960 and 1970 observations only = .069 × (share outside of agriculture [see AGRIC below]) × the natural log of the ratio of the state's average earnings per man-hour in manufacturing to the same earnings average for the U.S.

DYCAPORI = decadal rate of growth in prior income per capita = the decadal rate of growth in the antilog of YCAPORIG.

DYWORK = decadal rate of growth in current income per person in the labor force = the decadal rate of growth in the antilog of YWORKER.

DRELCOST = decadal rate of change in the relative cost of a nonfarm third child, all U.S. The same value was applied to each state for a given decade. (DRELCOST was calculated from a time-series index of the relative cost of a third child, derived in Appendix F.)

UNIMPROV = an index of the availability of unimproved land in 1900, and a proxy for the relative cheapness of an extra farm child in 1900. (UNIMPROV was calculated as follows: The share of the highest acreage in the state ever in farms in the twentieth century that was not improved acreage in 1900 was divided by the same share for the contiguous U.S. This new ratio minus one was then weighted [multiplied] by the share of the state's working males who were employed in agriculture.)

LANDCOST = an index of the average labor cost of farm land in 1900, and a proxy for the relative cost of an extra farm child in 1900. (LANDCOST was calculated as follows: the ratio of the state's average value of farm real estate per acre to the annual average daily farm wage without board was divided by the same ratio for the contiguous U.S. This new ratio minus one was then weighted [multiplied] by the share of the state's working males who were employed in agriculture.)

SOCIOECONOMIC AND RELIGIOUS VARIABLES

NONWHITE = share of nonwhites in females 15–49, after adjusting for estimated underenumeration.

FORBORN = percentage* of the state's population born in other countries.

AGRIC = percentage* of working males employed in agriculture.

ILLIT = percentage* of all persons twenty-one and over who are illiterate (1900–30 only).

SCHOOLF = median years of schooling completed by females twenty-five and over.

SCHOOLF50,60 = SCHOOLF times 1 for each observation of the 1950 and 1960 censuses; 0 for other censuses.

SCHOOLF70 = SCHOOLF times 1 for each observation of the 1970 census; 0 for other censuses.

CATHOLIC = for 1900–40 only, the ratio of membership in the Roman Catholic church four years earlier to the population of the state at the time of the census.

CATH5050 = for 1950 only, the ratio of membership in the Roman Catholic church in 1936, the last year for state religious membership, to the state's 1950 population.

CATH5060 = the value of CATH5050, applied to each 1960 observation instead of to each 1950 observation.

* E.g., 12% = 12.0, not .12.

CATH5070 = the value of CATH5050, applied to each 1970 observation instead of to each 1950 observation.
DNONWHIT = the decadal change in the share of nonwhites in females 15–49.
DFORBORN = the decadal change in the percentage* of the state's population born in other countries.
DAGRIC = the decadal change in the percentage* of the state's working males employed in agriculture.
DSCHOOLF = the decadal change in the median years of schooling completed by females twenty-five and over.
SCHDY = interaction term relating schooling of females to the rate of growth in income = SCHOOLF times (YWORKER minus YCAPORIG).

OTHER VARIABLES

PILLETC(1970) = 1 if the observation is from the 1970 census, 0 otherwise.
IKE(1960) = 1 if the observation is from the 1960 census, 0 otherwise.
SOUTH = regional dummy for the South = 1 if the state is in the South Atlantic, East South Central, or West South Central division, except for Maryland, Delaware, and the District of Columbia, and 0 for other states (including Md., Del., D.C.).
NENG = regional dummy for New England.
WNCMN = regional dummy for the West North Central plus Mountain states.
CW2 = the child-woman ratio for the same state twenty years earlier.

* E.g., 12% = 12.0, not .12.

Table 5-1. Child-Woman Ratios: Regressions Using State Data, Various Censuses, 1900-1970.

(Dependent variable is CW)

Regression no.:	(1) postwar #		(1a) postwar #		(2) postwar #		(3) all 7 censuses		(4) all 7 censuses	
Sample: Indep. variable	coeff.	std.err.	coeff.	std.err.	coeff.	std.err.	coeff.	std.err.	coeff.	std.err.
Constant term	.870 ***	(.237)	1.208	(.244)	.419	(.222)	.887 ***	(.143)	.860 ***	(.139)
WED1529	.002 *	(.001)	–	–	–	–	–	–	.007 ***	(.0008)
WED3044	-.001	(.001)	–	–	–	–	–	–	-.001	(.0008)
PRIMAGE	-.007	(.079)	.289 *	(.138)	–	–	–	–	.228 **	(.076)
SEXWH	–	–	–	–	-.031	(.064)	.194 *	(.082)	–	–
SEXNW	–	–	–	–	.184 *	(.090)	.358 ***	(.082)	–	–
SEXGAP	–	–	.160 *	(.078)	-.097	(.160)	.013	(.038)	–	–
YCAPORIG	-.179 ***	(.027)	-.151 ***	(.033)	-.131 ***	(.026)	-.193 ***	(.017)	-.159 ***	(.016)
YWORKER	.074 *	(.033)	.009	(.045)	.084 **	(.029)	.086 ***	(.014)	.026	(.014)
RELCOST	–	–	–	–	–	–	–	–	–	–
NONWHITE	.013	(.026)	-.041	(.027)	.022	(.026)	.036	(.032)	.008	(.028)
FORBORN	-.0016	(.0014)	-.0005	(.001)	-.0012	(.0011)	-.0015 **	(.0006)	-.0030***	(.0007)
AGRIC	.0003	(.0004)	.0001	(.0005)	.0000	(.0004)	-.0012 **	(.0004)	-.0015***	(.0004)
SCHDY	–	–	.0045 a	(.0023)	–	–	–	–	–	–
SCHOOLF	.0117*	(.0045)	–	–	.0116 **	(.0038)	–	–	–	–
CATHOLIC	–	–	–	–	-.064	(.055)	–	–	–	–
CATH5050	.150 *	(.063)	–	–	–	–	–	–	–	–
CATH5060	.152 **	(.047)	–	–	.138 **	(.042)	–	–	–	–
CATH5070	.073	(.047)	–	–	.065	(.040)	–	–	–	–
PILLETC(1970)	-.015 ***	(.019)	.007	(.015)	-.086 ***	(.019)	-.063 ***	(.013)	-.079***	(.012)
IKE(1960)	.063 ***	(.012)	.091 ***	(.011)	.065 ***	(.011)	.144 ***	(.011)	.129***	(.010)
SOUTH	-.033 **	(.011)	-.039 ***	(.010)	-.028 **	(.009)	-.020	(.011)	-.041***	(.011)
NENG	–	–	–	–	–	–	.020	(.011)	.009	(.009)
WNCMN	–	–	–	–	–	–	.012	(.010)	.005	(.009)
CW2	–	–	–	–	.318***	(.057)	–	–	–	–
R^2_{adj} / std. error of estim.	.877 / .027		.854 / .029		.904 / .024		.712 / .051		.765 / .046	
no. of observations / deg. of freedom	135 / 119		147 / 135		135 / 118		307 / 293		307 / 293	

* = significant at 5% level. ** = signif. at 1% level. *** = signif. at 0.1% level.

= Censuses of 1950, 1960, 1970, excluding Alaska and Hawaii, and excluding the District of Columbia Mountain States, and Pacific States for 1950.

[149]

Table 5-1. Child-Woman Ratios: Regressions Using State Data, Various Censuses, 1900-1970.
(continued) (Dependent variable is CW)

Regression no.:	(5)		(6)		(7)		(8)		(9)	
Sample:	1900 census		1900 census		1900 census		1920 census		1920 census	
Indep. variable	coeff.	std.err.	coeff.	std.err.	coeff.	std.err.	coeff.	std.err.	coeff.	std.err.
constant term	-.231	(.373)	-.993	(.536)	1.615	(.315)	-.145	(.566)	.757	(.400)
WED1529	--	--	-.0068	(.0038)	--	--	-.0072	(.0035)	--	--
WED3044	--	--	.0183*	(.0067)	--	--	.014 *	(.006)	--	--
PRIMAGE	--	--	--	--	--	--	.089	(.589)	.993	(.497)
SEXWH	--	--	--	--	--	--	--	--	--	--
SEXNW	--	--	--	--	--	--	--	--	--	--
SEXGAP	.116	(.076)	--	--	--	--	--	--	-.008	(.035)
YCAPORIG	-.111	(.060)	-.091	(.082)	-.186 ***	(.050)	-.147 *	(.068)	-.130 *	(.061)
YWORKER	.161 *	(.074)	.082	(.083)	--	--	.071	(.077)	--	--
UNIMPROV/LANDCOST#	.239 **	(.081)	-.082	(.055)	--	--	--	--	--	--
NONWHITE	-.010	(.146)	.149	(.187)	.116	(.274)	-.258	(.68)	-.354 *	(.150)
FORBORN	--	--	--	--	--	--	--	--	--	--
AGRIC	.0034***	(.0006)	.0009	(.0013)	--	--	.0003	(.0009)	.0015*	(.0006)
ILLIT	.0055*	(.0027)	.0087*	(.0038)	--	--	.0089	(.0045)	.0068	(.0043)
SCHOOLF	--	--	--	--	--	--	--	--	--	--
CATHOLIC	--	--	.018	(.163)	--	--	-.182	(.189)	-.098	(.153)
CATH5050	--	--	--	--	--	--	--	--	--	--
CATH5060	--	--	--	--	--	--	--	--	--	--
CATH5070	--	--	--	--	--	--	--	--	--	--
PILLETC(1970)	--	--	--	--	--	--	--	--	--	--
IKE(1960)	--	--	--	--	--	--	--	--	--	--
SOUTH	--	--	--	--	--	--	--	--	--	--
NENG	--	--	--	--	--	--	--	--	--	--
WNCMN	--	--	--	--	--	--	--	--	--	--
CW2	--	--	--	--	--	--	--	--	--	--
$R^2_{adj.}$ / std. error of estim.	.881 / .040		.865 / .043		.597 / .074		.732 / .038		.693 / .040	
no. of observations / deg. freedom	37 / 29		37 / 27		37 / 34		37 / 27		37 / 29	

*significant at 5% level. ** significant at 1% level. *** significant at 0.1% level.

: AGRIC's coefficient was significant at the 6% level, YCAPORIG's at the 9% level, and ILLIT's at the 11% level.

#UNIMPROV for (5), LANDCOST for (6).

[150]

Table 5-1. Child-Woman Ratios: Regressions Using State Data, Various Censuses, 1900-1970. (Continued) (Dependent variable is CW)

Regression No.:	(10)		(11)		(12)		(13)		(14)	
Sample	1930 census		1930 census		1940 census		1940 census		1950 census	
Indep. variable	coeff.	std.err.	coeff.	std.err.	coeff.	std.err.	coeff.	std.err.	coeff.	std.err.
constant term	.873	(.653)	1.168 **	(.392)	2.186 ***	(.410)	1.276	(.427)	1.473 ***	(.402)
WED1529	.0024	(.0021)	-	-	-	-	.0034	(.0020)	-	-
WED3044	.0002	(.0046)	-	-	-	-	.0011	(.0037)	-	-
PRIMAGE	.157	(.103)	.117	(.100)	.524	(.572)	.832	(.545)	.913	(.491)
SEXWH	-	-	-	-	-	-	-	-	-	-
SEXNW	-	-	-	-	-	-	-	-	-	-
SEXGAP	-	-	.179	(.143)	.407 ***	(.113)	-	-	.196	(.159)
YCAPORIG	-.113 a	(.064)	-.133 *	(.058)	-.222 ***	(.059)	-.233 ***	(.060)	-.195 ***	(.044)
YWORKER	.002	(.070)	-	-	-.078	(.061)	-.012	(.063)	-.030	(.060)
RELCOST	-	-	-	-	-	-	-	-	-	-
NONWHITE	-.419 **	(.141)	-.349 *	(.132)	-.138 *	(.065)	-.237 **	(.068)	-.165 *	(.062)
FORBORN	-	-	-	-	-	-	-	-	-	-
AGRIC	.0021a	(.0010)	.0018***	(.0005)	-.0005	(.0007)	.0005	(.0007)	.0004	(.0008)
ILLIT	.0081a	(.0049)	.0078	(.0048)	-	-	-	-	-	-
SCHOOLF	-	-	-	-	.0037a	(.0020)	.0006	(.0022)	.0120*	(.0054)
CATHOLIC	-.057	(.126)	-.114	(.105)	.010	(.057)	.141 b	(.070)	.077	(.062)
CATH5050	-	-	-	-	-	-	-	-	-	-
CATH5060	-	-	-	-	-	-	-	-	-	-
CATH5070	-	-	-	-	-	-	-	-	-	-
PILLETC(1970)	-	-	-	-	-	-	-	-	-	-
IKE(1960)	-	-	-	-	-	-	-	-	-	-
SOUTH	-	-	-	-	-	-	-	-	-	-
NENG	-	-	-	-	-	-	-	-	-	-
WNCMN	-	-	-	-	-	-	-	-	-	-
CW2	-	-	-	-	-	-	-	-	-	-
R^2_{adj} / std. error of estim.	.767 / .034		.773 / .033		.826 / .029		.827 / .029		.734 / .030	
no. of observations / deg. of freedom	37 / 27		37 / 29		49 / 40		49 / 39		49 / 40	

*=significant at 5% level. **=significant at 1% level. ***=significant at 0.1% level.
a=significant at 7% level.
b=significant at 6% level.

[151]

Table 5-1. Child-Woman Ratios: Regressions Using State Data, Various Censuses, 1900-1970.
(Continued) (Dependent variable is CW)

Regression no.:	(15) 1950 census		(16) 1960 census		(17) 1960 census		(18) 1960 census		(19) 1960 census	
Indep. variable	coeff.	std. err.	coeff.	std. err.	coeff.	std. err.	coeff.	std. err.	coeff.	std. err.
constant term	.126	(.401)	.853	(.833)	.352	(.770)	.033	(.713)	-.061	(.665)
WED1529	-.0038	(.0024)	-	-	-.0018	(.0024)	-	-	-.0001	(.0021)
WED3044	.014 ***	(.004)	-	-	.0041**	(.0014)	-	-	.0023a	(.0012)
PRIMAGE	1.408 ***	(.317)	.295	(.210)	1.407	(.380)	.134	(.169)	.869	(.332)
SEXWH	-	-	-	-	-	-	-	-	-	-
SEXNW	-	-	-	-	-	-	-	-	-	-
SEXGAP	-	-	.225	(.208)	-	-	.042	(.172)	-	-
YCAPORIG	-.125 ***	(.042)	-.143 **	(.051)	-.085	(.054)	-.046	(.050)	-.019	(.048)
YWORKER	-.088	(.052)	.043	(.106)	-.029	(.103)	-.045	(.083)	-.021	(.083)
RELCOST	-	-	.503	(1.168)	.217	(1.060)	.879	(.949)	.900	(.899)
NONWHITE	-.060	(.056)	-.040	(.058)	-.060	(.054)	-.044	(.049)	-.037	(.049)
FORBORN	-	-	.0011	(.0027)	.001	(.003)	-.0008	(.0025)	-.0002	(.0025)
AGRIC	.0013*	(.0006)	.0008	(.0009)	.0014	(.0009)	.0014a	(.0008)	.0017 *	(.0007)
ILLIT	-	-	-	-	-	-	-	-	-	-
SCHOOLF	.011 *	(.005)	.014	(.008)	.011	(.008)	.015 *	(.006)	.011	(.006)
CATHOLIC	-	-	-	-	-	-	-	-	-	-
CATH5050	.179 **	(.060)	-	-	-	-	.188 **	(.062)	.189 **	(.064)
CATH5060	-	-	-	-	-	-	-	-	-	-
CATH5070	-	-	-	-	-	-	-	-	-	-
PILLETC(1970)	-	-	-	-	-	-	-	-	-	-
IKE(1960)	-	-	-	-	-	-	-	-	-	-
SOUTH	-	-	-	-	-	-	-	-	-	-
NENG	-	-	-	-	-	-	-	-	-	-
WNCMN	-	-	-	-	-	-	-	-	-	-
CW2	-	-	-	-	-	-	.484 ***	(.125)	.399 **	(.119)
R^2 adj. / std error of estim	.817 / .025		.466 / .036		.554 / .033		.672 / .028		.714 / .026	
no. of observations / deg. of freedom	49 / 39		49 /39		49 / 38		49 / 37		49 / 36	

*=significant at 5% level. **=significant at 1% level. ***=significant at 0.1% level.
a=significant at the 6% level.
b=significant at 6% level.

[152]

Table 5.1. Child-Woman Ratios: Regressions Using State Data, Various Censuses, 1900-1970. (Continued) (Dependent variable is CW)

Regression no.:	(20) 1970 census		(21) 1970 census		(22) 1970 census	
Sample: Indep.variable	coeff.	std.err.	coeff.	std.err.	coeff.	std.err.
Constant term	.182	(.534)	.738	(.744)	.232	(.606)
WED1529	-	-	-.0028	(.0023)	-.0001	(.0020)
WED3044	-	-	.0081	(.0049)	.0029	(.0043)
PRIMAGE	.344	(.254)	.238	(.325)	.237	(.267)
SEXWH	-	-	-	-	-	-
SEXNW	-	-	-	-	-	-
SEXGAP	-.182b	(.091)	-	-	-	-
YCAPORIG	-.030	(.048)	-.120 *	(.052)	-.075	(.047)
YWORKER	.006	(.055)	-.028	(.072)	.012	(.058)
RELCOST	.079	(.573)	.275	(.730)	.511	(.620)
NONWHITE	-.012	(.038)	.025	(.055)	.052	(.049)
FORBORN	.0008	(.0017)	.0008	(.0023)	-.0008	(.0018)
AGRIC	.00005	(.00006)	.0003	(.0007)	-.0001	(.0006)
ILLIT	-	-	-	-	-	-
SCHOOLF	.0003	(.0080)	.003	(.011)	.0029	(.0089)
CATHOLIC	-	-	-	-	-	-
CATH5050	-	-	-	-	-	-
CATH5060	-	-	-	-	-	-
CATH5070	.088 *	(.035)	-	-	.121 *	(.047)
PILLETC(1970)	-	-	-	-	-	-
IKE(1960)	-	-	-	-	-	-
SOUTH	-	-	-	-	-	-
NENG	-	-	-	-	-	-
WNCMN	-	-	-	-	-	-
CW2	.411***	(.080)	-	-	.330 **	(.097)
$R^2_{adj.}$ / std. error of estim.	.569 / .018		.260 / .023		.523 / .019	
no. of observations / deg. of freedom	49 / 37		49 / 38		49 / 36	

*=significant at 5% level. **=significant at 1% level. ***=significant at 0.1% level.
a=significant at 7% level.
b=significant at 6% level.

[153]

Table 5-2. Shares of Women Who Are Ever-Married or Single: Regressions using State Data, Various Censuses, 1900-1970.

Regression no.:	(23) postwar # WED1529		(24) postwar # LNSPINST		(25) all 7 censuses WED1529		(26) all 7 censuses LNSPINST		(27) 1900 census WED1529	
Indep. variable:	coeff.	std.err.	coeff.	std.err.	coeff.	std.err.	coeff.	std.err.	coeff.	std.err.
constant term	79.72 **	(24.29)	-4.33	(2.87)	6.40	(10.81)	-0.60	(0.83)	21.99	(21.09)
PRIMAGE	–		–		–		–		–	
SEXWH	29.83 **	(10.20)	-1.09	(1.21)	38.75***	(6.38)	-2.58***	(0.49)	–	
SEXNW	–		–		–		–		–	
SEXGAP	–		–		–		–		12.51 *	(4.79)
YCAPORIG	-7.39**	(2.81)	0.53	(0.33)	-4.70***	(1.35)	0.15	(0.10)	3.45	(3.47)
YWORKER	3.14	(3.51)	-0.18	(0.42)	9.90***	(1.08)	-0.34***	(0.08)	–	
UNIMPROV	–		–		–		–		16.83 **	(5.60)
NONWHITE	-12.75***	(2.60)	1.22***	(0.31)	1.20	(2.48)	0.53 **	(0.19)	13.20	(10.44)
FORBORN	- 0.53***	(0.13)	0.02	(0.02)	-0.70***	(0.05)	0.022***	(0.004)	-0.36***	(0.09)
AGRIC	- 0.11*	(0.50)	0.00	(0.01)	-0.00	(0.32)	-0.003	(0.002)	-0.14***	(0.04)
ILLIT	–		–		–		–		-0.12	(0.19)
SCHOOLF	1.00*	(0.47)	-0.07	(0.06)	–		–		–	
CATHOLIC	–		–		–		–		-0.53	(10.49)
CATH5050	-22.21**	(6.60)	1.58 *	(0.78)	–		–		–	
CATH5060	- 6.16	(5.13)	1.30 *	(0.61)	–		–		–	
CATH5070	-15.20**	(4.93)	1.43 *	(0.58)	–		–		–	
PILLETC(1970)	3.74	(1.91)	-0.42	(0.22)	-2.15 *	(1.01)	-0.45***	(0.08)	–	
IKE(1960)	- 1.40	(1.27)	-0.25	(0.15)	2.53**	(0.80)	-0.39***	(0.06)	–	
SOUTH	2.15	(1.12)	0.01	(0.13)	3.84***	(0.90)	-0.23***	(0.06)	–	
			NENG:		0.87	(0.84)	0.09	(0.07)		
			WNCMN:		1.11	(0.78)	-0.12 *	(0.06)		
R^2 adj.	.692 /	2.893	.407 /	0.342	.756 /	3.978	.607 /	.304	.886 /	2.40
std. error of estim.										
no. of observations / degr. freedom	135 /	121	135 /	121	307 /	295	307 /	295	37 /	28

*=significant at 5% level. **=significant at 1% level. ***=significant at 0.1% level.
#=Censuses of 1950, 1960, 1970, excluding Alaska and Hawaii, and excluding the District of Columbia and Mountain and Pacific states for 1950.

[154]

Table 5-2. Shares of Women Who Are Ever-Married or Single: Regressions Using State Data, Various Censuses, 1900-1970. (Continued)

Regression no.:	(28)		(29)		(30)		(31)		(32)	
Sample:	1900 census		1920 census		1920 census		1930 census		1930 census	
Dependent variable:	LNSPINST		WED1529		LNSPINST		WED1529		LNSPINST	
Indep. variable	coeff.	std.err.	coeff.	std.err.	coeff.	std.err.	coeff.	std.err.	coeff.	std.err.
constant term	0.95	(1.28)	48.35	(39.93)	-0.10	(2.56)	173.13 **	(51.07)	-8.02 **	(2.76)
PRIMAGE	-	-	-	-	-	-	-	-	-	-
SEXWH	-	-	-	-	-	-	-	-	-	-
SEXNW	-	-	-	-	-	-	-	-	-	-
SEXGAP	-0.68 *	(0.29)	4.86	(2.74)	-0.29	(0.18)	28.48 *	(13.33)	-1.95	(0.72)
YCAPORIG	-0.46 *	(0.21)	0.83	(5.61)	0.20	(0.36)	6.66	(5.96)	-0.20	(0.32)
YWORKER	-	-	0.08	(6.05)	-0.40	(0.39)	-19.87 **	(6.10)	0.86 *	(0.33)
UNIMPROV	-1.51 ***	(0.34)	-	-	-	-	-	-	-	-
NONWHITE	-1.40 *	(0.64)	5.46	(13.88)	-1.01	(0.89)	14.38	(12.71)	-0.35	(0.69)
FORBORN	0.010	(0.005)	-0.33 *	(0.14)	-0.003	(0.009)	- 0.54 ***	(0.15)	0.003	(0.009)
AGRIC	-0.016***	(0.003)	-0.03	(0.05)	-0.010**	(0.033)	- 0.34 **	(0.09)	0.009a	(0.005)
ILLIT	0.030*	(0.012)	0.23	(0.36)	0.015	(0.023)	- 0.25	(0.45)	0.008	(0.024)
SCHOOLF	-	-	-	-	-	-	-	-	-	-
CATHOLIC	0.27	(0.64)	-26.24	(15.82)	1.00	(1.01)	-10.38	(11.61)	1.061	(0.627)
CATH5050	-	-	-	-	-	-	-	-	-	-
CATH5060	-	-	-	-	-	-	-	-	-	-
CATH5070	-	-	-	-	-	-	-	-	-	-
PILLETC(1970)	-	-	-	-	-	-	-	-	-	-
IKE(1960)	-	-	-	-	-	-	-	-	-	-
SOUTH	-	-	-	-	-	-	-	-	-	-
$R^2_{adj.}$ / std. error of estim.	.883 /	.146	.791 /	3.094	.636 /	.198	.803 /	3.14	.684 /	.170
no. of observations / degr. of freedom	37 / 28		37 / 28		37 / 28		37 / 28		37 / 28	

*=significant at 5% level. **=significant at 1% level. ***=significant at 0.1% level.
a=significant at the 7% level.

[155]

Table 5-2. Shares of Women Who Are Ever-Married or Single: Regressions Using State Data, Various Censuses, 1900-1970. (Continued)

Regression no.:	(33)		(34)		(35)		(36)		(37)	
Sample:	1940 census		1940 census		1950 census		1950 census		1960 census	
Dependent variable:	WED1529		LNSPINST		WED1529		LNSPINST		WED1529	
Indep. variable	coeff.	std.err.	coeff.	std.err.	coeff.	std.err.	coeff.	std.err.	coeff.	std.err.
constant term	131.67 **	(40.94)	-5.77 *	(2.18)	81.66 *	(34.79)	-4.32	(2.84)	–	–
PRIMAGE	–	–	–	–	–	–	–	–	–	–
SEXWH	–	–	–	–	–	–	–	–	–	–
SEXNW	–	–	–	–	–	–	–	–	–	–
SEXGAP	60.75 ***	(12.52)	-3.43 ***	(0.67)	24.65 *	(11.07)	-1.97 *	(0.90)	–	–
YCAPORIG	4.53	(6.72)	-0.11	(0.36)	-14.56 ***	(3.99)	1.15 ***	(0.33)	-12.75 **	(4.33)
YWORKER	-14.28 *	(6.81)	0.54	(0.36)	8.25	(5.39)	-0.64	(0.44)	20.41 **	(7.27)
RELCOST	–	–	–	–	–	–	–	–	-45.37	(82.44)
NONWHITE	12.74 *	(6.28)	-0.11	(0.33)	- 5.09	(4.97)	0.86 *	(0.41)	- 4.58	(4.22)
FORBORN	- 0.56 **	(0.18)	0.002	(0.009)	- 0.56 **	(0.17)	0.011	(0.014)	–	–
AGRIC	- 0.20 *	(0.09)	0.005	(0.005)	- 0.14 *	(0.07)	0.011b	(0.006)	- 0.15 *	(0.06)
ILLIT	–	–	–	–	–	–	–	–	–	–
SCHOOLF	0.81 **	(0.24)	-0.027*	(0.013)	1.35 **	(0.48)	- .12 **	(0.04)	0.08	(0.55)
CATHOLIC	-19.12 *	(8.46)	1.46 **	(0.45)	-13.21 a	(6.70)	1.15 *	(0.55)	–	–
CATH5050	–	–	–	–	–	–	–	–	-17.71 ***	(4.71)
CATH5060	–	–	–	–	–	–	–	–	–	–
CATH5070	–	–	–	–	–	–	–	–	–	–
PILLETC(1970)	–	–	–	–	–	–	–	–	–	–
IKE(1960)	–	–	–	–	–	–	–	–	17.28	(10.63)
CW2	–	–	–	–	–	–	–	–	–	–
$R^2_{adj.}$ / std. error of estim.	.774 / 3.380		.669 / .180		.786 / 2.70		.656 / .220		.705 / 2.463	
no. of observations / degr. of freedom	49 / 40		49 / 40		49 / 40		49 / 40		49 / 38	

*=significant at 5% level. **=significant at 1% level. ***=significant at 0.1% level.
a=significant at the 6% level.
b=significant at the 7% level.

[156]

Table 5-2. Shares of Women Who Are Ever-Married or Single: Regressions Using State Data, Various Censuses, 1900-1970. (Continued)

Regression no.:	(38)		(39)	
Sample:	1960 census		1970 census	
Dependent variable:	LNSPINST		WED1529	
Indep. variable	coeff.	std.err.	coeff.	std.err.
constant term	-5.32	(11.24)	35.61	(71.85)
PRIMAGE	-	-	-30.82	(35.54)
SEXWH	-	-	-	-
SEXNW	-	-	-	-
SEXGAP	-1.28	(2.72)	25.35a	(12.79)
YCAPORIG	1.30a	(0.65)	1.53	(6.77)
YWORKER	-0.70	(1.44)	2.61	(7.23)
RELCOST	-2.06	(16.24)	-99.41	(79.93)
NONWHITE	1.01	(0.83)	-13.03 *	(5.42)
FORBORN	-	-	-	-
AGRIC	0.01	(0.01)	- 0.14	(0.08)
ILLIT	-	-	-	-
SCHOOLF	-0.10	(0.11)	- 0.68	(1.09)
CATHOLIC	-	-	-	-
CATH5050	-	-	-	-
CATH5060	1.12	(0.94)	-	-
CATH5070	-	-	-26.70	(4.48)
PILLETC(1970)	-	-	-	-
IKE(1960)	-	-	-	-
CW2	-	-	28.63	(10.85)
$R^2_{adj.}$ / std. error of estim.	103 / 491		.699 / 2.49	
no. of observations / degr. of freedom	49 / 40		49 / 38	

*=significant at 5% level. **=significant at 1% level. ***=significant at 0.1% level.
a=significant at 6% level.

[157]

Table 5-3. Decadal Changes in Child-Woman Ratios: Regressions Using State Data, Various Censuses, 1930-1970.[a] (Dependent variable is DCW)

Regression no.:	(40) postwar #		(41) postwar #		(42) 1940 census		(43) 1950 census		(44) 1950 census	
Sample: Indep. variable	coeff.	std.err.	coeff.	std.err.	coeff.	std.err.	coeff.	std.err.	coeff.	std.err.
constant term	.059 ***	(.009)	.061 ***	(.009)	-.005	(.010)	.049 **	(.015)	.095 ***	(.019)
DWED1529	.001	(.001)	.001	(.001)	.005 **	(.002)	.008 ***	(.001)	-	-
DPRIMAGE	-.010	(.042)	.056	(.053)	.025	(.078)	.495	(.209)	.878 *	(.354)
DSEXWH	.257 **	(.084)	-	-	-	-	-	-	.034b	(.142)b
DSEXNW	.060	(.129)	-	-	-	-	-	-	-	-
DYCAPORIG	-.065 ***	(.018)	-.063 ***	(.018)	-.086 **	(.026)	.022	(.031)	.010	(.042)
DYWORK	.015	(.019)	.012	(.018)	.096	(.059)	-.034	(.020)	.007	(.028)
DRELCOST	-.333 **	(.114)	-.243	(.147)	-	-	-	-	-	-
DNONWHITE	.195 *	(.083)	.197 *	(.086)	-.812	(.653)	.007	(.151)	.198	(.207)
DFORBORN	-.004	(.003)	-	-	-	-	-	-	-	-
DAGRIC	.002	(.001)	-	-	.008 ***	(.002)	-.0024	(.0014)	-.002	(.002)
DSCHOOLF	.023 ***	(.004)	-	-	-	-	.0015 *	(.0006)	.001	(.001)
CATHOLIC	-	-	-	-	.056	(.045)	-	-	-	-
CATH5050	.062	(.050)	.153 **	(.049)	-	-	.001	(.034)	.077	(.042)
CATH5060	-.001	(.042)	.082 *	(.041)	-	-	-	-	-	-
CATH5070	-.085 *	(.038)	-.038	(.041)	-	-	-	-	-	-
PILLETC(1970)	-.174 ***	(.011)	-.164 ***	(.011)	-	-	-	-	-	-
$R^2_{adj.}$ / std. error of estim.	.965 / .22		.952 / .026		.538 / .028		.647 / .016		.356 / .022	
no. of observations / degr. of freedom	135 / 120		135 / 124		49 / 41		49 / 40		49 / 40	

*=significant at 5% level, **=significant at 1% level, ***=significant at 0.1% level.
#=Census of 1950, 1960, 1970, excluding Alaska and Hawaii, and excluding the District of Columbia and Mountain and Pacific states for 1950.
a=For the 1930 census, all models with DCW as the dependent variable failed to yield any predictive power (i.e. R^2_{adj} was negative).
b=Independent variable is DSEXGAP.

[158]

Table 5-3. Decadal Changes in Child-Woman Ratios: Regressions Using State Data, Various Censuses, 1930-1970. (Continued) (Dependent variable is DCW)

Regression no.:	(45)		(46)		(47)		(48)		(49)	
Sample:	1960 census		1960 census		1970 census		1970 census		1970 census	
Indep. variable	coeff.	std.err.	coeff.	std.err.	coeff.	std.err.	coeff.	std.err.	coeff.	std.err.
constant term	.074 ***	(.014)	.070 ***	(.014)	-.131 ***	(.017)	-.141 ***	(.014)	-.127 ***	(.017)
DWED1529	-	-	.003 *	(.001)	-	-	.0056***	(.014)	-	-
DPRIMAGE	.223	(.127)	.448 *	(.184)	.206 b	(.110)	.794 ***	(.170)	.247 *	(.119)
DSEXWH	-	-	-	-	-	-	-	-	-	-
DSEXGAP	.243 *	(.114)	-	-	.259	(.149)	-	-	-	-
DYCAPORI	-.053	(.035)	-.030	(.037)	-.097 **	(.030)	-.023	(.030)	-.121 ***	(.023)
DYWORK	-.003	(.053)	.008	(.053)	.172 **	(.049)	.141	(.043)	.185	-
DRELCOST	-	-	-	-	-	-	-	-	-	-
DNONWHT	.269 *	(.127)	.272 *	(.127)	.035	(.128)	.091	(.113)	.009	(.130)
DFORBORN	-	-	-	-	-	-	-	-	-	-
DAGRIC	.0029	(.0015)	.0022	(.0015)	.0020	(.0019)	.0049**	(.0015)	-	-
DSCHOOLF	.021 **	(.007)	.014	(.008)	.0108	(.0065)	.0076	(.0058)	-	-
CATHOLIC	-	-	-	-	-	-	-	-	-	-
CATH5050	-	-	-	-	-	-	-	-	-	-
CATH5060	- a	-	- a	-	-	-	-	-	-	-
CATH5070	-	-	-	-	-.059	(.036)	-.023	(.032)	-.044	(.039)
PILLETC(1970)	-	-	-	-	-	-	-	-	.523	.025
R^2_{adj} / std. error of estim.	.475 / .023		.472 / .023		.612 / .021		.703 / .019		.523 / .025	
no. of observations / degr. of freedom	49 / 41		49 / 41		49 / 40		49 / 40		49 / 43	

*=significant at 5% level. **=significant at 1% level. ***=significant at 0.1% level.

a=A regression identical to this one except for the inclusion of CATH5060 yielded a lower R^2_{adj} and an insignificantly positive value for CATH5060.

b=significant at the 7% level.

[159]

Table 5-3. Decadal Changes in Child-Woman Ratios: Regressions Using State Data, Various Censuses, 1930-1970. (Continued) (Dependent variable is DCW)

Regression no.:	(50) 1970 census		(51) weighted postwar@	
Sample: Indep. variable	coeff.	std.err.	coeff.	std.err.
constant term	-.124 ***	(.016)	-	-
DWED1529	-	-	.389	(.095)
DPRIMAGE	.0047***	(.0016)	.118	(.066)
DSEXWH	.703 ***	(.186)	.094	(.170)
DSEXNW	-	-	-	-
DYCAPORI	-.090 ***	(.023)	-.061 ***	(.017)
DYWORK	.134 **	(.045)	.025	(.018)
DRELCOST	-	-	-.311 **	(.110)
DNONWHITE	.126	(.126)	.099	(.096)
DFORBORN	-	-	-.0045*	(.0020)
DAGRIC	-	-	.0012	(.0008)
DSCHOOLF	-	-	.0018a	(.0009)
SCHOOLF50,60	-	-	.0080***	(.0007)
SCHOOLF70	-	-	-.0223***	(.0058)
CATH5050	-	-	.039	(.041)
CATH5060	-	-	.036	(.040)
CATH5070	-.024	(.037)	.0005	(.0356)
PILLETC(1970)	-	-	.151 *	(.073)
$R^2_{adj.}$ / std. error of estim.	.591 / .022		.978@ / 17.17@	
no. of observations / degr. of freedom	49 / 41		147 / 131	

*=significant at 5% level. **=significant at 1% level. ***=significant at 0.1% level.

@: The state coverage of the weighted postwar sample is the same as for the unweighted postwar sample above. For the weighted sample, each variable, including the dependent variable, was multiplied by the square root of the number of females 15-49. This procedure assures that if the underlying individual observations are homoskedastic, the state aggregates used will also be homoskedastic, provided also that the constant term is omitted from the regression. The omission of a constant term, however, means that the R^2 statistic does not have its usual meaning.

[160]

Table 5.4. Decadal Changes in Shares of Woman Ever-Married or Single: Regressions Using State Data, Various Censuses, 1930-1970.

Regression no.:	(52)		(53)		(54)		(55)	
Sample:	postwar #		1950 census		1960 census		1970 census	
Dependent variable:	DWED1529		DWED1529		DWED1529		DWED1529	
Indep. variable	coeff.	std.err.	coeff.	std.err.	coeff.	std.err.	coeff.	std.err.
constant term	0.32	(1.26)	5.14	(1.35)	- 3.52 **	(1.24)	0.38	(1.54)
DPRIMAGE	-	-	-	-	-83.71 ***	(8.80)	-103.68****	(9.72)
DSEXWH	31.25 **	(11.34)	-	-	-	-	-	-
DSEXNW	28.92	(21.68)	-	-	-	-	-	-
DSEXGAP	-	-	23.68 **	(7.58)	50.15 ***	(7.95)	27.19 b	(13.55)
DYCAPORI	- 1.13	(2.41)	0.77	(3.09)	- 6.81 **	(2.45)	- 11.32***	(2.75)
DYWORK	0.69	(2.57)	3.46	(1.81)	- 3.17	(3.63)	7.14	(4.41)
DRELCOST	-75.87***	(15.42)	-	-	-	-	-	-
DNONWHIT	- 5.61	(11.35)	21.82	(13.97)	9.54	(8.92)	- 14.81	(11.51)
DFORBORN	- 0.96 **	(0.34)	- 1.02 ***	(0.23)	- 1.09 ***	(0.24)	- 0.96 *	(0.44)
DAGRIC	- 0.00	(0.12)	- 0.06	(0.13)	- 0.12	(0.12)	- 0.36 *	(0.17)
DILLIT	-	-	-	-	-	-	-	-
DSCHOOLF	1.07	(0.56)	0.35 **	(0.10)	2.51 ***	(0.50)	0.89	(0.59)
CATHOLIC	-	-	1.64	(3.54)	-	-	-	-
CATH5050	0.20	(6.88)	-	-	a		-	-
CATH5060	9.90	(5.64)	-	-	-	-	-	-
CATH5070	-11.19 *	(5.10)	-	-	-	-	-11.60 **	(3.99)
PILLETC(1970)	- 2.48	(1.39)	-	-	-	-	-	-
$R^2_{adj.}$ / std. error of estim.	.786 / 3.00		.542 / 1.61		.849 / 1.56		.731 / 1.88	
no of observations / degr. of freedom	131 / 121		49 / 40		49 / 40		49 / 39	

*=significant at 5% level. **=significant at 1% level. ***=significant at 0.1% level.
#=censuses of 1950, 1960, and 1970, excluding Alaska and Hawaii, and excluding the District of Columbia and Mountain and Pacific states for 1950.
a: A $_2$ regression identical to this one except for the inclusion of CATH5060 yielded a lower $R^2_{adj.}$ and an insignificantly negative value for CATH5060.
b: significant at the 6% level.

and past income variables—current income per person in the labor force (YWORKER) and income per capita in places of origin twenty years earlier (YCAPORIG)—and their rates of change between censuses. The level of current income is of inconsistent sign and seldom significant, while the past income variable always affects fertility negatively and usually passes the standard tests of statistical significance. This behavior of the income variables is consistent with the hypothesis about taste formation introduced above. The failure of current income per person in the labor force to show a consistently positive sign can be interpreted as an indication that current income often represents recent influences on couples' material standards (tastes) as much as it represents their current resources. The more consistently negative influence of past income experience (YCAPORIG) can be interpreted as a confirmation of the importance of income history as a determinant of the material standards that make couples limit family size.

This interpretation in favor of the hypothesis of taste formation through income and family input experience is consistent with the fact that the past income experience variable is statistically significant in some censuses and not in others. The YCAPORIG variable is significant in the censuses of 1920–50 and in the larger pooled samples, but not in the fertility cross sections of 1900, 1960, and 1970 (see Regressions 5, 6, 18–20, 22). (Hereafter references to the regressions in Tables 5–1 through 5–4 will be abbreviated: "R.3" for "see Regression 3," etc.) The failure of significance in these cases can be explained in a way that fits the view that past income experience is an important influence on controlled fertility in all settings. It so happened that in 1900 current income was almost perfectly correlated with the past income variable across states, and in 1960 and 1970 neither the past income variable nor current income varied nearly as greatly across states as they had varied earlier in this century. Therefore, in 1900 multicollinearity prevented confirmation of the statistical significance of past income experience, and the lack of significance for 1960 and 1970 regressions stemmed from the fact that past and current incomes did not happen to vary enough to show their influence in these single-census cross sections. For the censuses of 1920–50, by contrast, the American economy had been subjected to enough shocks to cause past incomes to vary considerably across states in ways not mirrored by current incomes, thus yielding a better test of the potential importance of prior income experience.

An alternative interpretation of the consistent influence of past income experience on fertility might be advanced. The performance of the

YCAPORIG variable might have reflected nothing more than the influence of past fertility on current fertility. This suspicion is fostered by the fact that YCAPORIG is a measure of prior incomes *per capita* and not per worker or per adult, thereby being negatively correlated with past fertility. It might be that its apparent explanatory power is in no way related to the hypothesis advanced above. Perhaps its negative signs only pick up the simple point that whatever affects past fertility for a state affects current fertility similarly. This possibility was tested in several regressions (R.2, 18–20, 22, and others not reported) which included the value of the state's child-woman ratio twenty years earlier as an additional explanatory variable. Not surprisingly, this variable is highly significant, representing as it does all the state-specific forces not captured in other variables. Yet when it is used in the postwar sample large enough to sort out the significance of highly correlated variables (R.2), the coefficient for past income experience still turns out to be highly significant and not much reduced in magnitude. Apparently the hypothesis about past income experience as a consistent determinant of couples' tastes toward childbearing is sustained.[13]

The other variable introduced by hypothesis above was the *relative cost* of a child. Its impact also shows up in the results, though its significance, like the manner in which it is measured, varies for different census samples. The direct measures of the rate of change in relative child costs (outside of agriculture) for the postwar era display a negative influence on both fertility and nuptiality, as theory had suggested (R. 40–41, 51, 52). Within single censuses, the relative cost variable, which is a variation on the wage rate, is not statistically significant (and of the "wrong" sign), owing to its high correlation with the current and past income variables used in the same regressions (R.16–22, 37–39). Across the postwar era, the *rate of change* in relative child cost is a clearly significant influence on the rate of change in fertility. Its significance stems essentially from the fact that the high fertility of the late 1940s accompanied a drop in relative child cost caused by the new relevance of the income tax exemption per child, while in later years no such drop occurred. We shall return to this point in re-examining the post-war fertility wave below.

[13] The issue of how the interplay of past and current incomes relates to nuptiality has been investigated by the regressions in Tables 5–2 and 5–4. The regressions from the large pooled samples and the single-census regressions from the postwar era show that marriage is encouraged by higher current incomes relative to past income experience, as one would have guessed. But this relationship does not hold for most earlier censuses.

The relative cost of a child must be measured differently for the era before World War I. In that less urbanized and industrialized setting the two main forces making children look more expensive relative to the things with which they competed were the migration out of agriculture and, within agriculture, the scarcity of land. The prewar influence of these two forces on relative child cost is incorporated into (but not necessarily equal to) the 1900 regression coefficients for the share of the male work force employed in agriculture (AGRIC) and two proxies for the relative availability of farm land (UNIMPROV and LANDCOST). These variables explain much of the variation of fertility and marriage among states in the 1900 census (R.5, 6, 27, 28), with one of the proxies for land availability (UNIMPROV) performing better than the other (LANDCOST). The clear tendency of the availability of unimproved land in West North Central and West South Central states to encourage marriage and fertility seems to confirm the argument of several authors that land availability is an important fertility determinant within largely agricultural societies. The interpretation taken here is that the importance of land availability, like that of the share of the population in agriculture, reflects a response of fertility and marriage to difference in relative child costs.[14]

In contrast to the relatively steady influence of present and past income on fertility and marriage, the impact of *agriculture and urbanization* has shown some striking changes over this century. Both of these forces must be represented by the single variable AGRIC in the present

[14] This conclusion is supported by the fact that AGRIC and UNIMPROV showed considerable explanatory power in regressions that included other independent variables for which they might have served as misleading proxies. The relevance of available land (UNIMPROV) is not to be explained away as merely reflecting the fact that the new farm areas to the west had higher ratios of males to females and a predominance of females in the prime childbearing age range (20–34). The importance of available unimproved land held up in regression also including the net excess of males over females (SEXGAP versus UNIMPROV in R.5), and there was in fact no correlation between the availability of new farm land and the share of females 15–49 in the prime 20–34 age group in 1900.

Nor is the share in agriculture or the availability of farm land an implicit proxy for the interplay between present and past incomes, since these variables were also given their due in the same regressions showing the importance of AGRIC and UNIMPROV for 1900. The suspicion that settlement on the frontier is another proxy for a jump in income prospects relative to past income experience is also countered by the fact that frontier states in 1900 failed to show any extraordinarily high ratio of current to past (place of birth) incomes in 1900. Hence the importance of AGRIC and UNIMPROV must bespeak either the relevance of relative child costs or an unidentified influence on tastes.

regressions, since data on the shares in cities are too highly correlated with the shares outside of agriculture for analysis of their separate roles. The cross-sectional impact of the agricultural variable on marriages has swung from positive to negative and back to insignificance between 1900 and 1970. In the 1900 census females tended to marry considerably earlier in more-agricultural states, other things equal (R.27, 28). In the 1920 census the share of women 30–44 who were ever married was again significantly higher in more-agricultural settings, other things equal (R.30), but this was no longer true for the younger (15–29) age group, suggesting that some sort of influence on the timing of marriage had tipped in favor of urban as opposed to farm marriage around World War I (R.29). By the time of the 1930 census, marriage seemed to be strongly discouraged by agricultural settings, especially for the younger age group (R.31, 32). The same was true for the next three decades, though the antinuptial impact of agriculture (or the positive impact of urbanization?) was smaller for 1940–60 than for the 1930 census. By 1970 the distribution of a state's population between agriculture and other sectors no longer seemed relevant to the share of females married (R.39).

The agricultural variable has a less pronounced and more erratic impact on fertility when the shares of females married are held constant. A more agricultural state, other things equal, has a level of fertility (for a constant married share) that is no different in most cases, but significantly greater in a minority of cases. The cases of positive relationship between agriculture and fertility for constant marriage were the censuses of 1930, 1950, and 1960 (R.10, 15, 19). The overall effect of agriculture on fertility, now combining its effect on marriage with its effect on fertility within and outside of marriage, appears to have declined across this country (R.5, 9, 11, 12, 14, 18, 20), from a strong positive stimulus in 1900 to irrelevance in 1970.

It is not clear why the role of agriculture-urbanization should have changed so. The mere fact that the population has migrated away from agriculture, for example, does not explain why the overall fertility impact of a given difference in the share in agriculture should have dropped. The patterns of effects on marriage do fit the swings in the relative economic fortunes of agriculture (downward from 1910 to 1940 and upward thereafter), but the long-run decline in agriculture's *unit* fertility relevance does not. Faced with this pattern and with the convergence in rural-urban differences in child-woman ratios from 1940 to 1960, one could construct an *ad hoc* hypothesis that across World

War II some social force made farm and urban tastes converge; but the issue must remain unresolved here.

Swings may also have occurred in the fertility and nuptiality effects of *Roman Catholicism*. We have state data, such as they are, on membership in the Roman Catholic church for years near each census from 1890 through 1940. At the risk of further distortion, one could also apply the last state-by-state membership figures, those for 1936, to states' 1950 population for an examination of the relevance of Catholicism in the postwar period. This information has been employed in various regressions in Tables 5–1 through 5–4. Taken at face value, the regressions on marriage patterns imply that Catholics between World War I and the 1950s had a greater tendency to postpone or completely avoid marriage than did others (R.29–36), this tendency being statistically significant for the censuses of 1940 and 1950. In the 1960 and 1970 censuses, as in 1900, the shaky measures of Catholic shares of population imply that marriage patterns were not statistically significant between Catholics and non-Catholics.[15]

When the shares married are held constant, the effect of higher concentrations of Roman Catholics on fertility seems to have swung from negative for 1900–30 to significantly positive for 1940–70 (R.6, 8, 10, 13, 15, 19, 22). These estimates, like recent fertility surveys, also suggest a marked dip in the marital fertility differential between Catholics and non-Catholics across the 1960s (R.19, 22, 40, 41, 47–51). When the effects on marriage and the effects on fertility for constant married shares are combined, it appears that the overall fertility effect of Roman Catholicism, other things equal, swung from negative in the 1920s to a statistically significant peak fertility stimulus in the late 1950s (i.e., in the 1960 census) and dropped off again across the 1960s (R.9, 11, 12, 14, 18, 20).

The observed pattern of fertility and nuptiality differentials by religion happen to fit expectations one might have had from swings in Catholic

---

[15] The statement about the absence of religious differences in marriage patterns in 1960 and 1970 is based on the fact that the impact of the Catholicism variable in these censuses seemed to be the same whether or not the shares married were held constant. This contradicts the regressions reporting a significant effect of Catholicism toward postponement of marriage in 1960 and 1970 (R.37, 39). These regressions happen to have no variable for sex ratios or immigration, which are correlated negatively and positively, respectively, with Catholicism in the state-by-state cross section. These variables may have caused the influence attributed to Catholicism in the regressions. At the same time, the postwar estimates of Catholic shares are particularly shaky, based as they are on state membership in 1936.

and Protestant policy and attitudes toward birth control. It was in 1930 that Pius XI's encyclical *Casti Connubii* firmly labeled any couples who attempt to frustrate the natural power of the sex act to generate life as "branded with guilt of grave sin." No such new toughness was apparent in official Protestant pronouncements. It is for the 1930s (1940 census) that the regression estimates begin to reveal greater fertility among Catholics than non-Catholics, holding marriage and other variables constant. It is also in the censuses of 1940 and 1950 that Catholicism appears to become a statistically significant factor postponing marriage. Both the fertility and the nuptiality effects associated with a large share of Catholics in the state appear to support the hypothesis that after *Casti Connubii* Catholics increasingly felt constrained not to limit births by effective means within marriage. The reduction in the fertility differential between Catholics and non-Catholics in the 1960s can be linked to a shift in lay Catholic attitudes. Around 1964 many American Catholics, probably encouraged by the publicized ecumenism and reform at the Second Vatican Council and by a series of lay American books defending modern contraception, shifted to the pill and other modern practices. This shift in attitude was not reversed by Pope Paul VI's condemnation of the pill in 1968.[16]

This view of the shifts in the impact of Catholicism should be treated with caution, however. As noted, the postwar estimates of the state shares of Catholics are not to be leaned on. And there is always the danger that Catholicism may be displaying influences that belong to omitted variables associated with heavily Catholic states.

The effect of *educational attainment* on fertility changed in a manner somewhat resembling the swing in the apparent fertility effect of Catholicism, whereas the effects of schooling and Catholicism on marriage moved quite differently. Education is represented inversely in the censuses up through 1930 by the share of persons over twenty-one who are illiterate, and directly for 1940 and beyond by the median years of schooling of females twenty-five and over. In 1900 education seems to have been a factor promoting earlier marriage but lowering fertility (see ILLIT in R.5, 6, 27, 28). Its negative effect on fertility remains essentially unchanged through 1930, though it appears to have no effect on

---

[16] For an annual series on the use of the pill and intrauterine devices by interviewed Catholics, see Norman B. Ryder, "Time Series of Pill and IUD Use: United States, 1961–1970," *Studies in Family Planning* 3 (October 1972), 233–240. On the shift in attitudes, see John T. Noonan, *Contraception: A History of Its Treatment by the Catholic Theologians and Canonists*, New York 1967, pp. 580–581, 595–597, 602–609.

marriage patterns in the censuses of 1920 and 1930 (R.8–11, 29–32). In the 1940 census, schooling shows no influence on the fertility patterns of the late 1930s when marriage is held constant (R.13). Yet it has again become a factor encouraging marriage (R.33, 34), as in 1900, so that its overall effect on fertility is positive and almost statistically significant (R.12).

In the postwar era, the relationship of fertility and marriage to schooling jumps and falls sharply. In the 1950 census schooling achieves its peak positive influence on both fertility and marriage (R.14, 15, 35, 36, 43, 44, 53). Where the census data had shown a reduction in the fertility differentials between low-education and high-education groups, in the baby boom, the regressions now add the observation that the effect of schooling on fertility became strongly positive for the late 1940s, other variables held constant. The same positive effects on marriage and fertility continue through the 1960 census, though their statistical significance and magnitude generally appear to have been lower than in the 1950 census (R.16, 18, 19, 37, 38, 45, 46, 51, 53). With the 1970 census, all such effects on fertility and marriage disappear (R.20, 21, 22, 39, 47, 48, 51, 55). The task of interpreting these swings in the impact of differences in schooling is undertaken in the next section.

The effect of *race* on fertility is left unclear by the regression results. The regressions of Tables 5–1 through 5–4 seem in general to argue that having a higher share of nonwhites may lower a state's aggregate fertility ratio, given the aggregate levels of income, schooling, and so forth. This antinatal effect is statistically significant about half the time. It occurs even in the censuses before World War II, despite some possible tendency for nonwhites to marry earlier then than their levels of income, etc., would have predicted for a white population. There is no obvious explanation for this tendency toward extra birth restriction, other things equal. The racial variable may well be playing the role of Southern residence (SOUTH), whose significantly negative influence removes any significance from the racial variable whenever both appear in the same regression (R.1–4). Accepting this interpretation, however, leaves the role of Southern residence itself unexplained.

The consistency of the likely impact of race, at any rate, suggests that over a long period the levels of fertility one would predict for nonwhites would generally follow the same trends as for white. Indeed one of the striking features of nonwhite fertility is that it did follow a trend very much like that of white fertility, declining from 1880 to the 1930s, then rising with the baby boom and falling again since. The similarity in the shape of the trends for different races suggests that their fertility rates may be responding to influences shared by all races. One set of roughly common influences, of course, is the growth path of incomes, education, and life expectancies. Perhaps the history of blacks' relative deprivation changed slowly enough so that forces felt by both blacks and whites governed trends in their fertility rates more visibly than did changes that discriminated against or for blacks. To make this point convincingly for the years before World War II, however, we would need better data on income and other variables by race than are now available.

IV. *The Postwar Baby Boom and Bust*

With these insights into changes in the determinants of fertility differences over time, one can better interpret some of the developments in the history of American population growth that have attracted attention and puzzlement.

The surge and crash of birth rates in the postwar era can be better understood in terms of interactions between past income experience, current incomes, relative child costs, and schooling. An explanation for most of or all the boom and bust swings seems implicit in the cross-sectional patterns already revealed by the regressions that examined one census at a time. But to make this explanation as clear as possible, it is best to look at pooled regressions covering more than one census and ask: "What combinations of other explanatory variables would be able to remove any significance from the *Zeitgeist* dummy variables identifying each recent decade's experience as a special case?" If no plausible combination of other variables can do that, then one would have to conclude that part of the explanation for the fertility swings lies in factors the models used here have failed to capture (or in measurement errors).

The pooled samples, like the single-census samples, show that the past income, current income, and relative cost variables indeed have a role to play in accounting for the rise and fall of fertility in the post war era (R.1–4, 40, 41, 51). In the late 1940s and 1950s fertility was promoted in part by the very high ratio of current to prewar incomes. By the 1960s, the relevance of the prewar experience for the decision-making of young couples was rapidly waning, and though the growth rate of the 1960s was somewhat higher than that for the 1950s, the fact remained that income prospects in the late 1960s were not so greatly improved over the experience of the previous two decades as was the case for the baby-boom cohorts of young couples. It thus appears that fertility was being adjusted to the ratio of current means over the material standards per family member that were formed by both recent and more distant past income experience. This is the same sort of conclusion reached by Easterlin on the basis of different measures. His measures of relative income status compare the recent incomes (and the unemployment history) of young adults with those of adults a generation older for the nation as a whole.

What we know about the movement of relative child costs also helps to explain the postwar fertility swings. As noted in Chapter 4, the relative cost of a third child was cut when World War II swept the majority of American families into the ranks of income-tax payers. This made the income-tax exemption per child suddenly relevant, cutting the relative cost of a third child in nonfarm families by 16 percent between 1940 and 1945, a cut that was partly offset by a 3 percent cost increase due to rising wage rates over the same years and a further 8 percent cost increase in the later 1940s. Taken by itself, the 16 percent wartime cut in the cost index due to the new income-tax-exemption effect raised the child-women ratio significantly. The coefficient on the relative-cost term in Regression 41 in Table 5–3 implies that this 16 percent cost reduction raised the child-woman ratio by .0533, or about 17 percent of the 1940 child-woman ratio for the entire U.S. For the 1940s as a whole, the net cost reduction of about 5 percent implies a fertility stimulus of a little over 5 percent of the 1940 level, again according to Regression 41. These cost effects account for only a small part, though a statistically significant part, of the observed baby boom, which saw fertility rise by about a third within the 1940s and rise further across the 1950s. Correspondingly, the slight postwar upward drift in relative child costs caused by the rise in wage rates had a slight tendency to reduce fertility, but was not large enough either to prevent the rise in the 1950s or to account for the sharp drop in fertility after the early 1960s.

When income history and relative costs have been entered directly into pooled regressions spanning the postwar period, with or without help from Catholicism variables specific to individual decades, it is still the case that there seems to be something significant and special—that is, something unexplained—about the fertility of the last two decades. Fertility was still higher in the late 1950s (1960 census) and lower in the late 1960s (1970 census) than the direct effects of the variables just mentioned would have predicted.

Another influence can be added to cut down the special unexplained differences between decades. The extra force to be added is suggested by the behavior of the schooling variables in the regressions. It will be recalled that the cross-sectional impact of the schooling variable within individual censuses varied noticeably from decade to decade. Schooling had a slight influence if any on fertility in both the 1940 and 1970 censuses, yet seemed to raise fertility greatly within the censuses of 1950 and 1960.

Why has the impact of differences in levels of schooling been so different for different periods? More specifically, why should it have become strongly positive across the 1940s and then insignificant across the 1960s? One possibility, of course, is that its influence is a mirage caused by omitting some other variables that happen to be strongly correlated with schooling levels across states in the baby boom years but not at other times. A simpler and more promising explanation is that the increased control over births at lower completed parities, an outcome strongly associated with schooling in the past, actually raises the sensitivity of fertility to economic and other changes affecting the desirability of extra births.[17]

There are two reasons for expecting such a pattern. First, a given percentage change in, say, incomes is likely to affect more strongly the demand for something that is a large commitment than the demand for something that takes little resources. Manufacturers of spices and other infrequent-purchase products have often noted a low price elasticity of demand for such products. It may well be that income elasticity of demand is also less strongly affected where the object of expenditure is a smaller share of total family resources. The marginal children in families that will be large with or without them will take a lower percentage of family resources than marginal additions to small families. Perhaps groups with lower parities, such as those with more schooling, find a greater effect on the desirability of one more child in response to a given percentage change in incomes.

Second, for any given change in the desirability of extra children, it seems likely that the responsiveness of birth probabilities will be greater for those groups who have invested more energy in gaining access to effective birth control options. These more informed and contracepting groups will tend to be those nearer their margins of desired family size. The smaller the likely completed parity, the greater the share of couples in the relevant group who are near their margins of wanted versus un-

[17] I am indebted to my colleague Larry L. Bumpass for suggesting that I test this hypothesis in connection with the fluctuations in American fertility since the Depression.

wanted births for any given state of income, costs, contraceptive technology, and so forth. More schooled, or higher-input,[18] couples will tend to be those who have fewer children on the average. Should conditions in the economy take a turn for the worse, they would cut their birth probabilities more effectively (as long as they had not already been preventing births altogether). Should conditions for raising a family seem to brighten, they would raise their birth probabilities considerably, while those groups who would tend to have had more anyway would tend to stick with a relatively ineffective method of contraception (rhythm, withdrawal) and end up wanting a greater share of a relatively constant number of births.[19] The same movements in income and costs can generate greater responses among those with greater control over their fertility.

This interpretation of the results suggests the following explanation of the relationship of education to the baby boom and bust. The more educated had achieved a considerably lower fertility than those with less education by 1940. Having greater control over fertility, they were able to raise their birth probabilities more sharply and certainly when the economy revived with World War II. They continued with levels of fertility that were historically not much lower than those of the less-educated groups, for as long as the climate seemed bright for large families. In the 1960s when the climate began to become less favorable, they were more prompt in once again cutting down on birth probabilities.

If this interpretation is accepted, it carries the important implication that modernizing countries, led by the more-educated and higher-input couples, acquire fertility patterns characterized by greater responsiveness to economic fluctuations and other changes, as well as by lower average fertility over the long run. Should conditions fluctuate, low-fertility groups and countries would show instability in their fertility patterns.

---

[18] For most censuses there is a high correlation between past income experience and schooling, as one would expect. This suggests that the role played by the schooling variable in the pooled regressions (e.g., R.51) might also have been played by variables measuring YCAPORIG separately for each census, or by interaction terms multiplying YCAPORIG by its own rate of growth.

[19] This argument might seem to draw support from the fact that the baby boom brought a greater response of births at lower than at higher birth orders (Dudley Kirk, "The Influence of Business Cycles on Marriage and Birth Rates," in Ansley J. Coale, ed., *Demographic and Economic Change in Developed Countries*, Princeton, 1960, p. 251). But the present hypothesis relates to differences in the responsiveness of different *completed* parities, not different current birth orders. There is little tendency for the share of "marginal" (last-born) children in any birth order to change from the second to the seventh order, so that the Kirk data on the responsiveness of different birth orders cannot serve as a proxy for the responsiveness of different completed parities.

Should conditions change slowly, this instability would not appear despite their keener sensitivity.

While it is plausible that more schooled and contracepting couples may be adjusting their fertility more sensitively to changing economic conditions, the present aggregate tests do not provide firm confirmation of the importance of this tendency for explaining recent experience. Regressions were run on the pooled postwar sample using interaction terms relating schooling to the rate of growth in incomes (SCHDY in R.1a, SCHOOLF50,60 and SCHOOLF70 in R.51). The theory just advanced predicts that such variables should pick up the pronatal effect of extra schooling when incomes are rising rapidly and the antinatal effect of extra schooling when they are not. The results do show the significance of the hypothesized effect on regressions reported here (R.1a,51), but in other (unreported) regressions the special interaction variable lost its significance when forced to compete with Catholicism proxies. The special argument about contraceptive sensitivity to changing economic conditions is thus consistent with the data, but one is left with the suspicion that other explanations could also fit the observed twists in the relationship of schooling to fertility.

It must also be noted that none of the regressions, even those with the special interaction terms, convincingly removed all that was special about individual postwar decades. In the pooled regressions on levels of the child-woman ratio, the Zeitgeist dummies for the 1960 and 1970 censuses accounted for only a small share of the shifts observed for the U.S. as a whole, (R.1-4), yet in the rate-of-change regressions (R.40, 41) the dummy for the 1970 census accounted for all of the observed decline in the child-woman ratio. It thus appears that income, education, and the other socioeconomic variables used here account for much of, but not all of, the special instability of postwar fertility.

V. *The Not-So-Puzzling Twenties*

To judge from the regressions, it appears that the same kinds of models that help to bring order to postwar fertility history fit the census of 1930 quite well. This seems to contradict the view of Coale and Sweezy that the experience of the 1920s does not fit the "economic" hypotheses used for explaining the baby boom. The puzzle they posed, again, was that the prosperity following World War II was accompanied by a surge in births while the prosperity following World War I brought a further decline in births.

The conundrum of the 1920s disappears when the economic history of that decade is examined. The prosperity of the 1920s could not compare to the boom of the 1940s. Output per man-hour rose 19.8 percent per decade between 1913 and 1929 or 28.2 percent in the decade of the 1920s (1919–29), whereas it rose 32.9 percent across the 1940s and at the rate of 36.0 percent per decade across the 1940s and 1950s combined.[20] The contrast in postwar eras is sharpened by the fact that unemployment, which is not reflected in the figures on output per man-hour, was at least as high in the 1920s as in 1913,[21] whereas unemployment dropped from over 14.5 percent to less than 6.0 percent in the 1940s.

What we know of the movement of the distribution of income in the 1920s also serves to account for the absence of a baby boom in that decade. The 1920s saw a widening of inequalities in wealth and income. The shift toward inequality was sufficiently pronounced, in fact, that the gains in real income were taken up almost entirely by the top 7 percent of nonfarm families.[22] Wage rates remained nearly fixed, and farm families suffered such large capital losses in the 1920–21 crash in land values that their small current income gains over the rest of the decade failed to bring an overall gain in purchasing power. In other words, for families that would account for nearly all of the nation's births, income was rising less rapidly than in previous decades. It is hardly surprising that fertility failed to surge in the 1920s the way it did in the ascent from depression to boom in the 1940s.

VI. *The Steady Decline, 1860–1935*

One historical development that helped to make the baby boom so unexpected was the steadiness of the previous long fertility decline. From the early nineteenth century to the middle of the Depression, the rate of decline in fertility fluctuated less than it has since. This is not to say that the decline was entirely uniform. As already noted, the fertility of native-born New Englanders was no lower in the 1920s than around the Civil War, and Southern white fertility fell less rapidly than the white national

---

[20] U.S. Bureau of Economic Analysis, *Long Term Economic Growth, 1860–1970*, Washington, 1973, Series A168.

[21] Robert M. Coen, "Labor Force and Unemployment in the 1920s and 1930s: A Re-examination Based on Postwar Experience," *Review of Economics and Statistics* 55 (February 1973), 46–55.

[22] Based on a reworking of the Simon Kuznets figures of upper-income groups' shares of total income by Charles F. Holt, "Size Distribution of Income and the Prosperity of the Twenties," manuscript, Duluth, Minnesota, 1972.

rate between 1870 and 1900. The national child-woman ratio had a slight sawtooth pattern, falling faster in the censuses of 1870, 1890, 1910, and 1930 than in 1880, 1900, or 1920. Each of these variations deserves to be studied by itself.

The theory advanced above cannot be tested against all of the features of the long fertility decline, owing to insufficient data. It is not difficult, however, to reconcile the present framework with the steadiness of the decline. All of the major influences on fertility identified by the models for the twentieth-century censuses moved more steadily before 1935 than since. Incomes fluctuated in response to local harvest failures, World War I, and short recessions marked by bank panics. But each of these fluctuations was too brief to affect fertility behavior greatly. The rise of schooling and the decline of agriculture also proceeded too evenly to cause major swings in fertility. The relative stability of the downward trend may also be explained in part by the interaction hypothesized above between the degree of control over fertility and the sensitivity of fertility response to changing conditions. In the later nineteenth century fertility was still controlled by the few crude means known to most young adults—postponement of marriage, abstinence, withdrawal, rhythm. As economic prospects varied, they had less ability than their descendants to vary their own birth probabilities. This greater imperfection of birth control may have dampened their responsiveness to economic fluctuations.

Used with care, the family of models tried out in Tables 5–1 through 5–4 could explain part of the variation in regional rates of fertility decline before 1935. One variation it *cannot* at present explain, because the necessary economic data are lacking, is the failure of the fertility of native-born New Englanders to decline from the 1860s to the 1920s. We lack series on the incomes, income history, agricultural employment share, and schooling of persons within a region classified by nativity. Another variation may prove more tractable. It has been noted that the fertility of Southern whites failed to drop much between 1870 and 1900. The same fact seems less anomalous if this period is broken at 1880. In the wake of the Civil War the Southern states experienced an abnormally low ratio of young males to young females. Southern whites also suffered from a loss of income from slaves and nonhuman capital, plus crop failures. All of these factors could easily have lowered fertility for the 1870 census. (The lower child-woman ratio for that census may also be due in part, but probably not entirely, to a bias in the serious undercount in Southern states in the 1870 census.) It is thus not surprising that

Southern white fertility dropped little if at all from the 1870 census to that of 1880. From 1880 on there is less of a drift of Southern white fertility to be explained, so that relative steadiness in the ratio of Southern white fertility holds during the era (after 1880) when there is no pronounced movement in the ratios of Southern to national income, schooling, share in agriculture, and so forth.

VII. Conclusion

It seems possible to use a single framework to tie together seemingly inconsistent patterns of American fertility. A framework featuring the interplay of past income experience, present income, relative costs, and the prior efficacy of fertility control seems capable of interpreting the baby boom and bust, the previous long decline in fertility, and cross-sectional fertility patterns. It provides these interpretations in a way that should strike historians as sensible: it makes the case for a general model by taking care to identify unique historical forces and changes in structure over time.

The same framework offers some conditional forecasts regarding American fertility. First, its reasons for predicting a negative relationship between fertility and modernization variables imply that over the long run fertility should indeed remain low, and at rates below those of the baby boom. It also points up the possibility, however, that instability in the economy will produce instability in fertility. As argued above, the more fertility becomes controlled in general, the more it moves from having a high random component for individual couples to having less randomness and more systematic response to the economic and other factors that govern the desirability of extra children. This hypothesis says, in effect, that if birth rates should jump in response to economic conditions in the future, we have good reason to hold back on cries of "Standing room only!" in the expectation that if the economic conditions producing the jump are temporary, so is the jump in fertility itself. Conversely, the record lows in fertility in the mid-1970s, which also seem affected by unfavorable short-run economic conditions, may be somewhat below the long-run average level of fertility to be expected.

When aligned with the present kind of model, the history of American fertility over the last 100 years also suggests a relationship between the rate of economic growth and the trend in fertility. Past fertility patterns have shown that the negative influence of income experience on desired family size outweighs the positive influence of family income prospects.

This suggests that as long as future American income growth resembles past growth in its degree of emphasis on investments in education, the faster the long-run rate of growth the greater the downward pressure on fertility will be, even though higher income growth can raise fertility in the short run. This forecast, however, is an extension of the present results beyond the sample on which they are based. Incomes are near record highs and fertility rates have never been lower. It is not implausible to argue that fertility cannot drop further because it is now as low as the natural desire of a majority of young adults to be parents will permit. Having not tested this hypothesis, the present tests cannot reject it. They do lead, however, to a presumption that the long-run trend in American fertility will at least not be upward.

Part III:

FROM FERTILITY TO INEQUALITY

CHAPTER 6. Fertility and Investments in Children

I. *What Theory Suggests*

The 1960s and the start of the 1970s were a period of agitation for less inequality and less discrimination, and also a period of concern over the consequences of high fertility and population growth. Yet the two sets of concerns were not joined. Christopher Jencks' monumental *Inequality* (New York: Basic Books, 1972), for example, passed over family size (and other factors) as sources of inequality. The concern about fertility and population growth remained tied to the fight for environmental quality. Only occasionally was it even suggested that fertility and the expansion of the labor force might have been major determinants of the degree of income inequality.

Yet there are several theoretical reasons for expecting reductions in fertility to turn into reductions in income inequality a generation later. There are, first, two microeconomic effects that should link declining fertility to a later leveling of incomes through the effects of family inputs on child achievements:

(1) A reduction in fertility lowers the dispersion of family sizes, since birth restriction typically reduces the number of children born into very large families by a greater percentage than it reduces the number of first and second children. Since larger family size seems like a factor that should retard the development of earning capacity in individual children, the reduction in family-size differences ought to reduce later earnings inequality.

(2) Since about 1910, birth restriction has on balance reduced the share of children born into poor and less-educated families. The same should be true of birth restrictions from 1970 into the future, since surveys have found that in the 1960s unwanted births were still a greater share of total births among the poor.[1] Birth restriction should thus tend to lower income inequality by cutting down on the share of children born into the extreme disadvantage of being unwanted members of large low-income families.[2]

---

[1] See the survey results reported by Larry Bumpass and Charles Westoff, "The 'Perfect Contraceptive' Population," *Science* (September 18, 1970), pp. 1177–1183; and by Westoff and Norman B. Ryder in *The Contraceptive Revolution*, Princeton, N.J.: Princeton University Press, 1977, based on the 1970 National Fertility Survey.

[2] A decline in fertility would tend to raise income inequality through a third

[181]

There is a "strain on public schools" reason for suspecting that lower fertility means less inequality:

> (3) If the total amount of philanthropic and taxpayer support for schooling is characterized by inertia, then the strain on school systems should be directly related to the share of the population that is of school age. Reducing births may reduce the ratio of children to adults more than it reduces public (and philanthropic) school expenditures per adult, so that the smaller cohort of school-age children enjoys greater public educational outlays per child. To the extent that this public-support effect is more relevant below college than it is for public funding of higher education, the extra public expenditures per child should help the most disadvantaged children the most. This should reduce inequalities of schooling and income.

There are also several macroeconomic reasons for believing in a long-run link between fertility and inequality. Some of these relate to the presumed effects of fertility, through labor supply, on the structure of wage rates and the level of profits:

> (4) A drop in fertility means fewer labor-force entrants a generation later. This in turn should accelerate the rise of all employee wage rates—skilled and unskilled—relative to profit rates and to rates of return on property. Since the ownership of property is almost always distributed less equally than is human earning power, a rise in employee wage rates relative to rates of return for property-holders and profit recipients makes income more equally distributed.
>
> (5) Among employees, the reduced dispersion, and higher average level, of skills caused by the microeconomic effects of birth reduction [see (1) and (2) above] should further reduce inequality of earnings by bidding down the premia earned by higher-paid

---

demographic effect. With lower fertility, both the average age and the dispersion in ages of the adult population would be higher. In a skill-based economy like that of twentieth-century America, the level and variance of earnings rise steeply with age. In such a setting, a lower level of prior fertility would be accompanied by higher inequality of income among adults, other things equal. This tendency is likely to be outweighed, however, by the effects (1) and (2). It would also be countered by the very tendency for this aging of the adult population to bid down the pay advantage of older and more experienced workers over younger, more recent labor force entrants. This last effect is implicit in effect (5) in the text.

employees. That is, fertility reduction should raise the wage rates of unskilled labor more than it raises skilled wage rates.

Other macroeconomic arguments relate to the effects of changes in fertility on the demand for final products. Extra children, like extra immigrants or a decline in incomes, tend to shift consumer demand somewhat toward agricultural products, especially food. This suggests that a decline in fertility should tend to have three effects on overall inequality:

(6) By shifting demand away from agricultural products, reductions in fertility may lower the relative price of these products. This would tend to reduce inequalities in real purchasing power to the extent that agricultural products are a greater share of the cost of living of poor families than of rich.

(7) The same demand shift would cause a shift of labor and capital out of agriculture, in proportions that would reduce the farm sector's share of total labor employment more noticeably than its share of total capital employment would be reduced. This shift of low-paid labor out of agriculture into what tend to be higher-paid jobs elsewhere should reduce inequality somewhat, farm labor being among the lowest-paid in the country.

(8) On the other hand, the shift in demand away from agriculture is a shift toward sectors that use low-paid labor less intensively. This might weaken the relative pay position of unskilled laborers somewhat, causing a counter-tendency toward inequality.

These three demand effects of fertility decline are each probably of less magnitude than the other macroeconomic effects, which operated through labor supply. The net demand effect is also not likely to be large, since the last demand effect pulls in the opposite direction from the first two.

For reasons like these, theory tends to favor the argument that fertility should be positively linked to inequality. Most general-equilibrium models imply that a rise in the labor force, as would result from rising fertility with a lag of one generation, would lower wage rates and raise returns on capital. Econometric models also suggest that an exogenous rise in the labor force should retard the advance of wage rates even in the short run.[3] A recent model simulating the effects of birth rates on inequality over the generations predicts what was predicted in (1) and (2)

---

[3] Charles E. Metcalf, *An Econometric Model of the Income Distribution*, Chicago: Markham Publishing Company, 1972.

above.[4] As far as theory goes, the arguments above seem reasonable. Do they fit the facts revealed by American experience?

The empirical link from fertility to inequality is traced in two stages. This chapter pursues the evidence relating to the microeconomic and strain-on-public-schools effects. The microeconomic influences of family size on child achievements are first confirmed by tests avoiding a potential weakness shared by earlier studies linking family size with achievement. The implied contribution of reduced fertility to equalization of educational attainment via family-input effects is then quantified. The final section of this chapter shows that the aggregate evidence for the United States is remarkably consistent with the strain-on-public-schools argument. The next chapter surveys the observed movements in income inequality in the United States since colonial times, and concludes that these movements are very consistent with the set of hypotheses above.

II. *Family Size and Sibling Achievement*

Many studies have concluded that children raised in larger families tend to have lower I.Q.'s, leave school earlier, and end up in lower-status, lower-paying jobs—other things equal.[5] This result is usually interpreted as showing that larger family size strains parents' ability to devote time, energy, and money to each child. The strain-on-family-resources interpretation seems to receive further support from studies of the consequences of birth order.[6] First-borns seem to have higher I.Q.'s and achievements than middle-born or last-born children, for any given

---

[4] Frederick Pryor, "Simulations of the Impact of Social and Economic Institutions on the Size Distribution of Income and Wealth," *American Economic Review* 63, no. 1 (March 1973), 50–72.

[5] For references to the vast empirical literature tying family size to subsequent achievement, see my earlier discussion paper "Family Inputs and Inequality among Children," Institute for Research on Poverty, University of Wisconsin, Discussion Paper no. 218–74, October 1974, available from the Institute (Madison, Wisconsin 53706). Hereafter this discussion paper is cited as "Family Inputs and Inequality." Two more recent contributions to the literature, not focusing on educational and career attainments, are Kenneth W. Terhune, *A Review of the Actual and Expected Consequences of Family Size*, U.S. Department of Health, Education, and Welfare, National Institutes of Health, Publication No. (NIH) 75–779, 1975; and Lillian Belmont and Francis A. Marolla, "Birth Order, Family Size, and Intelligence," *Science* 182 (1973), 1096–1101.

[6] For references to the debate over the effects of birth order, again see "Family Inputs and Inequality." Most of the literature focuses on the alleged advantage of first-borns over all later-born siblings. Only with respect to patterns of achievement, and not I.Q., emotional stability, or other variables, has it been argued that last-borns have an advantage over middle-borns for given family size.

family size. The last-borns tend to stay in school longer than middle-borns, though they have no I.Q. advantage. These patterns suggest that the middle-born children are disadvantaged by being forced to compete with siblings for parental resources throughout their childhood, while last-borns receive generous parental inputs only staying in school in their teens, after the other siblings have left the household. The birth-order results thus point to the same strains on parental resources emphasized by authors of studies of the effects of family size.

The family-size results clearly imply that reductions in fertility would raise average achievement levels. They further imply that any reduction in the dispersion of family size, a common accompaniment to reductions in average family size, will tend to equalize the educational and career attainments of children. If these implications are correct, then the "baby bust" that began in the 1960s should improve both the average achievement and the economic equality of the children born in this era of low fertility, even aside from the tendency of this restriction on future labor supply to cut down the percentage pay premia enjoyed by those with extra schooling and skills.

A. THE PROBLEM OF OMITTED VARIABLES

For all the attention devoted to the relationship of achievement to sibling position, the entire literature remains vulnerable to a single line of attack: other important variables have not been held constant, and any correlation between these omitted variables and sibling position (number of siblings and birth order) can yield misleading estimates of the impact of the latter. The most serious omitted variables are unobserved parental characteristics related to child orientation or tastes and ability for developing achievement in individual children. The danger of bias in estimates of the effects of sibling position can be seen most easily by supposing that sets of parents with the same observable attributes (e.g., occupation, education, race, region, religion) differ in their trade-offs between fertility and inputs per child. It could well be that parents with greater tastes or abilities for grooming achievers than other parents with the same observed attributes tend to have fewer children in order to pour more resources into each child. If so, then studies showing that greater family size (or middle-sib position, which is correlated with family size) depresses achievement may really be showing only the relevance of unobserved parental tastes and abilities for grooming achievers. This difficulty in interpreting the family-size and birth-order results would cause little harm if it were simply noted. Unfortunately, by not noting it, studies of the "consequences" of family size may overstate the positive effect on child achievement of such exogenous antinatal influences as improved access to birth control, improved job opportunities for women, and tougher tax policies toward dependents. We need to know how to divide up the apparent effects of family size on child achievement (holding constant the observable parental attributes) between the influence of unobserved parental attributes and all other influences on family size.

Until the problem of omitted parental variables is attacked with better tests, there exists an opportunity for a revisionist attack on the past studies that saw a link between family size (or birth order) and achievement. Pronatalists could raise the issue of omitted variables, add any of several suspicions about the data used in past studies, and advance the unresolved suggestion that being from a large family or being a later-born is not bad at all. Some initial steps have already been taken in this revisionist direction.[7]

The issue need not be left in such an uncertain state. The problem of unobserved parental attributes can be minimized by tests linking differences in achievement among siblings raised together to sibling positions and other variables. In what follows I shall: (1) retest the link between sibling position and educational and career attainments, using a cross section of pairs of siblings; (2) suggest and test a simple explanation of the observed patterns relating sibling position to achievement, an explanation focusing on family inputs into child development; and (3) quantify the impact of improved contraception on the subsequent level and inequality of a birth cohort's educational attainments.

It turns out that the link between sibling position and achievement is significant even when age and parents' attributes have been held constant. One reason for the importance of sibling position appears to be the fact that it affects the time inputs into the individual child more strongly than do the ages, status, and labor force participation of the parents. The impact of improved contraception on the distribution of achievements in the next generation turns out to be as important as, or possibly more important than, would be inferred from past studies. The family-inputs index which helps to underline these points emerges as a variable which some studies of achievement might profitably use as a

[7] Philip R. Kunz and Evan T. Peterson, "Family Size and Academic Achievement," and Darwin L. Thomas, "Family Size and Children's Characteristics," both in Howard M. Bahr, Bruce A. Chadwick, and Darwin L. Thomas, eds., *Population, Resources, and the Future: Non-Malthusian Perspectives,* Provo, Utah: Brigham Young University Press, 1972.

more efficient proxy for family-structure effects than the number of siblings.

B. THE NEW JERSEY SIBLING SAMPLE

A convincing test of whether and why sibling position matters to achievement requires a sample with data on intrafamily achievement differentials. The data should also allow one to make adjustments for age to take account of the fact that different cohorts of growing children experienced different access to schooling. A sample that meets these requirements is the sample of 1,087 siblings collected in 1963, when a Cornell Medical School team interviewed 312 senior male employees of a New Jersey utility company in search of information about the incidence of heart disease.[8] The 312 interview respondents were asked, among other things, for the age, sex, educational attainment, and most recent occupation of each of their siblings, living or dead. The respondents themselves ranged in age from 55 to 61, and the ages of their siblings ranged from 31 to 81. The sibling sample thus consists of persons old enough that their formal schooling had been completed. Furthermore, only a dozen siblings were under 40 in 1963, so that the boom in incomes and educational opportunity after Pearl Harbor (e.g., the GI bill) must have had no effect on the schooling or first jobs of almost all of the sample.[9]

The nature of the New Jersey sibling sample does complicate the present inquiry in one respect, however. The interview respondents were clustered into the higher educational and occupational classes, being all long-term employees of a company with a high average skill level. This high average status need not be a problem in itself, but two other facts

---

[8] For a more detailed description of the sample and for extensive analysis of the homogeneity of the siblings in the sample, see Albert I. Hermalin, "The Homogeneity of Siblings on Education and Occupation," Ph.D. dissertation, Princeton University, 1969.

The elimination of observations with incomplete information narrowed the sample from 1,087 siblings, including the 312 respondents, to 1,008 siblings, including 289 respondents.

Larger samples may soon be available which meet the requirement of having data on the age, sex, education, and occupation of each adult sibling. One possibility, being explored by Professor Hermalin, is that the original interview sheets of the 1965 Productive Americans survey will yield these data on all the grown children of several hundred elderly respondents. Another source of such data, apparently, will be the 1970 National Fertility Survey. These samples could be employed as a cross-check on the results reported here, but were not available at the time of writing.

[9] Unreported regressions showed that removing the twelve siblings under forty had no effect on intrafamily patterns of educational attainment.

make it a problem. First, the respondents had a higher average schooling and career achievement than the average levels they reported for their own siblings. Second, the likelihood that any given sibling in the sample was himself the interview respondent is closely related to his sibling position, and in particular to his family size. In the absence of any other information about an individual in the sample, we know that the probability of his being one of the high-achievement respondent group is $1/N$, where N is the number of siblings in his family. Thus all only children were interview respondents, as were half the siblings from two-child families, one-third of the siblings from three-child families, and so forth. Thus in this sample there is an unavoidable relationship between family size and respondent status, and another relationship between respondent status and predicted achievement.

The selection bias involved in the sample design can be handled in various ways. The range of options can be seen more clearly by referring to the casual relationships portrayed in Figure 6–1. The first option is the "reduced-form" strategy of arguing that the probability that an individual is the interview respondent for his family is itself simply one channel through which the true importance of sibling position for achievement shows up in this particular sample. Following this strategy, one would simply ignore who the respondents were, and run regressions explaining achievements in terms of the variables on the left in Part A of Figure 6–1: family background, sibling position, and sex. This procedure, of course, is likely to overestimate the importance of sibling position and sex. The interview respondents were not a random sample of males, nor were the only-child respondents a random sample of only children, nor the two-sibling respondents a random sample of persons from two-child families, and so forth. Such a strategy will be tried out below, but with the expectation that it overstates the importance of sibling position.

Two other testing options are likely to attribute less, and probably too little, importance to sibling position as a determinant of achievement. One is the device of adding a dummy variable for respondent status to the regressions explaining educational and career attainments. This is likely to understate both the unit impact and the statistical significance of sibling position. By mixing the respondents into the sample, this procedure is biased against sibling position by implicitly denying that sibling position was an influence in the likelihood of one's being a respondent in this survey, and by including a subsample (the respondents) selected

Figure 6-1. Influences on Predicted Achievement in the New Jersey Sibling Sample

A. *Achievements by Individuals in Different Families.*

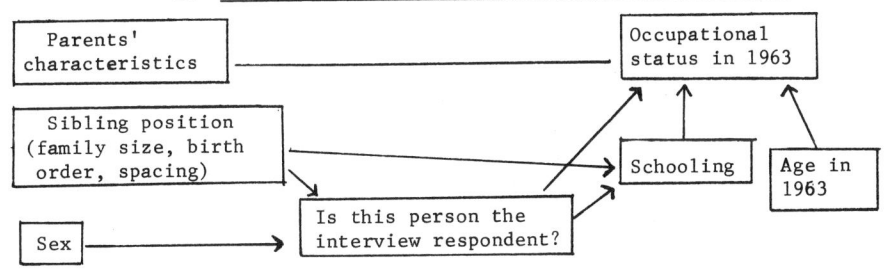

[Diagram: Parents' characteristics → Occupational status in 1963; Sibling position (family size, birth order, spacing) → Schooling; Sex → Is this person the interview respondent?; Schooling and Age in 1963 → Occupational status in 1963]

(The other possible arrows from left to right have been omitted because they failed to prove statistically significant.)

B. *Achievement Differentials within Families.*

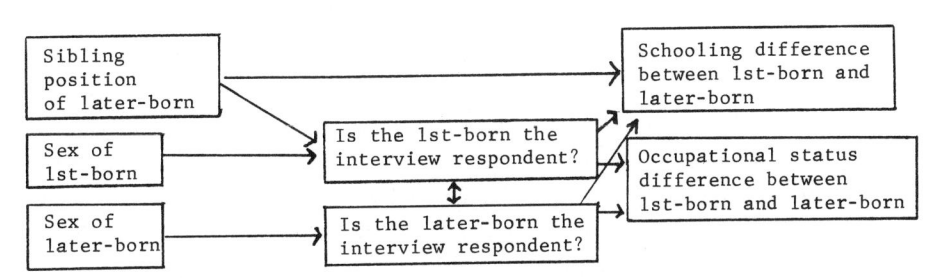

[Diagram: Sibling position of later-born → Schooling difference between 1st-born and later-born; Sex of 1st-born → Is the 1st-born the interview respondent?; Sex of later-born → Is the later-born the interview respondent? → Occupational status difference between 1st-born and later-born]

by occupational class, within which any independent variable has diminished explanatory power.

A better procedure is to run tests on the subsample of nonrespondents. This can keep the nature of the respondents from biasing the estimates of the impact of sibling position. Still, a test on a sample of siblings who are not respondents is a stern one for the sibling-position hypotheses. It cuts down the representation of the small families over which family size was supposed to matter most. A test from a sample of nonrespondents is thus likely to underestimate the significance (t-statistics) of sibling position variables.

FROM FERTILITY TO INEQUALITY

The best way of dealing with the special nature of the sample, however, is to run the kind of test that is also best for meeting the suspicions about omitted family variables raised by the past literature: examine *intrafamily* differentials in achievement. Part B of Figure 6–1 sketches a set of influences that could be tested by redefining all variables as differentials between the first-born and a later-born, to be employed over a sample consisting of all of the later-borns (non–first-borns) in the New Jersey sibling sample. Explaining intrafamily differences in achievement should give the most accurate indication of the importance of sibling position. The special nature of the group of interview respondents is a lesser problem in an intrafamily test. Since family size is the same for each first-born as for each of his own siblings, a first-born and each later-born in the same family have the same likelihood of being the interview respondent working for the New Jersey utility (except to the extent that birth order truly affects achievement). Therefore regressions following the scheme of Part B in Figure 6–1 should reveal the role of sibling position with or without dummy variables identifying the interview respondents. These intrafamily tests, and the other testing options just mentioned, will be probed next.

C. ACHIEVEMENT PATTERNS: REGRESSION RESULTS

When all of the different ways of correcting for the special nature of the New Jersey sibling sample have been tried, it turns out that sibling position is at least as significant an influence on achievement as past literature implied, and for the simple reason that sharing family time and money with siblings is a drag on achievement. This conclusion emerges from results like those given in Tables 6–1 through 6–3. To survey these results, let us examine the three tables in order.

Whenever the schooling levels of individuals in different families are analyzed, as in Table 6–1, certain background variables prove unmistakably significant. Schooling levels are higher, the higher the parents' schooling levels and occupational status are. A broken-home background significantly reduces one's likely educational attainment. Sex and age, on the other hand, were not significant influences on schooling in this sample. Both sex and age looked significant only in those regressions where they were allowed to act as proxies for interview respondent status, the respondents being all male and all over 55 [cf. Regressions (1) and (4) in Table 6–1].

Any of several specifications predicts that greater family size reduces the schooling expected for each sibling. The first three regressions also

FERTILITY AND INVESTMENTS IN CHILDREN

Table 6.1.   Patterns of Individual Educational Attainment: Regression Results from the New Jersey Sibling Sample

Independent variable	Regression number (dependent variable is ED):					
	(1)		(2)		(3)	
	coeff.	std.err.	coeff.	std.err.	coeff.	std.err.
Constant term	-1.815	(2.268)	1.198	(2.351)	1.233	(2.343)
MALE	.298**	(.109)	.076	(.116)	.078	(.118)
EDMA	.249**	(.052)	.226**	(.060)	.251**	(.052)
EDPA	.220**	(.046)	.260**	(.053)	.233**	(.046)
SEIPA	.018**	(.003)	.018**	(.003)	.018**	(.003)
BROKEN	-.505**	(.172)	-.582**	(.201)	-.526**	(.170)
AGE	.138	(.078)	.035	(.081)	.033	(.081)
AGESQ	-.0014*	(.0007)	-.0005	(.0007)	-.0005	(.0007)
RESP	---	---	---	---	.636**	(.140)
SIBLOSS	---	---	---	---	---	---
ONLY	1.071**	(.294)	---	---	.658*	(.305)
FIRST2	.742**	(.216)	.718*	(.316)	.512*	(.219)
FIRST3	.531*	(.238)	.533	(.283)	.410	(.237)
FIRST45	.209	(.217)	.248	(.232)	.178	(.215)
FIRST613	.638*	(.269)	.625*	(.287)	.589*	(.267)
MID3	.613*	(.236)	.644*	(.263)	.551*	(.234)
MID45CLO	.086	(.250)	.007	(.264)	.111	(.248)
MID45WID	.250	(.176)	.151	(.193)	.194	(.175)
LATTER	.454	(.215)	.365	(.252)	.369	(.214)
LAST3	.436	(.238)	.346	(.282)	.329	(.237)
LAST45	.480	(.221)	.489	(.248)	.387	(.220)
LAST613	.455	(.276)	.300	(.306)	.315	(.275)

$R^2_{adj.}$/s.e.e.   .3074/1.5866   .3144/1.5334   .3210/1.5709

degrees of freedom: 988   700   987

Sample: 1008 persons   719 nonrespondents   1008 persons

* = significant at the 5 percent level
** = significant at the 1 percent level.

NOTE: the coefficients on sibling-position binary variables show the impacts of these positions relative either to middle children in families of sic or more [in Regressions (1)-(3)] or to all children in families of six or more children [in Regression (7)].

Table 6-1 (cont.). Patterns of Individual Educational Attainment: Regression Results from the New Jersey Sibling Sample

Independent variable	Regression number (dependent variable is ED):					
	(4)		(5)		(6)	
	coeff.	std.err.	coeff.	std.err.	coeff.	std.err.
constant term	-1.252	(2.134)	1.919	(2.152)	1.770	(2.196)
MALE	.302**	(.108)	.058	(.115)	.063	(.117)
EDMA	.250**	(.052)	.229**	(.060)	.253**	(.052)
EDPA	.223**	(.046)	.261**	(.053)	.224**	(.045)
SEIPA	.018**	(.003)	.018**	(.003)	.018**	(.003)
BROKEN	-.482**	(.170)	-.572**	(.199)	-.505**	(.168)
AGE	.152*	(.074)	.039	(.075)	.034	(.077)
AGESQ	-.0015*	(.0007)	-.0005	(.0006)	-.0004	(.0007)
RESP	---	---	---	---	.680**	(.137)
SIBLOSS	-2.393**	(.611)	-2.236*	(.968)	-1.373*	(.638)
R^2_{adj}/s.e.e.	.3054/1.5889		.3128/1.5351		.3214/1.5705	
degrees of freedom:	999		710		998	
Sample:	1008 persons		719 non-respondents		1008 persons	

Independent variable	Regression number (dependent variable is ED):					
	(7)		(8)		(9)	
	coeff.	std.err.	coeff.	std.err.	coeff.	std.err.
constant term	-.387	(2.181)	.121	(2.250)	.596	(2.253)
MALE	.300**	(.109)	.333**	(.108)	.303**	(.108)
EDMA	.251**	(.052)	.248**	(.052)	.251**	(.052)
EDPA	.218**	(.046)	.228**	(.046)	.216**	(.046)
SEIPA	.018**	(.003)	.017**	(.003)	.018**	(.003)
BROKEN	-.511**	(.172)	-.489**	(.171)	-.492**	(.171)
AGE	.093	(.076)	.095	(.077)	.092	(.077)
AGESQ	-.0010	(.0007)	-.0010	(.0007)	-.0010	(.0007)
RESP	---	---	---	---	---	---
SIBLOSS	---	---	---	---	---	---
ONLY	.945**	(.291)	---	---	---	---
TWO	.464**	(.165)	---	---	---	---
THREE	.389*	(.154)	---	---	---	---
FOUR	.137	(.156)	---	---	---	---
FIVE	.109	(.155)	---	---	---	---
N	---	---	-.073**	(.022)	-.245**	(.075)
NSQ	---	---	---	---	.014*	(.006)
R^2_{adj}/s.e.e.	.3045/1.5899		.3025/1.5922		.3058/1.5884	
degrees of freedom:	995		999		998	
Sample:	1008 persons		1008 persons		1008 persons	

* = significant at the 5 percent level.
** = significant at the 1 percent level.

Definitions of Variables Used in Tables 6-1 and 6-2

Dependent Variables

ED = a one-digit schooling code, ranging in values from 1, for less than an eighth-grade education, to 8, for five or more years of college. (As explained in "Family Inputs and Inequality," an alternative scaling was also tried, one based on the logarithm of earnings predicted for levels of schooling, but it yielded results essentially identical to those reported here for ED.)

SEI = a two-digit index of socio-economic status, based on the individual's most recent occupation. The index number assignments were made by Professor Albert I. Hermalin.

Independent Variables

MALE = 1 if the individual is a male, 0 if female.

EDMA = the mother's educational attainment = ED for the mother.

EDPA = the father's educational attainment = ED for the father.

SEIPA = the socioeconomic status of the father's final occupation = SEI for the father.

BROKEN = dummy variable for a broken home during the individual's childhood = 1 if the parents were separated or divorced or if the interview respondent spent time in a foster home or an orphanage.

AGE = the individual's age in 1963, in years.

AGESQ = AGE squared.

RESP = 1 if this individual is the interview respondent, 0 if this is one of his siblings.

SIBLOSS = index of reduction in time inputs received by the child because of his having siblings = one minus the index given for the appropriate sibling position in Table 6-4. The indices calculated for one-year spacing in Table 6-4 were used whenever average child spacing was less than 1.5 years; the two-year indices were used for spacing from 1.5 years to 2.5; the three-year figures for spacing from 2.5 to 4.5; and the six-year figures for spacing over 4.5 years.

ONLY = 1 if the individual is an only child, 0 otherwise.

FIRST2, FIRST3, FIRST45, FIRST613 each = 1 when the individual is the first-born of two, three, four or five, and six through thirteen children, respectively.

MID3, MID45CLO, MID45WID = 1 when the individual is an intermediate-born child of three children, of four or five children spaced more closely than two years apart, or of four or five children spaced two years or more apart, respectively.

LATTER, LAST3, LAST45, LAST613 = 1 when the individual is the last-born of two, three, four or five, or six or more children, respectively.

TWO,THREE,FOUR,FIVE = 1 when the number of siblings (including the respondent) is two, three, four, or five, respectively.

N = number of siblings (including the respondent).

NSQ = N squared.

Table 6-2. Patterns of Individual Career Status Attainment: Regression Results from the New Jersey Sibling Sample

Independent variable	Regression number (dependent variable is SEI):							
	(1)		(2)		(3)		(4)	
	coeff.	std.err.	coeff.	std.err.	coeff.	std.err.	coeff.	std.err.
constant term	-190.66**	(39.11)	-90.16*	(40.26)	-179.26**	(37.68)	-81.72*	(38.57)
EDPA	1.78*	(0.74)	1.91**	(0.71)	1.80*	(0.73)	1.86**	(0.70)
EDMA	0.83	(0.84)	0.85	(0.81)	0.79*	(0.84)	0.84	(0.81)
SEIPA	0.22**	(0.04)	0.22**	(0.04)	0.22**	(0.04)	0.22**	(0.04)
BROKEN	-7.12*	(2.88)	-7.40**	(2.77)	-6.96*	(2.84)	-7.54**	(2.73)
AGE	8.11**	(1.35)	4.47**	(1.40)	8.09**	(1.29)	4.25**	(1.34)
AGESQ	-0.07**	(0.01)	-0.04**	(0.01)	-0.07**	(0.01)	-0.04**	(0.01)
RESP	---	---	13.35**	(1.88)	---	---	13.59**	(1.84)
SIBLOSS	---	---	---	---	-36.82**	(8.94)	-14.18	(9.13)
ONLY	13.08**	(4.03)	4.21	(4.08)	---	---	---	---
FIRST2	11.45**	(3.27)	5.38	(3.27)	---	---	---	---
FIRST3	3.94	(3.92)	0.35	(3.81)	---	---	---	---
FIRST45	4.78	(3.78)	3.65	(3.64)	---	---	---	---
FIRST613	10.01*	(4.63)	8.42	(4.47)	---	---	---	---
MID3	7.35	(4.04)	4.91	(3.90)	---	---	---	---
MID45CLO	-3.14	(4.20)	-2.52	(4.05)	---	---	---	---
MID45WID	1.24	(2.89)	-0.68	(2.80)	---	---	---	---
LATTER	4.58	(3.39)	1.84	(3.29)	---	---	---	---
LAST3	2.39	(3.87)	-0.87	(3.75)	---	---	---	---
LAST45	0.86	(3.68)	-1.91	(3.56)	---	---	---	---
LAST613	8.09	(5.03)	3.60	(4.89)	---	---	---	---
R^2_{adj}/s.e.e.	.2125/20.97		.2688/20.20		.2112/20.98		.2708/20.17	
degrees of freedom	640		639		651		650	

Sample: 659 males.

* = significant at the 5 percent level.
** = significant at the 1 percent level.

suggest that closer child spacing (for four- and five-child families) may be a disadvantage for educational attainment, but the spacing pattern was not statistically significant. As for birth order [in Regressions (1)–(3)], the hypothesized disadvantage of being a middle child shows up among families with more than three children, but fails to pass significance tests.

All family background variables tend to explain schooling levels better than they explain lifetime occupational achievements. The reason is that other events intervene between the completion of schooling and the peak of one's career. Accordingly, Table 6–2 shows that all background variables are less significant, and account for a smaller share of total variation, when it comes to explaining career status rather than schooling. Not surprisingly, age has much more to do with occupational status than

FERTILITY AND INVESTMENTS IN CHILDREN

with one's schooling. Respondent status is strongly significant as well, since the respondents were drawn from a fairly high-status occupational group. Sibling position, like the other background variables, is not statistically significant as a job status determinant [in Regressions (2) and (4) in Table 6–2], though its coefficients are still generally of the "right" sign.

The best tests for resolving suspicions about omitted variables are the intrafamily regressions reported in Table 6–3. These regressions convert the models of Table 6–1 into equivalent intrafamily differential form.[10]

One might expect that the intrafamily tests would be difficult ones for the sibling-position hypothesis to pass. When the dependent variable is a differential in the schooling of two siblings raised together, R^2 is going to be low. The dependent variable is a single digit, and some of the most powerful determinants of achievement across families—parents' education and occupational status, a broken-home history, and even completed family size—are of no help in accounting for intrafamily differentials. In view of the fact that family size was a more important determinant of predicted inputs into each child than were birth order and spacing, it would have been no surprise if Table 6–3 had reported only an insignificant influence of differences in family inputs on differences in schooling.

It is thus striking to find how much sibling position does seem to matter within families. Some predicted contrasts pass significance tests. First-borns end up with a significant edge in schooling over middle-borns of the same sex in families with six or more children [see first three terms in Regression (1) in Table 6–3]. Last-borns among four or five have an advantage over their eldest brothers and sisters that contrasts significantly with the disadvantage of middle-borns among six or more relative to their eldest siblings (LAST45 term in the same regression). Not significant, but of the "right" sign, are the advantages of last-borns over middle-borns within large families of given size (LAST613, and LAST45 versus the MID45's). In other words, a tough intrafamily test of the importance of birth order tends to support the same arguments about the disadvantages of sibling crowding that underlie the belief in a disadvantage of large family size.

Thus far, however, we have been retesting only the hypothesis that sibling position (family size, birth order, and child spacing) matters to

---

[10] The analogy between the models of Table 6–1 and those of Table 6–3 would be closer if terms corresponding to AGE and AGESQ had been included in the intrafamily regressions of Table 6–3. Regressions with the appropriate age-difference variables were run, but were not reported in Table 6–3 since the age-difference variables were never significant.

[195]

FROM FERTILITY TO INEQUALITY

Table 6-3   Intra-Family Differences in Educational Attainment:
Regression Results from the New Jersey Sibling Sample

Regression number (Dependent variable is EDDIF):

Independent Variable	(1) coeff. std.err.	(2) coeff. std.err.	(3) coeff. std.err.
constant term	.440 * (.200)	-.198 (.152)	-.208 (.152)
MALE1	.253 (.146)	.275 (.145)	.528 ** (.133)
MALEH	-.155 (.145)	-.144 (.145)	-.429 ** (.134)
RESPI	.479 * (.191)	.521 ** (.177)	-
RESPH	-.634 ** (.180)	-.657 ** (.178)	-
DIFINPUT	-	4.758 **(1.819)	4.983 **(1.813)
LATTER	-.112 (.261)	-	-
LAST3	-.347 (.260)	-	-
LAST45	-.719 ** (.232)	-	-
LAST613	-.428 (.280)	-	-
MID3	-.355 (.259)	-	-
MID45CLO	-.340 (.267)	-	--
MID45WID	-.304 (.195)	-	-
SPACEIN	-.065 (.043)	-	-
$R^2_{adj.}$/s.e.e.	.0785/1.7491	.0752/1.7522	.0396/1.7856
degrees of freedom	754	761	763

*=significant at the 5% level.
**=significant at the 1% level.

<u>The Sample:</u>

767 later-born (not first-born) siblings from 269 families, each compared in achievement with the first-born from the same family.

Note: the sibling-position binary variables in Regression (1) yield coefficients comparing the impact of assuming each later-born position relative to being a middle child in a family with six or more children. Thus, for example, the coefficient on LAST613 indicates the extent to which the schooling advantage of first-borns over last-borns in these large families differs from (in this case, is less than) the advantage of first-borns over middle children in families of six or more children.

achievement. The underlying presumption that it matters because sibling crowding strains family resources has not been tested, since we lack a quantification of just how the strain on family resources is supposed to vary over family sizes, birth orders, and child spacing. We next develop a set of indices of family inputs received by children in different sibling positions. These indices will then be examined as influences on achievement, influences represented by the special variables SIBLOSS and DIFINPUT in Tables 6–1 through 6–3.

FERTILITY AND INVESTMENTS IN CHILDREN

TABLE 6–3. INTRA-FAMILY DIFFERENCES IN EDUCATIONAL ATTAINMENT: REGRESSION RESULTS FROM THE NEW JERSEY SIBLING SAMPLE

DEFINITIONS OF VARIABLES USED

The Dependent Variable

EDDIF = the first-born's educational advantage = the difference between the schooling level attained by the first-born sibling and that attained by one later-born sibling in the same family. The schooling level in this case is a one-digit code with values from 1, for less than an eighth-grade education, to 8, for five or more years of college.

The Independent Variables

MALE1 = 1 if the first-born is a male, 0 if female.

MALEH = 1 if the later-born to whom the observation applies is a male, 0 if female.

RESP1 = 1 if the first-born is the (male) interview respondent working for the utility company in 1963, 0 otherwise. The function of this and the next variable is to quantify whatever distorting influences may have arisen from the facts that the interview respondents are a specially selected group of employees and that they may have systematically misreported their siblings' schooling.

RESPH = 1 if the later born to whom the observation applies is the interview respondent.

DIFINPUT = the difference between the index of time inputs that the first-born child is predicted to have received and the same index for the later-born child, where the input indices are those given in Table 6–4. The figures calculated for one-year spacing were used whenever average child spacing was less than 1.5 years; the two-year figures were used for spacing from 1.5 years to 2.5; the three-year figures for spacing from 2.5 to 4.5; and the six-year figures for spacing over 4.5 years.

LATTER = 1 if the later-born to which the observation applies is the second of two children.

LAST3 = 1 if the later-born is the last of three children, 0 otherwise.

LAST45 = 1 if the later-born is the last of four or the last of five, 0 otherwise.

LAST613 = 1 if the later-born is the last of from six to thirteen children (no families had more than thirteen children), 0 otherwise.

MID3 = 1 if the later-born is the second of three children, 0 otherwise.

MID45CLO = 1 if the later-born is a middle (intermediate-born) child in a family of four or five children and the number of years in age to the next oldest sibling plus the number of years to the next youngest sibling is less than 4, 0 otherwise.

MID45WID = 1 if the later born is a middle child in a family of four of five children and the number of years separating the next oldest sibling and the next youngest sibling is greater than or equal to 4, 0 otherwise.

SPACE1N = the average spacing between siblings in the same family = the years separating the oldest and the youngest in the family divided by (the number of siblings minus one).

D. THE LINK WITH FAMILY INPUT PATTERNS

There are many competing hypotheses about how sibling position affects achievement and other dimensions of child development. Some hypotheses feature differences in parental expectations by birth order. Others link family size with parental resort methods of behavior control that are external, autocratic, achievement-retarding, and labor-saving. Though the true origins of the influence of sibling position remain a legitimate subject for debate, most of the competing hypotheses agree on a *proximate* cause of whatever importance sibling position may seem to have. They share the belief that achievements (and some other personality traits) are influenced by the extent to which a child shares the time, emotional energy, and financial resources of adults with other children of similar age. It is generally believed, in other words, that a child receives from brothers and sisters less support for the development of career-relevant skills than he loses through their competition for the attention and support of adults.

Quantifying the above arguments about family inputs into a child requires using regression estimates from both time-use surveys and consumption surveys to calculate the expected effect of children in various sibling positions on family expenditures of time and money, given the attributes of the adults in the household. This procedure is complicated, time-consuming, and full of pitfalls, but reasonable estimates can be obtained. In what follows I shall focus mainly on the patterns of apparent time inputs into children and shall treat patterns of commodity inputs into children more briefly.

1. Time Inputs into Siblings. Using time-use surveys to infer how much time each child receives requires two steps. First, one must run regressions to determine how the total amounts of time spent by individual family members on child care vary with the numbers and ages of the children present. The second step is to rely on some key theoretical assumptions in order to convert the observed patterns of total child care into estimates of the amount of attention time received by each child per day or week or year. Theoretical assumptions are unavoidable in this second step, because of two problems of interpretation. The first problem is that it is often hard to decide whether a given activity constitutes caring for or interacting with children. The other main problem is in allocating to an individual child a part of the total time report as "child care."

Appendix C spells out at length my choice of key assumptions for estimating the amount of time inputs received by each sibling per day for different days of the week and seasons of the year. These assumptions have been applied to regressions on total child care time in a Cornell time-use survey of 1,296 Syracuse families in 1967–68.

Even without the aid of assumptions about the allocation of total child-care time among siblings, the regressions in Appendix C underline the importance of the ages as well as the numbers of children in determining parents' patterns of time use. The ages of the children dominate differences in child care time, with infants contributing far more to daily or annual hours of child care than children of school age, as noted in Chapter 4 above. Extra numbers of children also raise child care burdens at a decreasing rate, as one would expect. These patterns hold both for the mother's time and for the total time contributed by all persons to caring for the children of one family.

Attributes of the parents prove much less important than the ages and numbers of children as determinants of amounts of child care time. The mother's age, her education, and the father's socioeconomic status all fail to exert statistically significant influences on the total amount of care time given to children of given number and ages. It appears that the only way in which more-educated wives as a group manage to devote more time to each child is by having fewer children on the average.[11]

The importance of family composition even eclipses that of the mother's work status. It turns out that for given ages and numbers of children, mothers who work for pay outside the home spend only slightly less time in child care than nonworking mothers. The differences by work status are only near the border of statistical significance in the Cornell sample, though a much larger sample might make them clearly significant. Furthermore, for given family composition, children of working mothers receive more total time in child care from all persons. That is, the estimated deficit in mother's time is more than made up by extra (nonschool) time inputs by the husband and others. In addition, if the numbers of children are not held constant, it turns out that working mothers, having fewer children on the average, spend as much of their own time *per child* on child care as do nonworking mothers.

[11] This finding contradicts the conclusion of other authors that more-educated mothers spend more time with their children even for given ages and number of children (C. Russell Hill and Frank P. Stafford, "Allocation of Time to Preschool Children and Educational Opportunity," mimeographed, Ann Arbor, 1972; Arleen Leibowitz, "Education and Home Production," *American Economic Review* 64, no. 2, May 1974, 243–250). Appendix C gives my reasons for concluding that their results are based on inappropriately measured variables.

If the number and ages of children are such dominant influences on the total amount of time devoted to child care, there is good reason to look more closely at estimates of how the amount of time going into an individual sibling is affected by the number and ages of his siblings. In addition to estimating these time inputs from various caretakers into each child each year, one must aggregate over caretakers and over the years of the child's life in a way that requires further assumptions. I have opted for the simplest aggregation procedure, and have added up all of the hours received by a child from any person in any of the eighteen years he is assumed to spend in his parents' household. The total numbers of hours for a child in each of several sibling positions are given in Table 6–4 and illustrated in Figure 6–2.

Several patterns emerge from Table 6–4's estimates of the time received by children in different sibling positions. In general these patterns correspond to the simple formula mentioned at the start of this section: the presence of an extra sibling of similar or lower age reduces the amount of time (and attention) that a child receives. The appearance of a younger sibling lowers time inputs for a child in most sibling positions. It is interesting to note, though, that the estimates find this effect stronger for the arrival of the second and third child in the family than for the arrival of the fourth. It may be that a first-born or second-born suffers no further loss of attention from the appearance of the fourth and later siblings. Being the youngest of four or more siblings may similarly be no worse in this respect than being the latter of two or the last of three. Indeed, the estimates imply that the youngest of four receives more time inputs than the youngest of three, in part because the first-born is often old enough to help with the care of the fourth child. The table also asserts that middle-born children receive fewer hours of care than the eldest and youngest in all cases, primarily because they lack the opportunity to be the only child in the household at any time in their lives. The estimates also imply that wider child spacing provides more hours of attention for the eldest and youngest but has an ambiguous effect for the middle children. Finally, the estimates imply that a last-born receives at least as much care time as a first-born in families of the same size, by receiving enough more attention as a school-age child to make up for the first-born's advantage in the preschool years before the arrival of siblings.

A slightly transformed version of the indices in Table 6–4 has been used in regressions in Tables 6–1 through 6–3, as a means of testing the hypothesis that sibling position affects achievement by affecting family inputs into the child. The slight transformation involved is the introduction of a new variable, SIBLOSS, which equals one minus the appropriate index shown in parentheses for each sibling position in Table 6–4. This transformation is intended to cover against uniform percentage errors in the deviation of the time inputs received by each non-only child from those received by an only child. SIBLOSS, in other words, is assumed to equal the fraction of input reduction from the only-child norm times an unknown constant. As long as this assumption is correct, the value of the unknown constant is irrelevant to the ability of sibling position to help in explaining achievement differentials.

2. *Commodity Inputs into Siblings.* Having brothers and sisters is also likely to affect the amount of goods and services purchased on a child's behalf by his parents and others. A child who must share adult attention in any given year must also share their financial resources with his siblings. The greater the number of children present, the harder it is for parents to give each one extra medical care, extra lessons, and a room of his own. As with time inputs, closer child spacing and middle-child position should be a disadvantage for the child—the more so, the harder it is for the parents to spend on his behalf out of prior savings or out of borrowings against earnings that will come after the child has left home. It seems reasonable, then, to make calculations exactly analogous to those just summarized for time inputs, calculations yielding an index of the commodity inputs received for each sibling position as a fraction of those for an only child from parents of the same attributes.

There are two steps to the calculation of a sibling commodity input index, the same two steps taken for time inputs in the previous section. The first is to run regressions quantifying the impact of the number and ages of children, along with other variables, on family consumption patterns. The second is to impose *a priori* assumptions about how the expenditures predicted for different family compositions are shared among individual children and adults within the family. The resulting index for the commodity inputs predicted for each sibling position could then be combined with the index for time inputs by some appropriate choice of weights, yielding an overall index of family inputs into each sibling, to be compared to that for an only child in a similar family.

The first step is easy. In Appendix C, I have estimated the impacts of numbers and ages of children on total family expenditures and on expenditures on eleven commodity classes, using the 1960–61 Survey of Consumer Expenditures. The second step is also easy in principle, but extremely tedious to carry out. As with time inputs, the unobservability of

FROM FERTILITY TO INEQUALITY

Table 6-4. Predicted Child-Care Time Received over 18 Years by Children in Various Sibling Positions, as a Fraction of That Predicted for an Only Child, by Years of Spacing Between Adjacent Children (Based on 1967-68 data)

Child spacing (uniform)	Children ever born	1st born	2nd born	3rd born	4th born	5th born
	only child	8227 hrs. (1.000)	--	--	--	--
1-year	2	6518 hrs. (.791)	6518 (.791)	--	--	--
	3	5528 (.672)	5393 (.656)	5528 (.672)	--	--
	4	5757 (.700)	5555 (.675)	5664 (.688)	5761 (.700)	--
2-year	2	6662 hrs. (.810)	6662 (.810)	--	--	--
	3	5690 (.692)	5435 (.661)	5698 (.693)	--	--
	4	5799 (.705)	5407 (.657)	5625 (.684)	5819 (.707)	--
3-year	2	6790 hrs. (.825)	6794 (.826)	--	--	--
	3	5853 (.711)	5468 (.665)	5867 (.713)	--	--
	4	5834 (.709)	5256 (.639)	5443 (.662)	6003 (.730)	--
6-year	2	7172 hrs. (.871)	7188 (.874)	--	--	--
	3	6338 (.770)	6049 (.735)	6604 (.803)	--	--
	4	6338 (.770)	5544 (.674)	5794 (.704)	6604 (.803)	--
	5	6338 (.770)	5544 (.674)	4959 (.603)	5794 (.704)	6604 (.803)

Note: The figure in parentheses is the ratio of the estimated time received by this child to that received by an only child.

Source: Appendix C, using regression results from the 1967-1968 Syracuse time use survey conducted by Professor Kathryn E. Walker and others in the College of Human Ecology, Cornell University. I am indebted to Professor Walker for making the survey data available for the present study.

FERTILITY AND INVESTMENTS IN CHILDREN

Figure 6-2.

Predicted Child-care Time Received over 18 years by Children in Various Sibling Positions, as a Fraction of that Predicted for an Only Child: The Case of Three-year Child Spacing

Index of care-time inputs
(1.000 = 8226.5 hrs.)

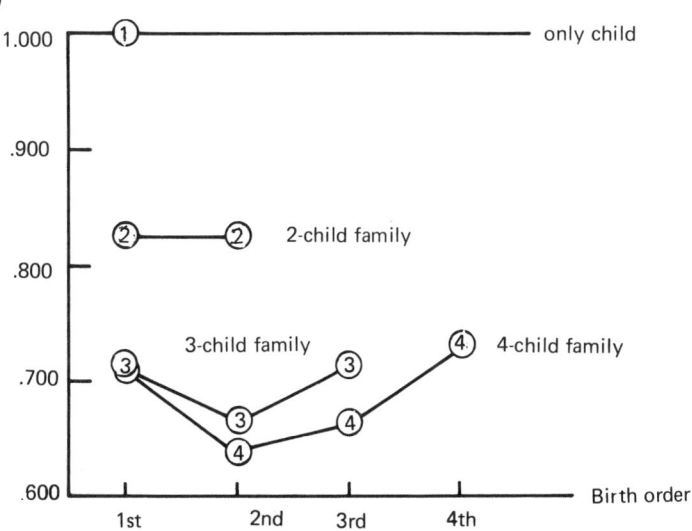

Source: Table 6-4 and Appendix C.

the amounts of inputs received by an individual child can be overcome if certain plausible assumptions are allowed. One can roughly assume, for example, that bedroom space and utilities are divided so as to give each child the same amount of space, heat, etc. One can approximate the expenditures on recreation and education for each child by dividing the total increment of expenditures for given family composition over that for a childless couple by the number of children. Expenditures on children's clothing could be allocated across the children in the family according to the ratios of only-child clothing expenditures for the different age groups. Finally, the USDA has made its own rough guesses as to the relationship of family size to the food and medical expenses of individual children. Plausible guesses like these can then be summed up to get a total value of commodity inputs for each sibling position. Unfortunately, that involves summing over eleven commodity categories, over eighteen years of childhood, and over the forty-two sibling positions represented in Table 6–4. The number of calculations involved proved more than patience and research budget could bear. In Appendix E, I made such calculations only for an only child and for the last of three children spaced at three-year intervals, for the purposes of Chapter 4.

Clues to the likely patterns of commodity inputs can be had, however, by noting some likely effects of family composition to the ratio of home time to commodities. First, it appears likely that children from families of different size differ slightly more in commodity inputs than in time inputs. The larger the family, the more time-intensive and the less commodity-intensive its home life. This follows from the fact that having an extra child tends to reduce the working hours and earnings of mothers by slightly more than it raises the average hours and earnings of husbands through moonlighting. Couples with more children tend to spend less money and more of their own (and older siblings') time in the home. What is true about the ratio of time to commodities in all home activities is also probably true of the raising of each child. One inference about commodities and child-rearing is thus that children in larger families may experience a greater percentage reduction in commodity inputs than in time inputs relative to an only child. This likely pattern is not equally shared by the different birth orders, however. Parents apparently spend slightly more on last-born children than on first-borns, and much more on the last-borns than on middle children.[12] If this is true, the main reason for it is probably the fact that by the time the last-born is growing up, his parents are older and earn more, allowing them to spend more on him (even if he does not go to college at their expense). There is no convenient way to adjust the SIBLOSS index for this likely relationship of birth order to commodity-intensity of child rearing, and the regression results must be examined to see if in fact the

---

[12] One shred of additional evidence that tends to support this conjecture is a set of calculations I have made of a proxy for the relationship between sibling position and the individual child's commodity inputs. I calculated the net impact of a sibling in each position on total family consumption over the eighteen years of his childhood (note again: this is not what the child received, but just his impact on total family expenditures). Last-borns tend to affect total family consumption more strongly than do first-borns or (especially) middle-borns. It seems likely that the true amount of commodities being received by a last-born is also larger than that received by each of his older siblings. The proxy was also enough higher for the last-born to suggest that his input advantage over earlier siblings was greater for commodity inputs than it was for time inputs. It thus appears that within each family size the last-borns are raised in a more commodity-intensive fashion than their older siblings.

achievements of last-borns are underexplained by the use of the SIBLOSS variable, which must be based on time-input calculations only.

3. *Family Time Inputs and Sibling Achievement.* When indices of predicted family time inputs are used as regressors in place of sibling-position variables, they prove to be a significant influence on schooling. This result is firmly established by tests on intrafamily schooling differences [DIFINPUT coefficients in Regressions (2) and (3) in Table 6-3] as well as by tests on individuals' schooling [SIBLOSS coefficients in Regressions (4)-(6) in Table 6-1].[13] The predicted-time-input index is also a significant influence on career attainments if one views respondent status as determined in part by sibling position [Regression (3) in Table 6-2], but not significant if respondent status is held constant [Regression (4) in Table 6-2]. These results are all consistent with the hypothesis that sibling position affects achievement because it strains family inputs, even though one could still choose to view the outcome as a possible coincidence produced by a strong correlation between the family-inputs index and some unspecified "true" influence on achievement.

---

[13] Adding an age differential (and the differential in the squares of ages) reduces the magnitude and significance of the DIFINPUT index. In a sample restricted to later-borns, the age difference between each sibling and the first-born is highly correlated with the DIFINPUT index, which predicts higher time inputs for a later-born child the further his birth lags behind the first birth. Thus neither age nor the DIFINPUT index appeared significant in the unreported regressions that included both. This result is interpreted as showing that age differentials themselves do not belong in the model used for intrafamily testing. Since age proved insignificant in the comparison of individuals from different families while SIBLOSS was significant (Table 6-1), it is viewed as an unimportant determinant of schooling differentials within families, and as a variable that just happens to be correlated with DIFINPUT in a sample of later-borns.

Other unreported regressions tested the hypothesis by William T. Smelser and Louis H. Stewart ("Where are the Siblings? A Reevaluation of the Relationship between Birth Order and College Attendance," *Sociometry* 31, 1968, 294-303) that the schooling advantage of the first-born is greater in families with children of both sexes than in families where all were of the same sex. Regressions were run with the variable ALLMALE added to sets of variables like those in Table 6-3. The ALLMALE variable did have the negative coefficient that Smelser and Stewart would predict, suggesting that when boys are raised without sisters, the first-born had less advantage than when both sexes are represented. But the coefficient for ALLMALE was never statistically significant. This leaves the issue unresolved. This interaction of sex with sibling position deserves further exploration, especially if the development of sex preselection technology leads to a shift toward first-born males followed by second-born females, as predicted by Charles Westoff and Ronald Rindfuss ("Sex Preselection in the United States: Some Implications," *Science* [May 10, 1974], 633-636). If Smelser and Stewart are right, sex preselection could be a minor force tending to widen male-female differentials in occupational status through an effect of sibling positions on schooling.

The present results are consistent with two other lines of inquiry into the consequences of sibling position. One is the quantification of the effect of family size on schooling by Beverly Duncan. On the basis of regressions using the 1962 survey of Occupational Change in a Generation, she estimated that children in two-child families had on the average 0.6 year more final schooling than children in five-child families when age and six other variables were held constant.[14] This degree of impact of family size on schooling is also predicted by the present regressions containing terms for age or age differences (Table 6–1 plus the unreported regressions referred to in footnotes 10 and 13), though larger effects of family size are predicted when age is not held constant (e.g., using DIFINPUT coefficients from Table 6–3).

The present results are also consistent with a second line of inquiry, despite what may seem like a contradiction. In their recent re-examination of "Birth Order and Intellectual Development,"[15] R. B. Zajonc and Gregory B. Markus noted several relationships between sibling position and intelligence test scores. As with the present achievement patterns, larger family size meant lower scores and middle-borns fell below first-borns for given family size. But unlike the achievement patterns, last-borns were found to have a much lower intelligence test score than earlier-borns for the same family size. Also unlike the achievement patterns, only children were not at any great advantage. Zajonc and Markus offered an index of home intellectual environment during childhood which was a transformation based on sibling position.

The patterns observed for intelligence are for the most part consistent with the view that sibling position is relevant to child development mainly through its effects on family time and commodity inputs into siblings, as long as one adds the plausible assumption that the inputs that shape intelligence are the inputs into the child's early, say preschool, development. Calculations like those summarized in Table 6–4 would show that the predicted pattern of time inputs by sibling position for the first six years of childhood match the patterns observed by Zajonc and Markus and others before them. Last-borns suffer in their early years, and only in their teens do they receive relatively generous attention and financial support. It seems reasonable to argue that they are indeed less intelligent (on tests) than earlier-borns yet at the same time achieve

[14] Beverly Duncan, "Trends in Output and Distribution of Schooling," in Eleanor Bernert Sheldon and Wilbert E. Moore, eds., *Indicators of Social Change*, New York: Russell Sage Foundation, 1968, pp. 648–649.
[15] *Psychological Review*, April 1975.

more than middle-borns by receiving more encouragement to stay in school. The only aspect of the Zajonc-Markus patterns not predicted by the time-inputs index is the failure of the only child to score higher, though unobserved parental attributes may explain this.

III. *Birth Control and the Schooling of Smaller Families*

If sibling position matters to schooling and career attainments, the decline in American birth rates must have raised levels, and reduced inqualities, of schooling, status, and income. To know how great a contribution it has made, one must decide on an appropriate hypothetical experiment. The experiment involves imagining how a given cohort would have been distributed over different completed family sizes if births were hypothetically restricted. That in turn requires knowledge of how both achievements and the incidence of prevented births are spread over different sibling positions.

To get a rough idea of the degree of impact of birth restriction on inequality in schooling, let us ask: How does the variability of schooling among the 1,008 individuals in the New Jersey sibling sample seem to compare with the variability of schooling in the hypothetical subset of those individuals out of the 1,008 who would have been born under conditions of more effective birth control? To imagine the situation with more effective birth control, let us first divide the sample of 1,008 individuals into each birth order and each of three classes based on the mother's schooling: less than high school graduation, high school graduate, and some college. For each birth-order-and-mother's-schooling group, let us assume that the percentage of births prevented is the percentage of such births between 1960 and 1965 found to have been unwanted in the 1965 National Fertility Survey.[16] This is presumably an underestimate of the incidence of unwanted births among those surviving in the New Jersey sample, since contraception was less effective in the prewar cohorts represented in the sample than in the early pill years investigated in the 1965 survey. The hypothetically prevented unwanted births turn out to be 21 percent of the total (23 percent for mothers in the lowest-schooling group, and 14 percent for mothers with some college). Let us next regroup the 798 wanted births into their new family size groups. Finally, we compare the standard deviations and means of the schooling of these 798 with the original 1,008, under the assumption that the means and variances within each family-size-and-mother's-education

[16] Bumpass and Westoff, "The 'Perfect Contraceptive' Population."

group is unchanged. The result is a measure of how the average level and variability of schooling would be affected if nothing changed but the numbers of persons falling in each group.

The impact of the hypothetical birth restriction is unimpressive according to some measures but more noteworthy according to others. The mean schooling index of the sample of 798 wanted births was 3.57 percent, or roughly 0.32 year, higher than that of the sample of all births.[17] The standard deviations hardly differed at all in absolute terms, being only 0.3 percent lower with the improved birth control. At first glance it appears that birth reduction could have raised average schooling noticeably while leaving the inequality of schooling unaffected. Yet for several reasons this appearance understates the contribution of birth reduction to the historic leveling of American educational attainment. One reason is that the level of the standard deviation is raised by the higher average schooling of the wanted-birth group. When the standard deviation is expressed as a share of mean years of schooling, it proves to be 3.74 percent lower with the smaller-family group. That represents a minor but noteworthy contribution to the total reduction in schooling inequality over successive twentieth-century cohorts, especially if one compares the New Jersey respondents' birth cohort (1905–11) with the cohort of thirty years later, which had a fertility rate that was about 37 percent lower, instead of the 21 percent used here.[18]

The impact of birth reduction on schooling inequality would also appear larger in a perspective spanning two or more generations. The higher average schooling, and slightly less variable schooling, of a generation

[17] The calculations were performed on the index of the mother's schooling, which assigned such values as 1 to 0–4 years of schooling, 3 to an eighth-grade education, 5 to a high school finisher, and 7 to a college graduate with no postgraduate schooling. The results in terms of this index were:

	Mean	Standard Deviation
All 1008 births	4.5000	1.9161
798 wanted births	4.6605	1.9103

If one starts from equating the index value of 5.0 with 12 years of schooling and equates each point of the index with 2 years of schooling, then it could be said that the respective means were 11.000 and 11.321 years, while the standard deviations were 3.8322 years and 3.8206 years.

[18] Average schooling rose from 9.6 years for the 1905–09 birth cohort to 12.1 years for the 1935–39 cohort (Duncan, "Trends," p. 611). The most comparable pair of figures available on standard deviations is the estimation of Barry Chiswick and Jacob Mincer that the standard deviation among adults fell from 3.70 years for 1949 to 3.04 years for 1970 ("Time-Series Changes in Personal Income Inequality in the United States from 1939, with Projections to 1985," *Journal of Political Economy* 80, no. 3, pt. II, May/June 1972, S43).

born into smaller families would not only transmit itself to the following generation for constant family size, but would also be a force reducing fertility further in the next generation, thereby making the cycle of fewer births and higher and more equal schooling become cumulative.

It should be further noted that this exercise understates the impact of birth reduction on the level and equality of schooling for two other reasons. First, it takes as fixed a reward structure that birth restrictions apparently tend to equalize. It thus ignores the macroeconomic contributions of fertility reduction to income equality introduced above. Second, it focuses only on family-input effects within a cohort and does not allow for the possibility that lower fertility can ease the strain on public school inputs into children. We turn next to this possibility.

IV. *Aggregate Fertility and Public School Inputs*

The micro-level evidence for the strain-on-family resources argument can be supplemented with aggregate evidence in favor of the strain-on-public-schools argument. The postwar baby boom and bust were so pronounced in the United States that one should examine this experience to see whether the switch from falling to rising fertility around World War II and the switch back to falling fertility in the early 1960s was echoed in any discernible change in the growth of public school inputs per child.

It was from 1950 through 1968 that the baby boom raised the share of the national population that was of school age (5–19). To see if this reversal in the long-run decline in children's share of the population really affected schooling inputs and attendance, we can compare educational expenditures and attendance rates in these years with the trends indicated by earlier years. To identify the effect of the baby bulge, it is important to give other independent variables their due weight. In particular, it is essential that the income of adults be taken into account, since all relevant studies have shown that adults' incomes are the strongest determinant of both educational expenditures and the length of school attendance by children.

Figure 6–3 and Table 6–5 are designed to reveal the possible impact of the age distribution of the population on educational expenditures per child. Figure 6–3 plots the ratio of expenditures per child to income (GNP) per adult, both for public elementary and secondary schooling and for all schooling, against real income per adult. The first pattern revealed by the course of these two variables is that expenditures for edu-

ECONOMIC INFLUENCES ON FERTILITY

Figure 6-3. The Relationship of Educational Expenditures per Child to Income per Adult and to the Share of Children 5-19 in the U.S. Population, 1840-1972.

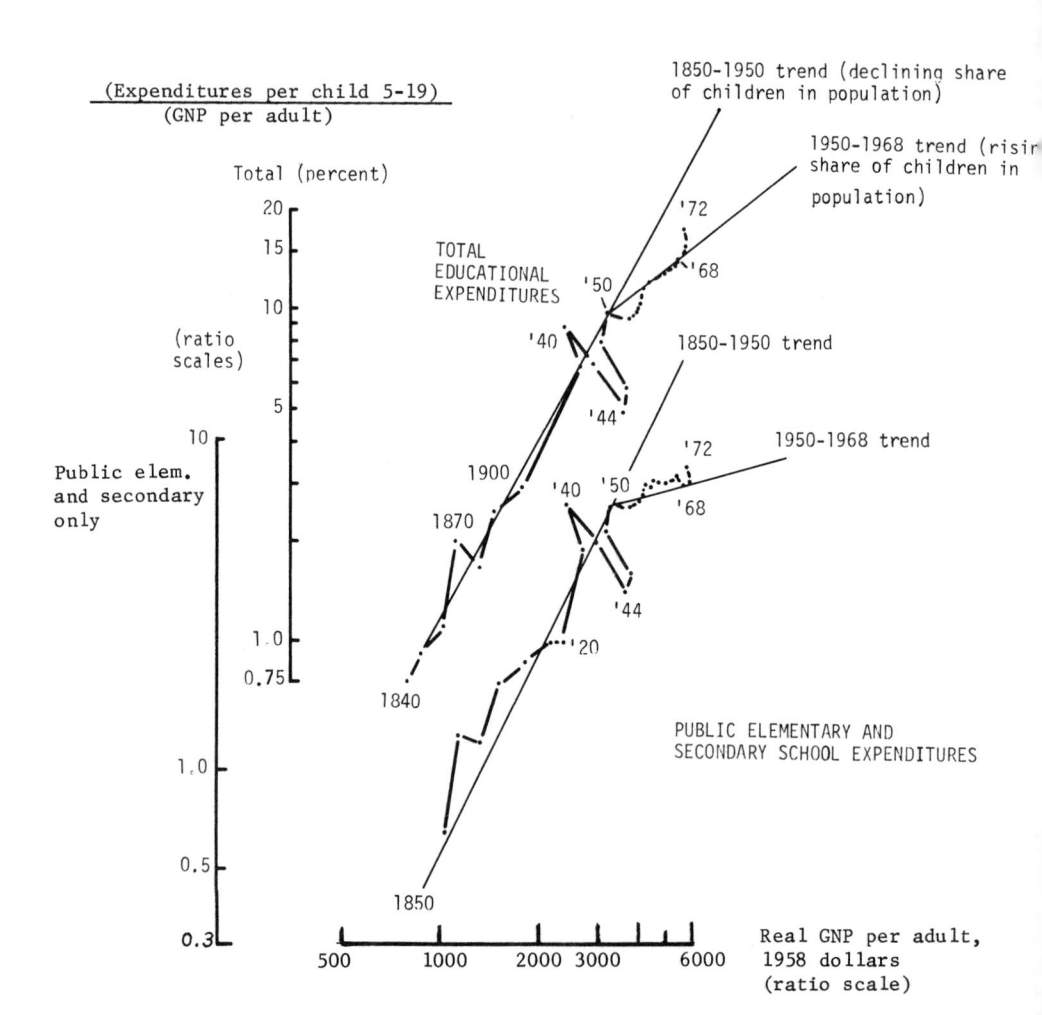

cation have been very elastic with respect to income, so much so that their ratio to income itself has risen sharply and systematically with income growth. This is true even though the data slightly overstate this elasticity by implicitly using the GNP price deflator to deflate educational expenditures, missing the fact that a service like education has risen in price more rapidly than GNP as a whole. A second pattern, to be documented in the next chapter, is the cyclical sensitivity of education's share of GNP. When prices shoot up, as in World War II, school budgets are very slow to respond, being locked into yearly pay contracts and some inertia in property tax receipts. The opposite happened when prices dropped in the Great Depression, for which data have not been presented here. When prices and wages fell off in the early 1930s, educational expenditures hardly changed at all, causing a sharp rise in their share of GNP. Over the longer run, however, this behavior cancels out, leaving a much more stable relationship between educational expenditures and income.

The possible role played by movements in fertility and the age distribution is shown in the shift of the trend in expenditures occurring in 1950. That was the year that children born toward the end of the war entered primary school, and the year in which the share of school-age children in the population stopped its historic decline and began rising. The trend in expenditure's relation to income remains less steep from then until 1968, when the share of the population that is of school age peaks and begins to decline again. The 1950–68 pattern represented an even sharper break for public elementary and secondary school expenditures than for total expenditures, suggesting (but not documenting) a shift to a less equal distribution of school inputs among children.

The consistency of this flatter trend over the eighteen-year period is striking in view of the good reasons one could have had for expecting no such dip in the long-run trend. The period 1950–68 was one in which a large share of voters had a direct parental stake in better schools and higher taxes. The decade 1958–68 was also the Sputnik decade, in which a whole nation cried for better schools to keep up with the Russians. Yet in these years the trend in expenditures, given the level of adult incomes, remained flatter than the trend for 1850–1950 or, so far, the trend from 1968 on.

The same peculiarity of the baby-boom wave is shown by other scraps of time-series data on education. There is some evidence of classroom crowding during the baby-boom wave. Pupil-teacher ratios rose above their long-term trend in nonpublic schools during this wave, though no

FROM FERTILITY TO INEQUALITY

Table 6-5. The Relationship of Educational Expenditures to Income per Adult and to the Share of Children 5-19 in the Population 1840-1972.

School year ending in	Share of GNP spent on (1) public elem.&sec. schooling	(2) all schooling	(3) ratio of children 5-19 to adults (20 & up)	Educational expenditures per child ÷ GNP per adult (4) pub. elem.+ sec.	(5) all expen.	(6) Exhibit: GNP per adult in 1958 dollars (previous yr.)
1840	..	0.6	.8008	..	0.75	799.9
1850	0.33	0.7	.7841	0.42	0.91	882.1
1860	0.46	0.8	.7335	0.63	1.09	1032.5
1870	0.84	1.3	.6601	1.28	1.97	1136.7
1880	0.81	1.1	.6611	1.22	1.67	1328.9
1890	1.13	1.5	.6210	1.81	2.42	1485.2
1900	1.23	1.7	.5787	2.14	2.89	1818.7
1910	1.28	..	.5224	2.44	..	2167.0
1920	1.23	..	.5018	2.42	..	2362.6
1930	2.25	3.1	.4776	4.70	6.74	2721.5
1940	2.59	3.5	.4006	6.46	8.73	2432.3
1942	1.87	2.6	.3783	4.93	6.87	2972.9
1944	1.28	1.8	.3633	3.52	4.96	3695.7
1946	1.37	2.0	.3508	3.91	5.70	3782.4
1948	1.86	2.8	.3513	5.31	7.97	3233.1
1950	2.28	3.4	.3507	6.49	9.70	3285.9
1952	2.24	3.4	.3612	6.20	9.42	3799.7
1954	2.49	3.8	.3828	6.51	9.92	4023.3
1956	2.75	4.2	.4017	6.86	10.45	4186.4
1958	3.10	4.8	.4224	7.34	11.36	4240.8
1960	3.20	3.2	.4417	7.24	11.55	4370.7
1962	3.40	3.4	.4617	7.36	12.13	4452.3
1964	3.50	3.5	.4713	7.39	12.89	4805.3
1966	3.80	3.8	.4891	7.76	13.49	5266.5
1968	3.80	3.8	.5119	7.42	14.07	5544.9
1970	3.56	3.6	.4785	7.44	15.68	5778.7
1972	3.80	3.8	.4539	8.37	17.63	5669.5

FERTILITY AND INVESTMENTS IN CHILDREN

Sources for Table 6-5 (and Figure 6-3)

Col. (1): For some years, the figures on public elementary and secondary school expenditures came from separate sources; for others, their ratio was given in a single source. The figures on public expenditures, 1840–70, of which less than 5 percent was for public support to higher education, are from Albert Fishlow, "Levels of Nineteenth-Century American Investment in Education," *Journal of Economic History* 26, no. 4 (December 1966), Table 1. For 1870–1920, the figures for public elementary and secondary expenditures come from U.S. Bureau of the Census, *Historical Statistics of the United States* . . . , Washington: GPO, 1960, Series H252. For 1930–68, the ratio of these expenditures to the previous year's GNP is given by Abbott L. Ferriss, *Indicators of Trends in American Education*, New York: Russell Sage Foundation, 1969, p. 184. The expenditure figures for 1970 and 1972, along with GNP for 1969 and 1971, are given in U.S. Bureau of the Census, *Statistical Abstract of the United States 1972*, Washington: GPO, 1972. The GNP figures for 1890–1970 are from U.S. Bureau of Economic Analysis, *Long-term Economic Growth, 1860–1970*, Washington: GPO, 1973, Series A7 and A8. For 1840–80, the estimates of GNP in current dollars are the Gallman estimates cited by Fishlow, op. cit., Table 3.

Col. (2): For 1840–1900, Fishlow, op. cit., Table 3. For 1930–72: U.S. Office of Education, *Digest of Educational Statistics*, 1972, Washington: GPO, 1972, p. 25.

Col. (3): For decennial census years, 1840–1950, *Historical Statistics*, pp. 8–10, with the 1840 ratio applying to males only. For all other years, various reports in *Current Population Reports*, Series P-25, P-45, and P-47.

Col. (4) = (1) ÷ (3).
Col. (5) = (2) ÷ (3).

Col. (6): For 1890–1970, Bureau of Economic Analysis, *Long-term Economic Growth*, Series A1 and A2, divided by the share of adults in the population, which was calculated from the same sources cited for Col. (3). This series was spliced at 1890 onto an index of NNP per member of the labor force from Lance E. Davis et al., *American Economic Growth*, New York: Harper and Row, 1972, p. 34, to derive estimates of the 1958-dollar GNP per adult for 1840–80. For 1972, *Statistical Abstract*, . . . *1972*.

deviation from trend was evident in pupil-teacher ratios for public schools.[19] The next chapter will also note that school enrollment rates and attendance rates grew more slowly in the baby-boom wave, and that the median schooling of the adult labor force decelerated a bit when the baby-boom cohort began to enter the labor force in recent years. These scraps of evidence are unimpressive by themselves, in part because they may reflect the other channels of influence as well as the strain-on-public schools channel, but they are at least consistent with the evidence on public school expenditures in Figure 6–3 above.

It can still be objected that the time series just reviewed do not prove that the extra births dragged down society's inputs into children's edu-

[19] Abbott L. Ferriss, *Indicators of Trends in American Education*, New York: Russell Sage Foundation, 1969, Figure 3.8 and Series A13–A16.

cational developments. Perhaps there were other factors that made 1950–68 look special, factors wholly unrelated to the rush of a large share of the population through the schools. In particular, perhaps the deceleration in both expenditures and years of schooling attained simply reflects a natural limit on the share of our lives and funds that can be profitably spent on formal education. Perhaps by 1950 Americans had raised formal education to such a high level that the population cannot find good reason to make the median child spend more than twelve or thirteen years in school, except for a very slow upward creep over the decades as teaching techniques improve and incomes rise. On this reasoning it is perfectly natural for the income elasticity of education to drop as a society becomes supereducated.

This argument about natural limits fails to fit another kind of evidence as well as does the argument that higher fertility puts a strain on educational inputs. The additional evidence comes not from a time series, but from a cross section. G. S. Tolley and E. Olson recently examined the interrelationship between educational expenditures per pupil and incomes per adult (employee) over a cross section of the states in the U.S. for 1960.[20] Their main purpose was to sort out the simultaneity of the income-education relationship. They found that educational expenditures per pupil were strongly affected by two variables in particular. One was income per employee, which was in turn affected by urbanization, population density, racial mixture, nonhuman wealth, and the schooling of the adult population. The other, always negative and significant at the one percent level, was the ratio of pupils to employees. This ratio, which varied across states in response more to fertility differences than to differences in enrollment rates, again reflected the greater pressure imposed on family and taxpayer resources for given income levels by a larger share of school-aged children in the population. Nor can their cross-sectional result be dismissed as further evidence on the natural limits to formal schooling: the states for which a higher ratio of pupils to employees kept expenditures down were states with lower average expenditures and lower average educational attainment.

V. *Conclusion*

There is thus a considerable body of evidence that reductions in fertility should raise the average level, and reduce the dispersion, of schooling.

[20] G. S. Tolley and E. Olson, "The Interdependence of Income and Education," *Journal of Political Economy* 79, no. 3 (May/June 1971), 460–480.

Fertility reduction has this effect by giving each child more inputs both from his family and from the public schools. The higher level and lower dispersion of schooling should in turn tend to equalize incomes by shifting labor supply toward the higher-skill occupations.

The tendency of lower fertility to raise schooling needs to be noted in any projections of the demand for higher education between now and the year 2000. It is now common knowledge that higher education is an industry strongly affected by movements in fertility. The college boom of the 1960s has already vanished, as was predicted by Allan Cartter and others.[21] Pessimism now rules the forecasts on demand for college, fed by the knowledge that the pronounced fertility decline will cut the size of the college-age cohort across the 1980s. This pessimism was reinforced by a recent article by Stephen P. Dresch, which correctly notes that the economic returns from college will continue to be depressed by the glut of college-educated members of the baby-boom cohorts.[22]

The results of the present chapter suggest a partial offset to the tendency of demand for college to be depressed by shrinkage in the size of the age group, even when this demand is further lowered by a previous baby-boom glut of degree holders. The fertility reduction itself will raise the attendance rates for a cohort that has had better access to family and public school inputs. Even in the face of possibly declining rates of return on a college degree, parents will tend to follow through to some extent on their prior decision to cut fertility for the sake of assuring each child higher inputs and earning potential. A smaller-family cohort will tend to have a higher rate of college attendance, even if this tendency itself makes college less an economic investment and more an act of consumption. This attendance effect needs to be considered, along with the more pessimistic arguments, in forecasting the demand for higher education.

[21] A. Cartter, "A New Look at the Supply of College Teachers," *Education Review* 46 (Summer 1965), 267–277.

[22] Stephen P. Dresch, "Demography, Technology, and Higher Education: Toward a Formal Model of Educational Adaptation," *Journal of Political Economy* 83, no. 3 (June 1975), 535–569.

Chapter 7. Fertility, Labor Supply, and Inequality: the Macroeconomic Evidence

Chapter 6 found empirical support for the microeconomic, or strain-on-family-resources, arguments and the strain-on-public-schools argument for expecting higher fertility to feed income inequality. These arguments stressed that higher fertility lowers the schooling and skills of labor-force entrants a generation later. This lowering of average labor-force quality and the accompanying acceleration in growth of the number of man-hours of labor available presumably bids down unskilled wage rates relative to skilled wage rates and especially relative to property returns, thereby heightening income inequality.

Do these effects really add up to a strong relationship running from fertility through labor-force size and quality to income inequality? This chapter shows that the apparent long-run movements in the distribution of income correspond quite well with movements in the quantity and quality of labor supplied, and with the demographic movements that govern labor supply. The correspondence is good enough to suggest that it is much more plausible to assign great importance to the combination of arguments above than it is to leave these arguments out of one's explanation of trends in inequality.

It should be stressed at the outset that the set of hypotheses linking inequality to fertility and labor supply will receive only a limited test here. When the variable to be explained is a long-run rate of change in something macroeconomic, like aggregate inequality, we are always short on historical experiments. A national economy seldom yields historical data on income distribution over more than two or three epochs long enough to span a generation. With only two or three observations it is difficult to choose among the ten or more leading variables whose influence should be tested. When long-run influences are at issue, empirical macroeconomics has no choice but to exploit its handful of case studies for all they are worth, and then leave it to readers to decide if they share the faith the researcher has expressed in the theory of his choosing. When the testing is done, what can be argued is that the facts fit the theory advanced—followed by the admission that the facts fit some other theories, too. Some competing explanations can be rejected, but others cannot.

The next section reviews the available evidence on what has happened to income inequality. After that the explanatory power of demographic and other variables will be judged.

I. *Trends in American Inequality*

The degree of aggregate inequality can be quantified in any of several ways that manage to reflect popular intuition about what makes inequality look great or small. Such measures as Gini coefficients, areas over the Lorenz curve, variances or standard deviations in logarithms, percentile shares, and entropy measures all tend to rank the inequalities of different situations similarly.[1]

Any measure of aggregate inequality can be broken down into two parts when the population is divided into classes. The first part consists of the inequalities (dispersion, variation) between classes or groups, and the second consists of the inequalities within groups. This means that the change in inequality over time equals the sum of three changes:

(1) Changes in inequalities within the classes or groups
(2) Changes in inequalities between classes caused by movements in their average rates of pay
(3) Changes in aggregate inequality caused by changes in the shares of the population falling into the various classes.

Breaking overall changes in inequality up into these three parts provides extra clues to the sources of changes in inequality over time. Many possible explanations of what forces have been altering the degree of overall inequality also carry implications about the directions in which each of these three parts should be moving. These implications can be tested against the movements of the three parts. For example, suppose that one wondered whether the most important influence reducing income inequality in a particular period might not be an exogenous shift of large numbers of farm workers to higher-paying jobs in industry. One could test this proposition by noting not only whether or not large numbers so moved, but also how overall inequality was affected by the shift in population alone [change (3) above] and by changes in the ratio of farm to nonfarm wage rates. For the hypothesis to be confirmed, it

[1] For comparisons of the mathematical properties of different measures of inequality, see Henri Theil, *Economics and Information Theory*, Chicago, Rand McNally, 1963; and Anthony B. Atkinson, "On the Measurement of Inequality," *Journal of Economic Theory* 2 (September 1970), 249–263.

should be the case that overall inequality was greatly reduced by the shift in population out of the farm sector, *and* that the ratio of nonfarm to farm wage rates did not rise, *and* that any decline in this ratio of wage rates did not raise the measure of overall inequality so greatly as to offset the effect of the population shift.[2] In this way, hypotheses that are competing for explanation of the movements in overall inequality can also be tested against the separate movements of rates of pay, of population between classes, and of inequality within classes.

Recent research has developed measures of trends in inequality within the United States at various levels. Since the beginning of federal income tax returns in 1913–14, and especially since the 1940 census, more and more data have become available on the overall distribution of income and wealth. Economic historians have also been coming up with suggestive results for the two and a half centuries before 1913, based on state income and wealth returns, local wealth tax assessments, probate and manuscript-census wealth samples, and time series on wage rate differentials. From these various sources, an intriguing long-run pattern is beginning to emerge. A recent paper by Jeffrey G. Williamson and myself has surveyed trends in American income and wealth inequality in some detail.[3] Its findings can be summarized more briefly here.

It is only for the years since 1913 that we have direct measures of overall income inequality. For earlier years it is nonetheless useful to follow the progress of cruder proxies for income inequality. As we have argued elsewhere,[4] the twentieth-century record has shown that move-

[2] In the example used here, it is presumed that the shift of population out of agriculture would reduce inequality, for constant rates of pay in each occupational class. That would be likely to be the case as long as the previous farm incomes of the migrants were not above the farm average, and as long as the nonfarm sector was already a large share of the population. It cannot be concluded, however, that any migration of persons from lower to higher rates of pay will reduce inequality, even if the migrants' new rate of pay is below the overall average. Such migration can raise overall inequality in cases where the sector they are leaving (the farm sector here) dominates the economy and/or the migrants were better paid in that sector than were those who stayed behind. For a discussion of the conditions governing the net effect of migration on inequality, see Simon Kuznets' treatment of the shift out of agriculture in his "Economic Growth and Income Inequality," *American Economic Review* 45, no. 1 (March 1955), 1–28; and especially Theil's section on "Maxwell's Demon on Ellis Island," in *Economics and Information Theory*, pp. 114–120.

[3] Peter H. Lindert and Jeffrey G. Williamson, "Three Centuries of American Inequality," *Research in Economic History*, vol. 1, September 1976, hereafter cited as "Three Centuries."

[4] Ibid.

ments in income inequality are roughly paralleled by movements in such indirect indicators as (a) the ratio of skilled or professional wage rates to those of unskilled labor; (b) the inverse of unskilled labor's share of product, or national product per-man-hour of labor force divided by the unskilled hourly wage rate adjusted for unskilled unemployment; and (c) the inequality of wealth-holding, which serves as both a clue to the inequality of current property income and a reflection of earlier inequality in total income.

From this twentieth-century parallelism between inequality measures and cruder proxies for inequality, I draw two inferences. The first, already implied, is that any explanation of twentieth-century inequality trends must be consistent with the behavior of the crude proxies. The second is that the crude proxies offer good clues to the trends in income inequality before the onset of the federal income tax in 1913.

These proxies, the richer twentieth-century data on aggregate income inequality, and some other rough adjustments yield a chronology of inequality in real income before taxes and transfers. The main data series underlying this chronology are given in Figures 7–1 through 7–3. Figure 7–1 summarizes the direct measures of income inequality during the income tax era. Figure 7–2 proxies the inequality of earnings with selected occupational pay ratios. Figure 7–3 summarizes what is known about the share of wealth held by the richest decile and percentile of wealth-holders. From these data and a variety of others, the following chronology emerges.

A. THE DRIFT TO CONCENTRATED WEALTH BEFORE THE CIVIL WAR

Although reliable size distributions of income do not exist for the years before World War I, wealth distributions can be calculated from several kinds of source materials. Probate inventories can reveal the inequality of wealth-holding among the recently deceased. Used with care, they can also yield estimates of wealth inequality among living heads of households. The probate results must be adjusted for incomplete coverage of assets and decedents and for the fact that the population of living heads of households is younger, and less unequal in wealth-holding, than the probated decedents, by different degrees in different periods. A second kind of source material is the tax assessment list, available for certain cities, towns, and colonies. The assessments often fail to cover all wealth, and are suspected of underassessing the wealthiest households most, but can reveal wealth inequality trends if these biases can

Figure 7-1. Selected Measures of Income Inequality in the United States, since 1913 and in Seven Earlier Years.

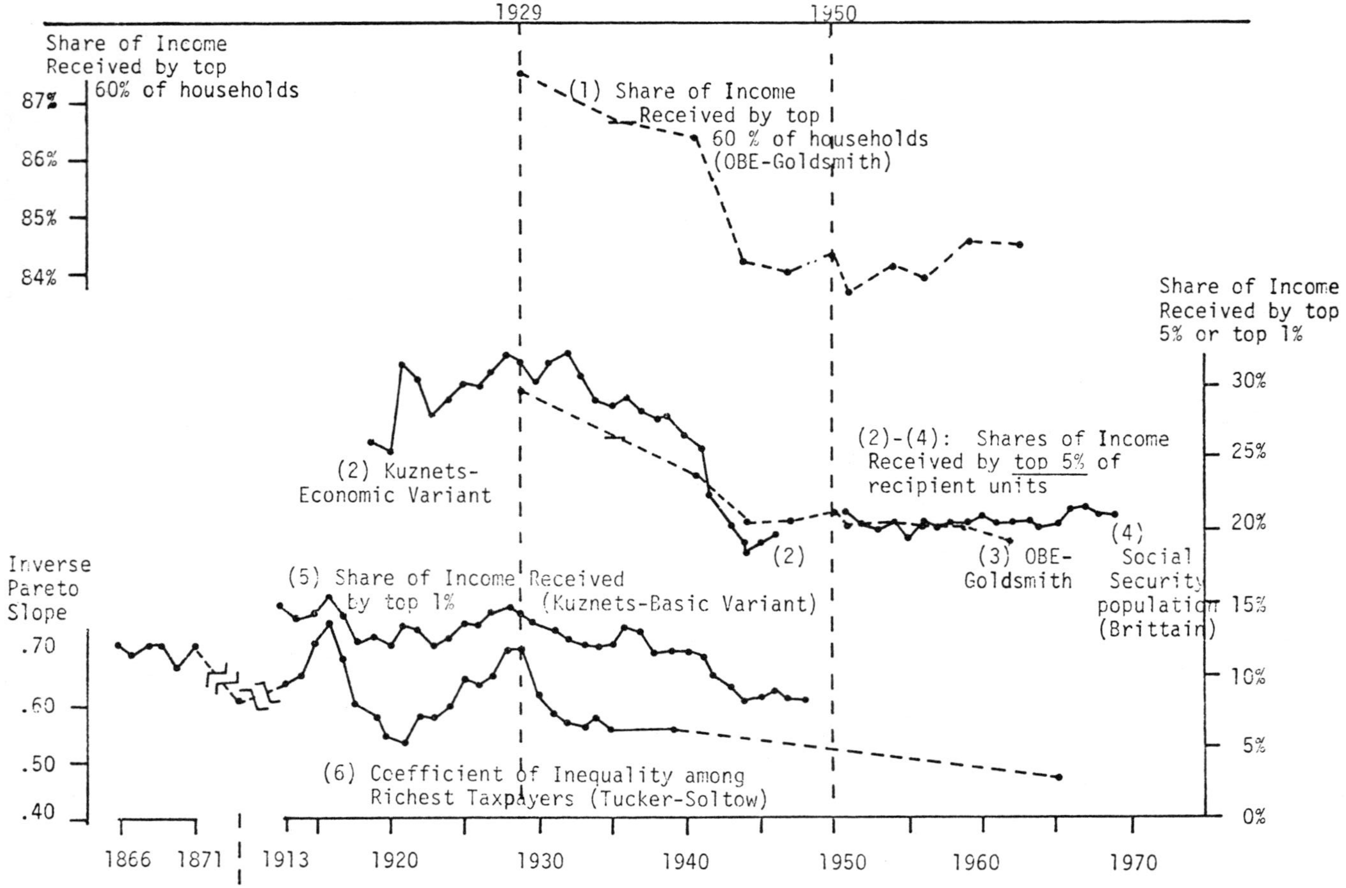

FERTILITY, LABOR SUPPLY, INEQUALITY

NOTES AND SOURCES TO FIGURE 7-1

(1) Share of income received by top 60% of households, 1929–62: the OBE-Goldsmith estimates extended to 1962, as given in Edward C. Budd, ed., *Inequality and Poverty*, New York: W. W. Norton, 1967, p. xiii. The OBE-Goldsmith estimates are a hybrid of different sets of primary data. For 1929 they mixed tax returns with an independent Brookings Institution estimate of the entire income distribution. For 1935/36 and 1941, they adjusted the results of two household surveys. For later years the results of the Census Bureau's Current Population Surveys were adjusted to the OBE-Goldsmith definitions of income and recipient unit.

(2) Share of national income received by top 5%, Kuznets' Economic Variant, 1919–46: Simon Kuznets, *The Shares of Upper Income Groups in Income and Savings*, New York: National Bureau of Economic Research, 1953, p. 635. Kuznets' economic variant measures income in a way corresponding more closely with the concept of income before taxes and transfers used here, for reasons given in his introduction, pp. xxxiv–xxxv. Unlike other main series on aggregate inequality, Kuznets' are based on a ranking of taxpaying units by income *per person*.

(3) Share of income received by top 5%, OBE-Goldsmith, 1929–62: same as (1) above.

(4) Share of income received by top 5%, Brittain, 1951–69: estimated by John A. Brittain, *The Payroll Tax for Social Security*, Washington: Brookings, 1972, p. 107, from unpublished data supplied by the Social Security Administration. The "income" in this case is earnings before payroll taxes, and the recipient unit is the earning individual rather than the family or household. Brittain's numbers show degrees of inequality very close to other main series because the reduction in inequality implicit in his use of data on earnings rather than total income roughly offsets the greater inequality implied by his exclusion of transfer payments and perhaps also by his use of data on earning individuals of all ages rather than on households.

(5) Share of national income received by top 1%, Kuznets' basic variant, 1913–48: Same source as (2) above. Kuznets' basic variant was used here in place of the slightly more appropriate economic variant in order to cover the extra years (1913–18, 1947, 1948) for which he could not estimate the economic variant.

(6) Coefficient of inequality among richest taxpayers, 1866–71, 1894, 1913–1935/39, 1965: Rufus S. Tucker, "The Distribution of Income among Income Taxpayers in the United States, 1863–1935," *Quarterly Journal of Economics* 52, no. 3 (August 1938), pp. 547–587; and Lee Soltow, "Evidence on Income Inequality in the United States, 1866–1965," *Journal of Economic History* 29, no. 2 (June 1969), Table 2. The coefficient is the inverse Pareto slope, which measures the percentage by which income must rise to cut by one percent the proportion of the population having incomes above this income in the year in question. Soltow gives this inverse Pareto slope, while Tucker gives its reciprocal.

Figure 7-2. Occupational Pay Ratios in the Nonfarm United States since Colonial Times.

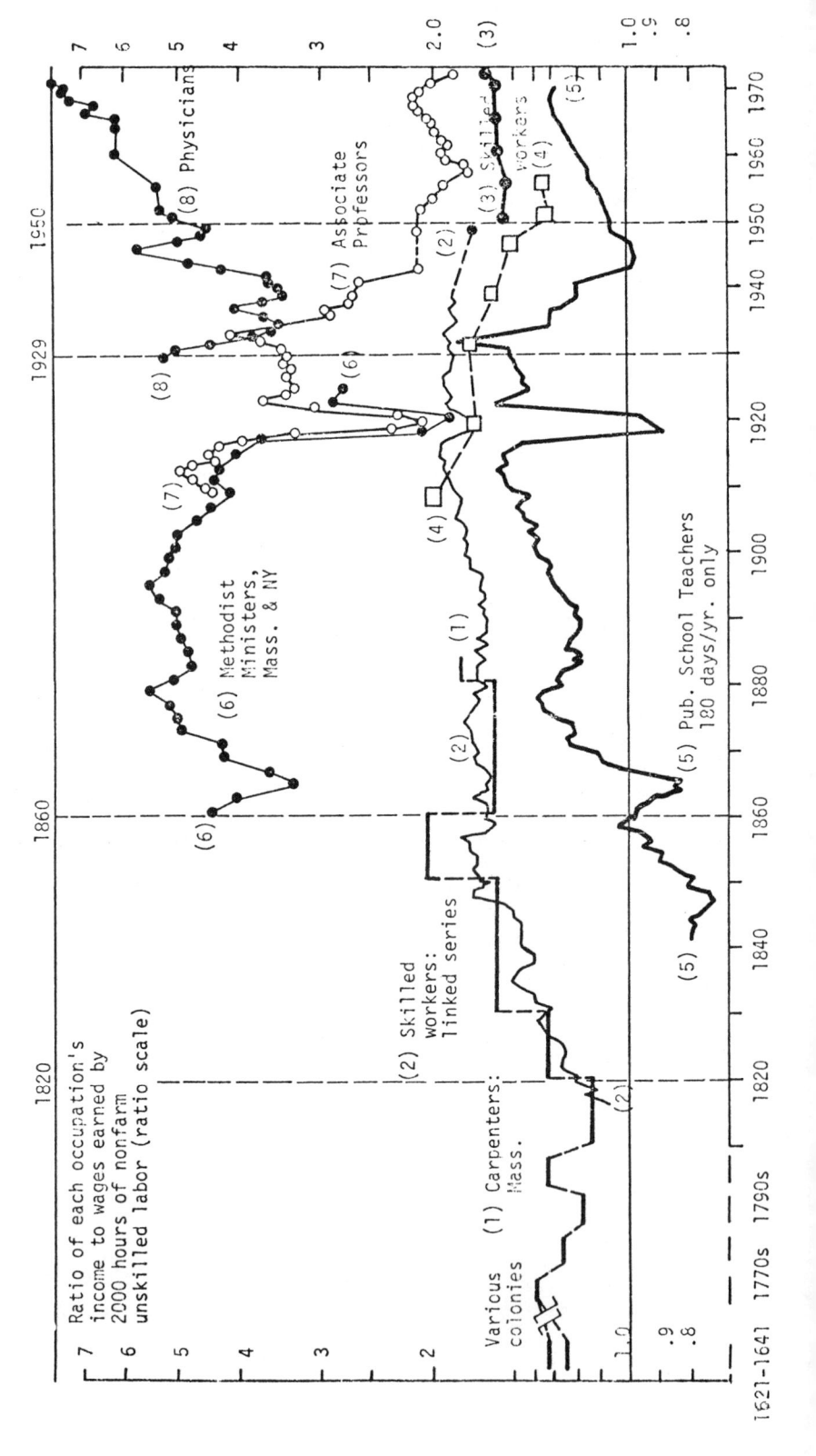

FERTILITY, LABOR SUPPLY, INEQUALITY

SOURCES AND NOTES FOR FIGURE 7-2

Series (1)—Carpenters: the ratio of carpenters' to common day laborers' daily wage rates. For 1621–41, the figures are the legal maximum rates reported for Virginia—1621, Massachusetts—1633, New Haven—1640, and New Haven—1641 in U.S. Bureau of the Census, *Historical Statistics of the United States, Colonial Times to 1957*, Washington: GPO, 1960, Series Z324, Z329. The ratios ranged from 1.25 to 1.33. For 1752–60 through 1880–83, the ratio is the Massachusetts average given in Massachusetts Bureau of Labor Statistics, *Sixteenth Annual Report of the Commissioner of Labor*, Boston, 1885, Massachusetts Public Documents, vol. III, no. 15.

Series (2)—Skilled workers, Williamson linked series: a spliced series of ratios of skilled workers' wage rates to those of unskilled workers, mainly in the manufacturing sector, for 1816–1939 and 1948. The ratios are calculated from daily wage rates for skilled and unskilled workers up to 1890, and from weekly rates thereafter. While a wide variety of sources was used, two main primary sources were the Aldrich Report of 1891 and the series constructed from BLS wage surveys by the National Industrial Conference Board. A detailed explanation of the construction of the series and its relationship to alternative series is given in Jeffrey G. Williamson, "The Relative Costs of American Men, Skills, and Machines: A Long View," University of Wisconsin-Madison, Institute for Research on Poverty, Discussion Paper, revised July 1975. An alternative series calculated from Aldrich Report and BLS data is given in Peter H. Lindert, "Fertility and the Macroeconomics of Inequality," University of Wisconsin-Madison, Institute for Research on Poverty, Discussion Paper no. 219-74, November 1974, Table 2, which uses skilled and unskilled wage series for 1841–1920 calculated from those primary sources by W. Randolph Burgess, *Trends in School Costs*, New York: Russell Sage Foundation, 1920, Table 8.

Series (3)—Skilled workers (1950–73): the average ratio of skilled to unskilled hourly wage rates, where the skilled wage rate is a weighted average of the rates for mechanics, electricians, and carpenters in six cities (Boston, New York, Atlanta, Chicago, Denver, and San Francisco-Oakland), and the unskilled wage rate is that for janitors and custodians in the same cities. The employment weights used are those for the skilled categories in the six cities in the 1960 census. The series was calculated from the BLS occupational wage surveys of metropolitan areas. The ratios: 1950/51—1.580, 1955/56—1.556, 1960/61—1.603, 1965/66—1.611, 1970/71—1.646, 1972/73—1.673.

Series (4)—Skilled workers in manufacturing (Ober-Miller): the ratio of hourly skilled to hourly unskilled wage rates in several manufacturing industries in several cities, from Harry Ober, "Occupational Wage Differentials, 1907–1947," *Monthly Labor Review*, vol. LXVII, August 1948, p. 130; and Herman P. Miller, *Income Distribution in the United States*, Washington: GPO, 1966, p. 79.

Series (5)—Public school teachers, 180 days/yr. only, 1841–1972: the ratio of school teachers' pay per 180 days to the wages received by industrial unskilled laborers per 2,000 hours. From 1890 through 1972, this ratio is calculated by dividing the annual rate of pay for primary and secondary public school teachers first by the number of days in the school year and then by 2,000 times the hourly unskilled wage rate in industry. For 1841–90, the ratio is calculated from the average weekly pay for urban public school teachers divided by the daily wage rate for common laborers in manufacturing, spliced onto the later series at 1890. For sources, further details on the method of calculation, and an alternative rural series covering 1841–90, see Peter H. Lindert, "Fertility and the Macroeconomics of Inequality," 1974, Table 2.

The wage rate series for unskilled labor differs slightly from the one used in this source. The unskilled hourly wage rate was computed as follows: (a) 1950/51–1972/73: the average hourly wage of unskilled custodial and maintenance workers in all industries, six cities (Boston, New York, Atlanta, Chicago, Denver, San Francisco-Oakland), using 1960 census employment weights, from BLS occupational wage surveys; (b) 1914, 1920–48: the NICB series for males in 25 industries, cited as Series 663 in *Historical Statistics of the United States*; (c) 1915–19: interpolated from the NICB series, using the Douglas series on weekly earnings, cited in Williamson, "The Relative Cost of Men, Skills, and Machines," divided by the all-manufacturing average daily hours given by Ethel Jones and the Aldrich Report, and adjusted so as to equal the NICB figure in dollars per hour for 1914.

Series (6)—Methodist ministers, Massachusetts and New York, 1860–1924: the average annual pay of Methodist ministers in the New England and New York Conferences, divided by 2,000 times the unskilled hourly wage series described for Series (5) above. The New England Conference data covered "the eastern part of New York, exclusive of Long Island and part of New York City." The figure plotted here is the simple average of the annual cash salaries in these two Conferences, times 1.25 to adjust for the estimated rental value of the parsonage, divided by 2,000 hours times the unskilled hourly wage rate. The series on ministers' pay is from Edward L. Thorndike and Ella Woodyard, "The Effect of Violent Price-Fluctuations upon the Salaries of Clergymen," *Journal of the American Statistical Association* 22, no. 157 (March 1927), pp. 66–74.

Series (7)—Associate professors, 1908–72: the median salaries of associate professors in large public universities, nine-month basis, divided by 2,000 hours times the unskilled hourly wage rate series described for Series (5) above. The pay series for associate professors is from Willis L. Peterson and Joseph C. Fitzharris, "The Organization and Productivity of the Federal-State Research System in the United States," University of Minnesota, Department of Agricultural and Applied Economics, Staff Paper P74–23, October 1974, Appendix Table 4. Peterson and Fitzharris used data from George Stigler, *Employment and Compensation in Education*, NBER Occasional Paper no. 33, 1950, for 1908–42; and the *Bulletin* of the American Association of University Professors, for 1948–72.

Series (8)—Physicians, 1929–69: the average annual income of self-employed physicians divided by 2,000 hours of pay for unskilled workers, as described for Series (5) above. The concept of physicians' income differs among the three series used for different subperiods. For 1929–51, the figure refers to the mean net income of independent physicians, given by George Stigler, *Trends in Employment in the Service Industries*, NBER General Series, no. 59, Princeton: Princeton University Press, 1955, Table 5. For 1955–66, the figure refers to the median income of self-employed physicians, multiplied by 1.02145 (the ratio of mean to median incomes in 1951), as reported by Elton Rayack, "The Physicians' Service Industry," in Walter F. Adams, ed., *The Structure of American Industry*, 4th edition, New York: Macmillan, 1971, Table 2. For 1966–69, the figure refers to the median income of self-employed physicians under sixty-five, from U.S. Department of Health, Education, and Welfare, *Income of Physicians and Osteopaths . . . 1966–1969*, as cited in *Medical Economics*, various issues, again multiplied by 1.02145. For 1966–69 the figures given in *Medical Economics* tended to run about 13 to 15 percent above those reported by the Internal Revenue Service and about 10 percent above those reported by the American Medical Association. Figures for 1969 on refer to the incomes of unincorporated physicians only, though a rapidly rising share of physicians, presumably those with higher incomes, became incorporated.

be shown to be about constant over time. Another source is the set of returns on total personal wealth in the manuscript censuses of 1860 and 1870.

Taken at face value, wealth inequality data like those in Figure 7–3 reveal a striking drift toward greater and greater concentration. Wealth inequality seems to have risen across the colonial period in Philadelphia, in nearby Chester County, in Boston,[5] and in a few other Massachusetts towns for which we have data. The main exception to the rule of rising colonial wealth inequality is Jackson T. Main's recent finding of no trend in inequality in Hartford County, Connecticut.[6] The drift toward inequality ostensibly continued from the eve of the Revolution to at least the eve of the Civil War.[7] The percentage share of personal wealth held by the richest 10 percent of potential wealth-holders in the thirteen colonies in the early 1770s was somewhere between 45 and the low 60s, to judge from the rough estimates made by Main and by Alice Hanson Jones. By contrast, the samplings from the 1860 manuscript census by Lee Soltow and Robert Gallman show that the top decile of wealth-holders then controlled over 70 percent of all wealth, regardless of how one treats slaves in the calculation. To judge from the Massachusetts probate returns and Gallman's estimates of the share of wealth held by the super-rich (the top .031 percent), wealth inequality may have reached its all-time peak still later, around the 1880s.

The extent of the apparent movement toward sharp inequalities in wealth is very impressive. The figures seem to show that the inequality of income from property drifted toward inequality for two centuries before the 1880s, as long as one accepts the plausible assumption that the inequality trend was the same for the returns from property as for the value of property. The figures also carry the suggestion that total income, earnings plus returns to property, was becoming more unequally distributed as well: wealth inequality is likely to follow earlier trends in

[5] Inequality in probated Boston wealth rose after a trough in the 1680s and 1690s, though the highest inequality in the colonial era was recorded by the earliest returns, in the 1650s and 1660s. See Gloria L. Main, "Inequality in Early America: The Evidence of Probate Records from Massachusetts and Maryland," ms., 1975, Tables IV, V.

[6] Jackson T. Main, "The Distribution of Property in Colonial Connecticut," in James Kirby, ed., *The Human Dimensions of Nation Making*, Madison, Wis.: The State Historical Society of Wisconsin, 1976, p. 88.

[7] The main demonstrated exception to the rule that wealth inequality rose from the eve of the Revolution to the eve of the Civil War is Lee Soltow's finding of no change in the inequality of slaveholding in the South from 1790 (and probably from 1770) to 1860. See Lee Soltow, "Economic Inequality in the United States in the Period from 1790 to 1860," *Journal of Economic History* XXXI, no. 4 (December 1971), 822–839.

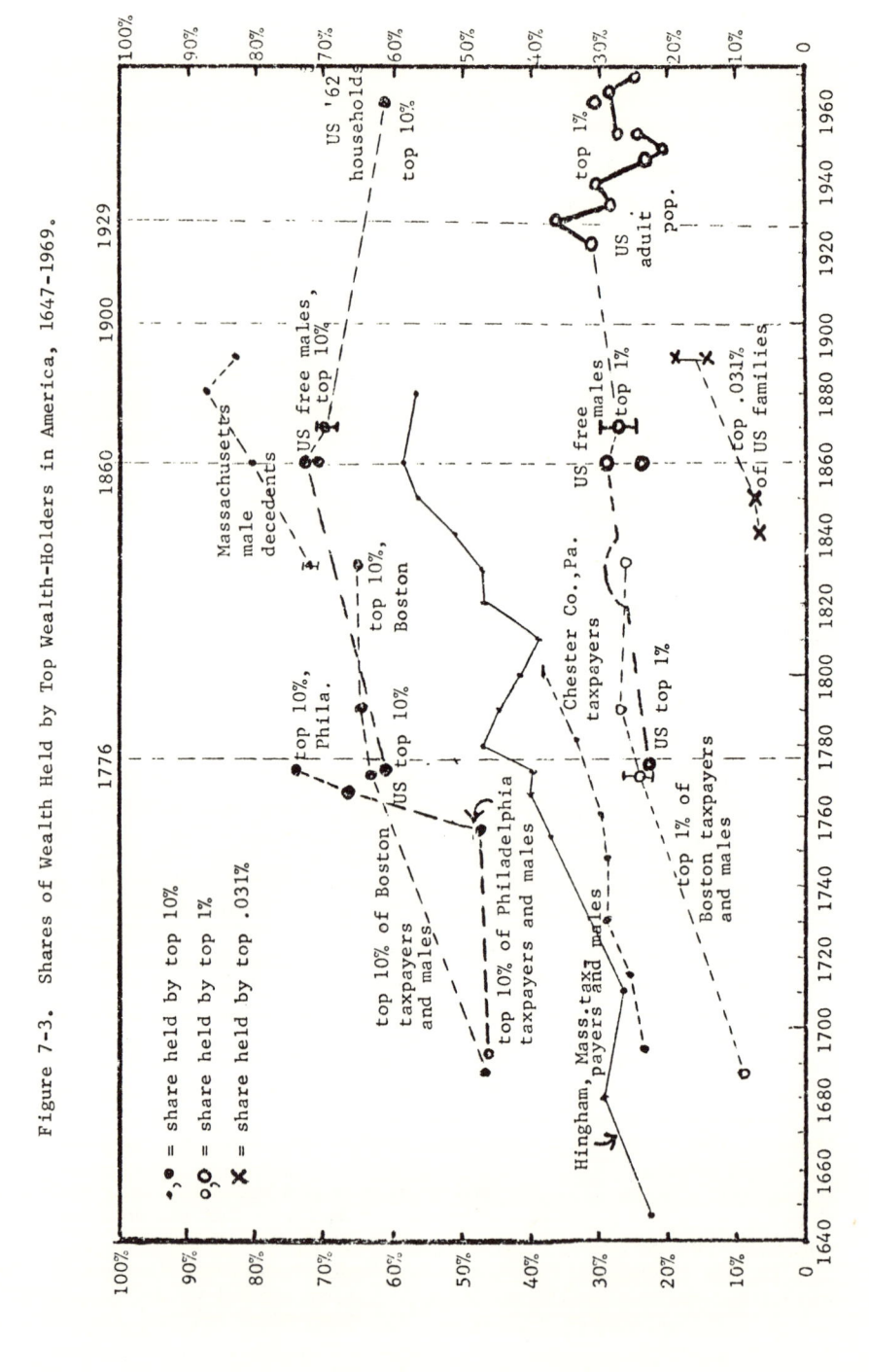

Figure 7-3. Shares of Wealth Held by Top Wealth-Holders in America, 1647-1969.

[226]

FERTILITY, LABOR SUPPLY, INEQUALITY

NOTES AND SOURCES FOR FIGURE 7-3

(1) *Total US pop., 1922–69*: share of gross assets held by richest 1% of adult population of the U.S., from Robert Lampman, *The Share of Top Wealth-Holders in National Wealth, 1922–1956*, Princeton: Princeton University Press, 1962, p. 204; and James D. Smith and Stephen D. Franklin, "The Concentration of Personal Wealth, 1922–1969," *American Economic Review* 64, no. 2 (May 1974), p. 166. Lampman gives: 1922—31.6%, '29—36.3, '33—28.3, '39—30.6, '45—23.3, '49—20.8, '53—24.3. Smith and Franklin give: 1953—27.5%, '65—29.2, '69—24.9, using the total U.S. population as a base.

(2) *US '62 households*: the shares of gross assets held by the top 10% and top 1% of households, calculated from the Federal Reserve survey results reported in Dorothy S. Projector and Gertrude A. Weiss, *Survey of Financial Characteristics of Consumers*, Washington: Federal Reserve Board, 1966, Federal Reserve Technical Paper, Table A2. Share of top 10%—between 60.41 and 62.71%; share of top 1%—between 30.10 and 31.10%. The results of a 1953 survey conducted by the Federal Reserve (*Federal Reserve Bulletin*, 1953) showed somewhat less inequality in wealth-holding. Yet the earlier survey appears to have underestimated the inequality of holdings of total assets (Lampman, *Share of Top Wealth-Holders*, pp. 195–196), so that the 1953 distribution may have resembled that for 1962.

(3) *US free males, 1860 and 1870*: shares of gross assets held by richest 10% and richest 1%, from samples drawn from manuscript U.S. censuses. The upper dots for 1860 and the dots for 1870 give Lee Soltow's estimates for free males 20 and older, generously provided to the present author by Professor Soltow in personal correspondence. His estimates are presented in more detail in his *Men and Wealth in the United States, 1850–1870*, New Haven: Yale University Press, 1975. In 1860 the top 10% and the top 1% held 73% and 29% of the personal wealth, respectively. In 1870 their respective shares were 68% and 25% for white adult males, or 70% and 27% among all adult males. The lower dots for the U.S. in 1860 are the shares of wealth held by the top decile and top percentile of *families*, as estimated from the manuscript census by Robert E. Gallman, "Trends in the Size Distribution of Wealth in the Nineteenth Century: Some Speculations," in Lee Soltow, ed., *Six Papers on the Size Distribution of Wealth and Income*, New York: NBER, 1969, Table 1. The top decile held 71 or 72%, depending on whether one treats slaves as property or as penniless potential property owners, while the top percentile held 24% with slaves viewed as either property or penniless potential property owners (but not both).

(4) *Top .031% of US families, 1840–90*: their shares of total national wealth, from Gallman, "Trends in Size Distribution," Table 2. 1840: 6.9%, '50—7.2 to 7.6%, '90: 14.3—19.1%.

(5) *Massachusetts male decendents*: the shares of total estimated wealth held by the richest decile of adult males dying in Massachusetts in the periods 1829–31, 1859–61, 1879–81, and 1889–91. The values held at death show greater inequality than would the values held by living adult males at any point in time. The primary data on the values of probated estates are from Massachusetts Bureau of Statistics of Labor, *Twenty-Fifth Annual Report*, Boston, 1895, Mass. Public Documents for 1894, vol. XI, Doc. 15. The figures for the latter three periods were adjusted for estimated deaths of males without wealth and for assumed distributions of wealth among uninventoried estates by W. I. King, *The Wealth and Income of the People of the United States*, New York: Macmillan, 1915, Tables IX and X and accompanying text. A careful scrutiny of King's estimates

revealed the specific assumptions he made. These assumptions were not given any careful justification but do not seem implausible. I applied the same King assumptions to the 1829–31 distribution of probated wealth. For 1829–31 it was assumed that the total number of adult male deaths was in the same ratio to the adult male population of Massachusetts as in 1859–61, an assumption based on a reading of Maris A. Vinovskis, "Mortality Rates and Trends in Massachusetts before 1860," *Journal of Economic History*, 32, no. 1 (March 1972), pp. 202–213. The top decile shares: 1829–31, 71.27–73.11%; 1859–61, 80.4%; 1879–81, 87.15%; 1889–91, 82.45–83.39%.

(6) *Top 10% and top 1% of Boston taxpayers*: Allen Kulikoff, "The Progress of Inequality in Revolutionary Boston," *William and Mary Quarterly*, 3rd series, 28, no. 3 (July 1971), Table II, and James A. Henretta, "Economic Development and Social Structure in Revolutionary Boston," *William and Mary Quarterly*, 3rd series, 22, no. 1 (January 1965), Tables I, II, p. 185. The estimates, adjusted to include adult males without wealth:

	1687	1771	1790	1830
share held by top 10%:	46.60%	63.46	64.70	65.14
share held by top 1%:	9.51%	25.98	27.14	26.15

In personal correspondence dated November 20, 1975, Gerard B. Warden has warned that one takes great risks in trying to infer the level and trend of wealth inequality from Boston's tax assessments. His own work with the tax lists of 1681 and 1771 suggests that the undervaluation ratios varied greatly (e.g., 1:20 for some kinds of assets, 1:12 for others), while many assets escaped assessment altogether. His own adjustments yield top-decile shares of 42.3% for 1681 and 47.5 for 1771, but he presents these only as rough indications of how sensitive the estimates of wealth inequality are to possible biases in the tax lists.

Less fully explained estimates of the share of Boston's wealth held by the top percentile of "the population" in 1820, 1833, and 1848 are given by Edward Pessen in his *Riches, Class, and Power before the Civil War*, Lexington, Mass.: D. C. Heath, 1973, pp. 38–40.

(7) *Hingham, Mass. taxpayers and males, 1647–1880*: the share of total taxable wealth held by the top decile of Hingham property taxpayers plus adult males with zero property, from Daniel Scott Smith, "Population, Family, and Society in Hingham, Massachusetts, 1635–1880," unpublished Ph.D. dissertation, University of California, Berkeley, 1973, Table III-1 and Appendix Table III-2. Smith's samples from the Hingham tax lists ranged in size from 97 for 1711 up to 347 for 1790. His decile shares: 1647, 22.06%; 1680, 29.43; 1711, 26.49; 1754, 37.44; 1765, 40.09; 1772, 39.93; 1779, 46.52; 1790, 44.66; 1800, 41.86; 1810, 39.10; 1820, 46.22; 1830, 46.98; 1840, 51:40; 1850, 56.65; 1860, 58.80; 1880, 57.47.

(8) *Chester Co., Pa., taxpayers, 1693–1800–02*: James T. Lemon and Gary B. Nash, "The Distribution of Wealth in Eighteenth Century America: A Century of Changes in Chester County, Pennsylvania, 1693–1802," *Journal of Social History* 2, no. 1 (Fall 1968), Table 1. Their estimates of top-decile shares: 1693, 23.8%; 1715, 25.9; 1730, 28.6; 1748, 28.7; 1760, 29.9; 1782, 33.6; 1800–02, 38.3.

(9) *US top 10% and top 1%, 1774*: the estimated share of net worth held by the richest 10% and richest 1% of free potential wealth-holders for the thirteen colonies. The estimates are by Professor Alice Hanson Jones from her books on *Wealth of the Colonies on the Eve of the American Revolution*, New York: Columbia University Press, and *American Colonial Wealth: Documents and Methods*, New York: Arno Press, 1977. Professor Jones converted regional

wealth distributions for probated decedents into regional and all-colony distributions for living adult free wealth-holders using 1800 age distributions. She estimated the total population of potential wealth-holders as the number of adult free males plus 10% of adult free females. Her methods have been described in her article "Wealth Estimates for the New England Colonies about 1770," *Journal of Economic History* 32, no. 1 (March 1972), pp. 98–127.

Professor Jones' estimates differ from those of J. T. Main, which were also developed from probate records and tax lists (*The Social Structure of Revolutionary America*, Princeton: Princeton University Press, 1965, p. 276), and his note on "Trends in Wealth Concentration before 1860," *Journal of Economic History* 31, no. 2 (June 1971), pp. 445–447. Main estimated that the top decile of wealth-holders held around half, and not more than 55%, of total wealth in the early 1770s. It is not clear, however, how he adjusted for differences in regional currencies, differences in regional average wealth, the difference between the age distribution of living adults and probated decedents, or the number of free potential wealth-holders having zero wealth.

(10) *Top 10% of Philadelphia taxpayers and males*: the share of total wealth held by the richest decile of taxpayers plus adult males without wealth, from Gary B. Nash, "Urban Wealth and Poverty in Pre-Revolutionary America," *Journal of Interdisciplinary History* VI, no. 4 (Spring 1976), Tables 1 and 2. I am indebted to Professor Nash for supplying a prepublication copy of these estimates, which he developed from Philadelphia tax lists. Excluded from the measure of taxable wealth are "ships, stock in trade, the values of commissions in merchandise, and money at interest." The estimated top-decile shares: 1693, 46.0%; 1756, 46.6; 1767, 65.7; and 1774, 72.3. Nash's article also gives taxable-wealth distributions for colonial New York and Boston and distributions of probated wealth of decedents in Philadelphia and Boston.

---

income inequality as long as the distribution of saving rates and rates of capital gain and loss across income quantiles does not change much over time.

Is the trend toward unequal wealth a real one? Does it really reflect growing inequalities in the wealth held by people of given age and residential history? Or is it a mirage created by movements in the age distribution and by geographic shifts in population?

Movements in age distribution can change wealth inequality even if the wealth inequality for any age group does not change at all. The old hold vastly greater average wealth than young adults, and whatever creates greater dispersion in the ages of adult heads of households can make inequality look greater. To judge what has been happening to the inequality of economic rewards, one must try to hold the age distribution constant.

It turns out that changes in age distribution cannot explain away the observed drift toward wealth concentration before 1860. Lee Soltow's recent work on the 1870 manuscript census has compared the wealth inequality among all adult males with the wealth inequality within certain age groups. Not surprisingly, wealth was less unequally distributed among the 30–39 age group than among all males.[8] Yet any aging or increasing dispersion in age among adult males falls far short of explaining the historic trend toward wealth concentration before the Civil War. Even if all of the adult male colonial free population had been crammed into the 30–39 age group, its wealth could not have been so equally distributed as in the actual colonial data, if there had been no change in the wealth inequality within age groups before 1860 or 1870. And the actual changes in age distribution were far less dramatic than in this hypothetical change from everybody's being 30–39 in the colonial period to the observed age distribution of 1870. In fact, within the colonial period it is not clear that the adult male population got any older or more dispersed in age from the 1690s to the Revolution, and even in 1860 the age distribution of adult males (slave plus free) was not much older or more dispersed than in colonial times.[9] And even if the adult male population did age and become more dispersed in ages, this process could not account for the observed rise in the share of this population having zero wealth, first within colonial cities and then for the whole U.S. (with or without counting slaves in the population) between the 1770s and 1860.

Geographic population shifts may create the impression of a drift toward inequality where there has been no change in the inequality of wealth for persons of given age and prior residence. We must consider several possible influences of geographic mobility on measures of wealth inequality, first at the national level between 1770 and 1860 and then with respect to the local data from the colonial period.

It is possible that the apparent drift toward wealth inequality between 1770 and 1860 is the result of changes in the share of the population born abroad or changes in the share employed in agriculture. It might be that a rise in the share born abroad would raise aggregate wealth inequality without any change in inequality among persons with given

[8] Lee Soltow, *Men and Wealth in the United States, 1850–1870*, New Haven: Yale University Press, 1975, p. 107.

[9] This sentence is based on an examination of the following age distributions: (a) New England white males, c.1690 (Robert Paul Thomas and Terry Anderson, "White Population, Labor Force, and the Extensive Growth of the New England Economy in the Seventeenth Century," *Journal of Economic History* XXXIII, no. 3, September 1973, p. 654); (b) both sexes, Bedford and New Rochelle, New York, 1698 (Robert Wells, *The Population of the British Colonies in America before 1776*, Princeton: Princeton University Press, 1975, p. 117); (c) Connecticut whites, both sexes, 1774 (ibid., p. 92); (d) U.S. white males, 1800 (*Historical Statistics of the United States*, Series A71–A84); and (e) U.S. males, 1860 (ibid.).

birthplace, by making a higher share of the population have the disadvantage of much lower average wealth because of foreign birth and the costs of migration. Yet what we know about the link between wealth inequality and nativity suggests that changes in the share born abroad could not account for more than a trivial share of the observed drift toward inequality before 1860. Lee Soltow's results for 1870 show that the wealth inequality among native-born Americans was nearly as great as among all Americans. Thus even if the entire population of adult males had been native-born back in 1770, the rise in the foreign-born share to its actual values in 1860 or 1870 could not account for much of the observed drift toward inequality.[10]

The shift of families out of agriculture similarly fails to help explain the drift toward inequality between 1770 and 1860, even though one might have expected it to help. It is true that wealth was more equally distributed among farm families than among all families in the 1870 census sample drawn by Lee Soltow.[11] Yet the difference is small enough so that even if the entire population had lived on farms back in 1770, with the same separate degrees of inequality in and out of agriculture as in 1870, the shift away from farms observed by 1870 could not have raised inequality as much as inequality actually rose. The apparent rise in wealth inequality from 1770 to 1860 was a real rise in the inequality of wealth outcomes for people of given age, nativity, and sector of residence.

Within the colonial period it is harder to know whether geographic shifts could explain away the apparent rise in wealth concentration. We have no aggregate inequality measures before the 1770s. What we have are time series on a few cities, towns, and counties along the seaboard. Geographic migration may have made the apparent rise in wealth inequality misrepresent the trend even within these areas themselves. Suppose, for example, that as Boston grew and the frontier moved westward, the rich and poor tended more and more to cluster in Boston, while a larger share of persons of medium wealth and talent migrated out of Boston in search of new opportunities elsewhere. This selectivity in migration to and from a growing city would cause inequality to rise in the city but not in the entire region. The lack of information about migrants to and from the areas where wealth inequality was greater, plus other miscellaneous doubts about the credibility of the underlying tax-assess-

---

[10] Soltow, *Men and Wealth*, p. 107. The Gini coefficient of wealth inequality for all males in 1870 was .833 and that for native-born males was .831.

[11] Ibid. The Gini coefficient for farm males alone was .765.

ment and probate data, prevents firm conclusions about the wealth inequality trend in the colonial era, beyond the likelihood the inequality was not falling between the late seventeenth century and the Revolutionary War.

It thus seems clear that wealth inequality, with or without adjustments for age, nativity, and residence, was rising between 1770 and 1860, and very possibly within the colonial period as well. The net change was great. In the late seventeenth century, wealth *may* have been more equally distributed among free households than it is today, though the distribution of wealth including slave values among all households, slave or free, was probably as unequal as today. By the time of the Revolution, wealth was distributed about as unequally among free households, and probably more unequally among all households, than today. And by the period 1860–90, wealth was clearly more concentrated than today.

B. THE ANTEBELLUM SURGE OF WAGE INEQUALITY

A very different kind of evidence also suggests a movement toward inequality before the Civil War. Yet the testimonial of the data on occupational wage gaps, unlike those on wealth, confines the trend toward inequality to the period 1816–60.

Wage data gathered by Zachariah Allen for the 1820s showed that skilled workers had less pay advantage over unskilled workers in America than in Britain or France.[12] About a decade later de Tocqueville remarked: "Among the novel objects that attracted my attention during my stay in the United States, nothing struck me more forcibly than the general equality of condition among the people."[13] Yet as the century wore on, such references to the relative equality among Americans became harder and harder to find, and for a good reason.

Time series on pay differentials between perennially highly-paid and low-paid groups, like those shown in Figure 7–2 above, confirm that the occupational gaps widened between 1816 and 1860, or roughly between the War of 1812 and the Civil War. Machinists, carpenters, and other skilled workers rose from a very slight advantage over common labor to

---

[12] Nathan Rosenberg, "Anglo-American Wage Differences in the 1820's," *Journal of Economic History* 27, no. 2 (June 1967), 221–229.

[13] Alexis de Tocqueville, *Democracy in America*, New York: Knopf, 1963 edition, p. 3. While his impression contrasted correctly with later travelers' impressions, one could just as easily have been impressed with the extent of trend toward inequality in de Tocqueville's own time. The trend toward inequality around that time has been stressed by Edward Pessen, *Riches, Class, and Power before the Civil War*, Lexington, Mass.: D. C. Heath and Company, 1973, Chap. 3.

a premium of 60 to 100 percent by the late 1840s, and held onto that edge thereafter. Teachers also began to pull away from unskilled laborers, both in and out of farm areas, in the 1850s. What was suggested by the upward drift of wealth data is also suggested by the separate data on pay gaps: income inequality apparently widened before the Civil War.

C. THE UNEVEN HIGH PLATEAU OF INEQUALITY, 1860–1929

A patchwork quilt of time series on wealth inequality, wage gaps, and inequality measures from early income tax returns covers the period from the Civil War to the Wall Street crash of 1929. Varied as these series are, it seems clear from Figures 7–1 through 7–3 and miscellaneous supporting evidence that the entire period was one of sharp inequalities in income and wealth. It is hard to tell when within this period inequality was the greatest. Between the Civil War and World War I, no clear trend in income inequality can be discerned. Yet two other considerations suggest that the 1880s be considered a possible era of all-time peak inequality. First, the share of total wealth held by the super-rich did rise from before the Civil War to 1880 or 1890, as already noted in connection with Figure 7–3. Second, regional income inequality was at its greatest in 1880, when the South was at its greatest disadvantage.[14] This regional effect may have made 1880, or a year soon thereafter, the year of widest inequalities. Yet the main point about the era between the eve of the Civil War and the eve of World War I is that inequality remained wide and changed little.

Between the wide inequalities shown for 1916 and those shown for 1929 in Figures 7–1 and 7–2, the economy passed through an unprecedented equalization of incomes and an equally pronounced, if slightly slower, reversion back to wide inequalities. For reasons to be considered below, World War I improved the relative income position of the lowest-paid. Unskilled laborers, both on and off the farm, gained ground on skilled workers and professionals, as shown by the series on skilled workers, teachers, professors, and ministers in Figure 7–2. Within three years' time, pay gaps dropped from historic heights to their lowest level since before the Civil War. Then all of this sudden leveling was undone across the 1920s. By 1929 income looked as unequal as ever (though, again, the 1880s may have seen the highest inequality).

[14] For an index of regional income inequality for selected years between 1840 and 1970, see Peter H. Lindert, "Fertility and the Macroeconomics of Inequality," University of Wisconsin-Madison, Institute for Research on Poverty, Discussion Paper no. 219–74, November 1974, Table 1.

FROM FERTILITY TO INEQUALITY

D. THE LEVELING ERA, 1929–51

The data in Figures 7–1 through 7–3 underline the point that income inequality apparently declined dramatically between 1929 and the Korean War. This leveling, first publicized in connection with the research of Simon Kuznets, has been doubted by critics contending that a rise in the tendency of the very rich to underreport their incomes explains away the seeming equalization of incomes.[15] Yet the evidence appears to come down on the side of the debate affirming the existence of an epochal leveling of incomes.

The timing of this leveling is peculiar. It occurred in stages over a historical experience spanning the nation's deepest depression, a sudden wartime recovery, and moderate postwar growth. While a large part of the leveling occurred during World War II, by no means did all of it come then. This timing suggests that the explanation of this drop in inequality must go beyond any simple models that try to relate inequality to either the upswing or the downswing of the business cycle. Also peculiar is the fact that the leveling seems to have been as great in incomes *before* taxes as the estimated redistributive effect of government. That is, there was as much leveling of income that is not directly explained by the rise of government taxes, transfers, and purchases as the amount of income leveling that was achieved through these means.

A comparison of the income inequality measures of Figure 7–1 with the pay ratios and wealth inequality measures of Figures 7–2 and 7–3 also confirms that movements in direct measurements of income inequality happen to be paralleled by movements in cruder proxies for income inequality. The leveling shows up in all three diagrams, the main exception being the ability of physicians to prevent any erosion in their formidable income advantage over the unskilled.

E. POSTWAR STABILITY

Since 1947 the scholar interested in the size distribution of income has had several series to consider—the tax-return data of the Internal Revenue Service, which now cover most of the population; the annual Current Population Survey data from the Census Bureau; and others. Though these series differ in coverage, they tell similar stories, at least when the postwar period as a whole is contrasted with earlier eras. It seems clear that the inequality of income before taxes and government spending was either stable or slightly increasing, with or without adjustments for age

---

[15] For a re-examination of the debate over the extent of the income equalization in this period, see "Three Centuries."

and sex.[16] The net redistribution of income through government budgets has come to level incomes more by 1970 than in the early postwar years, so that income inequality *after* the effects of government may have lessened slightly. The main impression conveyed by the available data, however, is the one suggested by a glance at the postwar years in Figures 7-1 through 7-3: there has been very little change in the degree of inequality since the Korean War, before or after the effects of government.

II. *The Correlation with Labor Force Growth*

What could explain these long-run trends? What changes were most important in accounting for the fact that inequalities and pay ratios reversed their long-run trend sometime near World War I? Were these changes at work in other countries as well? How do they relate to fertility?

I shall suggest in this and the next section that it is difficult to account for the change in trend without assigning a principal role to movements in the quantity and average "quality" of the labor force. Movements in the number of persons in the labor force affect overall inequality by affecting the ratio of profits to (all) wage rates, while movements in the average quality of labor should move the pay ratio.

Although labor supply is given the central role here, it must be stressed that a monocausal theory of income distribution is *not* being advanced. It is only over long periods of time, such as periods each a decade or longer, that the prominence of labor supply as a source of inequality seems to stand out. For shorter periods, and even for comparisons of certain decades, other factors seem to deserve equal emphasis. Even over the long run, it is incorrect to assume that other factors lack a strong unit impact on the distribution of income. Rather, what makes the long-run role of labor supply central is that of all the

---

[16] This statement directly contradicts Morton Paglin's finding that when one adjusts for changes in age distribution, the inequality of income (after transfers but before taxes) has decreased since 1947 ("The Measurement and Trend of Inequality: A Basic Revision," *American Economic Review* 65, no. 4, September 1975, 598–609). Paglin applied a correction for age that inadvertently mixes the effects of changes in labor force participation and genuine changes in pay structure in with age corrections. By correcting the overall inequality index for a different age-income profile each year, Paglin apparently subtracted out a contribution to inequality that grew over the postwar years in part because of a true decline in the relative full-time pay facing younger and less experienced workers of given age and in part because of rising college attendance and earlier retirement in the youngest and oldest age groups.

several forces having a strong unit impact on the degree of inequality, labor supply is the one that happens to have changed greatly.

With this warning about monocausality in mind, let us examine the raw correlation between trends in inequalities and trends in labor supply, in order to suggest what story might be told in terms of the labor supply trends alone. The next section takes up the issue of what other forces might really deserve the credit that this first simplified view attributes to labor supply.

A. PAY RATIOS AND THE GROWTH OF LABOR FORCE SIZE

Figure 7–4 and Table 7–1 compare movements in pay ratios to movements in two measures of labor force growth. The series on changes in pay ratios is again acting partly as a proxy statistic for the movements in overall inequality. For the period 1869/78 on, the more relevant series on the growth of the labor force is that showing the changes in total man-hours worked in peak employment years in the private economy. This series takes account of the trends in part-time work and in average full-time yearly hours, as well as trends in the number of persons in the labor force. We lack hard data on trends in total man-hours worked before 1869/78, but qualitative evidence suggests that man-hours per person employed changed little, making the growth of the number of persons in the labor force a good measure of the growth of man-hours supplied in the early and mid–nineteenth century.

Over long periods of time, there is a positive correlation between the growth of the labor force and the rate of movement toward income inequality. This is true whether labor force growth is being compared with the wage-ratio movements in Figure 7–4 or with changes in the inequality measures in Figure 7–1. In the antebellum period the labor force grew at an average rate as high as 3 percent a year, and inequalities widened. Labor force growth was somewhat less rapid and inequality virtually unchanged from 1860 to 1929. The period 1929–55 brought decreases in inequality on all fronts, along with much lower rates of growth in the labor force. After 1955 the expansion of the labor force picked up moderately, while measures of inequality showed little further change. Within each of these longer periods, to be sure, the correlation between labor force growth and income inequality is much less evident—but the long-run correlation is unmistakable nevertheless.

B. LABOR FORCE QUALITY GROWTH IN THE TWENTIETH CENTURY

To read causation into the correlation between rapid growth of the labor force and rising income inequality, one needs at least evidence that more

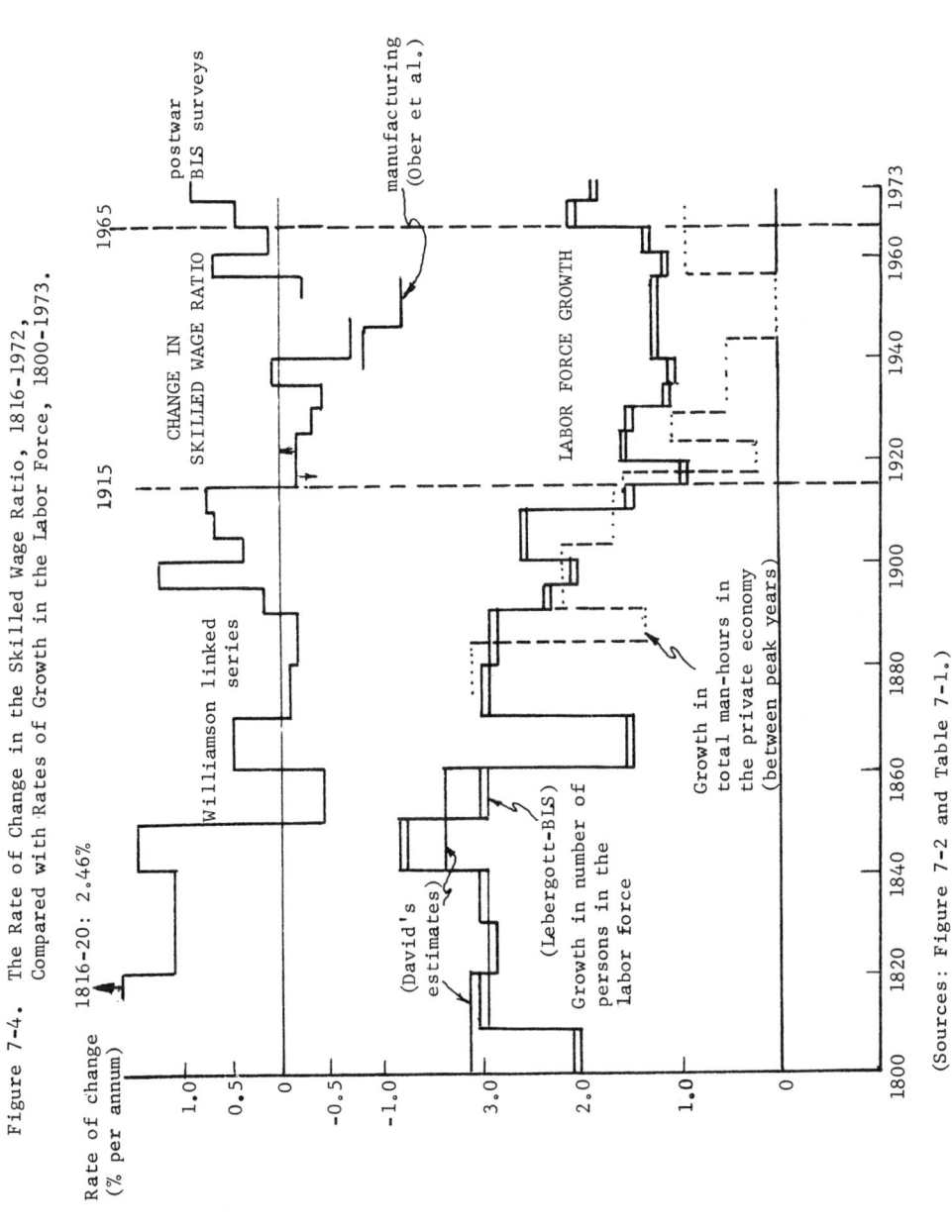

Figure 7-4. The Rate of Change in the Skilled Wage Ratio, 1816-1972, Compared with Rates of Growth in the Labor Force, 1800-1973.

(Sources: Figure 7-2 and Table 7-1.)

[237]

Table 7-1. Rates of Growth in the Size and Quality of the Labor Force, Selected Periods, 1800-1973.

(Percent per annum)

	SIZE			QUALITY		
Period	Total labor force, persons 10 and older	Period	Total private man-hours	Period	Denison's index of labor input/man-hr.	Period	Median Schooling of population 25 and over

Period	David estimates
1800-20	3.11
1820-40	2.95
1840-60	3.36

	Lebergott-BLS						
1800-10	2.04						
1810-20	2.97						
1820-30	2.92						
1830-40	2.98						
1840-50	3.77						
1850-60	2.98						
1860-70	1.52						
1870-80	2.96	1869/78-					
1880-90	2.93	1879-88:	3.22				
1890-95	2.35	1879/88-					
1895-00	2.10	1892:	1.39				
1900-05	2.57	1892-03:	2.21				
1905-10	2.57	1903-13:	2.21	1909-15:	0.57		
1910-15	1.53	1913-17:	1.70			1910-20:	0.12
1915-20	0.96	1917-23:	0.26				
1920-25	1.60			1915-29:	0.71	1920-30:	0.24
1925-30	1.53	1923-29:	1.15				
1930-35	1.19					1930-40:	0.24
1935-40	1.11	1929-43:	0.56	1929-48:	1.07		
1940-50	1.27a	1943-56:	-0.01			1940-50:	0.78
1950-55	1.28			1948-58:	0.88	1950-57:	1.87
1955-60	1.16	1956-69:	1.00				
1960-65	1.35			1958-65:	0.38	1957-65:	1.34
1965-70	2.14			1965-69:	0.58	1965-72:	0.48
1970-73	1.94						

a:	1940-45	1945-50
total labor force:	3.01	-0.65
civilian labor force:	-0.45	3.22

FERTILITY, LABOR SUPPLY, INEQUALITY

Sources for Table 7-1

Total labor force, persons ten and older: the David estimates for early periods are from Paul A. David, "The Growth of Real Product in the United States before 1840: New Evidence, Controlled Conjectures," *Journal of Economic History* XXVII, no. 2 (June 1967), p. 196. The Lebergott-BLS series is from U.S. Bureau of Economic Analysis, *Long-Term Economic Growth, 1860–1970*, Washington: GPO, 1973, Series A107 (to 1930) and A108 (from 1930 on), plus the *Economic Report of the President* for the most recent years and the Lebergott volume cited in *Long-Term* . . . for the early nineteenth century.

Total man-hours in the private economy: 1909–29—Edward F. Denison, *The Sources of Economic Growth and the Alternatives Before Us*, New York: Committee for Economic Development, 1962, p. 85. 1929–69—Edward F. Denison, *Accounting for United States Economic Growth, 1929–1969*, Washington: Brookings Institution, 1974, Table 4–1. Denison's index has been criticized as an overestimate of the rate of growth of labor quality attributable to schooling by David Schwartzman, "The Contribution of Education to the Quality of Labor, 1929–1963," *American Economic Review* LVIII, no. 3, pt. 1 (June 1968), pp. 508–514. Schwartzman's criticisms, however, do not seem to alter the ranking of different time periods according to their rates of growth in labor quality per man-hour.

Median years of schooling of population twenty-five and over: U.S. Bureau of Economic Analysis, *Long-Term* . . . , Series B40, reproducing the estimates of Folger and Nam and of the decennial censuses. Other estimates have been offered for 1960 and earlier census years by Susan O. Gustavus and Charles B. Nam, "Estimates of the 'True' Educational Distribution of the Adult Population of the United States from 1910 to 1960," *Demography* 5, no. 1 (1968), pp. 410–421. The Gustavus-Nam revisions lower the median level slightly for 1960 and increasingly for each earlier census. As a result, using their revised estimates raises the rate of growth in median schooling of adults for each decade from 1910–60, and slightly raises the rate for the early 1960s as well. Their revisions do not cover more recent years, and I have assumed that the recent estimates are not subject to the second-guessing they applied to the Folger-Nam backward projections based on the age distributions in 1950 and 1960.

rapid growth in the labor force was accompanied by slower growth in the average quality or skills of workers. If that can be shown, then there is a basis for believing that the immigration or baby boom that accelerated the growth of person-hours available also shifted labor supply toward lower skills than otherwise, thereby heightening inequalities of earnings and of total income.

Movements in the average skill level of the labor force have been estimated by Edward F. Denison for the period 1909–69. As shown in Table 7–1, his estimates suggest that the growth of labor quality accelerated from 1910 to the decade after World War II—a span of time over which the rate of growth in the size of the labor force had slowed down (and temporarily stopped in the period 1943–56). This acceleration in labor force quality stems mainly from trends in schooling, which are also represented in Table 7–1, by the rates of growth in median years of schooling. The series on schooling growth shows the same acceleration shown in Denison's series during the period of declining growth in the numbers of persons and man-hours in the labor force. The figures on schooling levels also show that in the 1960s and early 1970s, when the labor force was beginning to grow faster again, the rise in median and mean years of schooling for persons over twenty-five slowed down. A closer look at the advance of schooling suggests that slower rates of growth in the schooling of the labor force should continue through the 1970s. The reason is that the generation of children born in the postwar baby boom has thus far not shown enough more years of schooling than the immediately preceding cohorts to match the previous rates of growth in schooling.[17] The rate of growth in annual school days attended per child of school age has also been slower after World War II than earlier in this century, as shown in Table 7–2. It further appears unlikely that an acceleration of accumulated training on the job has been offsetting the deceleration of adults' total schooling since the 1960s, in view of the fact that the labor force is becoming younger and less experienced as postwar boom babies enter its ranks.

Within the twentieth century, then, it appears that the rate of growth of the "quality"—essentially, the schooling—of the labor force accelerated when that of the number of man-hours slowed down, and later slowed down when the growth in man-hours and persons picked up again. On both the "quality" and quantity fronts, a reversal in the growth rate trend came in the 1960s. This inverse relationship suggests a reason for the otherwise puzzling correlation between the trends in the skilled wage ratios and the trends in the growth of man-hours. It is not surprising that the skilled wage ratios and teachers' pay ratios declined rapidly in the 1940s and early 1950s, when the quality of the labor force was growing rapidly. Nor is it surprising that the same ratios also were dropping in the interwar period, when the supply of low-skilled immigrants was curtailed by the restrictive immigration laws of 1921, 1924, and 1929. The trends in the average quality of the labor supplied were in turn correlated inversely with the trends in man-hours, yielding a correlation in Figure 7–4 between the growth of the size of the labor force and the trends in pay ratios.

There even seems to be reason to believe that the concurrence of

[17] Beverly Duncan, "Trends in the Output and Distribution of Schooling," in E. B. Sheldon and W. E. Moore, eds., *Indicators of Social Change*, New York: Russell Sage Foundation, 1968, p. 611.

Table 7-2. Rates of Growth in School Enrollment Rates and Attendance Rates, 1850-1970.

(percent per annum)

Rate of growth in:

Period	(1) Pupils enrolled per child of school age	(2) Days attended per year per pupil enrolled	(3)=(1)+(2) Days attended per child of school age
1850-60	0.70a	..	..
1860-70	-0.44a	..	..
1870-80	1.77a	0.34	2.11
1880-90	0.46b	0.62	1.08
1890-00	0.08c	1.37	1.45
1900-10	0.15c	1.32	1.45
1910-20	0.48c	0.70	1.18
1920-30	0.68c	1.65	2.33
1930-40	0.47c	0.59	1.06
1940-50	-0.16c	0.39	0.55
(1940-44)	(-1.39)c	(-0.63)	(-2.02)
(1944-50)	(0.66)c	(1.09)	(1.75)
1950-60	0.27c	0.14	0.41
1960-70	0.22c	0.23	0.45

Notes and sources to Table 7-2:

a: based on ratio of enrollments for all ages to population 5-19.
b: based on ratio of enrollments 5-17, public schools only, to population 5-17.
c: based on ratio of public plus non-public school enrollments 5-17 to population 5-17.

Sources: U.S. Bureau of Economic Analysis, Long-term Economic Growth, 1860-1970 (Washington: GPO, 1973), Series B36 and B39; and U.S. Bureau of the Census, Historical Statistics for the United States... (Washington: GPO, 1960), pp. 207, 213.

changes in these various trends in the last half-century stems from the nature of growth in the labor force. The fall in fertility and the shutting off of immigration, both of which kept down the growth of the size of the labor force before the 1960s, may both have helped to accelerate the growth of its average skill level, thereby pushing down the skilled wage ratios between the 1920s and the 1960s. Both made the labor force rise in average age and experience. The reduction in fertility before World War II, like the shutting off of immigration, may have accelerated the advance of schooling from cohort to cohort. Conversely, the entrance of baby-boom cohorts into the labor force after the mid-1960s may help to explain the absence of any further leveling in income inequality before taxes and transfers in the postwar period.

C. LABOR FORCE QUALITY GROWTH IN THE NINETEENTH CENTURY

To judge how the rate of growth of skills before 1909 compared with more recent rates, one must use less direct measures of labor force quality. Instead of the schooling of the labor force itself, we have data on the enrollment and attendance rates of children, most of whom were to enter the labor force later, plus important data on immigration. The data on enrollment and attendance rates in Table 7–2 show no clear difference between the rates of growth in schooling per child between the second half of the nineteenth century and the first half of the twentieth. The only clear break comes around 1950, when the growth of both enrollment rates and days attended per enrolled pupil decelerates. Note that these indicators refer only to trends in the schooling of the part of the labor force that grew up in the United States.

A clearer contrast between the eras before and after, say, 1909 or 1915 is offered by what we know about immigration into the U.S. Before World War I fluctuations in the average skill level of the labor force were apparently dominated by changes in immigration. Immigration often accounted for a third of the growth in the U.S. labor force. More relevant for the history of skilled wage ratios, the level and nature of immigration fluctuated considerably. When the rate of new arrivals jumped, the economy was presented with a generous supply of workers with lower levels of skills and market contacts than characterized the U.S. labor force as a whole.[18] The shortfall in their relative skills also fluctuated across the nineteenth century and the early twentieth century.

Figure 7–5 illuminates the link between immigration, the growth of the labor force size, the growth of labor force quality, and trends in wage ratios. The period in which new arrivals from abroad had the greatest impact on the U.S. labor force was the decade 1846–55, when a flood of Irish (and Germans) came to America. The period of second greatest impact in proportion to the size of the U.S. labor force was the last decade of peace before World War I. These two decades of peak influx were special in other ways as well. They were the decades in which the relative occupational "quality" of the immigrants was lowest. The data

---

[18] Brinley Thomas, *Migration and Economic Growth*, 2nd edition, Cambridge: Cambridge University Press, 1973, Chap. IX; Robert Higgs, "Race, Skills, and Earnings: American Immigrants in 1909," *Journal of Economic History* 31, no. 2 (June 1971), pp. 420–428.

FERTILITY, LABOR SUPPLY, INEQUALITY

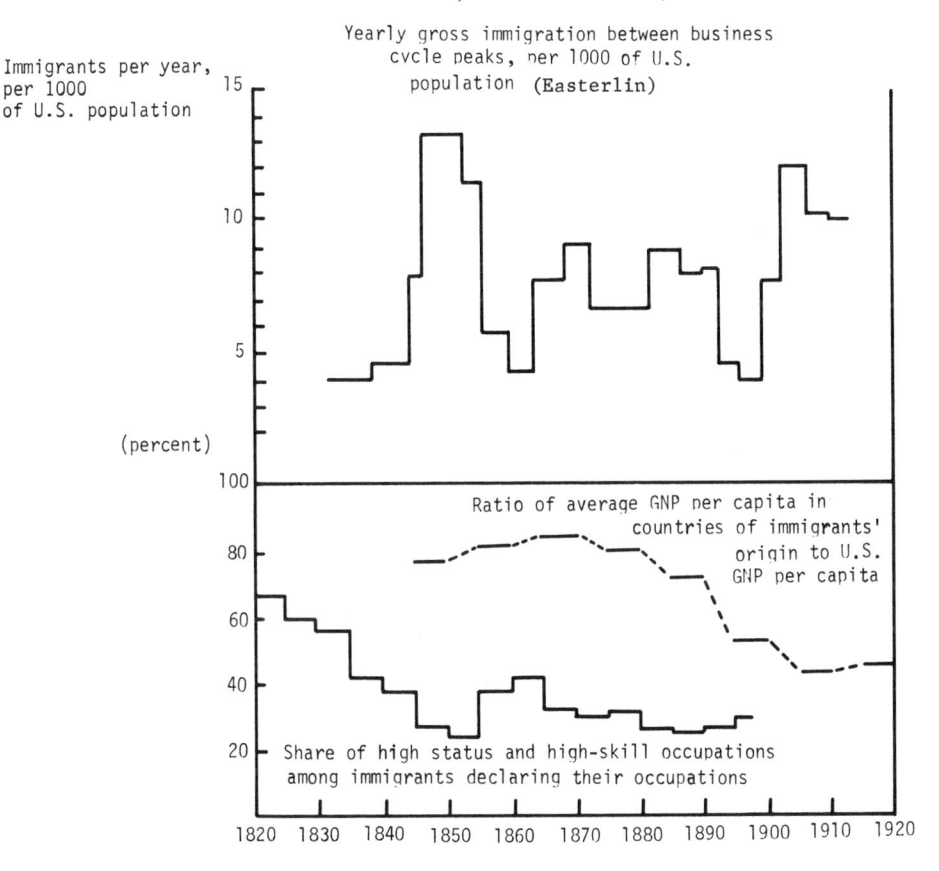

Figure 7-5. The Size and Economic Status of Immigration Flows into the United States, 1820-1920

NOTES AND SOURCES FOR FIGURE 7-5

(a) *Yearly gross immigration between business cycle peaks, per 1000 of U.S. population*: Richard A. Easterlin, *Population, Labor Force, and Long Swings in Economic Growth*, New York: Columbia University Press, 1968, Table B-2. The series stops with 1910-13.

(b) *Ratio of average GNP per capita in countries of immigrants' origin to U.S. GNP per capita*: Appendix G. The observations plotted refer to shares in immigration into the U.S. in the second halves of decades (e.g., 1846-50, 1856-60). The ratios of GNP per capita to that for the U.S., as explained in Appendix G, are for the preceding U.S. census years (e.g., 1840 for the 1846-50 immigrants).

(c) *Share of high-skill and high-status occupations among immigrants declaring their occupations*: U.S. Bureau of the Census, *Historical Statistics of the United States . . .* (1960), Series C115–C132. The figures refer to average quinquennial shares taken by the categories "professional," "commercial," and "skilled" in total declared occupations. The last observation is 1896-98, after which a new and non-comparable occupational classification was adopted.

on the occupational classes of immigrants single out the Irish wave in mid-century as one in which the unskilled occupations reached their highest share of the total declared occupations. The 1903–13 wave consisted primarily of immigrants from lower-income, non–English-speaking countries in eastern and southern Europe. Both waves helped to create the "labor aristocracy" that gave the English-speaking skilled native workers as high a pay advantage over the unskilled as skilled workers enjoyed in any other high-income country. The pay ratio series in Figure 7–2 also seem to mark out both the decade 1846–55 and the decade 1903–13 as periods of rising inequality.

It appears from this partial evidence that if we had a series on the rates of growth in the relative skill of the labor force from 1800 to the present, a consistent pattern would be seen. The periods in which the size of the labor force grew the fastest—in particular, the entire period before World War I—were periods in which the growth of the average skill level of the labor force grew slowly. And the period of slower growth in the labor force—roughly, the half-century from 1915 to 1965—was one of relatively rapid upgrading of the skill of the labor force. Furthermore, the periods in which numbers grew relatively fast and average skill relatively slowly were periods of rising (or steady) inequalities. The leveling of incomes was confined to the period of growth more in the quality than in the size of the labor force. There is a correlation, in other words, that points unmistakably at an explanation of inequality trends in which labor supply is the prime variable.

III. *Competing Explanations*

Correlation is not causation, and there are many completely different forces from those mentioned so far that may be the true causes of movements in American inequalities, movements that just happen to resemble movements in labor supply. These must be considered carefully before one can reach conclusions about the apparent long-run role of labor supply. Most of these competing explanations fail to fit the facts, but some do fit and cannot be rejected.

A. INFLATION AND EQUITY

If one ignores the employment and price twists of the Great Depression, there is a correspondence between periods of inflation and periods of leveling of incomes and wage rates. Furthermore, inflations in industrialized countries in this century have, until 1970, been tied to wars. It has been argued that inflation levels incomes and rates of pay in several ways. First, the postwar data clearly show a negative short-run cyclical relationship between inflation and measures of overall inequality of income. The reason is simply that inflation has been accompanied by reductions in unemployment great enough to govern the cyclical movement of inequality. The link between extra jobs and more equal incomes, however, is just a cyclical influence on aggregate inequality and lacks the scope to account for the parallel longer-run trends shown above.

A second variation on the inflation theme is that higher-level salaries are more fixed in money terms than unskilled wage rates. Higher-level salaries are often negotiated on long-term contracts and adjust only very slowly to unforeseen changes in the cost of living. This argument is supported by the fact that teachers' salaries, to take an example already implicit in Figure 7–2 above, failed to keep pace with the cost of living and unskilled wage rates during sudden inflations, and correspondingly failed to drop as fast when prices fell off in the early 1930s. The difficulty with this sticky-salary variation on the inflation argument is that it fails to explain why the equalizing that comes with sudden inflation should persist long after the inflation has stopped and all salaries have been renegotiated several times over (1920s, 1954–1960s).

Another variation on the inflation theme is one that sometimes relates to inflation and sometimes does not. It has been argued that in periods of wartime inflation the public considers it only fair that rates of pay should advance most rapidly (in percentage terms) for the poor. In part the argument seems to be that a fear that the poor will be especially damaged by inflation turns sentiments in favor of more egalitarian pay settlements. But in part the argument seems to say that major wars call for a sharing of national burdens that is inconsistent with prewar economic inequalities. The same band-together spirit encouraged by having rich and poor stand in the same ration lines, and by knowing during World War II that Princess Elizabeth was an auto mechanic, may well have been a force compelling a jump in unskilled wage rates up toward skilled levels.

This wartime-sharing variant has the strength of being an argument that is consistent with the persistence of an egalitarian pay structure for some time after the war has ended. Once equity-consciousness has been raised by the wartime experience, it is plausible that the spirit should linger on in postwar pay settlements. It is difficult to see, however, how such a shift in attitude could still be a prime determinant of the pay structure a decade later. Competition and profit-maximization would soon take their toll and reward those firms and workers who agreed on rates of pay re-establishing the old inequalities if nothing but social attitudes had changed. The new attitudes could only persist if something else in the postwar setting made lower pay differentials profitable to tens of thousands of employers. To persist in the private sector, equity must be profitable.

All of the inflation and equity theories about income inequalities suffer from the additional defect that inequalities have failed to drop during some wars and other inflations. Pay ratios showed little net movement during the Civil War and drifted upward during the gentle 1900–13 inflation. Inequalities and pay ratios were not greatly affected by the Vietnam war, except to the extent that fuller employment brought extra incomes to the poor. Thus far the inflation of the 1970s has apparently done little leveling, since it has been characterized by less-than-full employment and a relative rise in the food and fuel prices that take a greater share of poor budgets than of rich.

B. UNIONS

The greatest reductions in wage differentials and overall inequality came in a period of rising union power. And while American unions have lacked an explicit policy for changing wage differentials, their demands have seemed to favor the lower-skilled worker, more since the 1930s than before. It is reasonable to ask whether the impact of unions has been to raise the relative wages of the unskilled, while raising all wages at the expense of profits.

At the local level, one can find cases in which the impact of unions on the wage structure has been profound. For example, the patternmakers at the McCormick Works were able to win a handsome hike in their pay advantage vis-à-vis unskilled workers during World War II, at a time when skilled wage premia were dropping in most sectors.[19]

At the aggregate level, however, the union impact on income and wage rate inequalities has apparently been minor at most. Union members still make up less than 30 percent of the labor force, and pay differentials have moved similarly in unionized and nonunionized industries. Changes in union power provide no explanation for the apparent reduction in some measures of inequality between 1913 and 1929, or for the tendency of pay differentials to stabilize after the Korean War, when union membership was greater than ever before. Furthermore, even if unions had won for their members the maximum possible influence al-

[19] Robert Ozanne, "A Century of Occupational Differentials in Manufacturing," *Review of Economics and Statistics* 44 (August 1962), 293, 296, 298.

lowed them H. Gregg Lewis' study,[20] they could not have reduced aggregate measures of inequality as much as these measures have declined in this century, in part because unions offer no relative gains for large numbers of unskilled nonunion workers. Even what influence unions seem to have had is to be denied them in a longer-run perspective when one recognizes that union power can level rates of pay for decades only if the marketplace and/or the government somehow conspire to keep up the demand, or keep down the supply, of the kinds of labor that have become unionized. It thus appears, as other studies have concluded for pay ratios,[21] that union power can account for very little if any of the long-run aggregate movement in wage ratios or overall income inequalities.

Another form of union impact also seems to fall short as an explanation for trends in wage ratios and overall inequality. Unions have successfully pushed for the passage of minimum wage legislation ever since the New Deal, and it is reasonable to wonder whether or not this might not account for the leveling in the 1940s. Since the demand for unskilled labor always has some elasticity, especially over a decade or more, any ability of minimum wage legislation to drive up the relative price of unskilled labor would have to be reflected in either a sustained rise in unemployment specific to the unskilled or a retardation of the migration of workers from the legally exempt farm sector. Neither of these developments occurred in the 1940s and early 1950s, when wage differentials were shrinking.

If one entertains the further argument that these indications of the effectiveness of minimum wage legislation were prevented by government expansion aimed at preserving full employment along with legal minimum wages, it remains to be shown that the net result of this combination of policies would have somehow kept skilled wages and profits from rising during the inflation designed to employ all of the unskilled at the minimum wage rates. The minimum wage hypothesis would at that point become equivalent to the inflation argument already examined.

---

[20] H. Gregg Lewis, *Unionism and Relative Wages in the United States*, Chicago: University of Chicago Press, 1963.

[21] George Hildebrand and George E. Delahanty, "Wage Levels and Differentials," in Robert A. Gordon and Margaret S. Gordon, eds., *Prosperity and Unemployment*, New York: John Wiley and Sons, 1966, pp. 265–301; and Robert Evans, Jr., *The Labor Economies of the United States and Japan*, New York: Praeger, 1971, pp. 189–191.

FROM FERTILITY TO INEQUALITY

C. THE SUPPLY OF LAND

It is common to argue that the rapid expansion of available land in America before 1900 must have been a considerable democratizing and leveling influence. An unskilled worker who faced poor prospects in Eastern industry could flee to the opportunity of developing a farm on good soil relatively unencumbered with obligations to landlords and governments. As more and more farmland became accessible, it might have turned out that incomes leveled.

Yet this influence was apparently never the predominant one on the distribution of income among Americans. In the nineteenth century, when the supply of land grew rapidly, the distribution of wealth and skilled wage ratios moved toward inequality. Two decades after the rate of growth of farm acreage dropped off at the start of this century, income and wealth began to become more equally distributed. What we know about the supply of land reinforces, rather than solves, the task of explaining the historic trends in income distribution.

D. ENGEL'S LAW AND THE SHIFT OUT OF AGRICULTURE

Engel's Law has established that a given percentage increase in income per capita causes a smaller, but definitely positive, reduction in the share of household incomes spent on food. Largely for this reason, resources have been shifting out of agriculture for two centuries. Since agriculture tends to employ unskilled labor more intensively than the rest of the economy, it is reasonable to suspect that variations in the degree and impact of the shift in demand away from agriculture might affect the relative income of unskilled labor, thereby contributing to an explanation of trends in inequality. Other authors have previously pointed out that a growth-induced shift of resources out of agriculture affects the degree of overall inequality in more ways than one. The shift in demand away from farm products should tend to raise the ratios of nonfarm skilled wage rates and profit rates to the wage rate on unskilled labor. On the other hand, the same shift should hurt the returns to farmland more than the wage rates for the unskilled, a tendency that should help reduce inequalities, since farmland is less equally distributed than farm or total unskilled labor power. At the same time, for any given structure of rates of pay, the migration of persons and property from the farm to the nonfarm sector can itself shift the degree of overall inequality.

It seems reasonable to suspect that growth in incomes, by shifting resources out of agriculture,[22] should widen gaps between higher earning rates (and profit rates) and the unskilled rate, even though the effect on the returns to farm property should partly counteract this inegalitarian tendency. The difficulty with this explanation of trends in inequality comes on the empirical level rather than the theoretical. The shift out of agriculture has been proceeding rather steadily throughout our national history, and the rate of decline in agriculture's share was no greater when income inequality was widening before about 1910, or when it was steady after the Korean War, than when it was falling between the last prewar decade and the decade following World War II. It would appear that over the long run the growth of incomes and Engel's Law have had much less influence on the relative wage rate of unskilled labor than they have had on the returns to farmland ownership.

The other type of argument stressing the shift out of agriculture is the interesting suggestion by Kuznets[23] and others that a steady movement of the population out of agriculture, even with rates of pay constant, can first raise and then lower overall inequality. The suggestion should be taken seriously, in view of the movement of U.S. income and wealth first toward and then away from inequality.

Under certain conditions, but not under others,[24] a steady migration away from agriculture can indeed generate a curved path of inequality. To see how, let us imagine a simple example similar to that used by Kuznets. Suppose that everyone employed in agriculture earned $5,000 a year and everyone employed outside of agriculture earned $10,000 a year. Start from a situation in which everyone was employed in agriculture. The migration of the first person to the new higher-paying sector would create inequality where none had existed before. Further migration would for a while continue to raise most measures of inequality, such as the share earned by the top 5 percent of individuals. Ultimately,

---

[22] Note that the exogenous force here is not the shift in demand itself but instead the whole set of forces, such as improved technology, that raise income per capita. The shift in demand away from agriculture would be the parameter only if one were interested in comparing the actual course of economic growth with a hypothetical world in which there were no Engel effects on demand shares for different sectors. The universality of Engel's Law makes such a counterfactual hypothesis uninteresting.

[23] Simon Kuznets, "Economic Growth and Income Inequality," *American Economic Review* 45, no. 1 (March 1955), 1–28.

[24] Again see Theil, *Economics and Information Theory*, pp. 114–120, for a mathematical derivation of the conditions under which the migration from one sector to another raises inequality.

though, the migration must bring a return to equality in this simple example. When the last farmer had moved to the other sector, perfect equality would again be restored, since everyone would be earning $10,000.

It turns out that this possibility is not only mathematically fragile but also unhelpful in explaining what has happened to the American distribution of income. Data series like those shown in Figure 7–2 make it clear that the up-then-down movement of inequality holds *within* each major sector, and is not just an aggregate artifact of migration between sectors. The forces that first widened and then narrowed inequalities were more pervasive in their impact than the migration examples can imply.

E. BIASES IN TECHNOLOGICAL PROGRESS

A potentially powerful determinant of the distribution of income is the degree to which the course of technological progress tends to economize on certain factors of production and to favor the use of others. A bias toward saving on unskilled labor can widen income gaps by worsening job prospects and relative wage rates for the unskilled while bidding up rates of return on skills and property.

Econometric estimates of the aggregate bias in technological change in the twentieth century encourage the belief that in the pattern of bias we have discovered one of the keys to trends in American inequality. For the U.S. economy as a whole each of several studies has found considerable labor-saving bias from around the start of this century to 1929, followed by either neutrality or a labor-using bias from 1929 to World War II, and some debate over whether or not a strong labor-saving bias has resumed in the postwar period.[25] None of these studies actually made separate measurement of the use of unskilled and of skilled labor. This aggregation of all labor makes it more difficult to get inferences about the distribution of income, but it can be guessed that an era of labor-saving technological change is one in which the labor being replaced with other inputs by the change in techniques tends to be unskilled. The econometric literature thus suggests that the equalization of

[25] Paul A. David and Th. Van de Klundert, "Biased Efficiency Growth and Capital-Labor Substitution in the United States, 1899–1960," *American Economic Review* 55, no. 2 (June 1965), 357–394; Murray Brown, *On the Theory and Measurement of Technological Change*, Cambridge: Cambridge University Press, 1966, Chap. 10; M. Morishima and M. Saito, "An Economic Test of Sir John Hicks' Theory of Biased Induced Inventions," in J. R. Wolfe, ed., *Value, Capital, and Growth*, Chicago: Aldine, 1968, pp. 415–445.

FERTILITY, LABOR SUPPLY, INEQUALITY

incomes between 1929 and 1945 may have been due to a switch in the bias of aggregate technological progress from labor-saving to labor-using. The absence of any further equalization within the postwar era might be tied to the tendency of technology to drift toward labor-saving once again.

On closer examination, this explanation breaks down for longer-run movements, though it is still of considerable help in explaining certain decade-to-decade changes. To understand the causal role of technological bias, one must be careful to identify what part of the aggregate technological change is in fact exogenous rather than just a reflection of other forces already measured separately. The aggregate technological bias, say, toward labor-saving can for any time period be decomposed into the following more usable parts:

(1) Aggregate bias due to shifts in sectoral shares of output (e.g., the shift out of agriculture);
(2) Bias due to differences in the rate of neutral productivity advance between sectors using labor in different degrees;
(3) The labor-saving bias within sectors, (a) some of which is a response to movements in factor prices, and (b) some of which is exogenous.

All of the first source and some of the third source of aggregate technological bias [i.e., (1) and (3a)] are not causal influences. The shift of resources from, say, agriculture to other sectors is something that looks like an unskilled-labor–saving technological change, in that the receiving sectors use unskilled labor less intensively than does agriculture. But the shift of resources between sectors is not an exogenous determinant of the processes that determine incomes. It is instead an endogenous part of the same processes, and requires explanation. It may be that some other dimension of technological change, such as a rapid rate of technological progress outside of agriculture, is the cause of the shift between sectors, but the point remains that the sectoral shift itself [(1) above] is not a causal influence on the income distribution. The same point can be made about (3a): an apparent bias toward labor-saving that is just a response to rising wages does not deserve to be counted as a factor influencing wage rates and other incomes (unless one is for some reason comparing what actually happened with a hypothetical world in which substituting other factors for labor were impossible). Thus, to identify technological biases that are independent influences on the distribution of income, one must empirically isolate the exogenous factors, (2) and (3b) above.

Some authors have taken care to provide measures of technological bias that succeed in pointing out some of its exogenous components for the United States in this century.[26] One outcome of these studies is to show that most of the apparent aggregate bias is due to shifts in sectoral shares plus sectoral differences in rates of neutral productivity advance. It turns out that a prime determinant of demand for factors has been the difference in neutral productivity advance between agriculture, which uses unskilled labor intensively, and industry (all nonfarm nonservice sectors). For example, Keller and Williamson have shown that what looked like a jump in labor-saving bias from the years around World War I to the 1920s was the result of a jump in the difference between productivity growth in manufacturing and in agriculture. With productivity advancing much more rapidly in manufacturing, which used unskilled labor much less intensively than agriculture, aggregate measures recorded a bias toward techniques—actually, toward a sector—that used unskilled labor much more sparingly.

Over the longer period, the productivity estimates of Kendrick and others show that productivity continued to advance more rapidly in manufacturing, transportation, and utilities than in agriculture until sometime around World War II. There is some evidence that this intersectoral gap in neutral productivity advance favored the nonfarm sector more during periods of rising income inequality—1889–1909 and 1919–29—than during periods of declining inequalities—1909–19 and 1929–53.[27] The intersectoral gap in productivity growth may have been greatest in the antebellum surge toward wage inequality between the 1820s and 1860. In that era total factor productivity hardly changed at all in agriculture, while an assortment of studies of textiles, shipping,

---

[26] Kendrick has presented separate estimates of total factor productivity growth for several sectors and subsectors for several periods from 1889 to 1953. Morishima and Saito, Keller, and Williamson have all examined the decomposition of technological bias into the working parts listed above. See John W. Kendrick, *Productivity Trends in the United States*, Princeton: Princeton University Press, 1961, pp. 136–137; Morishima and Saito, "Economic Test of Hicks' Theory"; Robert Keller, "Factor Income Distribution in the United States during the 1920s: A Re-examination of Fact and Theory," *Journal of Economic History* 33, no. 1 (March 1973), 252–273; and Jeffrey G. Williamson, "War, Immigration, and Technology: American Distributional Experience, 1913–1929," University of Wisconsin-Madison, Graduate Program in Economic History, Discussion Paper EH 74-24, April 1974.

[27] Kendrick, *Productivity Trends*, pp. 136–137.

railroads, and firearms suggests very rapid rates of growth in total factor productivity in these manufacturing sectors, which had weaker demands for unskilled labor and stronger demands for skills and machinery.[28] The expansions and contractions of the intersectoral gaps in productivity growth have thus tended to correspond with movements toward and away from income inequality.

This parallelism has not continued after World War II, however. Farm mechanization, the diffusion of hybrid seed varieties, and other improvements have raised the rate of productivity growth in agriculture to what looks like its historic peak. The intersectoral gap in productivity growth has been virtually closed. If the intersectoral imbalance in technological progress were the main force driving movements in income inequality throughout American history, then the postwar era should have seen a dramatic leveling of incomes. Yet, as we have seen, the earlier leveling of the income distribution came to a halt in the postwar era, when inequality hardly changed. The postwar shift from leveling to stability fits the labor-supply argument better than it fits the technological-imbalance view of what has determined movements in equality.

Subject to this postwar exception, it appears that in the sectoral differences in productivity growth we have found a force that can compete with movements in the quantity and quality of labor supply as a partial explanation of changes in the trends in American inequality.

F. THE RATE OF CAPITAL ACCUMULATION

If the rate of accumulation of nonhuman capital were an exogenous force, it would seem attractive as an additional explanation for the observed trends in inequality. Between 1840 and 1860, when inequalities

---

[28] The articles by Robert Zevin on textiles and Douglass North on ocean shipping, both in Robert W. Fogel and Stanley L. Engerman, eds., *The Reinterpretation of American Economic History*, New York: Harper and Row, 1971; Paul A. David, *Technical Choice, Innovation and Economic Growth*, Cambridge: Cambridge University Press, 1975, Chaps. 2 and 3 on cotton textiles; Albert Fishlow, "Productivity and Technological Change in the Railroad Sector, 1840–1910," in Dorothy S. Brady, ed., *Output, Employment, and Productivity in the United States after 1800*, New York: Columbia University Press, 1966, NBER Studies in Income and Wealth vol. 30, pp. 583–646, especially Table 10; and Paul J. Uselding, "Technical Progress at the Springfield Armory, 1820–1850," *Explorations in Economic History* 9, no. 3 (Spring 1972), 291–316. The stagnation of antebellum agricultural productivity is discussed at length by Robert E. Gallman, "The Agricultural Sector and the Pace of Economic Growth; U. S. Experience in the Nineteenth Century," in David C. Klingaman and Richard K. Vedder, eds., *Essays in Nineteenth Century Economic History: The Old Northwest*, Athens, Ohio: Ohio University Press, 1975, pp. 35–76.

were widening, the capital stock grew faster than 6 percent a year. Across the plateau of high and roughly stable inequality from 1860 to 1929, the capital stock grew at about 4 percent a year. During the leveling era, roughly 1929–51, capital growth dropped to only 1 percent a year. During the postwar era of no change in inequality, the capital stock grew at about 3.3 percent a year.[29] These swings in the rate of capital accumulation were wide enough so that even the capital stock *per man-hour* grew faster during the drift toward inequality than during the leveling period. This correlation suggests that more rapid accumulation of nonhuman capital may raise inequalities by bidding up the return to skills of all sorts while displacing unskilled labor. That surmise is encouraged by the findings of Griliches[30] and Berndt and Christensen[31] that capital and skills tend to be complementary inputs, both of which tend to be substitutes for unskilled labor.

Yet the rate of capital accumulation is a variable that no explanation of trends in income inequality can afford to leave unexplained and exogenous. Both intuition and recent battles in economic growth theory point to the relationship between income distribution and capital accumulation as being a simultaneous, or reciprocal, one. It is as easy to argue that income inequality fosters rapid capital accumulation as it is to argue the reverse. To make good use of the information we have about trends in the rate of capital accumulation, one must identify long-run influences that could have altered both the rate of accumulation and the degree of income inequality together. Two basic changes in the economy could have caused the rate of accumulation, the trend in inequality, and the rate of profit all to take a long-term drop as they did around the time of World War I. Both changes were introduced above. One is the shift in the rate of growth in the labor force. The other is the movement in sectoral differences in total factor productivity advance.

The drop in the rate of growth in the labor force during World War I and again at the end of the twenties is a force that could have squeezed profits, wage and salary inequalities, and capital accumulation simultaneously. The reduction in the rate of growth of the labor force held back the supply of both unskilled and skilled labor. The tendency of the

[29] Lance E. Davis et al., *American Economic Growth*, New York: Harper and Row, 1972, p. 34.

[30] Zvi Griliches, "A Note on Capital-Skill Complementarity," *Review of Economics and Statistics* 51 (November 1969), 465–470.

[31] Ernst R. Berndt and Laurits R. Christensen, "Testing for the Existence of a Consistant Aggregate Index of Labor Input," *American Economic Review* 64, no. 3 (June 1974), 391–404.

slower growth of the labor force to raise the rate of improvement of its average skill level meant that the restriction in labor supply was more severe in the lower-skill job markets. Faced with this slower supply expansion, firms found it harder to keep profits up. The pressure on profits in turn cut into firms' ability to use inside funds to finance real capital formation. Since borrowed funds are in fact seldom available at the opportunity cost of inside funds, the reduction of profits cuts investments through the total supply of funds as well as through its influence on expectations about the returns from capital formation. If this argument is correct, then the reduction in labor supply growth lowered the pay advantage of skilled labor in two ways: directly, by encouraging the growth of the average skill of those who supply labor; and indirectly, by cutting into the accumulation of nonhuman capital, which is complementary in use with skills. This reduction in the inequality of household incomes may have reinforced itself: if marginal propensities to save are lower in lower-income groups, then the reduction in income inequality could further reduce the rate of household saving and aggregate investment.

It must be acknowledged, though, that this reasoning from labor supply through capital accumulation to inequality rests squarely on an unproven hypothesis: that faster growth in labor force size raises the rate of growth of capital *per man-hour of labor force*. The present argument resembles the belief by Charles P. Kindleberger and others that faster labor supply growth has raised the growth rate of capital per worker in recent times.[32] This belief stands in direct opposition to the vague intuition that faster labor supply growth should retard the substitution of capital for labor, thereby raising capital stock more slowly than the labor force itself grows. This intuition is suspect because it tries to draw an analogy between how an individual firm's investment responds to wage rates and how the entire economy's accumulation responds to labor supply shifts, without explaining how aggregate saving desires are affected. The point remains, nonetheless, that we still lack good evidence either for or against the present presumption that more rapid labor force growth raises the growth rate of capital per man-hour.

The other influence possibly driving skill premia, profits, and accumulation in the same direction is the history of sectoral differences in rates of productivity growth. Recall that productivity apparently advanced faster in industries using unskilled labor less intensively during

[32] Charles P. Kindleberger, *Europe's Postwar Growth: The Role of Labor Supply*, Cambridge: Harvard University Press, 1967, Chaps. I–VI.

the periods 1889–1909 and 1919–29, while this was not true during the decade 1909–19 or after 1929. This pattern, as noted, corresponded roughly with the time division between rising and falling inequalities. It could be that the shift in total factor productivity growth back toward sectors using unskilled labor intensively (agriculture, in particular), especially after 1929, not only depressed skills' pay advantage but also may have cut into profits and capital accumulation to the advantage of returns to farmers as well as to unskilled labor. It is not clear that a shift in the locus of productivity advance would have all these effects, but it is possible.

The effect of taking account of trends in the rate of capital accumulation is thus to add another channel through which movements in labor supply, and possibly sectoral differences in productivity advance, seem likely to have influenced trends in inequality.

G. THE RISE OF GOVERNMENT

The era in which inequalities shrank was also one in which the share of national product consumed by government rose. The wars were, of course, the main influence on government's share, but after each war that share failed to fall all the way back to its prewar position. How might the rise of government have fostered the leveling of personal incomes measured *before* taxes? One way is by raising the share of the labor force drafted or induced into the armed forces, thereby bidding up wages. This type of government influence is but another form of labor supply restriction. Its importance during wars reinforces the labor supply argument always discussed. The other kind of government impact is to shift the composition of demand for final products, both in war and in peace, by replacing what the government buys with what would have been bought were it not for the extra taxes and deficit financing.[33] If it could be shown that the government's purchases of goods and services created a much greater demand for labor, especially for more unskilled labor, than the same amount of displaced private demand, then the rise of government would have been a leveling influence on incomes even

[33] The government can also shift the labor-intensity of final demand with policies other than its own purchases. Tax and tariff policies are good examples. For an investigation of the relevance of tax and tariff policies for income distribution in the wake of the Civil War, see Jeffrey G. Williamson, "What *Should* the Civil War Tariff Have Done Anyway?" University of Wisconsin-Madison, Social Science Research Institute, Discussion Paper no. 73–23, 1973; and his "Watersheds and Turning Points: Nineteenth Century Capital Formation, Relative Prices, and the Civil War," University of Wisconsin-Madison, Graduate Program in Economic History, Discussion Paper no. 73–20, March 1973.

aside from its effects on troop levels, aggregate demand, and the progressiveness of taxation.

To compare the labor content of government demand with that of the demand it displaces, one needs data on the sectoral distribution of government demand and other demands, on the ratios of employment to sales in each sector, and an input-output table. A careful estimation of the labor content of government versus other demand cannot be performed here. A tentative judgment can be reached, however, by inspecting some of the features of the U.S. input-output structure in 1939, 1947, 1958, and 1963.[34] Casual inspection reveals no net difference between the man-hours of labor content of government demand and that of other sectors, whether the other sectors are all others or the private demands that declined in periods when government's share rose. More revealing is an input-output performed by Anne P. Carter. She calculated the changes in labor and capital demand that would have ensued in the periods 1939–47 and 1947–58 if the actual changes in final demand composition had been combined with an unchanged structure of prices and input-output ratios.[35] In none of the variants tried did the shift in demand have any noteworthy effect on the aggregate ratio of capital stock to man-hours. This result obtained even though the period 1947–58 was one in which the Cold War raised the government's share of real (1958-dollars) aggregate demand from 12.9 percent to 21.3 percent.[36] Apparently a shift in demand from private parties to the government affects the relative strength of demand for labor very little if at all. The tentative conclusion reached is that the government shifts demand toward unskilled labor and away from capital primarily or solely by pulling bodies into the armed forces and by raising aggregate demand in the short run.

IV. Conclusions

No other potential influence on the distribution of income fits the long-run movements in inequality as well as the behavior of the labor supply. The closest competitor is the sectoral distribution of advances in produc-

[34] Anne P. Carter, *Structural Change in the American Economy*, Cambridge: Harvard University Press, 1970, Chap. 8; and Roger Bezdek, Bruce Hannon, and Susan Nakagawa, "Derivation of the 1963 and 1967 Total Employment Vectors for 326 I/O Sectors," University of Illinois at Urbana-Champaign, Center for Advanced Computation, Document no. 63, April 1973.

[35] Carter, *Structural Change*, pp. 150, 151.

[36] U. S. Department of Commerce, Bureau of Economic Analysis, *Long Term Economic Growth, 1860–1970*, Washington: GPO, 1973, Series A2 and A34.

tivity, discussed above. Other forces presumably also have a strong unit impact on the degree of inequality. Exogenous shifts in demand, intrasectoral technological innovations that throw the unskilled out of work, and the political power of organized labor all *could have been* the dominant influences on inequality if they had moved in the right directions while the labor supply grew at a steady rate. But that did not happen. Instead the trends in American inequality and movements in labor supply happened to reveal the strong effect of the latter on the former. The marked changes in the rate of growth of man-hours supplied happened to govern changes in inequality trends, apparently through their effects on the rate of growth of skills and the rate of accumulation of capital.

There seems to be good reason for believing that extra fertility affects the size and "quality" of the labor force in ways that raise income inequalities. Fertility, like immigration, seems to reduce the average "quality" of the labor force, by reducing the amounts of family and public school resources devoted to each child. The retardation in the historic improvement in labor force quality has in turn held back the rise in the incomes of the unskilled relative to those enjoyed by skilled labor and wealth-holders.

These connections have been revealed by a comparison of trends in American income inequality with trends in fertility, immigration, and the growth in the size and quality of the labor force. Inequalities rose gradually on all fronts in the century before World War I, when the supply of unskilled labor was recurrently fed by large immigration inflows. As fertility continued to decline and immigration was shut off around World War I and again in the later 1920s, inequalities in income began to contract and continued to do so until the Korean War. Since then income inequality has shown no clear upward or downward trend. It appears likely, from data on their numbers and schooling, that the passage of baby-boom children into the labor force will counter any further equalization of incomes for the rest of the 1970s. Across the 1980s, a marked deceleration in labor-force growth should cause income equalization to resume—other things equal.

The historical evidence in favor of these conclusions is not airtight, however. It is always possible to construct other, more elaborate, hypotheses to explain the swings in American income inequality. Yet at some point simplicity is to be preferred, and the reasoning linking inequality to fertility and labor supply has fewer cumbersome working parts than others that happen to fit American experience.

If this reading of the macroeconomic evidence is correct, the case for collective policies to encourage birth restriction in countries with rapid population growth is strengthened. Greater equality in the distribution is a public good that political systems have great trouble purchasing directly through taxes and transfers. The social returns to a long-run investment in income through birth restriction, while quite distant, may be very high.

APPENDIX A. The Job-Interruption Effect on Wage Rates as a Part of Child Cost

In calculating the cost of children, one must take special care to take proper account of the effect of interrupting a job to have a child on the mother's subsequent wage rate. The basic importance of this effect for child cost is clear enough (as noted also by Michael and Lazear),[1] but quantifying it involves some details that should be discussed here.

How the Job-Interruption Effect Fits into the Relative Cost Measure

In most skilled and semiskilled occupations, the individual worker's rate of pay varies with the length and continuity of his or her prior employment, especially prior employment in the same firm. Employers offer pay increases based on seniority and experience because productivity is learned on the job and because turnover of workers involves costs. Dropping out of work for a while to have a baby therefore lowers a woman's rates of pay for the rest of her working career.

It is clear that this wage-rate effect should be included somehow in the total dollar cost of having a child. One could make such an adjustment by dividing up the total effect on her earnings in either of two ways. If one chooses to value the reduction in her hours of paid work at the wage rate she would earn *with* the extra child, then the job-interruption effect should be measured by multiplying the hours she would have worked *without* the child by the change in wage rate caused by the maternity interruption. If the hours of cost work are valued at the wage rate she would earn *without* having the child, than the job-interruption effect should be calculated by multiplying the hours she would work *with* the child by the change in wage rate. Either of these approaches yields the correct dollar cost adjustment, for reasons that can be clarified by reexpressing the matter algebraically. Let N represent women-hours worked per year and w represent the hourly wage rate. Use the $_0$ subscript for the situation without the child and the $_1$ subscript for the situation with the child. The total effect of the child on the mother's earnings in any given year is:

$$w_1 N_1 - w_0 N_0,$$

which is negative.

[1] Robert T. Michael and Edward Lazear, "On the Shadow Price of Children," paper presented at the 1971 meetings of the Econometric Society, New Orleans, December 1971.

APPENDIX A

As just stated in words, this total change in earnings can be expressed either as:

$$\underbrace{w_1(N_1 - N_0)}_{\substack{\text{mother works} \\ \text{less}}} + \underbrace{(w_1 - w_0)N_0}_{\substack{\text{her wage rate is lower} \\ \text{due to job interruption}}}$$

or as:

$$\underbrace{w_0(N_1 - N_0)}_{\substack{\text{mother works} \\ \text{less}}} + \underbrace{(w_1 - w_0)N_1}_{\substack{\text{her wage rate is lower} \\ \text{due to job interruption}}}$$

For the index of relative child cost, however, knowing the dollar magnitude of this job interruption effect is not sufficient. It must also be allocated to a particular input or inputs into the home, so that the effects of movements of inputs prices can be traced by the overall index. To what inputs and to what bundles should the extra wages be attributed?

Two principles should be followed in arriving at a decision on where to put the extra wages when deriving index weights for the base period. The first is that one should take a stand on a particular vector of prices and wages and apply the *same* prices and wages to both bundles. To use different wages for the two bundles is unhelpful because it mixes differences in marginal values (*given* family size) with differences in quantities. When both courses of action are being contemplated in advance by a couple, the quantities of time at stake in having a child or not should be valued consistently at a common wage rate, and not at the separate wage rates representing the margins given one or the other choice. The common wage rate appropriate to the extra-child margin can be anywhere in the range marked out by the wage rates with or without the child. The important point is that the same rate should be used in connection with both bundles.

The second principle is that the relative cost index should have in its two bundles the real base-period quantities of time and commodities consumed over a lifetime with and without the extra child. To decide where to inject the extra wages earned without the child, we need to identify exactly where estimates excluding these extra wages would fail to reflect the most likely course of life. This principle leads us to examine the ways in which specific expenditures of time and commodities are estimated empirically.

When examining such empirical estimates, one finds that the estimates which fail to allow for differences in pay due to wage rate effects are those used in quantifying the effect of an extra child on family commodity expenditures. These estimates, used to get to estimates of the commodity purchases involved in the activities that would take the place of an extra child, rest on an assumption of how much higher the family's income would be without the extra child. Clearly, this assumption must reflect the effect of job interruption on the wife's wage rate. Therefore the adjustment that must be made for the job-interruption effect would give an inaccurate picture of home inputs. Accordingly, I have allocated the change in income, including the job-interruption effect on the wage rate, across commodity groups on the basis of marginal propensities to consume when calculating the C^H's.

No such adjustments need to be made to the estimates of the other home inputs. The estimates of inputs into the child (the C^N's and L^N's in the text of Chapter 4) are our starting point, and do not hinge on how income would have been different without the child. The estimates of the effect of the child on hours worked (the $\triangle L$'s) and of the time inputs into the home activities in lieu of the child (the L^H's) have been derived from regressions that make further adjustments unnecessary. The key estimates of effects on labor force participation by Bowen and Finegan are *not* estimates that hold wage rates constant. Their regressions linking the presence of children (and other variables) to wives' work do not contain a wage-rate term. Thus the coefficients showing the impact of children on work implicitly embody the effects of the accompanying wage rate shifts on the amount of work supplied. This procedure makes the estimates of $\triangle L$'s and L^H's appropriate as they stand.

Quantifying the Wage Rate Impact of Job Interruption

Now that the way of treating the job interruption effect on wage rates is resolved, we must find plausible estimates of this effect to start with. This is not easy. One must have access to data on all of the following variables for a large sample of working-age women: wage rates, years of experience at present job, years of previous work experience, education, and number of children. Many samples, such as those tied to the census, fall short of this requirement, usually by having insufficient information on work experience.

At present I know of two recent studies with sufficient information to quantify the effect of job interruption on rates of pay. The first is the detailed study of wage determination in the Chicago area by Rees and

APPENDIX A

Shultz, based on a survey taken in early 1963. For a few occupations they trace out the effects of different levels of current-job seniority on wage rates. The other is a recent article by Jacob Mincer and Solomon W. Polachek, which applies a human capital model of wage determination to data from the "Parnes" longitudinal sample of work experience in the mid-1960s.[2]

While either study could be used for rough estimation purposes, the Mincer-Polachek paper seems to fit my present purpose a bit more closely. To use the Rees-Shultz results to estimate the impact of maternity leave, one would have to assume that the interruption simply postponed the date at which the woman entered each seniority rank at the *same* job, with no net effect on her rate of pay for a given seniority. The Mincer-Polachek model avoids this restrictive assumption. Mincer and Polachek specifically allow the rate of depreciation of human capital for stay-at-homes to differ from the rate of capital formation tied to on-the-job experience. They also quantify the importance of extra experience at previous jobs for the woman's rate of pay (for a *given* experience level) by raising employers' expectations of further job interruption. For these reasons I have relied more heavily on the Mincer-Polachek estimates.

Two assumptions have been made in adapting the Mincer-Polachek results to present purposes. First, I have assumed that their regressions are valid only up to age forty-four, at which the longitudinal sample ends. After that age, I have assumed, continuing to stay out of the labor force does not cause any further percentage reduction in her re-entry wage rate. In effect I have assumed that women who do work accumulate no further human capital after age forty-four. This seems consistent with the seniority-effect results of Rees and Shultz. Second, a set of arbitrary assumptions had to be made in interpreting the particular work history variables gathered from the Parnes longitudinal sample. These assumptions are a bit obscure, but are necessitated by the structure of the Parnes sample:

(a) It was assumed that the years of work lost with a first child would represent a substitution of "years not worked between school and marriage" for "years worked between school and

[2] Albert Rees and George W. Shultz, *Workers and Wages in an Urban Labor Market*, Chicago: University of Chicago Press, 1970; Jacob Mincer and Solomon Polachek, "Family Investments in Human Capital: Earnings of Women," *Journal of Political Economy* 82, no. 2, pt. II (supplement, March/April 1974), pp. S76–S108.

APPENDIX A

first marriage"; this assumption seems to make all first children prenuptially conceived, but it is the most realistic way of modelling the disruption of the job that the wife held from school to first birth.

(b) It was assumed that the years lost with each subsequent child were a substitution of "home time after first child" for "current job tenure" within samples of wives having some children.

The phrases quoted here are given concrete interpretations in the regression analysis of Mincer and Polachek.

Empirical studies relating job experience with earnings show that extra job experience raises earnings at faster percentage rates in more highly skilled jobs. How much effect job interruption has on rates of pay therefore depends greatly on the level of prior training of the individual. In what follows I shall quantify the job interruption effect for two kinds of couples: a "low income couple" consisting of a (nonfarm) husband and wife who have both graduated from high school, and a "high income" couple consisting of a husband who graduated from college and a wife who received some college education but who did not graduate. The couple in either case marry on the twenty-second birthday of both partners and have their first child, if they have any children, on their twenty-fourth birthday. This is the same pair of hypothetical couples, one "low income" and one "high income," referred to in Chapter 4 and in the next five appendixes.

The regressions reported by Mincer and Polachek yield the following expression for the fraction of wage rate deterioration experienced by the wife as a result of each child:

	first child	*each later child*
"low income" couple (wife is high school grad)	$.002 + .026T$	$.019 + .019T$
"high income" couple (wife has some college)	$.002 + .026T$	$.010 + .042T$

where T stands for the number of years the wife stays out of work because of the arrival of the extra child. There is reason to believe that these estimates somewhat overstate the impact of a career interruption on a woman's wage rates. The estimates come from a cross section of job histories, and thus compare the wage rates of women with few children and long job experience with those of women who have spent more time at home. This procedure may involve some unavoidable self-selection

APPENDIX A

bias: women who stayed out of work more may have personal attributes lowering their pay prospects even when the influence of work history and other variables have been separated out. Women with these extra individual reasons for having less experience and lower pay will earn less than would women with fuller work histories if they dropped out of the labor force for the same length of time. In other words, the observed effect of work experience on rates of pay probably adds to the true effect an implicit measure of personal differences in job qualifications and preferences not picked up in the measurable independent variables. Still, the Mincer-Polachek estimates are far more useful than anything else available for quantifying the job-interruption effect. They will be used in the knowledge that they may somewhat overstate the strength of the job-interruption effect.

Age-Wage Profiles for Wives with Different Numbers of Children

One can trace out the course of a wife's wage rate over her lifetime as a function of the number of children she has by applying the expressions above. These wage profiles can then be combined with estimates of hours worked and of husband's wage rates and hours to get a complete life cycle of incomes and wage rates as a function of family composition. Four steps are involved.

The starting point is the age-wage profile for a woman of given education who is married but has no children. This profile can be obtained from studies like that of Rees and Shultz, after adjustment for the marginal income tax rate.

The second step is to plot the lower wage rates that await a mother with a given number of children who has stayed out of work and wishes to re-enter the labor force. The positions of these child-burdened wage profiles will depend very much on the timing of the births. In order to derive indices of relative child cost, I shall assume three-year child spacing here. The first child is assumed to arrive on the couple's twenty-fourth birthday, the second on the twenty-seventh, the third on the thirtieth and the fourth on the thirty-third. To economize on calculations, higher parities and other spacing intervals are not examined here.

A third step must be taken if the child-burdened wage profiles are to reflect the mean, or "typical," prospects facing mothers. Once a woman re-enters the labor force, her earning power stops decaying (until she nears sixty). For the woman back at work, the sagging wage path calculated on the assumption that she is still at home is too pessimistic. What is needed is therefore a weighted-average wage rate profile for each number of children, where the weights reflect the probabilities of different lengths of job interruption. The procedure for computing the weighted average can be sketched as follows. For the first year of, say, the third child's life, I first determined the share of previously working mothers (with two children of the assumed spacing) who re-enter the labor force within this first year. For these women the Mincer-Polachek estimates are used, assuming the interruption lasted half a year. Their wage rates stop sagging below the two-child rates at that point. Most women, however, would remain out of work that whole first year, to judge from the results given by Bowen and Finegan (pp. 101–102). Their prospective wage rates continue to decay. For the second year, the share of those re-entering is again determined from Bowen-Finegan data. For these women the Mincer-Polachek expressions are applied, with the interruption period set at a year. Those still out of work are carried over to the third year, with further wage decay. The process is repeated for each subsequent year, the final result for each year being an average wage rate drop for a set of women, some of whom are back at work and some of whom are not.

The final step is to combine these wage profiles with those for hours worked and husband's hours and wage rates, in order to get the complete histories of pay to be used in calculating child costs. Table A–1 and Figure A–1 give the final estimates to be used.

APPENDIX A

Procedure for Selecting the Illustrative Values in Table A-1

The income levels for the "low income" and "high income" couples in Table A-1 were chosen in such a way that the low income couple would have an income just below the median income for urban childless high school graduates, while the high-income couple would have somewhat more than the median income for childless couples with college-graduate husbands. These income levels are such that the average income of the couple over the life cycle is about equal to the income levels used by the U.S. Department of Agriculture for its estimates of the "economy" and "moderate cost" child cost bundles. These considerations led to a choice of $3,500 as a disposable income for the "low income" couple at age twenty-four and $6,000 as the same for the "high income" couple.

The next step was to set an initial ratio of wife's to husband's wage rates. The Women's Bureau found that in 1964 the ratio of median full-time year-round female workers' earnings to full-time year-round male earnings was 59.5 percent.* This ratio is an average over all age groups and all family sizes. The appropriate ratio for the childless couple starting out at age twenty-four is apt to be higher. A ratio of 65 percent was assumed. This ratio was then combined with the family disposable income figures and with estimates of the partners' weekly hours of work to get absolute wage rate levels for each partner. The husband throughout was assumed to work a standard 2000 hours a year if there were no children in the household, and 2050 if children are present, the latter figure coming from the following appendix (Appendix B). The childless wife at age twenty-four was assumed to work 1046 hours per year, as predicted by the regressions run by Bowen and Finegan.** These figures on yearly hours, wage ratios, and total disposable income yielded the following initial hourly wage rates:

	Husband	Wife
low income couple	$1.31	$0.85
high income couple	$2.25	$1.46

Starting with these age-twenty-four wage rates, the procedures outlined above yielded estimates of the complete age-wage profiles for each number of children ever born.

* U.S. Department of Labor, Women's Bureau, *1965 Handbook of Women Workers,* Washington, D.C.: GPO, 1965, Women's Bureau Bulletin No. 290, p. 126.

** William Bowen and T. Aldrich Finegan, *The Economics of Labor Force Participation,* Princeton: Princeton University Press, 1969, p. 101.

TABLE A-1

Life Cycles of Hours and Earnings for Couples
with Various Numbers of Children (Three-Year Child Spacing)

(After-tax figures. Assume no outside property income
or out-of-home earnings by children within household.)

A. "Low Income" Couple

Couple's age	Children's ages (if applicable) 1st 2nd 3rd 4th	Husband's wage rate ($/hour)	With no Children wife's wage	wife's hrs/yr	family income	With one Child wife's wage	wife's hrs/yr	family income
23		(1.31)	(.85)	(1046)	(3500)	.85	826	3322
24	<1	1.31	.85	1046	3500	.83	174.5	2829.8
25	1	1.41	.88	↑	3740	.84	312	3152.1
26	2	1.52	.94		4023	.88	358.5	3431.5
27	3 <1	1.62	.96		4244	.89	389.5	3667.7
28	4 1	1.70	.97		4415	.88	456.5	3886.7
29	5 2	1.78	.99		4596	.89	472	4069.1
30	6 3 <1	1.86	1.00		4766	.89	620	4364.8
31	7 4 1	1.94	1.01		4936	.88	↑	4522.6
32	8 5 2	2.02	1.02		5107	.88		4686.6
33	9 6 3 <1	2.05	1.02		5167	.87		4241.4
34	10 7 4 1	2.09	1.03		5257	.87		4872.4
35	11 8 5 2	2.12	1.04		5328	.87		4885.4
36	12 9 6 3	2.16	1.04		5408	.86	↓	4961.2
37	13 10 7 4	2.20	1.05		5498	.85	620	5037.0
38	14 11 8 5	2.21	1.05		5518	.85	950	5337.5
39	15 12 9 6	2.22	1.06		5549	↑	↑	5358.5
40	16 13 10 7	2.23	1.06		5569		↓	5370.5
41	17 14 11 8	2.25	1.07		5619		950	5419.5
42	15 12 9	2.26	1.07		5639		1003	5372.6
43	16 13 10	2.26	↑		5639	↓	↑	5372.6
44	17 14 11	2.27			5659	.85		5392.6
45	15 12	2.27			5659	↑		
46	16 13	2.28			5679			5412.6
47	17 14	2.28			↑			↑
48	15	↑						
49	16							
50	17							
.								
.				↓	↓	↓	↓	↓
59		2.28	1.07	1046	5679	.85	1003	5417.6

Note: The effects of the per-child income tax exemption have not been added into the above figures. These effects are incorporated into the child cost estimates in Table E-5 of Appendix E.)

[269]

APPENDIX A

TABLE A-1 (continued)

A. "Low Income" Couple (continued)

With Two Children			With Three Children			With Four Children		
wife's wage	wife's hrs/yr	family income	wife's wage	wife's hrs/yr	family income	wife's wage	wife's hrs/yr	family income
.85	826	3322	.85	826	3322	.85	826	3322
.83	174.5	2829.8	.83	174.5	2830	.83	174.5	2830
.84	312	3152.1	.84	312	3152	.84	312	3152
.88	266	3350.1	.88	266	3350	.88	266	3350
.87	174.5	3472.8	.87	174.5	3473	.87	174.5	3473
.86	312	3753.3	.86	312	3753	.86	312	3753
.87	358.5	3960.9	.87	266	3881	.87	266	3881
.86	389.5	4147.9	.84	174.5	3960	.84	174.5	3960
.85	456.5	4365.0	.83	312	4236	.83	312	4236
.85	472	4482.0	.83	358.5	4437	.83	266	4361.8
.84	620	4722.8	.82	389.5	4521	.80	174.5	4341.6
.84	↑	4804.8	.81	456.5	4654	.79	312	4530.5
.84		4866.8	.81	472	4728	.79	358.5	4629.2
.83		4942.6	.80	620	4924	.77	389.5	4727.9
.82		5018.4	.79	↑	5000	.76	456.5	4856.9
.81		5032.2	.78		5014	.75	472	4834.0
.81	↓	5053.2	.78	↓	5035	.75	620	5016
.80	620	4967.0	.77		4948	.74	↑	4929.8
↑	950	5372.0	.77		5089	.74		5070.8
	↑	5393.0	.76	↓	5104	.73		5035.6
↓	↓	5393.0	.76	620	5104	.73		5035.6
.80	950	5413.0	.76	950	5375	.73	↓	5106
↑	1017	5353.6	↑	↑	5375	↑		4992.6
	↑	5373.6		↓	5396		620	5012.6
				950	5396		950	5254
				977	5303		↑	5368
				↑	5303		↓	5368
				↑			950	5368
							872	5197
							↑	↑
				↓				
				5303				
↓	↓	↓	↓	↓		↓	↓	↓
.80	1017	5374	.76	977		.73	872	5197

[270]

APPENDIX A

TABLE A-1 (continued)

B. "High Income" Couple

Couple's age	Children's Ages (if applicable) 1st 2nd 3rd 4th	Husband's Wage Rate ($/hour)	With no Children wife's wage	wife's hrs/yr	family income	With one Child wife's wage	wife's hrs/yr	family income
23		(2.25)	(1.46)	1046	6027.2	1.46	826	5706
24	<1	2.25	1.46	↑	6027.2	1.43	174.5	4867
25	1	2.44	1.63		6585.0	1.56	312	5488.7
26	2	2.63	1.73		7069.6	1.63	358.5	5975.9
27	3 <1	2.81	1.80		7502.8	1.66	389.5	6407.1
28	4 1	2.99	1.85		7915.1	1.68	456.5	6896.4
29	5 2	3.18	1.89		8336.9	1.69	472	7316.9
30	6 3 <1	3.36	1.93		8738.8	1.71	620	7948.2
31	7 4 1	3.54	1.96		9130.2	1.71	↑	8317
32	8 5 2	3.72	1.98		9511.1	1.71		8686.2
33	9 6 3 <1	3.85	2.01		9802.5	1.72		8958.4
34	10 7 4 1	3.98	2.03		10083.4	1.71		9219.2
35	11 8 5 2	4.11	2.05		10364.3	1.71		9485.7
36	12 9 6 3	4.24	2.07		10645.2	1.70	↓	9746
37	13 10 7 4	4.37	2.09		10926.1	1.69	620	10086.3
38	14 11 8 5	4.46	2.10		11117	1.70	950	10758
39	15 12 9 6	4.55	2.12		11317.5	1.71	↑	10952
40	16 13 10 7	4.63	2.13		11488	1.71	↓	11116
41	17 14 11 8	4.71	↑		11648	1.71	950	11280
42	15 12 9	4.80			11828	1.70	1003	11305
43	16 13 10	4.85	↓		11928	1.70	↑	11405
44	17 14 11	4.91	2.13		12048	1.70		11525
45	15 12	4.96	↑		12148	↑		11625
46	16 13	5.02			12268			11745
47	17 14	5.07			12368			11845
48	15	5.09			12408			11885
49	16	5.10			12428			11905
50	17	5.12			12468			11945
51		5.13			12488			11965
52		5.15	↑		12528	↑		12005
.								
.			↓		↓		↓	↓
59		5.15	2.13	1046	12528	1.70	1003	12005

[271]

APPENDIX A

TABLE A-1 (continued)

B. "High Income" Couple (continued)

With two Children wife's wage	wife's hrs/yr	family income	With three Children wife's wage	wife's hrs/yr	family income	With four Children wife's wage	wife's hrs/yr	family income
1.46	826	5706	1.46	826	5706	1.46	826	5706
1.43	174.5	4862	1.43	174.5	4862	1.43	174.5	4862
1.56	312	5488.7	1.56	312	5488.7	1.56	312	5488.7
1.63	266	5825.0	1.63	266	5825.0	1.63	266	5825
1.61	174.5	6041.4	1.61	174.5	6041.4	1.61	174.5	6041.4
1.62	312	6634.9	1.62	312	6634.9	1.62	312	6634.9
1.63	358.5	7687.2	1.63	266	6952.6	1.63	266	6952.6
1.63	389.5	7522.9	1.59	174.5	7165.4	1.59	174.5	7165.4
1.62	456.5	7996.5	1.57	312	7746.8	1.57	312	7746.8
1.61	472	8385.9	1.55	358.3	8181.7	1.55	266	8031.3
1.62	620	8896.4	1.54	389.5	8491.8	1.50	174.5	8153.8
1.61	↑	9157.2	1.52	456.5	8852.9	1.47	312	8617.6
1.61		9423.7	1.51	472	9138.2	1.45	358.5	8945.3
1.60		9654.0	1.50	620	9622.0	1.43	389.5	9248.9
1.59		9944.3	1.49	↑	9882.3	1.41	456.5	9602.2
1.58	↓	10122.6	1.48		10060.6	1.39	472	9799.1
1.56		10294.7	1.46		10232.7	1.37	620	10176.9
1.54	620	10446.3	1.45		10390.5	1.36	↑	10334.7
1.54	950	11118.5	1.43		10542.1	1.34		10486.3
1.53	↑	11293.5	1.41	↓	10714.2	1.33		10664.6
1.53	↓	11396	1.39	620	10804.3	1.31		10754.7
1.52	950	11509.5	1.37	950	11367.0	1.27		10857.9
↑	1017	11465.5	↑	↑	11469.5	↑	↓	10707.4
	↑	11588.8		↓	11592.5		620	10827.4
		11685.8		950	11695.0		950	11346.5
		11725.8		977	11518.5		↑	11641.0
		11745.8		↑	11536.5		↓	11661.5
		11785.8			11578.5		950	11702.5
		11805.8			11598.5		872	11367.4
		11845.8			11638.5		↑	11407.4
		↑			↑			↑
↓	↓	↓	↓	↓	↓	↓	↓	↓
1.52	1017	11845.8	1.37	977	11638.5	1.27	872	11407.4

[272]

APPENDIX A

Figure A-1. Effects of Number of Children on the Average Wage Rates Facing Wives (Three-Year Child Spacing).

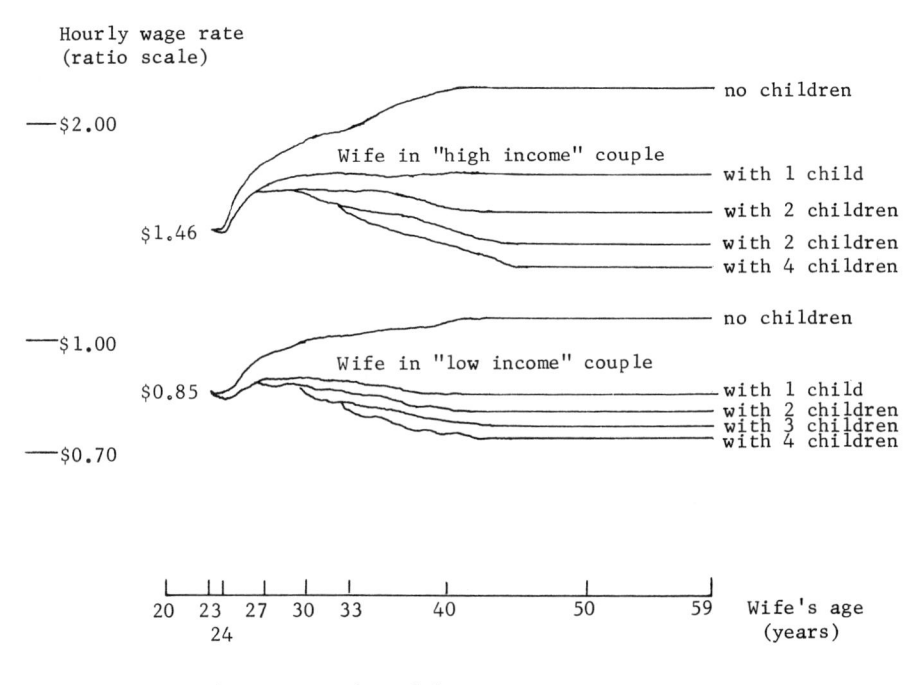

Hourly wage rate
(ratio scale)

—$2.00

no children
Wife in "high income" couple
with 1 child
with 2 children
$1.46
with 2 children
with 4 children

no children
—$1.00
Wife in "low income" couple
$0.85
with 1 child
with 2 children
with 3 children
with 4 children
—$0.70

20 23 27 30 33   40   50   59   Wife's age
    24   (years)

(Source: Table A-1.)

[273]

APPENDIX B. The Work-Time Effects of Children in the Home: Regression Results

This appendix provides further evidence to support some of Chapter 4's estimates of the effects of an extra child on paid work time by family members. The first section elaborates on the reasons for guessing, as in Chapter 4 and Appendix E below, that the presence of one or more children in the home raises the father's paid work time by 50 hours a year as a rough postwar average. The next two sections present regression estimates of the effects of an extra child on earnings by children and wives in a cross section of U.S. industrial workers' families in 1889–90.

EXTRA CHILDREN AND THE HOURS WORKED BY POSTWAR FATHERS

A number of authors have asserted that extra children cause fathers to "moonlight" more.[1] In trying to quantify this effect, one would logically start with the 1/1000 census samples, like the 1960 sample used by Bowen and Finegan and others to explain patterns in work by women and children. Bowen and Finegan themselves happen not to have collected the data on presence of children in the home when setting up regressions to account for patterns in hours worked by adult males. Julian Simon, however, did regress males' hours on presence-of-children variables plus education, race, age, occupation, and residence in the 1960 census sample. He found that an extra child raises the work time of fathers by 0.2 hour a week, or 10 hours a year. He felt this result was too low because of biases imparted by errors in measuring the dependent variable.[2]

Boone Turchi used the 1964 data in the 1965 Productive Americans survey to estimate the effects of different numbers and age ranges of children in the home on hours of market work by husbands, using regressions that also included the husband's wage rate, education, household work, and nonlabor income, and the wife's market work.[3] While

---

[1] Harvey R. Hamel, "Moonlighting—An Economic Phenomenon," *Monthly Labor Review* 90, no. 10 (October 1967), 17–22; Harold W. Guthrie, "Some Explanations of Moonlighting," American Statistical Association, Business and Economics Section, *Proceedings*, 1966.

[2] Julian L. Simon, "The Influence of Population Growth on Per-Worker Income in Developed Economies," University of Illinois at Urbana-Champaign, College of Commerce and Business Administration, Faculty Working Paper no. 33, November 1971, Appendix A.

[3] Boone A. Turchi, *The Demand for Children*, Cambridge, Mass.: Ballinger, 1975, pp. 105–108.

APPENDIX B

the dependent variable, husband's hours of paid work, may have a tangled simultaneous relationship to the wage rate and the wife's work, it is not clear that this simultaneity imparts any bias to the estimation of the effects of children. Turchi's regressions imply that a first child would have no net effect on the father's work time over the eighteen years of the child's growing up (actually, a small negative estimated effect, of − 1.44 hours per year). The tendency to work more grows with the second and third child, however. If we assume that the children are born three years apart, the second child makes the father work an extra 70.8 hours a year, or 1.42 hours a work week, over the eighteen years. The third child makes him work an extra 103.56 hours a year, or 2.07 hours a work week, by putting him into Turchi's large three-or-more children category for several years. The fourth and each year later child add 23.67 hours a year, or 0.47 hour a work week, to the father's paid work.

The 1967 Survey of Economic Opportunity has generated a variety of studies of labor supply functions by male household heads. As a by-product, this work has yielded three estimates of the effect of extra children on hours worked by husbands. The simplest estimate is that of Greenberg and Kosters, which simply included the number of children in the home as one of many independent variables, among them the wage rate earned by the husband. Their regression for hours worked by males aged 25–55 showed that the impact of an extra child on hours worked was 11.17 hours a year, or only 0.22 hour per working week, and this impact was significantly positive even at the one percent level.[4] This virtually matches the low estimate reported by Simon on the basis of the 1960 census.

A second set of results emerging from the SEO data file was reported by my colleague Irving Garfinkel. Like Greenberg and Kosters, Garfinkel simply included the number of children as one of many independent variables explaining work time patterns of adult males. He used different measures of work time, trying both hours worked in a survey week and these hours times a proxy for weeks worked per year based on some broad work-regularity categories. In his regressions an extra child added about 0.23 hour to the father's work in the survey week, and about 15.6 hours over a year, still quite near the estimates of Simon and

---

[4] David H. Greenberg and Marvin Kosters, "Income Guarantees and the Working Poor: The Effect of Income Maintenance Programs on the Hours of Work of Male Family Heads," Santa Monica, RAND Corporation, 1970, Table B-3A, Row 6. This and other detailed tables were omitted in the published version of their paper, which nonetheless describes their method (in Glen G. Cain and Harold W. Watts, eds., *Income Maintenance and Labor Supply: Econometric Studies*, Chicago: Markham, 1973, pp. 14–101).

APPENDIX B

of Greenberg and Kosters.[5] In some extra unpublished regressions on the same data, Garfinkel replaced the number-of-children variable with a set of dummies for each family size. It turned out that the first and second child each raised the hours worked by a male aged 25–54 by one hour a working week, or about 50 hours a year. The third through fifth children had no effect, while the sixth put the father into a larger-family category working 2.4 hours a week, or 120 hours a year, *less* than fathers of from three to five children. Garfinkel's results seem to imply the opposite progression of work effects by family size from those reached by Turchi: where Turchi found no effect of the first child and rising effects thereafter, Garfinkel's results imply that the effect of extra children starts out positive with the first child and dwindles away with succeeding children.

The final estimate emerging from the SEO file yields by far the largest predicted impact of an extra child on fathers' hours of paid work. Robert Hall found that the presence of preschool children made white husbands work an extra 122 hours a year and black husbands work an extra 72 hours a year on the average. Having children of school age evoked an extra 232 hours from white fathers and 179 hours from black fathers, while having both preschool and school-age children added 262 hours and 224 hours for white and black fathers, respectively.[6] These regression coefficients imply that a first-born white child would make his or her father work an extra 195.33 hours a year, or 3.91 hours a work week, on the average over the eighteen years of growing up. Any later-born would add 43.67 hours a year, or 0.87 hour a work week, to the father's work over the eighteen years if the children were born at three-year intervals.

If children made fathers work as much harder as Hall's estimates imply, then the phenomenon of moonlighting fathers would have obtained a more dominant position in the sociological and econometric literature on work than it has. Hall's high implied estimates of the impact of children seem to be only a reflection of his peculiar choice of regression variables. He has omitted continuous age and wage-rate variables, replacing them with dummy variables dividing the males into very broad age and wage-rate ranges. The only age division is between those aged

---

[5] Irving Garfinkel, "On Estimating the Labor-Supply Effects of a Negative Income Tax," in Cain and Watts, *Income Maintenance and Labor Supply*, Appendix 6, Regressions 20, 21, 23, and 24.

[6] Robert E. Hall, "Wages, Income and Hours of Work in the U.S. Labor Force," in Cain and Watts, *Income Maintenance and Labor Supply*, Table 3.5, Parts A and B.

APPENDIX B

20–59 and the two age groups above and below this one. In such regressions, having children at home becomes a proxy for being middle-aged, experienced, and settled in a job for whatever reason, in contrast with the irregularly employed males at both ends of the 20–59 age range. This model presumably attributes to fatherhood a larger effect than it really has on hours of work.

The final estimate comes from a special Current Population Survey reporting hours worked in 1966. Using this large sample Cohen, Rea, and Lerman ran elaborate regressions explaining hours of work in terms of the presence of children and many other variables. The presence of children under eighteen was represented by a simple binary dummy, both separately and in interaction terms involving family type and the husband's wage rate range. The effect of an extra child on the father's hours of work was greater in the low-wage group than in the middle-wage group starting at $2.50 an hour. Their results imply that a first-born child would make his or her father work an extra 134.1 hours a year (2.68 hours a work week) in low-wage cases and an extra 87.8 hours a year (1.76 hours a work week) in middle-wage cases. Any later-born child would add 22.35 hours a year (0.45 hour a work week) in the low-wage case and 14.63 hours a year (0.29 hour a work week) in the middle-wage case.[7]

While the estimates vary, there is general agreement that the impact of an extra child on the husband's work time is slightly but significantly positive. There is no agreement over which birth orders have the largest effect. This pattern of results emerges, it should be noted, from a set of regressions explaining hours worked by husbands who in fact worked. I have not seen any regressions quantifying the impact of fatherhood on the likelihood of being at work at all. For the first child, this might also be positive.

Table B–1 compares the results of these past studies with my own guesses as to the effect of an extra child on a husband's work time, assuming that children are born at three-year intervals and stay in their parents' home to their eighteenth birthday. It turns out that my own guess, made before most of the studies were available to me, is one of the higher estimates of the effect of a first-born and almost the lowest for most later-borns. This departure from the general range of estimates would not affect any of the conclusions reached in Chapters 4 and 5, as long as one rules out likely overestimates like those of Hall or Turchi's

[7] Malcolm S. Cohen, Samuel A. Rea, Jr., and Robert I. Lerman, *A Micro-Model of Labor Supply*, Washington, GPO, 1970, BLS Staff Paper 4, Table F-3.

APPENDIX B

Table B-1. The Impacts of Extra Children on Hours Worked by Husbands, Assuming Three-Year Child Spacing.

(hours of work per year, averaged over eighteen years of the child's growing up)

Source of estimate (see text)	Data year	1st	2nd	3rd	4th	5th	6th
(1) Simon	1960	10.0	10.0	10.0	10.0	10.0	10.0
(2) Turchi	1964	-1.4	70.8	103.6	23.7	23.7	23.7
(3) Greenberg-Kosters	1966-7	11.2	11.2	11.2	11.2	11.2	11.2
(4) Garfinkel, pub.	1966-7	15.6	15.6	15.6	15.6	15.6	15.6
unpub.	"	50.0	50.0	0	0	0	-120.0
(5) Hall	1966-7	195.3	43.7	43.7	43.7	43.7	43.7
(6) Cohen-Rea-Lerman,							
low-wage case	1966	134.1	22.4	22.4	22.4	22.4	22.4
middle-wage case	"	87.8	14.6	14.6	14.6	14.6	14.6
(7) Shisko and Rostker*	1969	35.5	35.5	35.5	35.5	35.5	35.5
(8) Present guess	(1960)	50.0	8.3	8.3	8.3	8.3	8.3

*R. Shisko and B. Rostker, "The Economics of Multiple Job Holding," American Economic Review, vol. 66, no. 3(June 1976), pp. 298-308.

third-born children. The only change is that first-borns would be slightly more time-intensive, and third-borns slightly less time-intensive, than I have estimated in Appendix E, Appendix F, and Chapter 4 if one were to use the average estimates from Table B-1.

Wives' Work and Earnings in Industry, 1889-90

In tracing the historical evolution of the effects of children on family work and earnings patterns, I have made use of the valuable survey of a few thousand U.S. and foreign industrial workers' families conducted by the U.S. Bureau of Statistics of Labor. This source, cited in Table 4-4 above, has been described and used at length by other scholars,[8] and

[8] Jeffrey G. Williamson, "Consumer Behavior in the Nineteenth Century: Carroll D. Wright's Massachusetts Workers in 1875," *Explorations in Economic History* 4, no. 2 (Winter 1967), pp. 98-135; Allen C. Kelley, "Demographic Changes and

APPENDIX B

need not be described at length here. In order to document the wages and living standards of "representative" industrial workers and to educate conjectures on how tariffs might affect these, the Bureau seems to have intercepted male and female industrial workers at the factory gates to solicit interviews. The Bureau went to the length of printing the entire schedules of individual household returns as well as countless summary tables in the public documents of Congress. They reported the husband's income, the wife's income, the children's income, income from boarders and lodgers, and other income separately. They also recorded the age and sex of every family member, along with a good deal of other detail on the head's occupation, whether or not the children were at school, and household expenditures and saving.

The 1889–90 survey allows us to run regressions explaining patterns in wives' labor force participation and income in terms of the presence of children in the home and other variables. In that prewar setting the wife's work and income can be defined in different ways. As noted in Chapter 4, many families earned significant amounts of income from taking in boarders and lodgers, an activity that can be viewed as paid work within the home by the wife and older children. We therefore need to explore the determinants both of wives' out-of-home earnings and of the income from boarders and lodgers.

Table B–2 gives the results of regressions explaining patterns in work and earnings by wives in the 1889–90 industrial sample. The results seem to assign plausible roles to nonchild variables as well as to child variables. Wives worked more, and took in more boarders and lodgers, the poorer were their husbands and other local male workers [see the coefficients for STATEINC and HOINC/STATEINC in Regressions (1) and (3)]. This pattern confirms the frequent observation that wives of poorer husbands had a much greater tendency to be in the labor force in the nineteenth century. The wife's age also affected her work and the family's income from boarders and lodgers. Wives between the ages twenty-five and forty-four worked more than younger or older wives, for any given ages of children present in the home. Taking in boarders

---

American Economic Development: Past, Present, and Future," in U.S. Commission on Population Growth and the American Future, *Research Reports*, vol. II, Washington, GPO, 1973, pp. 24–29; Albert Fishlow, "Comparative Consumption Patterns . . . ," in Eliezer Ayal, ed., *Micro-Aspects of Development*, New York: Praeger, 1973, pp. 41–80; and Michael R. Haines, "Industrial Work and the Family Cycle, 1889/90," paper presented at the annual Cliometrics Conference, Madison, Wis., April 22–24, 1976.

APPENDIX B

Table B-2. Determinants of Work and Earnings by Wives, U.S. Industrial Workers Survey, 1889-1890.

Regression Model Number

	(1)	(2)	(3)	(4)
Sample Constraint:	all husband-wife households	husband-wife households, wife works outside home	all husband-wife households	husband-wife households, with income from boarders
Dependent Variable:	Does the wife work outside the home?	Wife's out-of-home income, divided by STATEINC	Any income from boarders, etc.?	Income from boarders, etc., divided by STATEINC
Independent Variables:				
Constant	.406 *** (.031)	.709 *** (.123)	.451 *** (.044)	.498 *** (.076)
KID1 (0-1, no 14up)	-.052 *** (.012)	-.077 * (.036)	.027 (.018)	.012 (.032)
KID2 (2-5, no 14up)	-.000 (.012)	-.008 (.031)	.004 (.017)	.012 (.032)
KID3 (6-13)	-.013 (.010)	-.010 (.029)	-.001 (.014)	-.022 (.023)
KID4 (14 up, no<6)	-.045 ** (.014)	.026 (.046)	.062 ** (.020)	.048 (.032)
KID5 (0-1 and 14up)	-.027 (.028)	.010 (.118)	-.017 (.040)	.053 (.071)
KID6 (2-5 and 14up)	-.063 *** (.017)	-.064 (.065)	.067 ** (.024)	.014 (.039)
Own house?	.024 (.022)	.123 (.069)	.063 * (.031)	.098 * (.044)
STATEINC	-.0005*** (.0000)	-.0006** (.0002)	-.00021** (.00007)	-.0002* (.0001)
Wife is under 25	.027 (.017)	-.046 (.061)	-.134 *** (.024)	-.056 (.039)
Wife is 25-34	.078 *** (.015)	.036 (.054)	-.110 *** (.022)	-.052 (.035)
Wife is 35-44	.049 *** (.014)	-.009 (.050)	-.128 *** (.019)	-.010 (.029)
HOINC/STATEINC	-.097 *** (.011)	-.016 (.049)	-.102 *** (.016)	.014 (.029)
R^2 corrected/No. obs.	.055/ 3924	.029/ 319	.043/ 3924	.020/ 729
S.e.e./mean of dep.	.266/.0813	.227/.3820	.380/.1858	.270/.3670

*Significant at 5% level. **Significant at 1% level. ***Significant at 0.1% level.

(Figures in parentheses are the standard errors of the coefficients.)

APPENDIX B

DEFINITIONS OF SOME VARIABLES USED IN TABLE B–2

KID1 equals 1 if one or more children under the age of two years is present in the home and there is no child over 14 present; otherwise it equals 0.

KID2 equals 1 if one or more children aged 2-5 years is present in the home and there is no child over 14 present; 0 otherwise.

KID3 equals 1 if one or more children aged 6–13 is present in the home; 0 otherwise.

KID4 equals 1 if one or more children over the age of 14 is present and no children under 6 are present; 0 otherwise.

KID5 equals 1 if one or more children under the age of two years *and* one or more children over 14 are present; 0 otherwise.

KID6 equals 1 if one or more children aged 2–5 years *and* one or more children over 14 are present; 0 otherwise.

STATEINC equals the average household income among households interviewed in the state of this household's residence, in dollars per year.

HOINC/STATEINC equals the ratio of the sum of husband's income plus all "other" household income (aside from that of husband, wife, and children, and that earned from boarders and lodgers) to STATEINC, as a proxy for the husband's relative income position.

and lodgers was a much more common practice in households having a wife older than 44 than in younger homes, presumably because more space was available in homes from which grown children had already departed. The age of the wife had no significant effect, however, on her income given that she was working or given that she was tending to boarders and lodgers [Regressions (2) and (4)]. Home ownership had no separate effect on the tendency of the wife to earn income outside of the home, but it tended, as expected, to raise the family's income from boarders and lodgers.

The presence of children in the home also affected the wife's work and income. Her tendency to have work outside the home was reduced by children, as expected. Interestingly enough, teen-agers had as strongly negative an affect on her work as newborns, perhaps because their own ability to earn while living with their parents made it more likely that the family would decide to leave her at home with the still-heavy burdens of running a nineteenth-century household. The presence of teen-agers also significantly raised the likelihood that the family would take in boarders and lodgers. This might mean either that teen-agers helped to cook and clean for the boarders and lodgers, or that their outside earnings raised the wife's tendency to work at home for boarders and lodgers rather than outside the home, or that the data on boarder-lodger incomes actually included some charges levied on working teen-agers by their parents.

The net effect of an extra child on income attributable to the wife proves to have been quite small, in part because in their teens extra

APPENDIX B

children added to the family's incomes from boarders and lodgers an amount that partially offset the earnings that they cost their mothers in their infancy and in their primary-school years. The results of Table B-2 imply that a first-born child would cost $9 a year in wife plus boarder income over its first two years of life, add less than a dollar a year to age six, cost $5 a year across the primary-school years, and then add about $7 a year across ages 14–17. This comes to a net undiscounted cost of only $27 in family income. A third-born child would have a similar age-pattern of net income losses to the family, adding up to zero net effect (actually, a net gain of half a dollar) on income from wife plus boarders and lodgers over the eighteen years.

Children's Work and Earnings in Industry, 1889–90

The same 1889–90 survey also permits us to quantify how much earnings older children tended to bring back to their parents' household in the years before they left it. With the set of children, as with the wife, the survey reported total income earned. The number of children at work outside the home was also reported. What the survey did not tell us was the separate earnings of each child, so that it is not always possible to tell which of those children for which age and sex were recorded were the actual earners.

In using the survey to determine the likely labor force participation and earnings of a child by age and sex, I operated under some additional handicaps imposed by the computer-tape version of the data at hand. It was necessary to use the tape prepared by Professor Allen C. Kelley and his research assistants for his earlier work on demographic influences on household saving. This tape omitted several variables that would have been of use here: the industry and occupation of the household head, the sex of each child, and the number of children at work. In the future it will be possible to give these variables their due. Professor Michael R. Haines of Cornell has since extended the Kelley tape to cover all these variables plus all of the observations taken from European households by the American surveyors. Haines' preliminary results show that boys worked more than girls, as one would expect, and that children of parents in textiles worked much more, and children of parents in mining and metals worked less, than children whose parents worked in the glass industry.[9] The same ranking of industries shows up for wives' employment as well as for children's, but the effect is larger for children than for wives.

[9] Haines, "Industrial Work and Family Cycle."

APPENDIX B

In the absence of the data on number of children at work and the sex of children, I had to limit the sample in a way that still allowed a fair picture of the labor force participation rate and the income of the individual child. The sample for investigating participation rates was limited to households where there was exactly one child over the age of nine, along with the husband and wife and possibly children under nine years in age. In this way I retained the ability to attribute work and earnings to the individual child of known age, assuming that no children under nine earned significant amounts. The results for each age group were assumed to be the simple averages of the results that would have obtained for boys and girls separately in that age group.

A constrained sample of 644 households with exactly one child over nine yielded the following regression equation explaining patterns in the older children's labor force participation (standard errors in parentheses):

(Does the child have income?) = .557 − .00060 STATEINC − .195 HOINC/STATEINC
(.098) (.00015) (.032)
*** *** ***

+ .581 (18 or older, work not limited by state law) + .445 (18 or older, work limited by state law)
(.046) (.082)
*** ***

+ .542 (16–17, work not limited by state law) + .432 (16–17, work limited by state law)
(.080) (.064)
*** ***

+ .164 (14–15, work not limited by state law) + .391 (14–15, work limited by state law)
(.072) (.045)
*** ***

+ .072 (9–13, work not limited by state law) − .008 (number of children under 9)
(.050) (.012)

($R^2_{corr.}$ = .410, s.e.e. = .327, mean of dep. var. = .238)

* = significant at the 5% level.
*** = significant at the 0.1% level.
(Figures in parentheses are standard errors of coefficients.)

The STATEINC and HOINC/STATEINC variables are defined as in Table B–2, and the dummies for the different age groups refer to whether or not laws were passed before 1889 in the state of residence limiting, or in some cases prohibiting, work in manufacturing by children of this age.

APPENDIX B

The impact of these laws appears to have been questionable. The regression results imply that the child-labor laws did bind the hiring of children over sixteen, but there is certainly no evidence of a reduction in child labor under the age of sixteen where laws had been passed. These results must be treated with care, however, since the age–state-law dummies may be picking up influences of omitted variables that are correlated with state of residence.

The incomes of working children had to be estimated in a different way, given the computer tape at hand. It was not possible to stick with the sample of households with exactly one child over nine, since this would have yielded only 153 households with earning children. Instead it was necessary to revert to a larger sample consisting of all households having some child incomes and exactly one child who is allowed by law to work in manufacturing or who is over eighteen, even if there are other children over nine. This oddly truncated sample of 396 households with same child income yields *underestimates* of the average earnings of a working child, since it mixes participation-rate effects for some of the over-nine children with the average earnings effect of a working child of the same age. The regression resulting from this sample is:

$$\frac{\text{(Earnings from children)}}{\text{STATEINC}} = \underset{(.206)}{.406} - \underset{(.00040)}{.00048} \text{STATEINC} - \underset{(.035)}{.230} \frac{\text{HOINC}}{\text{STATEINC}} + \underset{(.095)}{.011} \text{(Own house?)}$$

$$+ \underset{\substack{(.063) \\ ***}}{.272} \text{(No. of kids over 18)} + \underset{\substack{(.047) \\ ***}}{.199} \text{(No. of kids 16–17)} + \underset{\substack{(.036) \\ ***}}{.164} \text{(No. of kids 14–15)}$$

$$- \underset{(.027)}{.026} \text{(No. of kids under 9)} \qquad (R^2_{corr.} = .209, \quad \text{s.e.e.} = .486,$$
$$\text{mean of dep. var.} = .651)$$

This earnings equation plus the previous equation for the labor force participation rate have been used to predict the age profile of expected earnings of a child in New York and in Georgia. The resulting earnings profile, which underestimates actual earnings, has been reported in Table 4–5 above. Even though these estimates are probably too low, both in dollars and as a share of the average value of husband plus property income (or 85% of STATEINC in the 1889–90 sample), they easily overshadow the effects of a child on the earnings of a wife. Thus the 1889–90 results show that in that era extra children in industrial families raised, rather than lowered, the family income for any reasonable rates of discount used to compare early and later effects on family income.

Appendix C. Time Inputs into Siblings, 1967–68: Hypotheses and Estimates

The task of measuring family time inputs into children is basic to any study of the costs of children and the relationship between the inputs they receive and their subsequent achievements. The necessary measurements must be based on time-budget studies that peer into the allocation of time within the home. A child takes time away from many things—from care of other children, from other household work, and from paid work. The amount of time involved cannot be determined at all just by measuring the effect of the child on either paid work time or total household work time. Only a detailed survey of the allocation of time within the home will do as a basis for measuring time inputs into children.

The Basic Identification Problem

There is an unavoidable difficulty involved in any attempt to measure what one child receives or takes away from other things when more than one child is present in the home: all that we can reasonably measure is the time spent on the care of all children or all family members. Regressions therefore can show us only the net effect of an extra child on total care time. We cannot directly observe the time inputs into one child unless he is an only child. The problem is not just that children divide up total child care time in unknown proportions. The problem is also that some of that time they do not divide up at all. Often parental attention is a joint good shared by more than one sibling, with its enjoyment by one sibling detracting not at all from its enjoyment from the other(s). Thus even before confronting any data on time use one must realize that only a leap of faith, only *a priori* assumptions, can lead to quantitative estimates of the time that a non-only child receives or the time he takes away from other activities.

There are, however, two plausible assumptions that allow us to establish upper and lower bounds on the child care time received by a sibling:

(a) It can be assumed that a sibling does not receive more care time than would be received by an only child of the same age and parental attributes. This assumption might be violated if somehow the presence of an only child in the home placed demands on adult time that fell below some threshold necessary to divert

APPENDIX C

the adults away from other activities (e.g., paid work) while the presence of more children would force a major shift toward care of each child. That seems unlikely, however, for large samples.

(b) It can be assumed that a sibling does not receive less care time, or take less care time from other siblings, than he adds to total child-care time. It seems likely that he takes more from others, and receives more, than his *net* addition to *total* child care time. Therefore, regression estimates of the effects of a non-only child on total child care time can be used to establish a lower bound on the child care time put into a sibling.

These two assumptions are made here, and yield upper and lower bounds on the time inputs into a child when other children are present in the home. The true magnitudes lie somewhere between these two bounds. To create specific estimates of the child care time inputs, I shall arbitrarily assume the midpoint between the two bounds to be the best measure of the care time received by the individual sibling. That is, I shall assume that he receives something midway between his contribution to total child care time (the lower bound) and the time he would have received as an only child (the upper bound). These estimates are used in Chapters 4 and 6 in ways that do not seem to require that this mid-range estimate be accurate.

The effects of an extra child on time use, however, go beyond the child care time he receives. The child forces others, usually his mother, to engage in extra household chores just to keep his presence from damaging other household pursuits, such as cleanliness and disease prevention. The time spent on these extra chores is truly part of the time cost of the extra child, even though he does not personally receive them as inputs relevant to his later development. These chore time burdens can be estimated by regressions explaining total chore time in terms of the presence of children and other variables. That procedure is followed here. Part of the estimated time cost of an extra child is the net addition to the mother's time at meal preparation, meal cleanup, and washing prompted by his presence in the home. These three tasks are ones that regressions show take more time with each extra child. (It turns out, not surprisingly, that the extra chore burden, like most home burdens, falls almost entirely on Mother.) Note that the chore burden has to be measured as the *net* addition to time spent on these specific chores by persons other than the extra child. It is practically impossible to observe gross chore burdens for an extra child. We would need unrealistically detailed survey

APPENDIX C

data to find out, for example, to what extent cleaning up the baby's house mess made a wife not only spend more total time on house care but also cut back on her cleaning up after herself and her husband. Selected measures of net chore increases will have to do, even though these underestimate the gross time cost of an extra child.

As an offset to this net chore effect, the child also helps out with chores that the family would have to perform in any case. He also, as a teen-ager, works for pay outside the household while still a member of it. His house work contribution can be estimated directly from time-use surveys. His paid work can be measured from census and labor market data. These contributions of time, like the net effect on family chore loads, are relevant to the time cost of a child, but not to the time inputs into his development.

The Cornell Syracuse Survey, 1967–68

Gathering believable survey data on how time is allocated within the home is not easy. To be useful, the survey data must represent an annoying bother and invasion of privacy to many respondents. The researcher must go to great pains to keep respondents from putting down just any old thing to get the interviewer to go away. Respondents may give answers that are less than candid. Some may exaggerate the amount of time they spend on socially laudable things like reading to their children or fixing dinner as opposed to watching television. Nor do the surveys offer any positive evidence that people go to the bathroom or have intercourse, although these activities presumably get discreetly buried under "other personal activities." To maximize its credibility a time-use survey must have respondents fill out a time clock. Only by recording or reconstructing a twenty-four-hour stretch will respondents make the effort to unravel just what it was they did with their time. If the interviewer asks cheap quick questions like "How much time did you spend on house work (or taking care of the children) yesterday?" he will get cheap quick answers. Another valuable precaution is to be prepared for the fact that respondents often do two things at once. A mother who is ironing while watching the kids is engaged in a primary activity (ironing) and a secondary activity (supervising the children). Any study pursuing what time is taken away from some tasks for others must allow for this distinction. (The present study will focus on the "primary" time use only.)

The only survey currently available that has clearly taken all the nec-

APPENDIX C

essary precautions is the survey of time use in 1,296 Syracuse families in 1967–68.[1] Each family had to account for the activities of each family member six and older on two dates. The sample was not random, but was spread evenly over family sizes, days of the week, and months of the year. It turned out that the sample was somewhat younger and more educated than would have been true for Syracuse as a whole in that year.

The survey gathered very detailed data on time use itself plus extensive information on the family's endowment of home equipment, right down to electric barbecue grills. Three lacunae stand out: nothing was recorded about religion, race, or income. That last omission was offset by the availability of information on the educational attainment, occupation, and age of both husband and wife.

To use the Cornell survey to determine the effects of children on home time use, one should begin by dividing the sample into different days of the week and time of the year. The effects (coefficients) of a child on patterns of time use are likely to vary over the calendar. A school-age child takes more attention, and helps out more as well, on weekends than on weekdays, and more in the summer than over the rest of the year. Accordingly, I divided the 2,592 interview observations (2 interviews times 1,296 families) into three mutually exclusive samples:

Sample 1: nonsummer weekdays
Sample 2: weekend days (any month of the year)
Sample 3: summer weekdays (June, July, August)

Doing so raised the number of observations to twice the number of families. On the other hand, some of the observations were discarded from the set of three samples. This happened whenever both interviews with the same family occurred in the same sample (e.g., on nonsummer weekdays). It was felt that including both observations would raise unresolvable issues about correlation among individual error terms. The second interview for the family was thus discarded. The net results of this sample design procedure were a sample of 925 nonsummer weekdays, a sample of 734 weekend days, and a sample of 362 summer weekdays.

Since the focus of this study is on the changes in behavior associated with extra children, it is important to specify the family composition

[1] A time-use survey currently underway at the University of Michigan may prove to meet the same standards. Past Michigan surveys, however, have not been of sufficient detail and care regarding home time use to support the kind of child time cost estimates sought here.

variables carefully. Children must be broken down into different age groups, since a newborn requires far more time inputs than a teen-ager. It is also likely (as the results below confirm) that a child of given age has less effect on the parents' use of time the more siblings there are in the home. There is thus a need for presence-of-children variables that count the number of children in a particular age group within families of a given total number of children; e.g., there should be a variable counting the number of children aged 6–11 within families that have four children in the home. This precaution is taken in the regression models below, and the results confirm that a 6–11-year-old child has less effect on family time use, and appears to receive less attention, in a family of four children than when he is an only child of the same age.

Time Use Regression Results

Table C–1 displays selected regressions showing the effects of children in the home and other variables on the amounts of time given to various home tasks. Long as the list of independent variables may be, some variables are not displayed here. Table C–1 leaves out the NKIDS coefficients and standard errors for families having more than four children (NKIDS50 through NKIDS74). These were included in the regressions, but are omitted here because some of them proved less reliable than the NKIDS coefficients for families with four or fewer children. Specifically, it turned out that the samples had too few children under two years of age within families of five or more children. Rather than report coefficients for age-and-parity classes represented by only four or fewer positive observations, I dropped all of the larger-family coefficients from Table C–1.

Also omitted from the list of independent variables, even in the full regressions, were variables relating to the labor force participation of the wife. It might seem natural to include them, in order to be able to ask to what extent a working wife gives less time to each specific household chore than a nonworking wife. The influence of the mother's work status on child care is taken up later in this appendix. For present purposes, however, this is an inappropriate specification. The issues of key importance here are the influences of the presence of children and the education of the couple on their time use in and out of the home. Children and the couple's education affect all their time use patterns simultaneously. To quantify their impact on, say, child care time, it is a lot simpler *not* to include the wife's work status as a competing variable, in

APPENDIX C

order to avoid having to ask, after the regression, to what extent this work status itself is shifted by the presence of children, thereby further shifting the amount of child care time given by the wife. Similar reasoning led me to exclude the wife's preference ratings for different home tasks from the list of independent variables: her stated preferences, like her labor force participation, are simultaneously determined along with her home time use by the couple's background, and including the preference variables would only lead to the further task of asking how responsive these were to the couple's background.

Some of the patterns revealed by the regressions are not surprising. It turns out that virtually all of the housework and virtually all child care are done by the wife. Husbands, older children, and nonfamily females (primarily baby-sitters) do help out, especially on weekends and summer weekdays. Yet over half of any indoor task gets done by the wife. This pattern is consistent enough that most of the regressions for time inputs by the husband or hired females yielded such low R^2's, low average time inputs, and low significance of coefficients that they were not worth reporting here. Total time inputs into a child or other indoor chore were so closely governed by the wife's inputs that it is valid and expedient in Appendix E to value total child care by all persons at the wife's wage rate. The higher unit dollar value of the little bit of her husband's time put into child care is offset by the lower wage rate for the little bit of child care time logged for older siblings and baby-sitters.

Some of the patterns regarding the home's less rewarding chores also square with intuition. Meal preparation, meal cleanup, and washing are performed mainly by the wife, and her burden in these areas is raised by pre–teen-age children. Teen-agers help out enough so that her total time on these chores is raised only 0.6 hour per week as a year-round average by the presence of each teen-ager. Teen-agers in turn put in more home chore time than they seem to add to the mother's total chores—though

DEFINITIONS OF VARIABLES USED
Characteristics of Husband and Wife
PREDWAGE = predicted hourly wage rate of the husband in 1969, in dollars per hour. The wage rate is a transformation on the educational attainment, occupational class, and exact age of the husband, using the detailed table of predicted values given in Boone A. Turchi, "The Demand for Children: An Economic Analysis of Fertility in the United States," unpublished doctoral dissertation, University of Michigan, Ann Arbor, 1973, Table VII–1.
COLLEGEW = 1 if wife has received a college degree, 0 otherwise.
HSW = 1 if wife graduated from high school but does not hold a college degree, 0 otherwise.

… APPENDIX C

AGEWIFE1 = 1 if wife is under 35, 0 otherwise.
AGEWIFE2 = 1 if wife is 35 but less than 45, 0 otherwise.
AGEWIFE3 = 1 if wife is 45 but less than 55, 0 otherwise.
DISABLEW = 1 if wife is ill or handicapped on the day of the interview data, otherwise = 0.

Date of Interview

SUMMER = 1 if the interview data refer to a date in June, July, or August, 0 otherwise.
SUNHOL = 1 if interview refers to a Sunday, 0 otherwise. Because of a coding error, about half of the Sunday observations were incorrectly recorded as non-Sunday observations. There is no known relationship between the incidence of this error and other independent variables, so that its only effect appears to be to cast doubt on the SUNHOL coefficient itself within the samples confined to weekend observations.

Time Spent on Various Kinds of Household Work (all variables in min./da.)

DRUDGEW = time spent by wife on all household work.
DRUDGEH = time spent by husband on all household work.
DRUDGE27 = time spent by children 12–17 on all household work.
DRUDGE61 = time spent by children 6–11 on all household work.
DRUDGES = total time spent on all household work by all persons.
CARE1W = time spent on physical care of family members by the wife.
CARE1H = time spent on physical care of family members by the husband.
CARE1S = time spent on physical care of family members by all persons.
CARE2W = time spent on other care of family members by the wife.
CARE2H = time spent on other care of family members by the husband.
CARE2S = time spent on other care of family members by all persons.

Numbers and Ages of Children in the Home

NUMKIDS = number of children in the home.
KIDS0 = number of children in the home under 1 year in age.
KIDS1 = number of children in the home 1 year old.
KIDS2 = number of children in the home 2–5 years old.
KIDS3 = number of children in the home 6–11 years old.
KIDS4 = number of children in the home 12–17 years old. (None in the sample were 18 or older.)
NKIDSij: the number of children in a family with i children who are in the jth age group. That is, the NKIDSij variables are a transformation on the total number of children (NUMKIDS) and the number in each age group (KIDSj) as follows:

Value of NKIDSij = Value of:	Total number of children (NUMKIDS):					
	1	2	3	4	5	6	7
KIDS0 :	NKIDS10	NKIDS20	—	—	—	—	NKIDS70
KIDS1 :	NKIDS11						—
KIDS2 :	NKIDS12						
KIDS3 :	NKIDS13						
KIDS4 :	NKIDS14	—	—	—	—	—	NKIDS74

[Thus, for example, a family of four children aged 7, 5, 3, and 1 would have NKIDS43 = 1 (the 7-year-old), NKIDS42 = 2 (the two middle children), NKIDS41 = 1, and all other NKIDSij variables = 0.]

APPENDIX C

TABLE C-1

Selected Home Time Use Regressions, Syracuse Survey, 1967-68
(Dependent variables in minutes per day)
(Standard errors of regression coefficients in parentheses)

	Dependent Variable:			
Independent Variables:	(1) DRUDGEW: wife's total home work time	(2) DRUDGEW: wife's total home work time	(3) DRUDGEW: wife's total home work time	(4) DRUDGES: total home work time by all persons
CONSTANT	247.6 (37.1)	228.4 (87.1)	258.8 (47.5)	368.8 (51.0)
COLLEGEW	-17.6 (22.6)	.058 (38.5)	23.7 (27.1)	.0 (31.1)
HSW	22.6 (18.0)	14.1 (27.9)	-15.6 (21.2)	13.6 (24.7)
PREDWAGE	10.0 (4.9)	5.5 (10.3)	6.9 (6.2)	5.5 (6.8)
AGEWIFE1	-37.0 (32.1)	71.0 (81.2)	-7.7 (41.5)	-98.4 (44.2)
AGEWIFE2	-19.5 (32.9)	57.9 (82.3)	-6.7 (42.4)	-76.6 (45.2)
AGEWIFE3	6.9 (32.0)	104.7 (83.2)	25.7 (42.1)	-42.2 (44.0)
DISABLEW	-20.1 (42.0)	226.8 (79.4)	-8.4 (58.7)	63.9 (57.9)
NKIDS10	287.9 (32.7)	182.6 (56.1)	150.3 (38.6)	349.9 (45.0)
NKIDS11	241.9 (31.8)	148.9 (62.4)	97.5 (38.7)	296.4 (43.7)
NKIDS12	101.2 (32.3)	-34.8 (58.8)	59.9 (38.5)	172.8 (44.4)
NKIDS13	108.4 (31.3)	116.6 (63.9)	58.2 (38.6)	178.8 (43.1)
NKIDS14	57.7 (32.3)	6.1 (60.8)	68.8 (38.3)	166.4 (44.5)
NKIDS20	184.7 (22.7)	181.8 (37.3)	133.0 (27.0)	217.6 (31.2)
NKIDS21	161.4 (22.7)	145.0 (34.7)	109.8 (26.0)	203.6 (31.3)
NKIDS22	122.1 (13.9)	83.6 (24.4)	82.7 (16.6)	166.6 (19.1)
NKIDS23	92.5 (13.7)	59.6 (26.4)	58.0 (16.6)	148.9 (18.8)
NKIDS24	36.1 (14.7)	13.2 (28.5)	45.2 (18.2)	96.1 (20.3)
NKIDS30	106.9 (31.4)	223.5 (56.0)	177.7 (42.2)	125.6 (43.3)
NKIDS31	151.5 (27.6)	140.4 (44.0)	93.6 (30.0)	140.8 (38.0)

APPENDIX C

TABLE C-1 (cont.)

Independent Variables:	(1) DRUDGEW: wife's total home work time	(2) DRUDGEW: wife's total home work time	(3) DRUDGEW: wife's total home work time	(4) DRUDGES: total home work time by all persons
NKIDS32	101.9 (13.1)	65.5 (22.2)	46.1 (15.4)	123.3 (18.1)
NKIDS33	68.9 (9.4)	46.0 (15.4)	53.5 (10.9)	121.1 (12.9)
NKIDS34	20.3 (9.4)	5.6 (17.5)	16.9 (11.8)	83.1 (13.6)
NKIDS40	144.1 (31.9)	68.4 (51.8)	107.3 (36.4)	243.1 (43.9)
NKIDS41	123.8 (33.7)	93.1 (50.7)	35.1 (33.3)	136.7 (46.4)
NKIDS42	86.1 (11.5)	53.5 (17.9)	62.2 (13.5)	91.6 (15.8)
NKIDS43	55.4 (7.6)	51.1 (14.2)	30.4 (9.3)	106.4 (10.4)
NKIDS44	12.5 (11.2)	10.6 (15.8)	24.9 (11.4)	53.9 (15.4)
SUMMER	--- ---	--- ---	−24.5 (13.7)	--- ---
SUNHOL	--- ---	--- ---	−87.0 (13.9)	--- ---

.
.
.

Sample constraint:	nonsummer weekdays	summer weekdays	weekend days	nonsummer weekdays
$R^2_{adj.}$/s.e.e.	.3240/152.44	.2248/164.70	.1713/160.15	.2978/209.84
no. of obs./ d.f.	925/882	362/320	734/689	925/882

Note: In all regressions involving the set of NKIDS variables, the coefficients for variables NKIDS50 through NKIDS74 have been omitted here, for reasons mentioned in the text of this Appendix.

[293]

APPENDIX C

TABLE C-1 (cont.)

	Dependent Variable:			
Independent Variable:	(5) DRUDGES: total home work time, all persons	(6) DRUDGES: total home work time, all persons	(7) CARE1W: wife's physical care of family members	(8) CARE1W: wife's physical care of family members
NKIDS33	116.7	121.4	5.3	5.7
	(23.9)	(20.6)	(3.0)	(4.6)
NKIDS34	52.4	102.8	2.2	7.0
	(27.2)	(22.2)	(3.1)	(5.2)
NKIDS40	185.8	221.9	123.7	65.5
	(80.5)	(68.8)	(10.1)	(15.4)
NKIDS41	113.1	75.7	66.8	66.0
	(78.8)	(62.9)	(10.7)	(15.1)
NKIDS42	46.7	74.5	23.8	24.4
	(27.8)	(25.4)	(3.6)	(5.3)
NKIDS43	71.2	89.8	6.2	7.6
	(22.1)	(17.6)	(2.4)	(4.2)
NKIDS44	53.5	105.3	1.9	6.2
	(24.6)	(21.6)	(3.5)	(4.7)
SUMMER	---	-29.0	---	---
	---	(25.9)	---	---
SUNHOL	---	-129.9	---	---
	---	(26.2)	---	---

.
.
.

Sample constraint:	summer weekdays	weekends	nonsummer weekdays	summer weekdays
R^2_{adj}/s.e.e.	.1854/255.87	.2135/302.58	.6173/48.23	.5998/49.02
no. of obs./ d.f.	362/320	734/689	925/882	362/320

APPENDIX C

TABLE C-1 (cont.)

	Dependent Variable:			
Independent Variable:	(5) DRUDGES: total home work time, all persons	(6) DRUDGES: total home work time, all persons	(7) CARE1W: wife's physical care of family members	(8) CARE1W: wife's physical care of family members
CONSTANT	315.2 (135.2)	267.0 (89.8)	-7.9 (11.7)	-1.9 (25.9)
COLLEGEW	-114.3 (59.8)	20.0 (51.2)	10.0 (7.1)	9.2 (11.4)
HSW	0.5 (43.4)	-48.2 (40.1)	6.8 (5.7)	1.3 (8.3)
PREDWAGE	15.5 (15.9)	26.6 (11.7)	.4 (1.6)	-0.4 (3.1)
AGEWIFE1	57.1 (126.1)	41.7 (78.4)	.0 (10.2)	0.1 (24.2)
AGEWIFE2	81.0 (127.8)	19.1 (80.1)	0.5 (10.4)	-12.6 (24.5)
AGEWIFE3	130.1 (129.3)	43.1 (79.6)	4.5 (10.1)	-5.7 (24.8)
DISABLEW	231.6 (123.4)	-33.4 (110.8)	-6.9 (13.3)	-0.7 (23.6)
NKIDS10	182.3 (87.1)	220.7 (72.8)	145.6 (10.3)	123.3 (16.7)
NKIDS11	165.9 (97.0)	125.0 (73.2)	89.0 (10.1)	73.4 (18.6)
NKIDS12	21.1 (91.4)	141.7 (72.8)	32.6 (10.2)	30.1 (17.5)
NKIDS13	80.4 (99.2)	94.8 (72.8)	7.1 (9.9)	16.7 (19.0)
NKIDS14	87.5 (94.5)	263.0 (72.4)	-2.0 (10.2)	17.9 (18.1)
NKIDS20	188.3 (58.0)	159.3 (51.0)	130.6 (7.2)	162.3 (11.1)
NKIDS21	221.2 (53.8)	203.5 (49.1)	77.9 (7.2)	67.0 (10.3)
NKIDS22	72.2 (37.9)	114.2 (31.3)	29.2 (4.4)	24.3 (7.3)
NKIDS23	87.0 (41.0)	122.6 (31.3)	14.3 (4.3)	12.1 (7.8)
NKIDS24	74.4 (44.3)	177.4 (34.3)	4.1 (4.7)	12.7 (8.5)
NKIDS30	160.6 (87.0)	267.2 (79.7)	117.6 (9.9)	128.4 (16.7)
NKIDS31	95.8 (68.3)	136.2 (56.6)	65.2 (8.7)	71.7 (13.1)
NKIDS32	68.1 (34.5)	74.9 (29.0)	26.5 (4.1)	39.5 (6.6)

[295]

APPENDIX C

TABLE C-1 (cont.)

Independent Variable:	Dependent Variable:			
	(9) CARE1W: wife's physical care of family members	(10) CARE1H: husband's physical care of family members	(11) CARE1H: husband's physical care of family members	(12) CARE1H: husband's physical care of family members
NKIDS33	7.2 (3.0)	1.8 (1.1)	0.3 (1.9)	1.8 (1.4)
NKIDS34	1.7 (3.3)	-0.9 (1.1)	0.2 (2.1)	-0.6 (1.5)
NKIDS40	97.9 (10.1)	11.3 (3.6)	2.6 (6.3)	11.3 (4.6)
NKIDS41	35.4 (9.2)	2.6 (3.8)	10.4 (6.1)	9.1 (4.2)
NKIDS42	26.7 (3.7)	5.2 (1.3)	0.3 (2.2)	7.3 (1.7)
NKIDS43	4.8 (2.6)	-0.3 (0.8)	0.4 (1.7)	1.6 (1.2)
NKIDS44	0.5 (3.2)	0.1 (1.3)	1.3 (1.9)	-0.6 (1.5)
SUMMER	-2.8 (3.8)	---	---	-0.6 (1.7)
SUNHOL	-6.3 (3.9)	---	---	0.3 (1.8)
.				
.				
.				
Sample constraint:	weekend days	nonsummer weekdays	summer weekdays	weekend days
R^2_{adj}/s.e.e.	.5941/44.42	.0807/17.07	.0403/19.91	.1492/20.37
No. of obs./ d.f.	734/689	925/882	362/320	734/689

[296]

APPENDIX C

TABLE C-1 (cont.)

	Dependent Variable:			
Independent Variable:	(9) CARE1W: wife's physical care of family members	(10) CARE1H: husband's physical care of family members	(11) CARE1H: husband's physical care of family members	(12) CARE1H: husband's physical care of family members
CONSTANT	-2.2	-1.4	2.8	-4.4
	(13.2)	(4.2)	(10.1)	(6.0)
COLLEGEW	4.7	-4.1	5.2	4.9
	(7.5)	(2.5)	(4.6)	(3.4)
HSW	-3.9	-2.4	1.1	-0.3
	(5.9)	(2.0)	(3.4)	(2.7)
PREDWAGE	1.4	0.7	-1.0	1.2
	(1.7)	(.6)	(1.2)	(0.8)
AGEWIFE1	-2.8	1.5	-2.4	-1.8
	(11.5)	(3.6)	(9.8)	(5.3)
AGEWIFE2	0.5	2.3	0.9	-2.7
	(11.8)	(3.7)	(9.9)	(5.4)
AGEWIFE3	2.8	0.7	-0.4	.0
	(11.7)	(3.6)	(10.0)	(5.4)
DISABLEW	-10.2	-0.3	4.7	1.7
	(16.3)	(4.7)	(9.6)	(7.5)
NKIDS10	131.1	13.9	30.3	9.3
	(10.7)	(3.7)	(6.8)	(4.9)
NKIDS11	78.0	6.0	9.3	2.7
	(10.7)	(3.6)	(7.5)	(4.9)
NKIDS12	34.6	6.1	3.1	6.0
	(10.7)	(3.6)	(7.1)	(4.9)
NKIDS13	4.2	-1.0	2.4	-0.5
	(10.7)	(3.5)	(7.7)	(4.9)
NKIDS14	2.2	0.5	1.1	-0.8
	(10.6)	(3.6)	(7.3)	(4.9)
NKIDS20	123.3	8.8	4.7	12.0
	(7.5)	(2.5)	(4.5)	(3.4)
NKIDS21	63.4	1.4	12.6	11.6
	(7.2)	(2.5)	(4.2)	(3.3)
NKIDS22	31.4	3.5	2.5	7.1
	(4.6)	(1.6)	(2.9)	(2.1)
NKIDS23	10.8	0.8	1.0	-0.0
	(4.6)	(1.5)	(3.2)	(2.1)
NKIDS24	3.4	-0.3	1.1	-0.9
	(5.0)	(1.6)	(.34)	(2.3)
NKIDS30	129.1	14.9	16.4	11.3
	(11.7)	(3.5)	(6.8)	(5.4)
NKIDS31	70.5	-0.0	2.5	7.4
	(8.3)	(3.1)	(5.3)	(3.8)
NKIDS32	20.5	1.3	8.8	6.5
	(4.3)	(1.5)	(2.7)	(2.0)

[297]

APPENDIX C

Table C-1 (cont.)

	Dependent Variable:			
Independent Variables:	(13) CARE1S: phys. care of family, by all persons	(14) CARE1S	(15) CARE1S.	(16) CARE2W: other care of family members, by wife
CONSTANT	-11.2 (12.8)	5.0 (32.0)	-4.8 (15.2)	-9.5 (11.7)
COLLEGEW	7.3 (7.8)	17.9 (14.2)	10.0 (8.7)	5.8 (7.1)
HSW	5.8 (6.2)	3.0 (10.2)	-3.3 (6.8)	2.5 (5.7)
PREDWAGE	1.3 (1.7)	-2.7 (3.8)	2.1 (2.0)	2.3 (1.6)
AGEWIFE1	2.2 (11.1)	-2.8 (30.0)	-5.1 (13.3)	2.1 (10.1)
AGEWIFE2	2.8 (11.4)	-1.4 (30.3)	-4.9 (13.6)	1.6 (10.4)
AGEWIFE3	4.6 (11.1)	-5.0 (30.6)	1.5 (13.5)	5.7 (10.1)
DISABLEW	-3.1 (14.6)	7.5 (29.2)	-8.7 (18.8)	-2.4 (13.3)
NKIDS10	161.3 (11.3)	153.8 (20.6)	146.8 (12.3)	64.5 (10.3)
NKIDS11	94.4 (11.0)	112.7 (23.0)	80.2 (12.4)	62.2 (10.0)
NKIDS12	39.1 (11.2)	34.2 (21.6)	40.3 (12.3)	36.9 (10.2)
NKIDS13	6.0 (10.8)	25.8 (23.5)	4.8 (12.3)	27.5 (9.9)
NKIDS14	-0.9 (11.2)	20.8 (22.4)	2.3 (12.3)	16.9 (10.2)
NKIDS20	139.7 (7.8)	172.4 (13.7)	135.3 (8.6)	26.9 (7.2)
NKIDS21	82.2 (7.9)	90.5 (12.8)	80.8 (8.3)	31.2 (7.2)
NKIDS22	32.2 (4.8)	26.5 (9.0)	37.9 (5.3)	19.7 (4.4)
NKIDS23	15.5 (4.7)	15.4 (9.7)	14.3 (5.3)	24.8 (4.3)
NKIDS24	5.1 (5.1)	18.1 (10.5)	4.6 (5.8)	9.1 (4.7)
NKIDS30	134.2 (10.9)	146.4 (20.6)	159.3 (13.5)	16.2 (9.9)
NKIDS31	65.7 (9.6)	73.8 (16.2)	79.9 (9.6)	32.3 (8.7)
NKIDS32	27.8 (4.5)	48.4 (81.7)	27.3 (4.9)	20.1 (4.1)
NKIDS33	7.0 (3.2)	7.7 (56.6)	8.9 (3.5)	20.3 (3.0)
NKIDS34	1.8 (3.4)	8.8 (64.4)	3.1 (3.8)	3.3 (3.1)
NKIDS40	134.6 (11.0)	72.6 (19.1)	108.1 (11.6)	18.3 (10.1)
NKIDS41	74.2 (11.7)	76.3 (18.7)	47.4 (10.6)	35.2 (10.7)
NKIDS42	29.6 (4.0)	25.3 (65.8)	34.1 (4.3)	22.4 (3.6)
NKIDS43	5.9 (2.6)	9.4 (52.3)	7.2 (3.0)	13.2 (2.4)
NKIDS44	2.4 (3.9)	7.6 (58.2)	.2 (3.7)	6.0 (3.5)
SUMMER	-- --	-- --	-- --	-- --
SUNHOL	-- --	-- --	-- --	-- --
Sample Constraint:	nonsummer weekdays	summer weekdays	weekend days	nonsummer weekdays
R^2/s.e.e.	.6261/52.76	.5512/60.62	.6044/51.21	.1846/48.17
no. of/ obs./ d.f.	925/882	362/320	734/689	925/882

[298]

APPENDIX C

Table C-1 (cont.)

	Dependent Variable:			
Independent Variables:	(17) CARE2W	(18) CARE2W	(19) CARE2H: other care of family members, by husband	(20) CARE2H
CONSTANT	24.3 (27.5)	-1.5 (11.8)	-.6 (7.9)	-2.5 (15.3)
COLLEGEW	13.9 (12.1)	3.8 (6.7)	4.8 (4.8)	-3.2 (6.7)
HSW	7.3 (8.1)	2.3 (5.3)	2.3 (3.8)	3.1 (4.9)
PREDWAGE	-2.0 (3.2)	.2 (1.5)	.9 (1.0)	1.9 (1.8)
AGEWIFE1	-23.2 (25.6)	-.2 (10.3)	-4.0 (6.8)	-1.2 (14.2)
AGEWIFE2	-12.1 (26.0)	7.6 (10.5)	-4.5 (7.0)	-2.2 (14.4)
AGEWIFE3	-17.3 (26.3)	3.8 (10.5)	.7 (6.8)	6.1 (14.6)
DISABLEW	-4.9 (25.1)	6.4 (14.6)	1.5 (8.9)	0.8 (13.9)
NKIDS10	28.2 (17.7)	31.0 (9.6)	29.8 (6.9)	10.7 (9.8)
NKIDS11	30.7 (19.7)	30.7 (9.6)	20.6 (6.7)	11.4 (11.0)
NKIDS12	37.1 (18.6)	20.5 (9.6)	25.1 (6.9)	-2.9 (10.3)
NKIDS13	13.4 (20.2)	20.8 (9.6)	12.8 (6.6)	5.6 (11.2)
NKIDS14	6.1 (19.2)	8.1 (9.5)	6.1 (6.9)	-9.3 (10.7)
NKIDS20	11.4 (11.8)	27.7 (6.7)	6.7 (4.8)	7.2 (6.5)
NKIDS21	59.7 (10.9)	14.3 (6.5)	9.4 (4.8)	18.6 (6.1)
NKIDS22	35.1 (7.7)	11.2 (4.1)	8.0 (2.9)	4.8 (4.3)
NKIDS23	15.2 (8.3)	11.7 (4.1)	8.0 (2.9)	6.5 (4.6)
NKIDS24	-0.7 (9.0)	4.8 (4.5)	2.5 (3.1)	-6.1 (5.0)
NKIDS30	27.9 (17.7)	-9.8 (10.5)	-2.0 (6.7)	-5.1 (9.8)
NKIDS31	42.2 (13.9)	20.2 (7.4)	-.6 (5.9)	0.3 (7.7)
NKIDS32	5.1 (7.0)	12.7 (3.8)	10.4 (2.8)	-2.0 (3.9)
NKIDS33	9.8 (4.9)	11.1 (2.7)	4.2 (2.0)	1.5 (2.7)
NKIDS34	5.4 (5.5)	.8 (2.9)	1.2 (2.1)	-2.2 (3.1)
NKIDS40	-8.9 (16.4)	4.2 (9.1)	23.5 (6.8)	25.8 (9.1)
NKIDS41	-2.2 (16.0)	-4.5 (8.3)	-9.0 (7.2)	9.8 (8.9)
NKIDS42	18.9 (5.6)	13.8 (3.3)	5.3 (2.4)	-2.0 (3.1)
NKIDS43	11.7 (4.5)	7.7 (2.3)	1.7 (1.6)	0.1 (2.5)
NKIDS44	4.0 (5.0)	5.6 (2.8)	2.2 (2.4)	-1.9 (2.8)
SUMMER	-- --	-- --	-- --	-- --
SUNHOL	-- --	-- --	-- --	-- --
Sample Constraint	summer weekdays	weekend days	nonsummer weekdays	summer weekdays
R^2/s.e.e.	.0989/51.98	.0774/57.18	.0700/32.38	.0407/28.89
no. of obs./d.f.	362/320	734/689	925/882	362/320

[299]

APPENDIX C

Table C-1 (cont.)

Independent Variables:	(21) CARE2H		(22) CARE2S: other care of family, by all persons		(23) CARE2S		(24) CARE2S	
CONSTANT	-16.5	(13.5)	-14.7	(19.3)	0.7	(56.3)	-19.0	(31.1)
COLLEGEW	4.0	(7.7)	18.7	(11.7)	16.8	(24.9)	26.4	(17.7)
HSW	2.4	(6.0)	10.6	(9.4)	17.8	(18.1)	11.2	(13.9)
PREDWAGE	3.3	(1.8)	2.9	(2.6)	2.4	(6.6)	2.4	(4.0)
AGEWIFE1	0.9	(11.8)	-4.2	(16.7)	-22.7	(52.5)	-1.6	(27.2)
AGEWIFE2	-.3	(12.1)	-5.3	(17.1)	-4.6	(53.3)	2.5	(27.8)
AGEWIFE3	4.1	(12.0)	7.9	(16.6)	-4.9	(53.8)	7.6	(27.6)
DISABLEW	-2.1	(16.7)	17.8	(21.9)	17.1	(51.4)	7.9	(38.4)
NKIDS10	29.8	(11.0)	96.2	(17.0)	54.2	(36.3)	119.5	(25.2)
NKIDS11	21.0	(11.0)	87.8	(16.5)	67.7	(40.4)	59.4	(25.3)
NKIDS12	8.4	(11.0)	85.4	(16.8)	93.8	(38.1)	46.1	(25.2)
NKIDS13	18.4	(11.0)	60.1	(16.3)	20.1	(41.4)	47.5	(25.2)
NKIDS14	1.1	(10.9)	25.1	(16.8)	-4.8	(39.4)	13.7	(25.1)
NKIDS20	19.0	(7.7)	48.4	(11.8)	36.0	(24.2)	75.4	(17.7)
NKIDS21	20.7	(7.4)	61.2	(11.8)	105.0	(22.4)	68.8	(17.0)
NKIDS22	12.7	(4.7)	38.5	(7.2)	63.7	(15.8)	29.4	(10.8)
NKIDS23	9.4	(4.7)	44.2	(7.1)	18.6	(17.1)	37.6	(10.8)
NKIDS24	7.0	(5.2)	14.4	(7.7)	-8.2	(18.5)	16.2	(11.9)
NKIDS30	7.2	(12.0)	36.0	(16.3)	-2.2	(36.2)	10.1	(27.6)
NKIDS31	35.9	(8.5)	32.6	(14.4)	26.3	(24.5)	80.5	(19.6)
NKIDS32	9.6	(4.4)	33.4	(6.9)	14.8	(14.4)	35.6	(10.1)
NKIDS33	4.9	(3.1)	30.4	(4.9)	29.6	(10.0)	28.1	(7.1)
NKIDS34	0.1	(3.3)	8.9	(5.1)	8.7	(11.3)	3.7	(7.7)
NKIDS40	16.6	(10.4)	56.7	(16.6)	74.7	(33.6)	47.5	(23.8)
NKIDS41	5.8	(9.6)	34.9	(17.5)	11.2	(32.8)	9.4	(21.8)
NKIDS42	5.7	(3.8)	30.8	(6.0)	34.7	(11.6)	29.4	(8.8)
NKIDS43	4.6	(2.6)	18.9	(3.9)	20.9	(9.2)	20.9	(6.1)
NKIDS44	4.5	(3.2)	10.9	(5.8)	0.8	(10.2)	13.8	(7.5)
SUMMER	--	--	--	--	--	--	-10.5	(9.0)
SUNHOL	--	--	--	--	--	--		
Sample Constraint	weekend days		nonsummer weekdays		summer weekdays		weekend days	
R^2adj/s.e.e.	.0967/45.54		.1566/79.31		.0833/106.62		.1602/104.70	
no. of obs./d.f.	734/689		925/882		362/320		734/689	

APPENDIX C

Table C-1 (cont.)

	Dependent Variable:			
Independent Variables:	(25) DRUDGE61: home chore time by children 6-11	(26) DRUDGE61	(27) DRUDGE61	(28) DRUDGE27: home chore time by children 12-17
CONSTANT	-17.5 (20.8)	-24.5 (44.9)	4.0 (29.9)	-32.3 (29.2)
COLLEGEW	22.8 (18.3)	5.8 (34.0)	6.0 (24.8)	33.5 (25.5)
HSW	9.9 (13.9)	-6.4 (21.5)	-17.1 (18.3)	23.9 (18.5)
PREDWAGE	-2.9 (3.8)	2.1 (8.9)	0.5 (5.3)	-0.2 (5.2)
KIDS0	11.7 (13.3)	39.7 (31.3)	41.2 (20.9)	30.9 (28.0)
KIDS1	11.6 (11.1)	-3.4 (21.3)	12.8 (14.0)	17.9 (22.5)
KIDS2	-3.3 (5.4)	-4.7 (13.1)	-1.1 (7.6)	-7.1 (10.8)
KIDS3	37.6 (3.8)	50.7 (8.7)	38.4 (5.3)	8.3 (5.6)
KIDS4	7.2 (4.3)	6.1 (9.2)	12.5 (6.0)	51.9 (6.5)
SUMMER	--- ---	--- ---	-12.1 (11.9)	--- ---
SUNHOL	--- ---	--- ---	-14.1 (12.2)	--- ---
Sample constraint:	at least 1 child, 6-11; nonsummer weekdays	at least 1 child, 6-11; summer weekdays	at least 1 child, 6-11; weekend days	at least 1 child, 12-17; nonsummer weekdays
R^2_{adj}/s.e.e	.1867/79.56	.1664/102.44	.1411/95.87	.1978/95.83
no. of obs./d.f.:	419/410	172/164	335/324	282/273

	Dependent Variable:	
Independent Variables:	(29) DRUDGE27	(30) DRUDGE27
CONSTANT	-60.1 (62.5)	45.6 (57.9)
COLLEGEW	14.8 (49.4)	-72.1 (46.0)
HSW	-16.5 (27.6)	-73.1 (31.2)
PREDWAGE	15.1 (12.3)	7.8 (10.4)
KIDS0	110.7 (63.2)	111.9 (58.9)
KIDS1	-6.1 (43.6)	40.6 (37.0)
KIDS2	21.3 (20.9)	-11.6 (19.6)
KIDS3	9.2 (11.3)	6.7 (10.5)
KIDS4	67.5 (12.0)	78.8 (12.1)
SUMMER	--- ---	-9.9 (23.3)
SUNHOL	--- ---	-44.8 (24.2)
Sample constraint:	at least 1 child, 12-17 summer weekdays	at least 1 child, 12-17; weekend days
R^2_{adj}/s.e.e.	.2136/121.43	.1791/159.81
no. of obs./d.f.:	130/121	236/225

APPENDIX C

Table C-1 (cont.).

Means of Selected Variables for the Three Main Samples:

Variable:	Nonsummer weekday sample	Summer weekday sample	Weekend day sample
COLLEGEW	.187	.182	.183
HSW	.717	.678	.718
AGEWIFE1	.548	.611	.569
AGEWIFE2	.272	.227	.252
AGEWIFE3	.145	.149	.151
DISABLEW	.015	0.014	0.011
SUNHOL	.145	.138	.251
DRUDGEW	468.010	476.560	378.280
DRUDGEH	75.319	84.807	141.380
DRUDGE27	27.458	50.069	51.308
DRUDGE61	24.643	37.251	32.016
DRUDGES	614.120	681.930	630.810
MEALW	78.989	79.116	72.568
MEALH	3.978	6.671	8.740
DISHESW	45.059	42.459	46.124
DISHESH	2.389	1.519	2.882
HOUSEW	71.465	70.981	51.792
HOUSEH	1.111	.746	3.018
WASHW	31.719	35.649	23.849
IRONW	.784	.331	.552
CARE1W	58.168	56.561	50.484
CARE1H	5.460	5.428	7.970
CARE127	.741	.345	.313
CARE161	.443	.925	.456
CARE1S	65.395	65.622	60.838
CARE2W	48.697	36.188	27.234
CARE2H	15.827	11.340	23.072
CARE227	2.005	4.599	3.161
CARE261	2.151	3.232	2.227
SUMMER	.000	1.000	.278
PREDWAGE	4.763	4.614	4.718
NUMKIDS	2.304	2.384	2.315
KIDS0	.166	.155	.155
KIDS1	.183	.199	.202
KIDS2	.554	.530	.544
KIDS3	.851	.865	.838
KIDS4	.550	.635	.576

APPENDIX C

Table C-1 (cont.)

Means of Selected Variables for the Three Main Samples:

Variable:	Nonsummer weekday sample	Summer weekday sample	Weekend day sample
NKIDS10	.032	.033	.033
NKIDS11	.036	.025	.033
NKIDS12	.034	.030	.033
NKIDS13	.036	.025	.033
NKIDS14	.032	.033	.033
NKIDS20	.060	.064	.060
NKIDS21	.069	.086	.076
NKIDS22	.158	.166	.158
NKIDS23	.174	.144	.163
NKIDS24	.128	.133	.128
NKIDS30	.028	.028	.023
NKIDS31	.042	.050	.050
NKIDS32	.149	.160	.155
NKIDS33	.234	.354	.266
NKIDS34	.179	.229	.192
NKIDS40	.032	.025	.030
NKIDS41	.024	.033	.034
NKIDS42	.146	.122	.142
NKIDS43	.230	.193	.207
NKIDS44	.104	.135	.127
NKIDS50	.001	.003	.003
NKIDS51	.003	.003	.003
NKIDS52	.013	.019	.011
NKIDS53	.057	.080	.076
NKIDS54	.034	.047	.037
NKIDS60	.009	.003	.005
NKIDS61	.004	.003	.003
NKIDS62	.020	.033	.022
NKIDS63	.043	.069	.040
NKIDS64	.020	.058	.020
NKIDS70	.004	.000	.001
NKIDS71	.004	.000	.003
NKIDS72	.034	.000	.023
NKIDS73	.077	.000	.053
NKIDS74	.053	.000	.040
Number of observations	925	362	734

(As noted at the start of this table, a coding error mismeasured the SUNHOL variable. About half of the Sunday observations were given SUNHOL=0 in the weekend sample, and a similar number of observations has SUNHOL=1 in the weekday samples, even though all observations in the weekend sample truly refer to weekend observations and no weekend observations were included in the weekday sample. The only effect of the coding error was to throw some suspicion on the SUNHOL coefficient and standard error for each model run on the weekend sample.)

[303]

APPENDIX C

one can wonder whether their rate of home production per hour matches hers. Regressions were also run for other chores—chauffeuring, ironing, and regular house care—but too many zeros were recorded in these time-use categories for interesting regression results to show up.

Several clear patterns in child-care time emerge from Table C-1. The impact of a child on total care time is much greater for an infant than for an older child. A newborn requires tremendous physical care, a one-year-old requires large amounts of both physical and other (interactive) care, and the demands drop off for each older age group. A glance at the coefficients further suggests that the impact of a child of given age on total care time tends to be lower the more children there are. One of two children in the home seems to affect total care time less than does an only child, and one of three less than one of two. The pattern does not continue, however, from three-child families to four-child families. Each child in a four-child family seems to have an impact on total care time the same as or greater than that of each child of the same age in a three-child family. There is no obvious explanation for this result. The unreported coefficients for larger families do suggest that the net impact of a child of any age above one year (i.e., for any age group well-represented in the large-family observations) is lower for five- and six-child families than for four-child families. The prevailing pattern appears, at a glance, to be one of declining impact of one child on total care time the more siblings he or she has. This pattern is examined more carefully below.

Class Differences in Child Care Time?

As noted in the text of Chapter 4, past authors have suggested that a wife with more schooling and socioeconomic status will tend to put more hours of time into the care of each child. This conclusion was reached, with varying degrees of qualification, by the U.S. Bureau of Human Nutrition and Home Economics (1944), Leibowitz (1972, 1974), Hill and Stafford (1972), Vanek (1973), and Szalai and others (1972).[2] The issue is one that might raise class sentiments, and deserves a closer look.

The literature to date has advanced two related hypotheses about class differences in child care time. The first is that a higher-status wife

---

[2] See Footnotes 7 and 8, Chapter 4, for U.S. Bureau of Human Nutrition and Home Economics, Leibowitz, and Hill and Stafford citations; Joann Vanek, "Keeping Busy: Time Spent in Housework, United States, 1920–1970," Ph.D. dissertation, University of Michigan, 1973; Alexander Szalai et al., *The Uses of Time*, The Hague: Mouton, 1972.

tends to put more hours into child care per child. The second is that she tends to devote more time to each child than would a lower-status wife having the *same number of children*. The first hypothesis is correct. The second is incorrect.

The regressions in Table C–1 demonstrate that when one has held the number and ages of children constant, the education of the wife and the status (predicted wage rate) of the husband have a small and insignificant effect on total time put into care of family members. The signs of the coefficients for extra education and status are usually positive, as past authors have implied, but the difference between the wife's having a college degree and her having dropped out of high school has less predicted impact on child care time per child than, say, the difference between having two and having three children for given parental characteristics. The unimpressiveness of the effects of the couple's education and status on child care time shows up consistently. It shows up for all times of the week and year. It shows up both for the wife's child care time and for child care time by all persons. It shows up when the current regressions are cross-checked by (unreported) regressions yielding predicted care time impacts of children in samples restricted to high- and then to low-education wives. The Cornell survey data clearly imply, then, that the tendency of higher-status wives to put in more child-care time per child is primarily or even entirely due to the fact that they have fewer children on the average. Here, as elsewhere in this book, we encounter the conclusion that the mechanisms governing family size are prime determinants of the inputs that one generation gives to each member of the next.

This finding can be reconciled with the cited findings to the contrary by other authors. Some of the studies noting class differences in childcare time were simply based on raw averages too crude for reliable conclusions about class differences. This is true of the study by Guilbert and others (1967) and by the international team of Szalai and others (1972, pp. 263, 382, 383).[3] Authors who took enough care to use regressions based on large samples often masked the present finding by their choices of variables. Professors Hill and Stafford, for example, used total household work time as a dependent variable, since the Michigan survey they used did not yield any breakdown between child care and other tasks. The apparent extra impact of a child of a more-educat-

---

[3] M. Guilbert, N. Lowit, and J. Creusen, "Les budgets-temps et l'étude des horaires de la vie quotidienne." *Revue française de sociologie* 8 (1967), 169–183; Szalai et al., *The Uses of Time*.

ed and higher-income couple might reflect not differences in time inputs into a child but a greater tendency of low-education wives to find time for the child at the expense of other home chores instead of leisure or paid work. This is especially true since the independent variables used by these authors fail to identify parity effects properly. By using the same variable for the impact of a child of given age whatever the number of his siblings, Hill and Stafford seem to have passed over the point that lower-status wives, having more children and less leisure on the average, might find the time for an extra child more at the expense of other household work, thereby showing a lower impact of the extra child on total household work even if the extra child received the same amount of care time as a higher-status child of the same parity.

Professor Leibowitz, using the better Cornell survey data, chose more appropriate dependent variables than Hill and Stafford had at their disposal. She divided the Syracuse sample into subsamples consisting of families with high-education wives and families with low-education wives. It turned out that the predicted values of care time were higher for the high-education group, though not always significantly so. This result hinged on the fact that the high-education sample had a greater intercept value (care time with no children), even though that sample had lower apparent impacts of each child on total care time than did the low-education group. In Leibowitz' formulation, as in that of Hill and Stafford, children are presented by the numbers of them within each age group, with no recognition of the fact that the impact of an extra child on each age group depends strongly on how many siblings are present. The likelihood that this simplification of the independent variables affected Leibowitz' conclusions is underlined by another property of the Syracuse sample. In that sample it turns out that the families having *no* children have less schooling on the average than the sample as a whole, while those having *one* child had higher than average schooling. This explains why the regressions for care time among higher-education families had higher intercepts and higher predicted values for small family sizes: the intercepts and predicted values were buoyed up by the relative absence of childless couples and the greater representation of one-child couples. This twisting of the regression line is avoided by making all the presence-of-children variables specific to the total number in the family.

Another study purporting to show marked class differences in child care time is that of the U.S. Bureau of Human Nutrition and Home Economics (1944). That study found that rural households spent quite a bit less time on child care for each age of the youngest child in the family than did urban alumnae of six prestigious Eastern women's colleges. This result is hard to interpret, given the nature of the sample and the impossibility of inspecting the original data behind these averages. I strongly suspect that the differences do not relate at all to education, but only to rural-urban differences in the reporting of time use to survey takers. Rural wives may report the large amounts of time spent both supervising the children and working about the house and farm as primarily time spent in chores other than child care, while the urban wives record such multiple-use time mainly as child care. Or it might be that there are true rural-urban differences in the devoting of time and energy to child care. It is hard to tell, but it does appear that the differences observed in this study hinged more on the rural-urban split than on the split by educational class.

Though past studies have underemphasized the extent to which differences in child care time hinge on differences in fertility, the present results uphold other patterns asserted by others. It is still true that a wife with more schooling will tend to put more care into each child if numbers and ages of children are *not* held constant across classes. And the present regressions allow one to reject the hypothesis that children of more-schooled parents receive markedly *less* time than children of less-schooled parents. In addition, nothing in Table C–1 denies (or confirms) the plausible argument that a more-schooled wife is more productive in developing a child's achievement potential with each hour and each bundle of commodities she spends on him or her. That issue is hard to test, given the multicollinearity between her unobserved productivity and such influences as the amount of purchased inputs given to the child.

Working Mothers and Child Care

To determine how child care time is influenced by family composition and by the age and education of the parents, it has proved convenient to omit the mother's work status from the list of independent variables, as noted above. Yet it is reasonable to wonder how a mother's working for pay outside the home affects the amount of time spent on child care by herself and by others. The movement of mothers into the labor force has been one of the most conspicuous changes in work habits in this century, and the relative pay prospects for women remain bright enough to make it likely that the trend toward having careers and children at the same time will continue, even without any further exogenous shifts in at-

APPENDIX C

titudes.[4] This trend raises curiosity about the effects of mothers' careers on child development, a curiosity that is reinforced by the absence of evidence that husbands have begun to devote a greater share of their lives to child care and other home tasks than in the past.

The Cornell time use data cannot directly appraise the effects of mothers' careers on a child's later development. Indeed, few bodies of data are up to this task, since it requires having information on the mother's work history, other family attributes, *and* the child's own achievements or emotional history in much later years. Only if one settles for school grades or test scores as early indicators of child development can one expect to get all the necessary information on family history into one sample. The time use data can, however, give useful clues on the extent to which the time inputs into children of given numbers and ages are affected by the mother's labor force participation. If her working seems to reduce time spent by herself on child care by more than the extra time that others devote to the same set of children because she has a job, there is good reason to suspect that her work may be depriving the children of attention needed for development. If her work takes away from the children less of her time than the extra care time provided by others, the case for suspecting a net deprivation seems weakened. If this latter result holds, children might still suffer on balance from a mother's working outside the home, but to show it one would have to show that the greater number of others' hours plus the extra commodities bought with the mother's pay were not enough to offset the reduction in contact with the mother.

To estimate the effects of a mother's work status on child care time, I divided the observations of the Cornell survey into four subsamples:

(a) 421 weekday observations, families with working[5] wives and 0–4 children
(b) 789 weekday observations, families with nonworking wives and 0–4 children
(c) 254 weekend observations, families with working wives and 0–4 children
(d) 438 weekend observations, families with nonworking wives and 0–4 children

[4] See Victor R. Fuchs, "Recent Trends and Long-Run Prospects for Female Earnings," *American Economic Review* 64, no. 2 (May 1974), 236–242.
[5] Wives were defined as working if they had worked for pay outside the home in the seven days preceding the date of the first interview.

For each subsample regressions were run on the amounts of physical care and of other care given to family members by the wife and by all persons. These regressions use the same independent variables as those used for Models (1)–(24) in Table C–1. The coefficients for the effects of various numbers and ages of children, converted into total annual hours, are shown in Table C–2. The implications of these coefficients for the inputs of time in children over their entire childhood are illustrated in Figure C–1, which follows the coefficients from Table C–2 over the childhood of two siblings born three years apart.

The estimates bring out several contrasts in the time devoted to child care in families differing by the mother's work status. First, the underlying averages show that working mothers have fewer children, and older children, than nonworking mothers, as one would expect. A prime mode of reconciling home time demands with a mother's job is thus the simple option of having fewer children. By having fewer children, working mothers are able to provide the same amount of their own time and of others' time (and more commodities) for each *individual* child, compared to nonworking mothers. Another means of adjusting to the job is the tendency of working mothers to spend less time at non-child home tasks, since the effect on child care time is much smaller than the average number of hours worked for pay (25.5 hours a week). Yet it remains true, even when the numbers and ages of children are held constant, that working mothers spend less of their own time on child care. The difference is on the border of statistical significance, though a mammoth sample would probably show clear significance.

The striking result in Table C–2 and Figure C–1, however, is that the reduction in the mother's child care time appears to be more than matched by an increase in the time spent by the husband and others caring for her children. In the two-child case illustrated in Figure C–1 it appears that each hour of contact the children lose with her is matched with about an hour and a half of care from others. This outcome can be interpreted in either of two ways. It could be the result of a reporting bias, as would occur if every single minute of baby-sitters' time were reported as child care while only part of the time spent by a nonworking mother at home with the children was reported as child care. Alternatively, it may actually be that working mothers spend more of their nonworking hours of the week on child care than nonworking mothers do, in an attempt to avoid shortchanging the children. Either interpretation, though, tends to leave little confirmation for the suspicion that children are deprived by a mother's work. If the reporting bias were responsible

APPENDIX C

Table C-2. Hours of Child-Care Time per Year Associated with Various Numbers and Ages of Children Present in the Home, Working versus Non-Working Mothers (Based on Data from the Cornell Time Use Survey, 1967-68)

A. On Weekdays, Families with Working Mothers

(Figures in parentheses are standard errors of regression coefficients)

		Physical Care by: Mother	Physical Care by: All Persons	Other Care by: Mother	Other Care by: All Persons	All Care by: Mother	All Care by: All Persons
For the only child present, aged:	<1:	a	a	a	a	a	a
	1:	a	a	a	a	a	a
	2-5:	139.4 (33.5)	170.3 (43.2)	132.4 (41.0)	404.5 (93.1)	271.8	574.8
	6-11:	43.4 (33.9)	58.4 (43.8)	88.6 (41.6)	231.8 (94.5)	132.0	290.2
	12-17:	-10.7 (35.7)	8.8 (46.0)	40.3 (43.7)	75.4 (99.3)	29.6	84.2
With 2 children present, for each child aged	<1:	516.5 (35.9)	508.3 (46.3)	68.7 (44.0)	96.4 (100.0)	585.2	604.7
	1:	248.8 (33.6)	371.2 (43.3)	177.6 (41.2)	409.8 (93.5)	426.4	781.0
	2-5:	89.9 (17.8)	94.3 (23.0)	95.0 (21.8)	263.6 (49.6)	184.9	357.9
	6-11:	30.7 (16.9)	59.7 (21.8)	105.6 (20.6)	194.4 (47.0)	136.3	254.1
	12-17:	8.9 (16.7)	26.4 (21.6)	10.0 (20.5)	4.1 (46.6)	18.9	30.5
With 3 children present, for each child aged	<1:	a	a	a	a	a	a
	1:	a	a	a	a	a	a
	2-5:	131.6 (19.2)	154.4 (24.7)	50.0 (23.5)	77.4 (53.4)	181.6	231.8
	6-11:	34.6 (11.2)	45.2 (14.5)	63.8 (13.8)	160.0 (31.3)	98.4	205.2
	12-17:	7.9 (10.8)	9.8 (14.0)	11.5 (13.2)	22.2 (30.0)	19.4	32.0
With 4 children present, for each child aged	<1:	a	a	a	a	a	a
	1:	a	a	a	a	a	a
	2-5:	21.5 (37.5)	64.3 (48.4)	158.8 (46.0)	170.3 (104.4)	180.3	234.6
	6-11:	19.5 (9.6)	20.9 (12.4)	53.9 (11.7)	69.1 (26.6)	73.4	90.0
	12-17:	15.8 (11.7)	23.3 (14.8)	29.3 (14.1)	29.7 (32.0)	45.1	53.0

APPENDIX C

Table C-2 (cont.). Hours of Child-Care Time per Year Associated with Various Numbers and Ages of Children Present in the Home, Working versus Non-working Mothers (based on data from the Cornell Time Use Survey, 1967-68)

B. On Weekdays, Families with Non-working Mothers

(Figures in parentheses are standard errors of regression coefficients)

		Physical Care by: Mother / All Persons	Other Care by: Mother / All Persons	All Care by: Mother / All Persons
For the only child present, aged	< 1:	597.0 / 677.2 (52.3) / (58.4)	247.0 / 387.0 (51.8) / (86.1)	844.0 / 1064.1
	1:	356.0 / 389.9 (55.0) / (61.3)	240.1 / 382.0 (54.4) / (87.2)	596.0 / 771.9
	2-5:	110.0 / 131.1 (64.8) / (72.2)	190.2 / 339.7 (64.1) / (102.7)	300.2 / 470.8
	6-11:	26.6 / 19.2 (64.0) / (71.4)	110.7 / 182.0 (63.4) / (101.5)	137.3 / 201.2
	12-17:	26.1 / 32.3 (62.6) / (69.8)	71.7 / 75.6 (62.0) / (99.3)	97.8 / 107.9
With 2 children present, for each child aged	< 1:	615.6 / 669.2 (35.5) / (39.6)	99.7 / 222.4 (35.2) / (56.3)	715.3 / 891.6
	1:	316.4 / 340.4 (35.1) / (39.1)	177.2 / 316.5 (34.7) / (55.6)	493.6 / 656.9
	2-5:	114.2 / 127.8 (24.6) / (27.4)	103.7 / 173.6 (24.3) / (39.0)	217.9 / 301.4
	6-11:	61.5 / 55.5 (24.7) / (27.8)	86.7 / 138.1 (24.4) / (39.1)	148.2 / 193.6
	12-17:	49.0 / 51.1 (27.9) / (31.1)	40.5 / 53.8 (27.7) / (44.3)	89.5 / 104.9
With 3 children present, for each child aged	< 1:	499.2 / 548.7 (48.3) / (53.7)	127.5 / 146.3 (47.7) / (76.4)	626.7 / 695.0
	1:	280.8 / 289.0 (39.2) / (43.7)	132.2 / 122.1 (38.8) / (62.1)	412.4 / 411.0
	2-5:	116.3 / 126.7 (21.4) / (23.9)	76.3 / 139.0 (21.2) / (34.0)	192.6 / 265.7
	6-11:	8.3 / 12.5 (16.3) / (18.1)	73.8 / 115.7 (16.1) / (25.8)	82.1 / 128.2
	12-17:	16.4 / 13.4 (18.6) / (20.7)	17.3 / 41.0 (18.3) / (29.4)	33.7 / 54.4
With 4 children present, for each child aged	< 1:	446.5 / 500.0 (42.7) / (47.6)	43.2 / 251.7 (42.3) / (67.7)	489.7 / 751.7
	1:	264.4 / 294.1 (45.1) / (50.3)	66.0 / 121.3 (44.7) / (71.6)	330.4 / 415.4
	2-5:	105.4 / 122.8 (16.4) / (18.3)	91.1 / 133.5 (16.3) / (26.1)	196.5 / 256.3
	6-11:	24.9 / 24.7 (13.3) / (14.9)	53.9 / 86.8 (13.2) / (21.2)	78.8 / 111.5
	12-17:	13.3 / 15.7 (19.1) / (21.3)	12.4 / 21.0 (19.0) / (30.3)	25.7 / 36.7

APPENDIX C

Table C-2 (cont.). Hours of Child-Care Time per Year Associated with Various Numbers and Ages of Children Present in the Home, Working versus Non-working Mothers (based on data from the Cornell Time Use Survey, 1967-68)

C. On Weekend Days, Families with Working Mothers

(Figures in parentheses are standard errors of regression coefficients)

	Physical Care by: Mother	Physical Care by: All Persons	Other Care by: Mother	Other Care by: All Persons	All Care by: Mother	All Care by: All Persons
For the only child present, aged < 1:	a	a	a	a	a	a
1:	a	a	a	a	a	a
2-5:	58.6 (16.6)	64.3 (23.4)	21.6 (18.7)	74.2 (51.1)	80.2	138.5
6-11:	13.8 (16.4)	21.0 (23.1)	24.9 (18.4)	64.6 (50.4)	38.7	85.6
12-17:	9.2 (18.0)	15.8 (25.3)	13.2 (20.2)	20.5 (55.3)	22.4	36.1
With 2 children present, for each child aged <1:	227.3[b] (16.6)	251.2[b] (23.4)	-3.8[b] (18.7)	227.2[b] (51.1)	225.1b	478.4b
1:	86.1[c] (15.7)	148.0[c] (22.1)	40.0[c] (17.6)	225.3 (48.3)	126.1c	373.3c
2-5:	50.3 (8.9)	52.5 (12.4)	22.6 (9.9)	24.8 (27.2)	72.9	77.3
6-11:	10.4 (9.1)	27.9 (12.8)	15.0 (10.2)	101.7 (28.1)	25.4	129.6
12-17:	7.5 (8.5)	13.6 (12.0)	6.6 (9.6)	9.7 (26.2)	14.1	23.3
With 3 children present, for each child aged <1:	a	a	a	a	a	a
1:	a	a	a	a	a	a
2-5:	25.0 (9.3)	31.6 (13.0)	27.8 (10.4)	115.1 (28.5)	52.8	146.7
6-11:	12.9 (6.0)	15.4 (8.4)	6.0 (6.7)	16.9 (18.4)	18.9	32.3
12-17:	8.0 (5.9)	11.6 (8.3)	1.4 (6.6)	0.9 (18.2)	9.4	12.5
With 4 children present, for each child aged <1:	a	a	a	a	a	a
1:	a	a	a	a	a	a
2-5:	23.7 (15.8)	64.5 (22.2)	-14.3 (17.7)	67.6 (48.4)	9.4	132.1
6-11:	12.1 (4.9)	13.4 (6.9)	12.2 (5.5)	14.1 (15.0)	24.3	27.5
12-17:	1.4 (5.2)	3.9 (7.3)	3.6 (5.9)	21.4 (16.1)	5.0	29.2

[312]

APPENDIX C

Table C-2 (cont.). Hours of Child-Care Time per Year Associated with Various Numbers and Ages of Children Present in the Home, Working versus Non-working Mothers (based on data from the Cornell Time Use Survey, 1967-68)

D. On Weekend Days, Families with Nonworking Mothers

(Figures in parentheses are standard errors of regression coefficients)

		Physical Care by: Mother / All Persons	Other Care by: Mother / All Persons	All Care by: Mother / All Persons
For the only child present, aged	<1:	236.2 (26.6) / 271.1 (29.1)	64.8 (21.7) / 249.8 (53.4)	301.0 / 520.9
	1:	146.1 (27.7) / 155.4 (30.4)	62.4 (22.6) / 121.8 (55.7)	208.5 / 277.2
	2-5:	54.5[b] (33.6) / 73.5[b] (36.8)	66.4[b] (27.4) / 74.6[b] (67.5)	120.9b / 148.1b
	6-11:	a / a	a / a	a / a
	12-17:	3.6[d] (30.6) / 2.5[d] (33.5)	8.5[d] (24.9) / 7.9[d] (61.4)	12.1d / 10.4d
With 2 children present, for each child aged	<1:	210.4 (18.8) / 234.9 (20.6)	68.4 (15.3) / 110.8 (37.7)	278.8 / 345.7
	1:	117.2 (18.1) / 138.0 (19.8)	19.9 (14.7) / 81.9 (36.3)	137.1 / 219.9
	2-5:	54.6 (12.6) / 71.1 (13.8)	20.8 (10.3) / 61.4 (25.4)	75.4 / 132.5
	6-11:	20.8 (12.4) / 22.6 (13.6)	23.6 (10.1) / 47.1 (24.9)	44.4 / 69.7
	12-17:	6.4 (14.6) / 5.5 (16.0)	3.5 (11.9) / 27.8 (29.4)	9.9 / 33.3
With 3 children present, for each child aged	<1:	224.1 (27.7) / 290.9 (30.3)	19.9 (22.6) / 30.0 (55.7)	244.0 / 323.9
	1:	122.1[d] (19.0) / 135.9[d] (20.9)	40.7[d] (15.5) / 138.3[d] (38.3)	162.8d / 274.2d
	2-5:	38.4 (11.1) / 53.9 (12.1)	21.0 (9.0) / 47.8 (22.3)	59.4 / 101.7
	6-11:	10.7 (8.2) / 14.4 (9.0)	25.2 (6.7) / 60.1 (16.5)	35.9 / 74.5
	12-17:	0.1 (9.1) / 2.8 (9.9)	2.5 (7.4) / 7.5 (18.2)	2.6 / 10.3
With 4 children present, for each child aged	<1:	166.6 (21.5) / 173.6 (23.6)	11.8 (17.6) / 107.6 (43.3)	178.4 / 281.2
	1:	59.7 (19.9) / 90.0 (21.8)	-13.1 (16.2) / -8.3 (39.9)	46.6 / 81.7
	2-5:	48.1 (8.7) / 58.0 (9.5)	29.2 (7.1) / 55.9 (17.5)	77.3 / 113.9
	6-11:	5.4 (7.0) / 10.9 (7.6)	14.3 (5.7) / 47.1 (14.0)	19.7 / 58.0
	12-17:	1.8 (9.8) / -1.6 (10.7)	13.6 (8.0) / 21.2 (19.7)	15.4 / 19.6

[313]

APPENDIX C

Table C-2 (cont.). Hours of Child-Care Time per Year Associated with Various Numbers and Ages of Children Present in the Home, Working versus Non-working Mothers (based on data from the Cornell Time Use Survey, 1967-68)

E. Total Year-Round Child Care Time		Families with Working Mothers		Families with Non-Working Mothers	
		By Mother	By All Persons	By Mother	By All Persons
For the only child present, aged	<1:	a	a	1145.0	1585.0
	1:	a	a	804.6	1049.1
	2-5:	352.0	713.3	421.1	618.9
	6-11:	170.7	375.8	a	a
	12-17:	52.0	120.3	109.9	118.3
With 2 children present, for each child aged	<1:	810.3	1083.1	994.1	1237.3
	1:	552.8	1154.3	630.7	876.8
	2-5:	257.8	435.2	293.3	433.9
	6-11:	161.7	383.7	192.6	263.3
	12-17:	33.0	53.7	99.4	138.2
With 3 children present, for each child aged	<1:	a	a	870.4	1018.9
	1:	a	a	575.2	685.2
	2-5:	234.4	387.5	252.0	367.4
	6-11:	117.3	237.5	118.0	202.7
	12-17:	28.8	44.5	36.3	64.7
With 4 children present, for each child aged	<1:	a	a	668.1	1032.9
	1:	a	a	377.0	497.1
	2-5:	189.7	366.7	273.8	370.2
	6-11:	97.7	117.5	98.5	169.5
	12-17:	50.1	82.2	41.1	56.3

Notes:

a: figures omitted, since the underlying regression coefficients were based on fewer than 10 children of the appropriate age, family size, and interview day of the week.
b: based on only 10 children in the appropriate category.
c: based on only 14 children in the appropriate category.
d: based on only 12 children in the appropriate category.

The figures are calculated from unreported regressions using the independent variables shown in Table A-1. Each weekday coefficient in those models was multiplied by 4.348 to convert from minutes per weekday to weekday hours per year. Each weekend coefficient was correspondingly multiplied by 1.739. Note that each coefficient is not the same thing as the child-care impact of that one child, as explained in the text of this appendix. Rather each is the contribution of one child that age to the total effect of having that many children (versus having none) in the home. (This distinction is unimportant, of course, for only children.)

APPENDIX C

Figure C-1. Child-Care Time in Hypothetical Two-Child Families, Working versus Non-Working Mother (Three-Year Child Spacing).

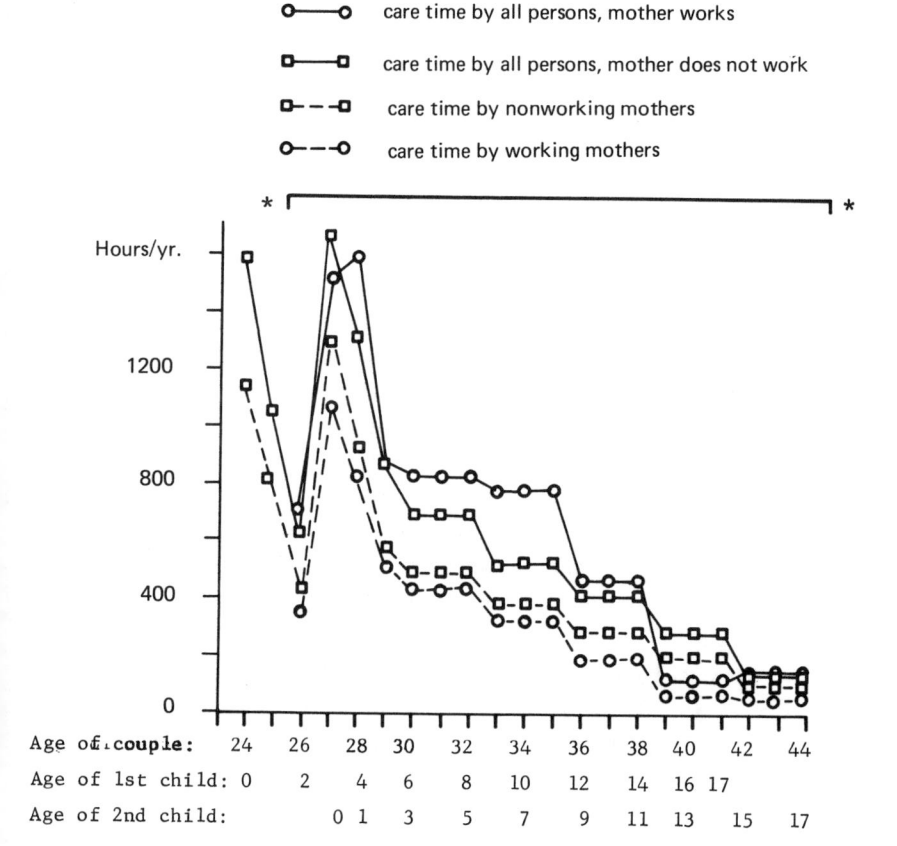

o——o   care time by all persons, mother works
□——□   care time by all persons, mother does not work
□– – –□   care time by nonworking mothers
o– – –o   care time by working mothers

Total hours of child care, over the 19 bracketed years:*

    o——o - 11,446.6 hours (11.6 hrs./wk.)

    □——□ - 10,528.6 hours (10.6 hrs./wk.)

    □– – –□ - 7,634.5 hours (7.7 hrs./wk.)

    o– – –o - 5,913.1 hours (6.0 hrs./wk.)

*(Figures for the first two years in the life of the first child could not be compared, since the sample for working mothers included almost no only children under two years in age.)

[315]

APPENDIX C

for the greater total care hours for children of working mothers, one must recognize that underlying this reporting bias is the fact that much of the time spent by the nonworking mother at home when her children are at home involves no more contact with them than a passive type of baby-sitting. If, on the other hand, working mothers actually concentrate more of their off-hour attention to their children, the result is the same: we find little hint of a net overall reduction in total child care time, even when holding the numbers and ages of children constant. The hypothesis of deprivation from a mother's career is not rejected, but it must find evidence not implying a serious reduction in total adult attention.

Estimating Time Inputs Into Siblings

The comments made thus far about the relationship of child care time to numbers and ages of children could be made on the basis of casual inspection of the coefficients in Table C–1. Yet a proper quantification of the child care time received by individual children, and the time costs of individual children, requires a more careful processing of the regression estimates. The coefficients for minutes per day of time spent on different days of the week and seasons of the year first need to be aggregated to yield hours of time use per year. That involves multiplying each figure on minutes per nonsummer weekday by 3.261 [= (365.25/60) × (3/4 of the yr.) × (5/7 of the week)], each figure on minutes per summer weekday by 1.087, and each figure on minutes per weekend day by 1.739. Next, the spacing of births determines which coefficients are relevant for each year of a child's life in appraising his impact on time use. For example, the first of two siblings born two years apart is an only child for his first two years, while the other is an only child for his last two years in the home, assuming they both leave home at the same age. The coefficients for a two-child family should therefore be used only for the years in which they are both present in the home.

Another complication to be introduced in processing the estimates of time inputs into children is that the regression coefficient for a given age group and number of children is not exactly the impact of a child that age on time use in a family achieving that number of children with his presence. Were he not present, that family would be smaller and a different set of child coefficients would be relevant. An example should help clarify this subtlety:

The net impact on total care time caused in a given year by a three-year-old who is the second of two children is not just the coefficient

[316]

NKIDS22, which is associated with a three-year-old in a family with two children present. If the other child is, say, six years old, the net impact of the three-year-old is the difference between the predicted value of care time inputs for the family with this pair of children and the predicted value that would obtain if the six-year-old were an only child. This difference, the net impact of the younger child on care time, equals NKIDS22 + NKIDS23 − NKIDS13, which does not exactly equal NKIDS22. Correspondingly, the net impact of the older child on care time in the same family equals NKIDS22 + NKIDS23 − NKIDS12, which is not exactly equal to NKIDS23.

The impact of children on various birth orders on total child care time (physical care plus other care) was calculated for different spacing intervals in accordance with these guidelines. The estimates are given in Table 6–4 in Chapter 6. An examination of the figures there confirms that a child tends to make a greater difference to total care time the fewer in number are his siblings. First-born and last-born children also appear to have greater impacts on total child care time than do middle children, because the first-born and last-born spend part of their childhood as the only child in the household. Again, as with the raw regression coefficients, there appears to be little difference between the care-time use impact of a third versus a fourth child.

Note that the figures in Table 6–4 refer to the estimated impact of the child on total care time during his presence in the home, and not to the time inputs he himself receives. The net impacts are thus low numbers where three or four children are present. In some cases, in fact, the values are negative for individual years (unreported here), implying that the presence of the extra child for such years lowers total care time. The negative values are counter to intuition. They stem from the inability of a less-than-mammoth sample of families to generate coefficients so finely tuned that they imply positive net impacts for all children in all spacing and parity combinations in all years. None of the negative predicted impacts, at any rate, are as negative as one standard error of estimate.

To convert these impacts on total care time into estimates of the inputs of care time received by an individual sibling, it is necessary to employ the assumptions made above about upper and lower bounds on the inputs of time into a child. The upper bound on the care time he receives is the time he would receive as an only child with similar parents. The lower bound is his impact in Table 6–4. The preferred estimate of the

APPENDIX C

care time he receives is the average of these two extreme estimates.[6] For each sibling position the average can be computed as the average of his column in Table 6–4 and the only-child column. The individual-year averages are omitted here. At the bottom of the table are presented the raw eighteen-year sums of the hours put into each child's care according to these mid-range estimates.

The estimates for total care time inputs into children in different family settings suggest that a child receives more care time by having fewer siblings, by having greater age gaps between siblings, and by being first or last. The ratios shown in Table 6–4 confirm that an only child receives much more time than a sibling. Either child in a two-child family also receives a good deal more than each child in larger families. Middle children receive less time than first or last children, especially in wider-spaced families, where the first and last each spend several years as the only child in the household. And the wider the average spacing, the more each child receives. These patterns are discussed at greater length in Chapter 6, where they are compared with the apparent effects of sibling position on adult achievement.

The estimates in Table 6–4 imply that a last-born receives more time inputs than a first-born when the average spacing between siblings is three years or wider. This result stems from the ability of the oldest siblings to care for the youngest when the age gaps are wide. What needs to be clarified is how the extent of this care of younger siblings by older siblings was calculated and incorporated into the overall estimates of time inputs. The complicated estimation procedure described above was based on regression estimates of the effects of the presence of each child on the total child care time logged by *all persons* [in Regressions (13)–(15) and (22)–(24) of Table C–1]. The use of the all-persons regressions was dictated by the necessity of cutting down on the number of

---

[6] The same mid-range estimates would also be appropriate for measuring the child care part of the total net time cost of a child. I used a more conservative procedure, however, when calculating the time cost of a third child in Chapter 4 and Appendix E. There I used the lower-bound estimate, which is the net impact of the third child on the time spent caring for all family members. The choice between the lower-bound estimate and the mid-range estimate, however, affects only the absolute cost of the third child and not the measure of relative cost that is the focus of Chapter 4. Using the mid-range estimate would only raise the absolute time cost of both the third child and the alternatives to having the third child by the same amount. (The extra amount of time represents time taken away from the care of the first two children.) The behavior of the relative cost index would not be affected by substituting the mid-range estimates for the lower-bound estimates.

APPENDIX C

calculations. The more logical procedure of working up separate estimates of the hours of care time by the wife, the husband, older siblings, and all others was just too time-consuming to be practical. The decision to use the all-persons regression results means that part of the net impact of older siblings on child care time by all persons is not really related to the care *of* him, but instead reflects care *by* him. It is thus necessary to subtract estimates of the care of younger siblings by older siblings in order to get a more accurate picture of what time the older siblings are receiving over their childhood. This subtraction was done. Table C–3 reports my estimates of the total amounts of child care supplied by older siblings. These estimates come from unreported regressions covering subsamples consisting of those families in the Cornell survey having at least one child in the relevant older age group (6–11 or 12–17). The figures in Table C–3 are sums of the amounts of care time supplied by each older sibling over the years from his eighth birthday to his eighteenth birthday.[7]

Chore Effects

An extra child adds to a mother's chore loads in many ways familiar to any parent. To quantify these burdens, regressions were run on the time spent by the wife and the husband at meal preparation, meal cleanup, regular care of the house and yard, washing, ironing, and chauffeuring (transportation). Of these only the regressions for the wife's meal preparation, her meal cleanup, and her washing turned up significant amounts of time spent and significant coefficients relating to the numbers of children in different age groups. The regressions have been omitted from Table C–1 to conserve space. While these chore time increases are not viewed as inputs relevant to the child's own development, they are included in the total time cost of the child in Table 4–1 and in Appendix E.

Also relevant to the cost of the child is his own contribution to family chores and his paid work time outside the home. The child's chore con-

[7] Readers wanting to know how much care was received from older siblings by each younger sibling can use the same figures: the figures on the total care of a last-born by a next-to-last-born (e.g., 32.88 hours for six-year spacing) are in fact the amounts received by any sibling from the sibling just ahead of him in birth order; the figures on the care supplied by a third-to-last-born (e.g., the second of four siblings) add together his care of the child next in line (e.g., the same figure of 32.88 hours for six-year spacing) and his care of the last-born (for six-year spacing, 533.17 − 32.88 = 500.29 hours). Following this procedure, one can derive the care received from older siblings for each younger sibling.

APPENDIX C

Table C-3. Predicted Care of Younger Siblings by Older Siblings, Various Numbers and Spacing of Children: (hours of care over the 18 years spent in the household by the older sibling)

Child Spacing (Uniform)	Children ever born	Care of all Younger Siblings by			
		1st born	2nd born	3rd born	4th born
1-year	4	8.22	0	0	0
	5	n.c.	n.c.	n.c.	n.c.
2-year	3	16.44	0	0	--
	4	41.10	8.22	0	0
	5	271.89	24.66	8.22	0
3-year	2	8.22	0	--	--
	3	28.77	8.22	0	--
	4	323.62	28.77	8.22	0
	5	733.99	225.48	28.77	8.22
6-year	2	32.88	0	--	--
	3	533.17	32.88	0	--
	4	533.17	533.17	32.88	0
	5	533.17	533.17	533.17	32.88

Notes:

n.c. = not calculated, because the the Cornell time-use sample did not include families with such numbers and spacing of children.

The estimates are based on unreported regressions relating sibling care time to the numbers of siblings in each of five age groups and to other variables. It was found that the number of children in each older age group (6-11, 12-17) had no significant effect on the total time spent by such age groups in caring for family members. The only significant influences on care time by older children were the numbers of children in each of the preschool age brackets (<1, 1, 2-5). Thus for each of the later years of the older sibling's life in the household, I summed the appropriate pre-school coefficients to find how much sibling-care burden to assign to each older age group. The total burden for the year was then divided among the siblings in that age-range. (In the case of the 6-11 age range, I arbitrarily attributed all of the care of preschool siblings to those who were 8-11 years old.) Each sibling's care time was then summed over the years he lived in his parents' household (here ages 8-17).

tribution has been estimated on the basis of Regressions (25) through (30) in Table C–1, and is included in the cost calculations in Table 4–1 and Appendix E. His paid work contribution was estimated from other unreported regressions. It turned out that his paid work contribution, as one would expect, was significant only beyond age 12. The average child in the 12–17 age group had a predicted probability of working of .1077, and the predicted weekly hours of paid work for those who worked was 12.88 hours, making the predicted value of paid work 1.39 hours/week, or 72.2 hours/yr., for all children 12–17 on the average. This estimate was used in the child cost calculations of Appendix E.

APPENDIX D. Net Effects of Children on Family Consumption Patterns, 1960–61 and 1889–90

The net effects of children of different ages in different family sizes on consumption patterns govern the relationship between the movements of relative commodity prices and the relative cost of a child. The regression estimates needed to derive these net effects (the $\triangle C$'s) are also to be used as a basis for guessing at the commodity inputs into the child (the C^N's). Some of the net effects of children on consumption patterns are already known from existing literature. As noted in Chapter 4, it is clear that the family-size elasticity of food is positive and the family-size elasticities for shelter and luxuries appear negative. Yet to develop estimates of how these effects vary with the age and sibling position of a child, a more careful set of regressions is in order. Two such sets are supplied here, one from the 1960–61 Survey of Consumer Expenditures and one from the 1889–90 survey of workers' families. The first set is used to estimate child commodity inputs in Appendix E.

Children and Consumption Patterns in 1960–61

For present purposes the variables that need to be set up most carefully are those capturing the presence and numbers of children. It would be very desirable to be able to employ the same definition of the NKIDS variables used for time use regressions in Appendix C. There each NKIDS variable counted the number of children in a particular age group in families of a given total number of children. The same approach can be followed for the 1889–90 survey but not for the general-purpose tape of the 1960–61 Survey of Consumer Expenditures. This tape does not give the exact ages of the children. It does, however, give a child-age-class code based on the ages of the oldest and youngest children. These can be combined with the number of children of all ages in the family to give a fairly good accounting of how family consumption patterns are affected by children in various sibling positions. Each NKIDS$_{ij}$ variable is thus defined so that i = the child-age-class code and j = the number of children in the family. The child-age-class codes are defined as on the chart on page 323.

Thus, for example, NKIDS23 = 1 will stand for a family with three children in the household, the oldest of whom is 6–11 and the youngest of whom is under 6; NKIDS91 = 1 represents a family where the only child in the home is 18 or older; and so forth. It turned out to be neces-

APPENDIX D

Age of the oldest child

		0-5	6-11	12-17	18 and up
Age of the youngest child	0-5	1	2	5	7
	6-11		3	6	8
	12-17			4	
	18 and up				9

sary to limit the sample to families with four or fewer children (and no adults other than the husband and wife), since coverage of all the age classes became spotty for larger families.

The variable definitions and selected regression results for the 1960–61 sample are given in Table D–1. The fits are generally satisfactory and the coefficients correspond to expectations based on intuition or on past consumption studies. The income elasticities reveal that furniture, adult clothing, transportation, recreation, and the indirectly represented category of "all other" expenditures are luxury goods. As couples age, they demand more medical care and less recreation. For any given level of income, extra schooling (of the husband in this case) significantly raises total consumption, with significant increases occurring in expenditures for shelter, utilities other than fuel and light, medical care, recreation, and education. The only expenditure class significantly shifted downward by education is fuel and light. Why education should significantly reduce saving is not clear. It does appear, at any rate, that we can sustain one hypothesis about the effects of education on child inputs that could not be sustained for its effects on time inputs: more-educated parents with a given number of children do spend considerably more on education itself, with most of the extra private education apparently going to their children.

The reported effects of children on expenditures are plausible and generally not surprising. The older a child becomes the more he raises total expenditures and expenditures on food, education, recreation, and children's clothing. This is brought out by Table D–2, which presents predicted expenditures for three-year child spacing in the "low-income" and "high-income" families introduced in Chapter 4 and Appendix A. Table D–2 also underlines the point that a child causes a much greater impact on total expenditures and expenditures in many categories when

[323]

APPENDIX D

he is the only child than when he is added to other siblings. This suggests, as did the time-input estimates in Appendix C, that the inputs a child receives depend greatly on the share of his childhood that he can spend as the only child in the household. This in turn suggests higher commodity (as well as time) inputs into first and last children than into middle children. This point is pursued further in Chapter 6.

The estimates of commodity inputs into a child that come from Table D–2 are given in Tables E–1 through E–4 in Appendix E.

Children and Consumption Patterns in 1889–90

It was inexpensive to run regressions like those for 1960–61 on data from the survey of workers' families conducted in 1889 and 1890 by the U.S. Bureau of Labor Statistics. In one respect the earlier gave better data: the exact age and sex of each child were given. This allowed a specification of the presence-of-children variables (NKIDS) that was analogous to that used in Appendix C. The NKIDS variables used for the 1889–90 survey are defined more precisely in Table D–3. In other respects the earlier survey necessitated a more limited range of variables. Data on education and regional price relatives were lacking. So were data on the expenses of home ownership, so that the sample had to be restricted to renters. As for dependent variables, the earlier survey went into just as much detail as the 1960–61 survey. However, the data tape available to me only gave food, rent, and total expenditures, limiting my regressions to these variables. The data on other expenditures exist, however, and await the efforts of scholars wanting to pursue other nineteenth-century themes than those followed here.

With these limitations, the results shown in Table D–3 look quite reasonable and quite analogous to those given for 1960–61 in Table D–1. Food expenditures are significantly raised by the presence of children in the home, though by lower percentages than in the 1960–61 survey of consumer expenditures. Older children tend to add more to food bills, though the percentage increases rise less steeply with age than in the 1960–61 results shown in Table D–1. Rent expenditures clearly tend to be reduced by the presence of an extra child. Each of these impacts of an extra child tends to diminish as family size rises. The presence of boarders, like the presence of children, tends to raise food expenditures and to lower rent expenditures. But in the case of boarders and lodgers, there is an institutional reason for this pattern: boarders consumed meals prepared within the household, and apparently agreed in many cases to pay part of the tenant family's rent rather than paying the homemaker cash for her services.

APPENDIX D

Definitions of Variables Used

Dependent Variables

LNFOOD = the natural logarithm of food expenditures deflated by the price index for food in the urban area of the individual observation (price relative to U.S. ave.).

LNSHEL = the natural logarithm of expenditures for shelter (rent or homeowning costs) deflated by the urban area's price index for shelter.

LNFUEL = the natural log of expenditures for fuel and light deflated by the urban area's price index for "other" commodities.

LNOTUT = the natural log of expenditures for other utilities, deflated as for LNFUEL.

LNFURN = the natural log of expenditures for furniture, deflated as for LNFUEL.

LNADULT = the natural log of expenditures for adult clothing deflated by the urban area's price index for clothing.

LNKIDC = ditto, children's clothing.

LNTRANS = the natural log of transportation expenditures deflated by the urban area's price index for transportation.

LNMED = the natural log of medical care expenditures deflated by the urban area's price index for medical care.

LNREC = the natural log of recreational expenditures deflated as for LNFUEL.

LNEDUC = the natural log of education expenditures deflated as for LNFUEL.

LNCONS = the natural log of total consumption expenditures deflated by the urban area's overall cost of living index.

Independent Variables

$\ln(P_i/CPI)$ = the natural log of the commodity's relative price, which is the ratio of the urban area's price index for the appropriate commodity class divided by its overall cost of living index (the U.S. ave. = 1.00 for both numerator and denom.). The price indices are for metropolitan areas in 1960 as reported by the BLS in the *Handbook of Labor Statistics*. In the case of the food price, a programming slip left P_i/CPI in absolute unlogged form. But its mean was 1.00 and all values were near that, so that its behavior is the same as if it were logged.

$\ln(Y_d)$ = the natural log of family disposable income deflated by the urban area's cost of living index.

AGE2 = 1 if the husband is 25–34 years old, 0 otherwise.

AGE3 = 1 if the husband is 35–44 years old, 0 otherwise.

AGE4 = 1 if the husband is 45–54 years old, 0 otherwise.

AGE5 = 1 if the husband is 55–64 years old, 0 otherwise (husbands over 64 excluded from the sample).

EDHEAD = index of the husband's educational attainment.

OWNER = 1 if the couple owns their house, zero if they rent. The "low-income" couple followed in these appendices rents, while the "high-income" couple owns.

NKIDSij's: as explained in the text of Appendix D, these are binary dummies based on the ages of the oldest and youngest child and the number of children in the family. The i subscript refers to the age-of-oldest-and-youngest code and the j subscript (and the second number) refers to the number of children.

Definitions of Variables Used

lnFOOD = the natural logarithm of family expenditures on food.

lnRENT = the natural logarithm of family expenditures on rent.

lnTOTEXP = the natural logarithm of family expenditures on all commodities.

lnTOTINC = the natural logarithm of total family income.

APPENDIX D

NOBRDRS = the number of boarders and lodgers staying in the household.
AGE1 = 1 if the husband is 25–34 years old; 0 otherwise. (No husbands were under 25.)
AGE2 = 1 if the husband is 35–44 years old; 0 otherwise.
AGE3 = 1 if the husband is 45–54 years old; 0 otherwise.
NKIDSij: these number-of-children variables are defined as the number of children in families of a given size that are in a given age range:

		Number of children in the family(i) =			
		1	2	3	4
	(1) 0–5 :	NKIDS11	NKIDS21	NKIDS31	NKIDS41
Age	(2) 6–11:	NKIDS12	NKIDS22	NKIDS32	NKIDS42
Groups (j):	(3) 12–17:	NKIDS13	NKIDS23	NKIDS33	NKIDS43
	(4) 18–up:	NKIDS14	NKIDS24	NKIDS34	NKIDS44

Examples: a family with children of ages 7, 5, and 1 has NKIDS31 = 2 (the two younger children), NKIDS32 = 1 (the eldest), and all other NKIDS variables = 0; a childless couple has all NKIDS variables = 0.

Sample Constraint

The sample was limited to those families for which (a) income, food expenditures, and rent expenditures were all positive; (b) as implied by (a), the family rented its housing and did not own it; (c) the husband was older than 24 and younger than 65; and (d) the number of children was 0, 1, 2, 3, or 4.

Data Source

The original data come from U.S. Commissioner of Labor, *Sixth Annual Report* and *Seventh Annual Report* (Washington: GPO, 1891 and 1892). I am indebted to Allen C. Kelley for permission to use computer tapes of these data.

APPENDIX D

Table D-1. The Impacts of Children and Other Variables on Family Consumption Patterns: Regressions Based on the 1960-61 Survey of Consumer Expenditures

Dependent Variable:	(1) LNFOOD (food)		(2) LNSHEL (shelter)	
Independent Variables	coeff.	std. error of coeff.	coeff.	std.error of coeff.
CONSTANT	3.310	(0.169)	1.5946	(0.1690)
$\ln(P_i/CPI)$	-0.678	(0.132)	-0.6222	(0.0866)
$\ln(Yd)$	0.498	(0.012)	0.5593	(0.0205)
AGE2(25-36)	0.042	(0.022)	0.0488	(0.0385)
AGE3(35-44)	0.099	(0.023)	0.0067	(0.0410)
AGE4(45-54)	0.103	(0.024)	-0.0564	(0.0431)
AGE5(55-64)	0.149	(0.025)	-0.1250	(0.0448)
EDHEAD	-0.002	(0.003)	0.0654	(0.0058)
OWNER	-0.012	(0.010)	-0.2222	(0.0183)
1 NKIDS11	0.102	(0.019)	0.1166	(0.0346)
k NKIDS21	0.146	(0.025)	0.1136	(0.0441)
i NKIDS41	0.203	(0.021)	0.0339	(0.0371)
d NKIDS71	0.182	(0.021)	-0.0269	(0.0368)
2 NKIDS12	0.196	(0.021)	0.1248	(0.0369)
c NKIDS22	0.253	(0.025)	0.0967	(0.0437)
h NKIDS32	0.279	(0.029)	-0.0114	(0.0510)
i NKIDS42	0.380	(0.030)	-0.0656	(0.0528)
l NKIDS52	0.310	(0.043)	-0.0617	(0.0771)
d NKIDS62	0.338	(0.026)	0.0045	(0.0456)
r NKIDS72	(0.000)*	(0.000)*	(0.0000)*	(0.0000)*
e NKIDS82	0.295	(0.025)	-0.0360	(0.0454)
n NKIDS92	0.245	(0.037)	-0.1242	(0.0663)
3 NKIDS13	0.289	(0.033)	0.0751	(0.0588)
c NKIDS23	0.345	(0.022)	0.0554	(0.0400)
h NKIDS33	0.399	(0.072)	0.0916	(0.1282)
i NKIDS43	0.448	(0.076)	-0.2147	(0.1361)
l NKIDS53	0.353	(0.035)	0.0190	(0.0617)
d NKIDS53	0.446	(0.027)	0.0080	(0.0478)
r NKIDS73	0.361	(0.132)	0.0416	(0.2345)
e NKIDS83	0.369	(0.030)	-0.1019	(0.0540)
n NKIDS93	0.300	(0.079)	-0.4440	(0.1411)
4 NKIDS14	0.405	(0.065)	0.1688	(0.1163)
c NKIDS24	0.386	(0.031)	-0.0153	(0.0547)
h NKIDS34	0.201	(0.208)	0.2227	(0.3697)
i NKIDS44	0.216	(0.132)	-0.3208	(0.2344)
l NKIDS54	0.411	(0.037)	0.0501	(0.0663)
d NKIDS64	0.413	(0.449)	0.0256	(0.0799)
r NKIDS74	(0.000)*	(0.000)*	(0.0000)*	(0.0000)*
e NKIDS84	0.467	(0.049)	-0.1142	(0.0868)
n NKIDS94	0.581	(0.147)	-0.0201	(0.2616)
R^2_{adj}/s.e.e.	.5155 / .2930		.2693 / .5219	

(The sample used for all of the models in this table was limited to families consisting of a husband under age 65, a wife, and 0-4 children living in an urban area. The number of observations is 4,410.)

(*It turned out that there were no two-child or four child families in which both a child over 18 and a child under 6 were present. Therefore NKIDS72=NKIDS74=0 for all observations.)

[327]

APPENDIX D

Table D-1 (Cont.)

Dependent Variable:	(3) LNFUEL		(4) LNOTUT (Other utilities)	
Independent Variables:	coeff.	std.error of coeff.	coeff.	std.error of coeff.
CONSTANT	1.8593	(0.2041)	-1.1422	(0.1591)
$\ln(P_i/CPI)$	-0.6536	(0.2138)	-0.4521	(0.1666)
$\ln(Y_d)$	0.3250	(0.0248)	0.7504	(0.0193)
AGE2(25-34)	0.1421	(0.0466)	0.0609	(0.0363)
AGE3(35-44)	0.2507	(0.0496)	0.0518	(0.0386)
AGE4(45-54)	0.2898	(0.0520)	0.0612	(0.0405)
AGE5(55-64)	0.3389	(0.0541)	0.0866	(0.0421)
EDHEAD	-0.0230	(0.0070)	0.0585	(0.0054)
OWNER	0.5153	(0.0221)	0.0626	(0.0172)
1 NKIDS11	0.2061	(0.0418)	0.1854	(0.0326)
k NKIDS21	0.1327	(0.0534)	0.1088	(0.0416)
i NKIDS41	0.0763	(0.0449)	-0.0018	(0.0350)
d NKIDS71	0.1388	(0.0446)	-0.9203	(0.0347)
2 NKIDS12	0.2753	(0.0446)	0.1629	(0.0348)
c NKIDS22	0.2852	(0.0529)	0.1855	(0.0412)
h NKIDS32	0.2790	(0.0617)	0.0214	(0.0481)
i NKIDS42	0.2315	(0.0639)	-0.0426	(0.0498)
l NKIDS52	0.3350	(0.0932)	0.1911	(0.0726)
d NKIDS62	0.1756	(0.0552)	0.0106	(0.0430)
r NKIDS72	(0.0000)	(0.0000)	(0.0000)	(0.0000)
e NKIDS82	0.1895	(0.0549)	-0.0189	(0.0428)
n NKIDS92	0.0696	(0.0802)	-0.0744	(0.0625)
3 NKIDS13	0.3657	(0.0711)	0.1437	(0.0554)
c NKIDS23	0.2554	(0.0483)	0.1618	(0.0377)
h NKIDS33	0.0920	(0.1551)	0.2006	(0.1208)
i NKIDS43	0.3479	(0.1646)	0.1261	(0.1283)
l NKIDS53	0.2631	(0.0746)	0.1230	(0.0581)
d NKIDS63	0.2155	(0.0578)	0.0140	(0.0450)
r NKIDS73	-0.1752	(0.2836)	0.3072	(0.2210)
e NKIDS83	0.1441	(0.0653)	-0.0001	(0.0509)
n NKIDS93	0.1230	(0.1706)	-0.0484	(0.1329)
4 NKIDS14	0.2618	(0.1406)	0.2074	(0.1096)
c NKIDS24	0.3985	(0.0661)	0.2298	(0.0515)
h NKIDS34	0.1021	(0.4470)	-0.2840	(0.3483)
i NKIDS44	0.3707	(0.2834)	0.1127	(0.2208)
l NKIDS54	0.2505	(0.0802)	0.1021	(0.0625)
d NKIDS64	0.3145	(0.0966)	-0.0102	(0.0753)
r NKIDS74	(0.0000)	(0.0000)	(0.0000)	(0.0000)
e NKIDS84	0.3016	(0.1050)	-0.0813	(0.0818)
n NKIDS94	0.1551	(0.3163)	-0.1611	(0.2465)

$R^2_{adj.}$/s.e.e.   .2597 / .6311   .4095 / .4917

APPENDIX D

Table D-1 (Cont.)

Dependent Variable:	(5) LNFURN (furniture)		(6) LNADULT (adult clothing)	
Independent Variables:	coeff.	std.error of coeff.	coeff.	std.error of coeff.
CONSTANT	-4.1293	(0.4183)	-3.9241	(0.2208)
ln(P$_i$/CPI)	-0.9027	(0.4381)	-1.0540	(0.2548)
ln(Yd)	1.1243	(0.0508)	1.1445	(0.0268)
AGE2(25-34)	-0.3433	(0.0955)	-0.0977	(0.0504)
AGE3(35-44)	-0.5646	(0.1016)	-0.1464	(0.0537)
AGE4(45-54)	-0.8201	(0.1066)	-0.2403	(0.0564)
AGE5(55-64)	0.9609	(0.1108)	-0.3094	(0.0586)
EDHEAD	-0.0226	(0.0143)	-0.0031	(0.0075)
OWNER	0.1353	(0.0454)	-0.0917	(0.0240)
NKIDS11	0.1830	(0.0856)	-0.1927	(0.0452)
NKIDS21	0.0532	(0.1094)	-0.0919	(0.0577)
NKIDS41	0.1967	(0.0920)	-0.0693	(0.0486)
NKIDS71	-0.0499	(0.0913)	0.3705	(0.0482)
NKIDS12	-0.0432	(0.0914)	-0.2552	(0.0483)
NKIDS22	0.1292	(0.1083)	-0.2742	(0.0572)
NKIDS32	-0.1134	(0.1265)	-0.2589	(0.0668)
NKIDS42	0.1059	(0.1308)	-0.1635	(0.0691)
NKIDS52	0.1073	(0.1910)	-0.1782	(0.1008)
NKIDS62	0.0717	(0.1130)	-0.2376	(0.0597)
NKIDS72	(0.0000)	(0.0000)	(0.0000)	(0.0000)
NKIDS82	0.1624	(0.1125)	0.2704	(0.0594)
NKIDS92	0.0786	(0.1643)	0.4971	(0.0867)
NKIDS13	0.3852	(0.1457)	-0.2519	(0.0769)
NKIDS23	-0.0052	(0.0990)	-0.3743	(0.0523)
NKIDS33	0.1371	(0.3178)	-0.1516	(0.1677)
NKIDS43	0.5634	(0.3373)	-0.1937	(0.1781)
NKIDS53	0.0286	(0.1528)	-0.3638	(0.0807)
NKIDS63	-0.0099	(0.1184)	-0.3314	(0.0625)
NKIDS73	0.4481	(0.5811)	0.4291	(0.3068)
NKIDS83	-0.0051	(0.1339)	0.1543	(0.0707)
NKIDS93	0.0415	(0.3496)	0.5129	(0.1846)
NKIDS14	0.1887	(0.2882)	-0.3166	(0.1522)
NKIDS24	0.0419	(0.1354)	-0.3622	(0.0715)
NKIDS34	-1.3423	(0.9160)	-0.4728	(0.4836)
NKIDS44	0.3783	(0.5808)	-0.4274	(0.3066)
NKIDS54	0.1078	(0.1643)	-0.5273	(0.0867)
NKIDS64	0.4074	(0.1980)	-0.2422	(0.1045)
NKIDS74	(0.0000)	(0.0000)	(0.0000)	(0.0000)
NKIDS84	0.0667	(0.2152)	0.0896	(0.1137)
NKIDS94	-0.5949	(0.6482)	0.6191	(0.3422)
$\bar{R}^2_{adj.}$/s.e.e.	.1574 / 1.2932		.4184 / 6826	

APPENDIX D

Table D-1 (Cont.)

Dependent Variable:	(7) LNKIDC (child clothing)		(8) LNTRANS (transportation)	
Independent Variables	coeff.	std.error of coeff.	coeff.	std.error of coeff.
CONSTANT	-3.0195	(0.3270)	-3.5852	(0.3341)
$\ln(P_i/CPI)$	-1.1594	(0.3773)	0.4547	(0.2663)
$\ln(Yd)$	0.8010	(0.0397)	1.1724	(0.0406)
AGE2(25-34)	0.0914	(0.0746)	-0.2435	(0.0762)
AGE3(35-44)	0.0720	(0.0796)	-0.3300	(0.0812)
AGE(45-54)	-0.0907	(0.0835)	-0.4231	(0.0852)
AGE4(55-64)	-0.2514	(0.0868)	-0.5274	(0.0885)
EDHEAD	0.0137	(0.0111)	-0.0069	(0.0114)
OWNER	-0.0888	(0.0355)	-0.1826	(0.0362)
1 NKIDS11	0.8151	(0.0669)	-0.0068	(0.0684)
k NKIDS21	1.3435	(0.0855)	-0.1724	(0.0874)
i NKIDS41	1.6722	(0.0719)	-0.0153	(0.0734)
d NKIDS71	0.1499	(0.0714)	-0.1403	(0.0730)
2 NKIDS12	0.0208	(0.0715)	-0.0657	(0.0730)
c NKIDS22	1.4526	(0.0846)	-0.1395	(0.0865)
h NKIDS32	1.5117	(0.0988)	-0.1694	(0.1010)
i NKIDS42	2.0032	(0.1023)	-0.0527	(0.1045)
l NKIDS52	1.6325	(0.1493)	-0.3367	(0.1526)
d NKIDS62	1.8080	(0.0884)	-0.2813	(0.0903)
r NKIDS72	(0.0000)	(0.0000)	(0.0000)	(0.0000)
e NKIDS82	1.5019	(0.8795)	0.0220	(0.0898)
n NKIDS92	0.3459	(0.1284)	0.2611	(0.1312)
3 NKIDS13	1.2712	(0.1138)	-0.1921	(0.1163)
c NKIDS23	1.5567	(0.0774)	-0.2254	(0.0791)
h NKIDS33	1.9372	(0.2483)	-0.0765	(0.2538)
i NKIDS43	2.1891	(0.2637)	-0.1972	(0.2694)
l NKIDS53	1.7873	(0.1194)	-0.2226	(0.1221)
d NKIDS63	1.9781	(0.0925)	-0.2358	(0.0946)
r NKIDS73	2.0973	(0.4543)	-0.5559	(0.4641)
e NKIDS83	1.7476	(0.1047)	-0.1130	(0.1069)
n NKIDS93	0.8207	(0.2733)	-0.4075	(0.2792)
4 NKIDS14	1.6195	(0.2253)	0.1609	(0.2301)
c NKIDS24	1.6982	(0.1058)	-0.4284	(0.1082)
h NKIDS34	1.9838	(0.7160)	-0.0129	(0.7316)
i NKIDS44	2.4354	(0.4540)	-0.8940	(0.4639)
l NKIDS54	1.9112	(0.1284)	-0.3072	(0.1312)
d NKIDS64	2.1887	(0.1547)	-0.3257	(0.1581)
r NKIDS74	(0.0000)	(0.0000)	(0.0000)	(0.0000)
e NKIDS84	1.8034	(0.1683)	0.1053	(0.1719)
n NKIDS94	2.2741	(0.5067)	0.8563	(0.5177)
$R^2_{adj.}$ / s.e.e	.4552 / 1.0107		.2441 / 1.0328	

APPENDIX D

Table D-1 (Cont.)

Dependent Variable:	(9) LNMED (medical care)		(10) LNREC (recreation)	
Independent Variables	coeff.	std.error of coeff.	coeff.	std.error of coeff.
CONSTANT	-2.6039	(0.3068)	-4.7238	(0.3183)
$\ln(P_j/CPI)$	-0.0645	(0.2353)	-1.4286	(0.3334)
$\ln(Y_d)$	0.8890	(0.0373)	1.1225	(0.0387)
AGE2 (25-34)	-0.0541	(0.0701)	-0.2279	(0.0726)
AGE3 (35-44)	-0.1252	(0.0746)	-0.3388	(0.0773)
AGE4 (45-54)	-0.0292	(0.0782)	-0.5610	(0.0811)
AGE5 (55-65)	0.2223	(0.0813)	-0.7675	(0.0843)
EDHEAD	0.0506	(0.0104)	0.0643	(0.0109)
OWNER	0.2142	(0.0332)	-0.0203	(0.0345)
NKIDS11	0.3460	(0.0628)	0.0157	(0.0652)
NKIDS21	0.1843	(0.0803)	0.3633	(0.0832)
NKIDS41	0.1288	(0.0675)	0.4688	(0.0700)
NKIDS71	-0.1004	(0.0670)	0.2850	(0.0695)
NKIDS12	0.3698	(0.0670)	0.1065	(0.0695)
NKIDS22	0.2787	(0.0794)	0.3179	(0.0824)
NKIDS32	0.3426	(0.0927)	0.3316	(0.0962)
NKIDS42	0.1613	(0.0960)	0.3778	(0.0996)
NKIDS52	0.3534	(0.1402)	0.3862	(0.1453)
NKIDS62	0.1873	(0.0829)	0.4169	(0.0860)
NKIDS72	(0.0000)	(0.0000)	(0.0000)	(0.0000)
NKIDS82	0.1846	(0.0825)	0.4806	(0.0856)
NKIDS92	-0.1353	(0.1205)	0.4344	(0.1250)
NKIDS13	0.3498	(0.1068)	0.1940	(0.1109)
NKIDS23	0.2967	(0.0726)	0.3169	(0.0754)
NKIDS33	0.4027	(0.2331)	0.1124	(0.2418)
NKIDS43	0.1235	(0.2475)	0.4059	(0.2566)
NKIDS53	0.1631	(0.1121)	0.2694	(0.1163)
NKIDS63	0.1648	(0.0869)	0.3806	(0.0901)
NKIDS73	-0.8434	(0.4264)	0.0624	(0.4421)
NKIDS83	0.0472	(0.0982)	0.4383	(0.1019)
NKIDS93	-0.1999	(0.2565)	0.5070	(0.2660)
NKIDS14	0.5471	(0.2114)	0.3864	(0.2193)
NKIDS24	0.2250	(0.0994)	0.1213	(0.1030)
NKIDS34	0.4252	(0.6721)	-0.8264	(0.6970)
NKIDS44	-1.6455	(0.4264)	-0.5909	(0.4419)
NKIDS54	0.0076	(0.1205)	0.3274	(0.1250)
NKIDS64	0.0509	(0.1452)	0.4322	(0.1506)
NKIDS74	(0.0000)	(0.0000)	(0.0000)	(0.0000)
NKIDS84	0.0205	(0.1579)	0.4498	(0.1637)
NKIDS94	0.1609	(0.4756)	0.2448	(0.4932)
$R^2_{adj.}$/s.e.e.	.2232 / .9478		.3073 / .9840	

APPENDIX D

Table D-1 (Cont.)

Independent Variables	(11) LNEDUC (education) coeff.	std.error of coeff.	(12) LNCONS (total consumption expenditures) coeff.	std.error of coeff.
CONSTANT	-3.977	(0.621)	2.6310	(0.0961)
$\ln(P_i/CPI)$	0.317	(0.650)	0.0209*	(0.0595)*
$\ln(Y_d)$	0.449	(0.075)	0.6775	(0.0093)
AGE2(25-34)	-0.258	(0.142)	-0.0172	(0.0175)
AGE3(35-44)	-0.344	(0.151)	-0.0172	(0.0187)
AGE4(45-54)	-0.389	(0.158)	-0.0507	(0.0196)
AGE5(55-64)	-0.699	(0.164)	-0.0772	(0.0204)
EDHEAD	0.334	(0.021)	0.0177	(0.0026)
OWNER	0.075	(0.067)	-0.0076	(0.0083)
1 NKIDS11	-0.125	(0.125)	0.0366	(0.0157)
k NKIDS21	1.505	(0.163)	0.0762	(0.0201)
i NKIDS41	1.808	(0.136)	0.0995	(0.0169)
d NKIDS71	1.848	(0.135)	0.1274	(0.0168)
2 NKIDS12	-0.131	(0.136)	0.0555	(0.0168)
c NKIDS22	1.303	(0.161)	0.0822	(0.0199)
h NKIDS32	1.934	(0.187)	0.0583	(0.0232)
i NKIDS42	1.825	(0.194)	0.1494	(0.0240)
l NKIDS52	1.329	(0.283)	0.1232	(0.0351)
d NKIDS62	2.195	(0.168)	0.1119	(0.0208)
r NKIDS72	(0.000)	(0.000)	(0.0000)	(0.0000)
e NKIDS82	2.995	(0.167)	0.2013	(0.0207)
n NKIDS92	2.365	(0.244)	0.2089	(0.0302)
3 NKIDS13	-0.004	(0.216)	0.0785	(0.0268)
c NKIDS23	1.166	(0.147)	0.0810	(0.0182)
h NKIDS33	2.158	(0.471)	0.2084	(0.0584)
i NKIDS43	2.452	(0.500)	0.1771	(0.0620)
l NKIDS53	1.872	(0.227)	0.1157	(0.0281)
d NKIDS63	1.892	(0.176)	0.1276	(0.0218)
r NKIDS73	2.213	(0.862)	0.1712	(0.1068)
e NKIDS83	3.076	(0.199)	0.2197	(0.0246)
n NKIDS93	2.556	(0.519)	0.1394	(0.0642)
4 NKIDS14	0.115	(0.428)	0.1852	(0.0530)
c NKIDS24	1.040	(0.201)	0.0885	(0.0249)
h NKIDS34	1.109	(1.359)	-0.0097	(0.1683)
i NKIDS44	0.826	(0.862)	-0.0388	(0.1067)
l NKIDS54	1.757	(0.244)	0.1088	(0.0302)
d NKIDS64	2.323	(0.294)	0.1588	(0.0364)
r NKIDS74	(0.000)	(0.000)	(0.0000)	(0.0000)
e NKIDS84	2.879	(0.319)	0.2249	(0.0395)
n NKIDS94	1.983	(0.962)	0.1783	(0.0191)
$R^2_{adj.}$ /s.e.e.	.3005 / 1.9186		.6858 / .2376	

*In the table-consumption model, the price variable was simply the log of the urban area's overall consumer price index (U.S. ave. = 1.00).

APPENDIX D

Table D-2. Predicted Family Expenditure Patterns over the Life Cycle, for "Low-Income" and "High-Income" Couples with Various Numbers of Children (3-year child spacing).

(Income estimates from Appendix A; expenditure values from Table D-1.)

(A.) Food Expenditures

Couple's Age	Children's Ages 1st 2nd 3rd 4th	"Low-Income" Couple 0 kids 1 kid 2 3 4 kids	"High-Income" Couple 0 kids 1 kid 2 3 4 kids
23	pr.	$ 779 778 778 778 778	$1030 1003 1003 1003 1003
24	<1	799 796 796 796 796	1030 1003 1000 1003 1003
25	1	826 876 876 876 876	1124 1136 1136 1136 1136
26	2 pr.	893 914 816 816 816	1164 1185 1057 1057 1057
27	3 <1	917 945 1010 1010 1010	1199 1227 1309 1309 1309
28	4 1	936 974 1050 1050 1050	1231 1273 1371 1371 1371
29	5 2 pr.	955 995 1078 878 878	1263 1311 1476 1154 1154
30	6 3 <1	972 1077 1168 1253 1253	1294 1428 1546 1656 1656
31	7 4 1	989 1096 1198 1295 1295	1322 1460 1593 1721 1721
32	8 5 2 pr.	1006 1115 1214 1326 930	1349 1492 1631 1769 1241
33	9 6 3 <1	1012 1122 1226 1338 1365	1369 1515 1725 1802 1838
34	10 7 4 1	1020 1131 1289 1357 1394	1389 1537 1750 1839 1890
35	11 8 5 2	1088 1205 1374 1448 1492	1490 1631 1879 1978 2031
36	12 9 6 3	1096 1285 1469 1633 1546	1510 1770 2019 2242 2121
37	13 10 7 4	1104 1295 1480 1645 1567	1530 1793 2046 2272 2165
38	14 11 8 5	1107 1332 1482 1647 1572	1543 1859 2064 2292 2186
39	15 12 9 6	1109 1335 1444 1651 1595	1557 1875 2023 2311 2232
40	16 13 10 7	1112 1338 1431 1482 1581	1568 1889 2039 2330 2249
41	17 14 11 8	1117 1343 1337 1568 1604	1579 1903 2103 2346 2266
42	15 12 9	1119 1092 1340 1451 1659	1591 1556 1904 2064 2360
43	16 13 10	1119 1092 1340 1451 1659	1598 1563 1913 2073 2370
44	17 14 11	1121 1094 1342 1489 1662	1606 1571 1922 2126 2380
45	15 12	1125 1098 1095 1343 1441	1619 1584 1573 1926 2072
46	16 13	1127 1100 1096 1345 1231	1627 1592 1581 1937 2084
47	17 14	1345 1478	1633 1599 1588 1945 2133
48	15	1089 1342	1636 1601 1590 1577 1941
49	16	1342	1638 1603 1592 1578 1943
50	17	1342	1640 1605 1595 1581 1946
51		1078	1641 1607 1596 1582 1567
52		↓	1644 1609 1599 1585 1569
53		↓ ↓ ↓ ↓	↓ ↓ ↓ ↓ ↓
54		1127 1100 1096 1089 1078	1644 1609 1599 1585 1569
55		1180 1151 1148 1140 1129	1721 1685 1674 1659 1642
.		. . . . .	. . . . .
.		. . . . .	. . . . .
59		1180 1151 1148 1140 1129	1721 1685 1674 1659 1642

[333]

APPENDIX D

Table D-2 (Cont.) Predicted Family Expenditure Patterns over the Life Cycle, for "Low-Income" and "High-Income" Couples with Various Numbers of Children (3-year child spacing).

(B.) Shelter Expenditures

Couple's Age	Children's Ages 1st 2nd 3rd 4th	"Low-Income" Couple 0 kids 1 kid 2 3 4 kids	"High-Income" Couple 0 kids 1 kid 2 3 4 kids
23	pr.	614 596 596 596 596	769 774 774 774 774
24	<1	614 643 643 643 643	760 795 795 795 795
25	1	669 684 684 684 684	839 851 851 851 851
26	2 pr.	796 717 630 630 630	873 892 783 783 783
27	3 <1	718 744 728 728 728	902 883 905 905 905
28	4 1	735 768 760 760 760	929 967 954 954 954
29	5 2 pr.	751 788 783 683 683	959 999 1035 864 864
30	6 3 <1	766 817 781 730 730	982 1044 995 929 929
31	7 4 1	782 837 804 758 758	1006 1070 1030 970 970
32	8 5 2 pr.	797 851 816 779 730	1030 1096 1057 1001 937
33	9 6 3 <1	802 856 754 786 717	1047 1115 981 1022 930
34	10 7 4 1	810 864 761 799 739	1064 1137 997 1045 960
35	11 8 5 2	782 835 735 773 718	1036 1105 971 1020 940
36	12 9 6 3	789 782 754 743 696	1052 1041 1002 986 924
37	13 10 7 4	796 788 760 749 706	1067 1056 1017 1000 944
38	14 11 8 5	798 814 761 750 709	1077 1100 1027 1011 955
39	15 12 9 6	800 816 714 752 737	1088 1111 970 1020 1000
40	16 13 10 7	802 818 707 745 730	1097 1120 978 1029 1008
41	17 14 11 8	806 821 739 756 742	1106 1130 1013 1037 1016
42	15 12 9	808 786 819 718 756	1115 1087 1130 992 1044
43	16 13 10	808 786 819 718 756	1121 1093 1136 997 1049
44	17 14 11	809 788 821 739 758	1127 1099 1142 1025 1054
45	15 12	760 740 737 768 666	1063 1037 1029 1070 931
46	16 13	761 741 738 769 667	1069 1043 1035 1077 937
47	17 14	↓ ↓ ↓ 769 685	1074 1048 1040 1082 962
48	15	↓ ↓ ↓ 762 767	1076 1050 1042 1032 1079
49	16	↓ ↓ ↓ ↓ 767	1077 1051 1043 1033 1080
50	17	↓ ↓ ↓ ↓ 767	1079 1053 1045 1035 1083
51		↓ ↓ ↓ ↓ 724	1079 1054 1046 1036 1024
52		↓ ↓ ↓ ↓ ↓	1082 1056 1048 1038 1026
53		↓ ↓ ↓ ↓ ↓	↓ ↓ ↓ ↓ ↓
54		761 741 738 762 724	1082 1056 1048 1038 1026
55		711 692 689 684 676	1010 986 979 969 958
.		. . . . .	. . . . .
59		711 692 689 684 676	1010 986 979 969 958

APPENDIX D

Table D-2 (Cont.) Predicted Family Expenditure Patterns over the Life Cycle, for "Low-Income" and "High-Income" Couples with Various Numbers of Children (3-year child spacing).

(C.) Fuel and Light Expenditures

Couple's Age	Children's Ages 1st 2nd 3rd 4th	"Low-Income" Couple 0 kids 1 kid 2 3 4 kids	"High-Income" Couple 0 kids 1 kid 2 3 4 kids
23	pr.	83 94 94 94 94	159 156 156 156 156
24	<1	83 95 95 95 95	159 182 182 182 182
25	1	98 114 114 114 114	188 189 189 189 189
26	2 pr.	100 117 94 94 94	192 224 181 181 181
27	3 <1	102 119 126 126 126	196 229 241 241 241
28	4 1	103 122 129 129 129	200 235 248 248 248
29	5 2 pr.	105 124 131 99 99	203 239 252 191 191
30	6 3 <1	106 117 133 129 129	206 228 257 250 250
31	7 4 1	107 119 137 132 132	209 232 264 256 256
32	8 5 2 pr.	108 120 138 134 103	212 235 268 261 201
33	9 6 3 <1	109 121 140 134 153	214 237 279 264 300
34	10 7 4 1	109 121 140 136 155	216 240 277 266 306
35	11 8 5 2	122 136 157 152 174	243 270 311 301 345
36	12 9 6 3	123 129 142 148 151	245 264 284 294 301
37	13 10 7 4	124 130 143 149 153	247 267 286 297 304
38	14 11 8 5	124 132 143 149 153	248 268 287 298 306
39	15 12 9 6	124 132 168 149 164	250 270 339 300 331
40	16 13 10 7	124 132 167 148 163	251 271 340 302 332
41	17 14 11 8	125 133 168 150 165	252 272 347 303 334
42	15 12 9	125 123 133 169 150	254 254 270 343 304
43	16 13 10	125 123 133 169 150	254 254 270 344 305
44	17 14 11	125 123 133 172 150	255 255 271 350 306
45	15 12	130 128 127 138 174	266 262 261 282 357
46	16 13	130 128 128 138 174	267 263 262 283 358
47	17 14	↑ ↑ ↑ 138 177	268 264 263 284 364
48	15	│ │ │ 127 138	268 264 263 261 283
49	16	│ │ │ ↑ 137	268 264 263 261 283
50	17	│ │ │ │ 137	268 265 263 262 284
51		│ │ │ │ 126	268 265 263 262 260
52		│ │ │ │ ↑	269 265 264 262 261
53		↓ ↓ ↓ ↓ ↓	↓ ↓ ↓ ↓ ↓
54		130 128 128 127 126	269 265 264 262 261
55		136 134 134 133 133	282 278 277 275 274
.		.	.
.		.	.
59		136 134 134 133 133	282 278 277 275 274

[335]

APPENDIX D

Table D-2 (Cont.) Predicted Family Expenditure Patterns over the Life Cycle, for "Low-Income" and "High-Income" Couples with Various Numbers of Children (3-year child spacing).

(D.) Expenditures for Other Utilities

Couple's Age	Children's Ages 1st 2nd 3rd 4th	"Low-Income" Couple 0 kids 1 kid 2 3 4 kids	"High-Income" Couple 0 kids 1 kid 2 3 4 kids
23	pr.	184 177 177 177 177	331 318 318 318 318
24	<1	184 157 157 157 157	331 282 282 282 282
25	1	206 179 179 179 179	376 328 328 328 328
26	2 pr.	217 193 189 189 189	397 350 343 343 343
27	3 <1	226 203 229 229 229	415 369 415 415 415
28	4 1	233 217 243 243 243	432 390 445 445 445
29	5 2 pr.	240 219 253 212 212	449 454 497 392 392
30	6 3 <1	247 257 267 252 252	467 483 501 471 471
31	7 4 1	252 264 278 265 265	481 500 524 500 500
32	8 5 2 pr.	260 271 284 275 231	496 516 543 521 437
33	9 6 3 <1	262 274 250 279 289	507 528 482 535 556
34	10 7 4 1	265 277 253 285 299	518 540 492 552 580
35	11 8 5 2	266 278 254 286 301	524 590 498 560 590
36	12 9 6 3	269 251 254 254 269	535 500 503 503 533
37	13 10 7 4	272 254 257 257 275	545 509 513 513 548
38	14 11 8 5	273 266 257 257 276	552 538 523 520 556
39	15 12 9 6	274 266 309 258 251	560 545 631 526 512
40	16 13 10 7	275 267 305 255 248	566 551 638 533 517
41	17 14 11 8	277 269 324 260 253	572 558 668 538 523
42	15 12 9	277 267 268 312 260	579 559 558 650 543
43	16 13 10	277 267 268 312 260	582 563 562 655 546
44	17 14 11	278 268 268 324 261	587 567 566 680 550
45	15 12	281 271 269 270 309	633 613 606 605 698
46	16 13	282 271 270 270 310	638 617 611 610 703
47	17 14	↑ ↑ ↑ 270 321	642 622 615 614 729
48	15	↑ ↑ ↑ 267 269	643 623 616 609 612
49	16	↑ ↑ ↑ ↑ 269	644 624 617 609 613
50	17	↑ ↑ ↑ ↑ 269	646 625 619 611 615
51		↑ ↑ ↑ ↑ 263	646 626 620 612 603
52		↑ ↑ ↑ ↑ ↑	648 628 622 613 604
53		↓ ↓ ↓ ↓ ↓	↓ ↓ ↓ ↓ ↓
54		282 271 270 267 263	648 628 622 613 604
55		289 278 277 274 270	626 606 600 592 583
.		. . . . .	. . . . .
59		289 278 277 274 270	626 606 600 592 583

[336]

APPENDIX D

Table D-2 (Cont.) Predicted Family Expenditure Patterns over the Life Cycle, for "Low-Income" and "High-Income" Couples with Various Numbers of Children (3-year child spacing).

(E.) Expenditures for Children's Clothing

Couple's Age	Children's Ages 1st 2nd 3rd 4th	"Low-Income" Couple 0 kids 1 kid 2 3 4 kids	"High-Income" Couple 0 kids 1 kid 2 3 4 kids
23	pr.	36 34 34 34 34	52 49 49 49 49
24	<1	36 30 30 30 30	52 44 44 44 44
25	1	41 36 36 36 36	61 53 53 53 53
26	2 pr.	44 38 38 38 38	64 56 55 55 55
27	3 <1	45 40 108 108 108	68 59 157 157 157
28	4 1	47 42 114 114 114	70 63 170 170 170
29	5 2 pr.	48 44 119 42 42	73 66 191 64 64
30	6 3 <1	50 178 191 204 204	76 271 289 309 309
31	7 4 1	51 183 199 215 215	79 281 304 329 329
32	8 5 2 pr.	53 189 203 224 47	82 291 315 343 71
33	9 6 3 <1	53 191 225 227 253	84 298 351 354 394
34	10 7 4 1	54 193 228 232 262	86 305 359 366 412
35	11 8 5 2	54 191 226 231 261	86 306 360 368 417
36	12 9 6 3	54 269 307 363 329	88 435 495 584 529
37	13 10 7 4	55 272 311 368 336	89 444 506 597 546
38	14 11 8 5	55 285 312 369 338	91 470 513 605 554
39	15 12 9 6	55 286 263 370 455	92 477 436 614 754
40	16 13 10 7	55 287 259 365 449	93 483 442 622 764
41	17 14 11 8	56 289 276 373 459	94 489 464 629 773
42	15 12 9	56 54 288 265 373	95 92 489 451 635
43	16 13 10	56 54 288 265 373	96 93 493 454 639
44	17 14 11	56 54 288 276 374	97 93 497 472 643
45	15 12	48 46 46 244 221	83 80 79 421 383
46	16 13	48 46 46 245 222	83 81 80 425 386
47	17 14	245 230	84 81 80 428 401
48	15	45 244	84 81 80 79 426
49	16	244	84 81 81 79 427
50	17	244	85 82 81 80 428
51		45	85 82 81 80 79
52			85 82 81 80 79
53		↓ ↓ ↓ ↓ ↓	↓ ↓ ↓ ↓ ↓
54		48 46 46 45 45	85 85 81 80 79
55		41 39 39 39 38	72 70 69 68 67.
.		. . . . .	. . . . .
.		. . . . .	. . . . .
59		41 39 39 39 38	72 70 69 68 67

[337]

APPENDIX D

Table D-2 (Cont.) Predicted Family Expenditure Patterns over the Life Cycle, for "Low-Income" and "High-Income" Couples with Various Numbers of Children (3-year child spacing).

(F.) Transportation Expenditures

Couple's Age	Children's Ages 1st 2nd 3rd 4th	"Low-Income" Couple 0 kids 1 kid 2 3 4 kids	"High-Income" Couple 0 kids 1 kid 2 3 4 kids
23	pr.	386 363 363 363 363	863 809 809 809 809
24	<1	386 236 236 236 236	863 671 671 671 671
25	1	327 267 267 267 267	751 606 606 606 606
26	2 pr.	356 295 287 287 287	816 670 650 650 650
27	3 <1	379 319 281 281 281	875 727 635 635 635
28	4 1	397 342 307 307 307	931 793 709 709 709
29	5 2 pr.	416 361 327 341 341	990 850 843 800 800
30	6 3 <1	434 329 321 279 279	1047 788 764 662 662
31	7 4 1	452 344 340 302 302	1101 831 820 725 725
32	8 5 2 pr.	471 358 351 319 391	1155 874 867 773 949
33	9 6 3 <1	477 363 362 326 254	1197 906 901 808 628
34	10 7 4 1	487 370 370 337 266	1238 938 961 847 671
35	11 8 5 2	454 345 344 315 251	1172 890 885 807 643
36	12 9 6 3	462 411 314 327 290	1210 1074 817 849 754
37	13 10 7 4	471 418 319 333 299	1247 1108 843 875 788
38	14 11 8 5	473 447 320 334 301	1272 1224 860 894 807
39	15 12 9 6	476 450 305 335 305	1299 1231 830 912 828
40	16 13 10 7	478 452 299 329 299	1322 1253 845 929 843
41	17 14 11 8	483 456 327 340 309	1344 1275 908 944 858
42	15 12 9	485 458 453 308 339	1368 1298 1276 890 958
43	16 13 10	485 458 453 308 339	1382 1311 1290 879 967
44	17 14 11	487 460 455 459 341	1399 1327 1305 932 977
45	15 12	443 419 416 412 274	1286 1222 1201 1184 793
46	16 13	446 421 417 419 275	1302 1236 1216 1199 803
47	17 14	↑ ↑ ↑ 419 290	1314 1249 1229 1212 848
48	15	411 411	1318 1254 1233 1209 1205
49	16	↑ 411	1322 1257 1236 1210 1207
50	17	417	1326 1261 1242 1216 1213
51		402	1328 1264 1243 1219 1191
52		↑	1334 1268 1249 1223 1195
53			↑ ↑ ↑ ↑ ↑
54		446 421 417 411 402	1334 1268 1249 1223 1195
55		402 379 376 370 362	1202 1143 1126 1102 1076
.		↑ ↑ ↑ ↑ ↑	↑ ↑ ↑ ↑ ↑
.		↓ ↓ ↓ ↓ ↓	↓ ↓ ↓ ↓ ↓
59		402 379 376 370 362	1202 1143 1126 1102 1076

[338]

APPENDIX D

Table D-2 (Cont.) Predicted Family Expenditure Patterns over the Life Cycle, for "Low-Income" and "High-Income" Couples with Various Numbers of Children (3-year child spacing).

(G.) Expenditures for Medical Care

Couple's Age	Children's Ages 1st 2nd 3rd 4th	"Low-Income" Couple 0 kids / 1 kid / 2 / 3 / 4 kids	"High-Income" Couple 0 kids / 1 kid / 2 / 3 / 4 kids
23	pr.	120 98 98 98 98	227 217 217 217 217
24	<1	120 85 85 85 85	227 188 188 188 188
25	1	109 94 94 94 94	246 209 209 209 209
26	2 pr.	116 101 99 99 99	262 226 221 221 221
27	3 <1	122 107 148 148 148	276 240 330 330 330
28	4 1	126 113 158 158 158	289 256 358 358 358
29	5 2 pr.	131 117 116 113 113	303 270 408 258 258
30	6 3 <1	135 150 158 154 154	316 349 366 356 356
31	7 4 1	139 155 165 164 164	328 363 386 382 382
32	8 5 2 pr.	143 160 169 171 175	340 377 402 401 293
33	9 6 3 <1	145 161 188 173 156	349 388 451 414 372
34	10 7 4 1	147 164 191 178 162	358 398 463 429 390
35	11 8 5 2	149 166 194 180 165	377 420 489 454 415
36	12 9 6 3	151 159 168 164 135	387 407 429 417 344
37	13 10 7 4	153 161 170 166 138	395 416 439 427 356
38	14 11 8 5	154 170 171 166 139	401 444 446 433 362
39	15 12 9 6	154 170 202 167 148	408 451 534 440 391
40	16 13 10 7	155 171 199 165 146	413 457 541 446 396
41	17 14 11 8	156 172 214 169 150	418 463 572 452 401
42	15 12 9	157 150 171 204 168	424 407 463 553 407
43	16 13 10	157 150 171 204 168	427 411 467 558 410
44	17 14 11	157 150 172 214 169	431 414 471 583 414
45	15 12	178 171 169 193 227	478 460 454 517 609
46	16 13	178 171 170 194 228	482 464 458 522 615
47	17 14	↑ ↑ ↑ 194 237	486 468 462 526 641
48	15	168 193	487 469 463 456 523
49	16	↑ 193	488 470 464 457 524
50	17	193	489 471 465 458 526
51		165	489 472 466 459 451
52		↑	491 473 468 460 452
53		↓ ↓ ↓ ↓ ↓	↓ ↓ ↓ ↓ ↓
54		178 171 170 168 165	491 473 468 460 452
55		230 220 218 216 212	632 609 602 592 582
.		. . . . .	. . . . .
.		. . . . .	. . . . .
59		230 220 218 216 212	632 609 602 592 582

[339]

APPENDIX D

Table D-2 (Cont.) Predicted Family Expenditure Patterns over the Life Cycle, for "Low-Income" and "High-Income" Couples with Various Numbers of Children (3-year child spacing).

(H.) Recreational Expenditures

Couple's Age	Children's Ages 1st 2nd 3rd 4th	"Low-Income" Couple 0 kids / 1 kid / 2 / 3 / 4 kids	"High-Income" Couple 0 kids / 1 kid / 2 / 3 / 4 kids
23	pr.	109 / 82 / 82 / 82 / 82	201 / 211 / 211 / 211 / 211
24	<1	109 / 69 / 69 / 69 / 69	201 / 176 / 176 / 176 / 176
25	1	94 / 77 / 77 / 77 / 77	197 / 160 / 160 / 160 / 160
26	2 pr.	102 / 85 / 83 / 83 / 83	213 / 177 / 172 / 172 / 172
27	3 <1	108 / 92 / 96 / 96 / 96	228 / 191 / 199 / 199 / 199
28	4 1	113 / 98 / 104 / 104 / 104	242 / 207 / 221 / 221 / 221
29	5 2 pr.	118 / 103 / 111 / 98 / 98	257 / 227 / 261 / 209 / 209
30	6 3 <1	123 / 160 / 144 / 137 / 137	271 / 350 / 314 / 297 / 297
31	7 4 1	128 / 167 / 153 / 148 / 148	284 / 368 / 337 / 324 / 324
32	8 5 2 pr.	133 / 173 / 158 / 156 / 111	298 / 386 / 355 / 345 / 246
33	9 6 3 <1	135 / 176 / 170 / 159 / 125	308 / 400 / 384 / 360 / 283
34	10 7 4 1	137 / 179 / 173 / 164 / 131	318 / 413 / 397 / 377 / 301
35	11 8 5 2	125 / 163 / 157 / 150 / 120	293 / 382 / 367 / 350 / 281
36	12 9 6 3	127 / 183 / 174 / 167 / 151	302 / 436 / 412 / 395 / 357
37	13 10 7 4	129 / 186 / 177 / 170 / 156	311 / 449 / 425 / 407 / 373
38	14 11 8 5	130 / 199 / 178 / 170 / 157	317 / 487 / 433 / 415 / 381
39	15 12 9 6	131 / 200 / 173 / 171 / 180	324 / 497 / 428 / 423 / 443
40	16 13 10 7	131 / 201 / 170 / 168 / 176	329 / 505 / 435 / 431 / 450
41	17 14 11 8	132 / 202 / 185 / 173 / 182	334 / 514 / 467 / 437 / 458
42	15 12 9	133 / 126 / 201 / 175 / 173	340 / 323 / 514 / 448 / 443
43	16 13 10	133 / 126 / 201 / 175 / 173	344 / 327 / 519 / 452 / 447
44	17 14 11	133 / 126 / 202 / 185 / 174	347 / 330 / 525 / 459 / 452
45	15 12	107 / 101 / 100 / 161 / 137	281 / 267 / 263 / 419 / 359
46	16 13	107 / 102 / 101 / 161 / 137	284 / 270 / 266 / 424 / 363
47	17 14	↑ / ↑ / ↑ / 161 / 145	286 / 273 / 269 / 428 / 383
48	15		/	/	/ 99 / 160	287 / 274 / 270 / 264 / 426
49	16		/	/	/ ↑ / 160	288 / 275 / 270 / 265 / 427
50	17		/	/	/	/ 160	289 / 275 / 271 / 266 / 429
51			/	/	/	/ 97	289 / 276 / 272 / 267 / 261
52			/	/	/	/ ↑	291 / 277 / 273 / 268 / 262
53			/	/	/	/	↓ / ↓ / ↓ / ↓ / ↓
54		107 / 102 / 101 / 99 / 97	291 / 277 / 273 / 268 / 262
55		87 / 83 / 82 / 81 / 79	236 / 225 / 222 / 218 / 213
.		. / . / . / . / .	. / . / . / . / .
.		. / . / . / . / .	. / . / . / . / .
.		. / . / . / . / .	. / . / . / . / .
59		87 / 83 / 82 / 81 / 79	236 / 225 / 222 / 218 / 213

APPENDIX D

Table D-2 (Cont.) Predicted Family Expenditure Patterns over the Life Cycle, for "Low-Income" and "High-Income" Couples with Various Numbers of Children (3-year child spacing).

(I.) Educational Expenditures (ignoring effect of children over 18)

Couple's Age	\multicolumn{4}{c}{Children's Ages}	\multicolumn{5}{c}{"Low-Income" Couple}	\multicolumn{5}{c}{"High-Income" Couple}
	1st	2nd	3rd	4th	0 kids	1 kid	2	3	4 kids	0 kids	1 kid	2	3	4 kids
23	pr.				3	3	3	3	3	7	7	7	7	7
24	<1				3	2	2	2	2	7	7	7	7	7
25	1				2	2	2	2	2	6	5	5	5	5
26	2	pr.			2	2	2	2	2	6	6	6	6	6
27	3	<1			2	2	2	2	2	6	6	5	5	5
28	4	1			2	2	2	2	2	7	6	5	5	5
29	5	2	pr.		2	2	2	2	2	7	6	6	6	6
30	6	3	<1		2	11	8	7	7	7	29	23	20	20
31	7	4	1		2	11	9	8	8	7	30	24	21	21
32	8	5	2	pr.	2	11	9	8	2	7	31	25	21	7
33	9	6	3	<1	3	11	17	8	7	7	31	47	22	19
34	10	7	4	1	3	11	18	8	7	7	31	48	22	19
35	11	8	5	2	2	10	16	7	6	7	29	45	20	18
36	12	9	6	3	2	14	21	15	13	7	40	59	43	37
37	13	10	7	4	2	14	21	15	13	7	40	59	44	38
38	14	11	8	5	2	14	21	15	13	7	42	60	44	38
39	15	12	9	6	2	15	9	15	24	7	42	25	44	68
40	16	13	10	7	2	15	9	15	23	7	42	26	45	69
41	17	14	11	8	2	15	9	15	24	7	43	26	45	69
42		15	12	9	2	2	15	8	15	7	7	43	26	45
43		16	13	10	2	2	15	8	15	7	7	43	26	46
44		17	14	11	2	2	15	9	15	7	7	43	27	46
45			15	12	2	2	2	14	8	7	7	7	41	25
46			16	13	2	2	2	14	8	7	7	7	41	25
47			17	14	↓	↓	↓	14	9	7	7	7	42	25
48				15				2	14	7	7	7	7	41
49				16					14	7	7	7	7	41
50				17					14	7	7	7	7	42
51									2	7	7	7	7	7
52										7	7	7	7	7
53					↓	↓	↓	↓	↓	↓	↓	↓	↓	↓
54					2	2	2	2	2	7	7	7	7	7
55					2	2	2	2	2	5	5	5	5	5
.					.	.	.	.	.	.	.	.	.	.
.					.	.	.	.	.	.	.	.	.	.
.					.	.	.	.	.	.	.	.	.	.
59					2	2	2	2	2	5	5	5	5	5

[341]

APPENDIX D

Table D-2 (Cont.) Predicted Family Expenditure Patterns over the Life Cycle, for "Low-Income" and "High-Income" Couples with Various Numbers of Children (3-year child spacing).

(J.) Total Consumption Expenditures

Couple's Age	1st	2nd	3rd	4th	"Low-Income" Couple 0 kids	1 kid	2	3	4 kids	"High-Income" Couple 0 kids	1 kid	2	3	4 kids
23	pr.				3755	3623	3623	3623	3623	5425	5283	5283	5283	5283
24	<1				3755	3251	3251	3251	3251	5425	4740	4740	4740	4740
25	1				3860	3438	3438	3438	3438	5823	5145	5145	5145	5145
26	2	pr.			4056	3642	3583	3583	3583	6111	5450	5358	5358	5358
27	3	<1			4204	3808	3881	3881	3881	6360	5715	5804	5804	5804
28	4	1			4320	3961	4089	4089	4089	6593	6008	6186	6186	6186
29	5	2	pr.		4438	4086	4241	3958	3958	6829	6253	6834	6041	6041
30	6	3	<1		4548	4624	4494	4263	4263	7055	7139	6919	6685	6685
31	7	4	1		4657	4738	4652	4553	4553	7264	7360	7211	7048	7048
32	8	5	2	pr.	4766	4852	4738	4700	4285	7468	7577	7445	7316	6665
33	9	6	3	<1	4805	4892	4792	4760	4665	7621	7738	7565	7501	7351
34	10	7	4	1	4860	4948	4847	4852	4800	7773	7892	7715	7713	7635
35	11	8	5	2	4859	4944	4843	4858	4825	7840	7991	7792	7806	7753
36	12	9	6	3	4909	5112	5165	5233	4995	7985	8159	8373	8471	8091
37	13	10	7	4	4962	5164	5218	5286	5087	8126	8309	8528	8622	8302
38	14	11	8	5	4970	5371	5229	5297	5108	8221	8457	8627	8728	8415
39	15	12	9	6	4993	5386	5302	5311	5465	8321	8880	8826	8829	9078
40	16	13	10	7	5006	5267	5242	5251	5402	8406	8991	8916	8925	9170
41	17	14	11	8	5037	5430	5526	5351	5506	8487	9081	9298	9009	9264
42		15	12	9	5051	4886	5411	5338	5517	8573	8304	9180	9068	9083
43		16	13	10	5051	4886	5411	5338	5517	8626	8316	9236	9124	9133
44		17	14	11	5061	4899	5422	5530	5532	8684	8367	9298	9438	9189
45			15	12	4942	4784	4761	5273	5136	8526	8276	8198	9055	8855
46			16	13	4955	4793	4771	5284	5150	8584	8332	8253	9123	8921
47			17	14				5284	5316	8631	8383	8304	9179	9210
48				15				4729	5266	8648	8400	8321	8225	9148
49				16					5266	8660	8411	8332	8231	9160
50				17					5266	8684	8428	8355	8253	9185
51									4665	8684	8440	8360	8264	8153
52										8707	8457	8383	8281	8170
53					↓	↓	↓	↓	↓	↓	↓	↓	↓	↓
54					4955	4793	4771	4729	4665	8707	8457	8383	8281	8170
55					4826	4668	4646	4605	4543	8479	8236	8164	8065	7956
.														
59					4826	4668	4646	4605	4543	8479	8236	8164	8065	7956

[342]

APPENDIX D

Table D-3. The Impacts of Children and Other Variables on Family Consumption Patterns: Regressions Based on the 1889-1890 Survey of Expenditures in Workers' Families.

Definitions of Variables Used

lnFOOD = the natural logarithm of family expenditures on food.
lnRENT =   "   "   "   rent.
lnTOTEXP =   "   "   "   all commodities.
lnTOTINC =   "   "   total family income.
NOBRDRS = the number of boarders and lodgers staying in the household.
AGE1 = 1 if the husband is 25-34 years old; zero otherwise. (No husbands were under 25.)
AGE2 = 1 if the husband is 35-44 years old; zero otherwise.
AGE3 = 1 if the husband is 45-54 years old; zero otherwise.

NKIDSij: these number-of-children variables are defined as the number of children in families of a given size that are in a given age range:

		Number of children in the family(i)=			
		1	2	3	4
	(1) 0-5 :	NKIDS11	NKIDS21	NKIDS31	NKIDS41
Age	(2) 6-11:	NKIDS12	NKIDS22	NKIDS32	NKIDS42
Groups(j):	(3) 12-17:	NKIDS13	NKIDS23	NKIDS33	NKIDS43
	(4) 18-up:	NKIDS14	NKIDS24	NKIDS34	NKIDS44

Examples: a family with children of ages 7,5, and 1 has NKIDS31=2(the two younger children), NKIDS32=1(the eldest), and all other NKIDS variables = 0; a childless couple has all NKIDS variables = 0.

Sample Constraint

The sample was limited to those families for which (a)income, food expenditures, and rent expenditures were all positive; (b)as implied by (a), the family rented its housing and did not own it; (c)the husband was older than 24 and younger than 65; and (d) the number of children was 0,1,2,3, or 4.

Data source

The original data come from U.S. Commissioner of Labor, Sixth Annual Report and Seventh Annual Report(Washington: GPO, 1891 and 1892). I am indebted to Allen C. Kelley for permission to use computer tapes of these data.

APPENDIX D

Table D-3 (Cont.) The Impacts of Children and Other Variables on Family Consumption of Patterns: Regressions Based on the 1889-1890 Survey of Expenditures in Workers' Families.

Dependent Variable:	(1) lnFOOD coeff.	standard error of coeff.	(2) lnFOOD coeff.	standard error of coeff.	(3) lnRENT coeff.	standard error of coeff.
CONSTANT	2.044	(.078)	.331	(.077)	.115	(.139)
NOBRDRS	.061	(.005)	.045	(.004)	-.040	(.008)
lnTOTINC	.518	(.012)	--	--	.665	(.022)
lnTOTEXP	--	--	.809	(.013)	--	--
AGE1 (25-34)	-.078	(.020)	-.093	(.016)	-.103	(.036)
AGE2 (35-44)	-.048	(.019)	-.053	(.015)	-.048	(.034)
AGE3 (45-54)	-.026	(.018)	-.029	(.015)	.005	(.033)
NKIDS11	.078	(.018)	.067	(.014)	-.037	(.032)
NKIDS12	.089	(.026)	.045	(.021)	.044	(.047)
NKIDS13	.124	(.026)	.070	(.021)	-.072	(.047)
NKIDS14	.080	(.034)	.024	(.027)	-.120	(.061)
NKIDS21	.075	(.009)	.052	(.007)	.027	(.017)
NKIDS22	.052	(.014)	.050	(.011)	-.021	(.025)
NKIDS23	.089	(.014)	.038	(.012)	.032	(.026)
NKIDS24	.085	(.019)	.041	(.015)	-.108	(.034)
NKIDS31	.068	(.008)	.044	(.006)	.011	(.014)
NKIDS32	.041	(.010)	.022	(.008)	.003	(.018)
NKIDS33	.065	(.011)	.033	(.009)	-.035	(.020)
NKIDS34	.077	(.015)	.049	(.012)	-.132	(.028)
NKIDS41	.065	(.008)	.046	(.007)	-.003	(.015)
NKIDS42	.061	(.009)	.033	(.008)	.009	(.017)
NKIDS43	.068	(.010)	.033	(.008)	-.060	(.018)
NKIDS44	.085	(.015)	.036	(.012)	-.044	(.027)

$R^2_{adj.}$ /std. error of estimate   .5803/.2245   .7260/.1810   .2791/.4024

Number of observations = 2,629.

APPENDIX D

Table D-3 (Cont.) The Impacts of Children and Other Variables on Family Consumption Patterns: Regressions Based on the 1889-1890 Survey of Expenditures in Workers' Families.

Dependent Variable:	(4) lnRENT coeff.	standard error of coeff.	(5) lnTOTEXP coeff.	standard error of coeff.	(6) sample means:
Independent Variables					
CONSTANT	-1.743	(.161)	2.083	(.056)	--
NOBRDRS	-.056	(.008)	.019	(.003)	0.4542
lnTOTINC	--	--	.647	(.009)	6.3064
lnTOTEXP	.981	(.026)	--	--	6.2842
AGE1 (25-34)	-.121	(.033)	.019	(.014)	0.4499
AGE2 (35-44)	-.052	(.032)	.006	(.014)	0.2857
AGE3 (45-54)	.002	(.031)	.004	(.013)	0.1746
NKIDS11	-.050	(.030)	.014	(.013)	0.1092
NKIDS12	-.009	(.044)	.055	(.019)	0.0331
NKIDS13	-.132	(.044)	.065	(.019)	0.0361
NKIDS14	-.193	(.057)	.081	(.024)	0.0202
NKIDS21	.000	(.016)	.028	(.007)	0.2313
NKIDS22	-.020	(.023)	.001	(.010)	0.1027
NKIDS23	-.024	(.024)	.063	(.010)	0.0813
NKIDS24	-.154	(.032)	.053	(.014)	0.0498
NKIDS31	-.017	(.013)	.029	(.005)	0.2784
NKIDS32	-.019	(.017)	.023	(.007)	0.2027
NKIDS33	-.071	(.018)	.039	(.008)	0.1484
NKIDS34	-.157	(.026)	.033	(.011)	0.0669
NKIDS41	-.026	(.014)	.023	(.006)	0.2126
NKIDS42	-.025	(.016)	.035	(.007)	0.2275
NKIDS43	-.099	(.017)	.042	(.007)	0.1693
NKIDS44	-.098	(.026)	.061	(.011)	0.0628
(lnFOOD):					5.4274
(lnRENT):					4.2041
$R^2_{adj.}$/s.e.e.	.3678/.3769		.7468/.1611		

Number of observations = 2,629.

APPENDIX E. Total Child Costs and Child Inputs, 1960–61

The estimates in Appendixes A through D can now be drawn together to yield a complete picture of the likely inputs into a child and the bundle of time and commodities involved in the alternative activities foregone in having the child. The estimates employ 1960 dollar values, since the work-effect regressions (Bowen and Finegan) and the commodity inputs and net consumption effects (Appendix D) are based on survey data from 1960 and 1961. The hours of time inputs and child work time from the 1967–68 Syracuse survey are thus given 1960 wage rates.

Four sets of estimates are developed in Tables E–1 through E–4. These represent estimates for a first child and for a third child. The effects of the first child are those that would obtain were he to remain an only child. Those of the third child are calculated on the assumption that he is three years younger than the second, who lags the first child by three years as well. The purpose of the only-child and third-child estimates was to allow comparison of the cost and input patterns for children sharing family inputs with siblings of slightly different ages with those for children having no siblings at any close age. The other distinction between estimates is that between the "low-income" and "high-income" couples introduced in Chapter 4 and Appendix A. The intent here is to allow clues at how the overall child input and cost estimates end up differing when the couples' incomes and education differ.

Tables E–1 through E–4 give the estimates of time and commodity inputs into the child (the L^N's and C^N's of Chapter 4) and the net effects of the child on total family paid work and consumption (the $\triangle L$'s and $\triangle C$'s). These values can be added together to reveal the time and commodities involved in the alternative activities foregone by couples having the extra child in each case (the L^H's and C^H's). The two sets of overall bundles in each case are compared directly in Tables 4–7 and 4–8. These input estimates in turn yield the weights to be assigned to each time and commodity category in deriving the time-series index of the relative cost of children in Appendix F.

The estimates for the commodities devoted to the child (the C^N's) are based on *a priori* hunches. As with the time inputs, data limitations make it very difficult to observe the commodity inputs directly. My own

APPENDIX E

TABLE E-1.

Child Costs and Net Work and Consumption Effects,
First Child, "Low-income" Couple

		\multicolumn{9}{c}{Time Costs}
Couple's Age	Child's Age	\multicolumn{3}{c}{Total Child Care Time}	\multicolumn{2}{c}{Other Chore Increases for Wife}	\multicolumn{4}{c}{Child's Chore and Paid Work Contrib. (−)}
		hrs/yr	wife's wage	value of care time	hrs/yr	value	chore time	work time	total (hrs/yr)	value*
23	preg.	0	.85	0	110.0	93.5	0	0	0	0
24	<1	1528.9	.83	1268.9	107.2	88.9	0	0	0	0
25	1	1033.0	.84	867.7	175.7	147.6	0	0	0	0
26	2	695.4	.88	611.9	136.2	119.8	0	0	0	0
27	3	695.4	.89	618.9	136.2	121.2	0	0	0	0
28	4	695.4	.88	611.9	136.2	119.9	0	0	0	0
29	5	695.4	.89	618.9	136.2	121.2	0	0	0	0
30	6	356.5	.89	317.3	93.5	83.0	−111.6	0	−111.6	−49.7
31	7	↑	.88	313.7	↑	82.3	−111.6	0	−111.6	−49.1
32	8		.88	313.7		82.3	−111.6	0	−111.6	−49.1
33	9		.87	310.2		81.3	−111.6	0	−111.6	−48.5
34	10	↓	.87	310.2	↓	81.3	−111.6	0	−111.6	−48.5
35	11	356.5	.87	310.2	93.5	81.3	−111.6	0	−111.6	−48.5
36	12	124.0	.86	106.6	31.1	26.7	−333.8	−72.2	−406.0	−261.9
37	13	↑	.85	105.4	↑	26.4	−333.8	−72.2	−406.0	−258.8
38	14		.85	105.4		26.4	−333.8	−72.2	−406.0	−258.8
39	15		↑	105.4		26.4	−333.8	−72.2	−406.0	−258.8
40	16	↓		105.4	↓	26.4	−333.8	−72.2	−406.0	−258.8
41	17	124.0		105.4	31.1	26.2	−333.8	−72.2	−406.0	−258.8
42		0		0	0	0	0	0	0	0
43		↑		↑	↑	↑	↑	↑	↑	↑
44										
⋮										
54		↓		↓	↓	↓	↓	↓	↓	↓
55–59		0	.85	0	0	0	0	0	0	0
TOTAL		8,226.5		7107.1	1685.3	1462.3	−2672.4	−433.2	3105.6	−1849.3

*Child's wage rate = 1/2 of wife's for ages 6–11, 3/4 for ages 12–17.

[347]

APPENDIX E

TABLE E-1 (cont.)

Child Costs and Net Work and Consumption Effects, First Child, "Low-Income" Couple

		\multicolumn{9}{c	}{Time Costs and Net Work Effects}
		\multicolumn{3}{c	}{Total value of net time cost (ΣL^N)}	\multicolumn{2}{c	}{Child's impact on husb. work}	\multicolumn{2}{c	}{Child's impact on wife's work}	\multicolumn{3}{c	}{Value of net work effect ($\Sigma\Delta L$) (husb. and wife only)}
		0%	13%	18%	hrs/yr	value	hrs/yr	value	0%	13%	18%
23	preg.	83.5	93.5	93.5	0	0	-220	-187.0	-187.0	-187.0	-187.0
24	<1	1357.8	1200.3	1150.7	50	65.5	-871.5	-723.3	-657.8	-531.5	-557.5
25	1	1015.3	703.6	729.0	↑	70.5	-734	-616.6	-546.1	-427.6	-392.1
26	2	731.7	507.1	445.6		76.0	-687.5	-605.0	-529.0	-367.0	-322.2
27	3	740.1	453.7	381.9		81.0	-656.5	-584.3	-503.3	-308.5	-259.7
28	4	731.8	397.4	319.8		85.0	-589.5	-518.8	-433.8	-235.6	-189.6
29	5	740.1	355.2	273.8		89.0	-574	-510.9	-421.9	-202.5	-156.1
30	6	350.6	149.0	110.1		93.0	-426	-379.1	-286.1	-121.6	-89.8
31	7	346.9	130.4	92.3		97.0	-426	-374.9	-277.9	-104.5	-73.9
32	8	346.9	115.5	78.1		101.0	-426	-374.9	-273.9	-91.2	-61.6
33	9	343.0	101.2	65.5		102.5	-426	-370.6	-268.1	-79.1	-51.2
34	10	343.0	89.5	55.6		104.5	-426	-370.6	-266.1	-69.5	-43.1
35	11	343.0	79.2	47.0		106.0	-426	-370.6	-264.6	-61.1	-36.3
36	12	-128.6	-26.6	-14.9		108.0	-426	-366.6	-258.4	-52.7	-30.0
37	13	-127.0	-23.0	-12.6		110.0	-426	-362.1	-252.1	-45.6	-25.0
38	14	-127.0	-20.3	-10.7		110.5	-96	-81.6	28.9	4.6	2.4
39	15	-127.0	-17.9	-9.0		111.0	-96	-81.6	29.4	4.1	2.0
40	16	-127.0	-15.9	-7.6		111.5	-96	-81.6	29.9	3.7	1.8
41	17	-127.0	-14.1	-6.5	50	112.5	-96	-81.6	30.9	3.4	1.6
42		0	0	0	0	0	-43	-36.6	-36.6	-3.6	-1.6
43		↑	↑	↑	↑	↑			↑	-3.2	-1.4
44										-2.5	-1.1
.										↑	↑
.											
.											
54		↓	↓	↓	↓	↓	-43	-36.6	-36.6	-.8	-.2
55-59		0	0	0	0	0	-215	-183.0	-183.0	-3.0	-.5
TOTAL		6720.1	458.2	3781.6	900	1734.5	-8799	-7700.3	-5965.8	-2946.9	-2477.0

APPENDIX E

TABLE E-1 (cont.)

Child Costs and Net Work and Consumption Effects, First Child, "Low-income" Couple

Commodity Inputs into the Child (C^N's)

Age of Couple	First Child's Age	Food i=0	Food 13%	Food 18%	Child's Clothing 0%	Utilities 0%	Shelter 0	Shelter 13%	Shelter 18%
24	<1	129	114	109	30	63	161	142	136
25	1	158	124	113	36	73	171	134	123
26	2	158	109	96	38	78	179	134	109
27	3	158	97	82	40	81	186	114	96
28	4	199	108	87	42	85	192	104	84
29	5	199	96	74	44	86	197	95	73
30	6	197	84	62	178	94	204	87	64
31	7	234	88	62	183	96	209	79	56
32	8	234	78	53	189	98	213	71	48
33	9	234	69	45	191	99	214	63	41
34	10	272	71	44	193	100	216	56	35
35	11	272	63	37	191	104	209	46	29
36	12	272	55	32	269	95	196	40	23
37	13	297	54	29	272	96	197	36	20
38	14	297	48	25	285	100	204	33	17
39	15	297	42	21	286	100	204	27	14
40	16	330	41	20	287	100	205	26	12
41	17	330	37	17	289	101	205	23	10
TOTAL		4,267	1,378	1,008	3,043	1,649	3,562	1,304	990

Basis: U.S.D.A.: economy, urban North Central | Predicted values, App. D. | Same basis as shelter | Predicted values, App. D, divided by (1 + family size)

[349]

APPENDIX E

TABLE E-1 (cont.)

Child Costs and Net Work and Consumption Effects,
First Child, "Low-income" Couple

		Commodity Inputs into the Child (c^N's)							
Age of Couple	Age of Child	Medical Care 0%	13%	18%	Recreation 0%	Education 0%	All but food, shelter, med. care 0	13%	18%
24	<1	439	388	372	0	0	93	82	79
25	1	38	30	27	0	0	109	85	78
26	2	38	26	23	0	0	116	80	71
27	3	38	23	20	0	0	121	74	62
28	4	38	21	17	0	0	127	69	55
29	5	38	18	14	0	0	130	62	48
30	6	40	17	13	37	9	315	135	100
31	7	40	15	11	39	9	327	123	87
32	8	40	13	9	40	9	336	112	76
33	9	40	12	8	41	8	339	100	65
34	10	40	10	6	42	8	343	90	56
35	11	40	9	5	38	8	341	79	47
36	12	40	8	5	56	12	432	88	50
37	13	40	7	4	57	12	437	79	43
38	14	40	6	3	69	12	466	75	39
39	15	40	6	3	69	13	468	66	33
40	16	39	5	2	70	13	470	59	28
41	17	39	4	2	70	13	473	53	24
TOTAL		1,107	618	544	628	126	5,446	1,511	1,041
Basis:		U.S.D.A.			Predicted increment over childless couple, div. by no. of children in household, from App. D. Negative values replaced by 0's (recr., ages 0-5).		(Sum of clothing, recr., education, utilities)		

[350]

APPENDIX E

TABLE E-1 (cont.)

Child Costs and Net Work and Consumption Effects, First Child, "Low-Income" Couple

Age of Couple	Age of Child	\multicolumn{3}{c}{Food}			\multicolumn{3}{c}{Shelter}			Util.	Child's Clothing	Trans-port'n
		i=0%	13%	18%	0%	13%	18%	0%	0%	0%
23	preg.	−21	−21	−21	−18	−18	−18	4	0	−23
24	<1	−3	−3	−3	29	26	25	−15	30	−150
25	1	50	39	36	15	12	11	−11	36	−60
6	2	21	15	13	20	14	12	−7	38	−61
7	3	28	17	14	26	16	13	−6	40	−60
8	4	38	21	17	33	18	14	3	42	−55
29	5	40	19	15	37	18	14	−2	44	−56
30	6	105	45	33	51	22	16	21	178	−105
1	7	107	40	28	55	21	15	23	183	−108
2	8	109	36	25	54	18	12	23	189	−113
3	9	110	32	21	54	16	10	24	191	−114
4	10	111	29	18	54	14	9	24	193	−117
35	11	117	27	16	53	12	7	26	191	−109
6	12	189	39	22	−7	−1	8	−12	269	−51
7	13	191	35	19	−8	−1	−1	−12	272	−53
8	14	225	36	19	16	3	1	−11	285	−26
39	15	226	32	16	16	2	1	0	286	−26
40	16	226	28	14	16	2	1	0	287	−26
1	17	226	25	12	15	2	1	0	289	−27
2		−27	−3	−1	−22	−2	−1	−12	0	−27
3		−27	−2	−1	−22	−2	−1	−12	0	−27
44		−27	−2	−1	−21	−2	−1	−12	0	−27
.		.	.	.	.	.	.	.	.	.
.		.	.	.	.	.	.	.	.	.
54		−27	−1	0	−20	0	0	−13	0	−27
(55−59)		−145	−2	−1	−105	−2	0	−65	0	−115
TOTAL		1599	470	307	141	179	147	−158	3043	−1806

[351]

APPENDIX E

TABLE E-1 (cont.)

Child Costs and Net Work and Consumption Effects, First Child, "Low-income" Couple

Age of Couple	First Child's Age	Recreation 0%	13%	18%	Recreation 0%	Education 0%	Total Expenditures 0%	13%	18%
23	preg.	378	378	378	-27	-27	+268	268	268
24	<1	-35	-31	-30	-40	0	-504	-446	-427
25	1	-15	-12	-11	-17	0	-422	-330	-303
26	2	-15	-10	-9	-17	0	-414	-287	-252
27	3	-15	-9	-8	-16	0	-396	-243	-204
28	4	-13	-7	-6	-15	0	-359	-195	-157
29	5	-14	-7	-5	-15	0	-352	-169	-130
30	6	15	6	5	-37	9	76	32	24
31	7	16	6	4	39	9	81	30	22
32	8	17	6	4	40	9	86	29	19
33	9	16	5	3	41	8	87	26	17
34	10	17	4	3	42	8	88	23	14
35	11	17	4	2	38	8	85	20	12
36	12	8	2	1	56	12	203	41	24
37	13	8	1	1	57	12	202	37	20
38	14	16	3	1	69	12	395	63	33
39	15	16	2	1	69	13	393	55	28
40	16	16	2	1	70	13	261	33	16
41	17	16	2	1	70	13	393	44	20
42		-7	-1	0	-7	0	-165	-16	-7
43		-7	-1	0	-7	0	-165	-14	-6
44		-7	-1	0	-7	0	-162	-12	-5
.		.	.	.	.	.	.	.	.
54		-7	0	0	-5	0	-162	-4	-1
(55-59)		-50	-1	0	-20	0	-790	-13	-3
TOTAL		308	341	336	389	126	-2727	-1093	-1020

APPENDIX E

TABLE E-2

Child Costs and Net Work and Consumption Effects,
Third Child, "Low-income" Couple (3-year child spacing)

Couple's Age	Third Child's Age	Time Costs									
		Total Child Care Time			Other Chore Increases for Wife		Child'e Chore and Paid Work Contrib. (-)			
		hrs/yr	wife's wage	value of care time	hrs/yr	value	chore time	work time	total (hrs/yr)	value*
29	preg.	0	.87	0	46.3	40.3	0	0	0	0
30	<1	1186.6	.84	996.7	107.2	90.0	0	0	0	0
31	1	789.5	.83	655.3	175.7	145.8	0	0	0	0
32	2	455.4	.83	378.0	136.2	113.0	0	0	0	0
33	3	442.0	.82	362.4	136.2	111.7	0	0	0	0
34	4	442.0	.81	358.0	136.2	110.3	0	0	0	0
35	5	442.0	.81	358.0	136.2	110.3	0	0	0	0
36	6	221.9	.80	177.5	93.5	74.8	-111.6	0	-111.6	-44.6
37	7	221.9	.79	175.3	93.5	73.9	-111.6	0	-111.6	-44.1
38	8	221.9	.78	173.1	93.5	72.9	-111.6	0	-111.6	-43.5
39	9	246.7	.78	192.4	93.5	72.9	-111.6	0	-111.6	-43.5
40	10	246.7	.77	189.9	93.5	72.0	-111.6	0	-111.6	-43.0
41	11	246.7	.77	189.9	93.5	72.0	-111.6	0	-111.6	-43.0
42	12	110.7	.76	84.1	31.1	23.6	-333.8	-72.2	-406.0	-231.4
43	13	110.7	.76	84.1	31.1	23.6	-333.8	-72.2	-406.0	-231.4
44	14	110.7	.76	84.1	31.1	23.6	-333.8	-72.2	-406.0	-231.4
45	15	124.0		94.2	31.1	23.6	-333.8	-72.2	-406.0	-231.4
46	16	124.0		94.2	31.1	23.6	-333.8	-72.2	-406.0	-231.4
47	17	124.0		94.2	31.1	23.6	-333.8	-72.2	-406.0	-231.4
48		0		0	0	0	0	0	0	0
49										
50										
51										
52										
53										
54										
55-59		0	.76	0	0	0	0	0	0	0
TOTAL		5,867.4		4,741.4	1,621.6	1,301.5	-2,672.4	-433.2	**-3105.6**	-1650.1

(mid-range estimate)

*Child's wage rate = 1/2 of wife's for ages 6-11, 3/4 of wife's for ages 12-17.

[353]

APPENDIX E

TABLE E-2 (cont.)

Child Costs and Net Work and Consumption Effects,
Third Child, "Low-Income" Couple (three-year child spacing)

Age of Couple	Age of Third Child	Total value of net time cost 0%	13%	18%	Child's impact on husband's paid work hrs/yr	value	Child's impact on wife's paid work hrs/yr	value	Value of net work effect 0%	13%	18%
29	preg.	40.3	40.3	40.3	0	0	-92.5	-80.5	-80.5	-80.5	-80.5
30	<1	1086.7	960.6	921.0	0	0	-215	-180.6	-180.6	-159.7	-153.1
31	1	801.1	627.3	575.2	↑	↑	-144.5	-119.9	-119.9	-93.9	-86.1
32	2	491.0	340.3	299.0			-113.5	-94.2	-94.2	-65.3	-57.4
33	3	474.1	290.6	244.6			-230.5	-189.0	-189.0	-115.9	-97.5
34	4	468.3	254.3	204.6			-163.5	-132.4	-132.4	-71.9	-57.9
35	5	468.3	224.8	173.3			-148	-119.9	-119.9	-57.6	-44.4
36	6	207.7	88.3	65.2			0	0	0	0	0
37	7	205.1	77.1	54.6			0	0	0	0	0
38	8	202.5	67.4	45.6			0	0	0	0	0
39	9	221.8	65.4	42.4			0	0	0	0	0
40	10	218.9	57.1	35.5			0	0	0	0	0
41	11	218.9	50.6	30.0			-330	-254.1	-254.1	-58.7	-34.8
42	12	-123.7	-25.2	-14.3			-330	-250.8	-250.8	-51.2	-29.1
43	13	-123.7	-22.4	-12.2	↓	↓	-330	-250.8	-250.8	-45.4	-24.8
44	14	-123.7	-19.8	-10.4	0	0	0	0	0	0	0
45	15	-113.6	-16.0	-8.0	50	113.5	-67	-50.9	62.6	8.8	4.4
46	16	-113.6	-14.2	-6.8	50	114.0	-67	-50.9	63.1	7.9	3.8
47	17	-113.6	-12.6	-5.8	50	114.0	-67	-50.9	63.1	7.0	3.2
48		0	0	0	0	0	-40	-30.4	-30.4	-3.0	-1.3
49		↑	↑	↑	↑	↑	-40	-30.4	-30.4	-2.6	-1.1
50							-40	-30.4	-30.4	-2.3	-.9
51							-40	-30.4	-30.4	-2.1	-.8
52							-40	-30.4	-30.4	-1.8	-.7
53							-40	-30.4	-30.4	-1.4	-.6
54		↓	↓	↓	↓	↓	-40	-30.4	-30.4	-1.4	-.5
55-59		0	0	0	0	0	-200	-152.0	-152.0	-5.6	-1.7
TOTAL		4392.8	3033.9	2673.8	150	341.5	-2778.5	-2189.7	-1848.2	-796.8	-661.8

[354]

APPENDIX E

TABLE E-2 (cont.)

Child Costs and Net Work and Consumption Effects,
Third Child, "Low-income" Couple (three-year child spacing)

		\multicolumn{3}{c}{Commodity Inputs into the Child (c^N's)}					
Age of Couple	Age of Third Child	\multicolumn{3}{c}{Food}	Child's Clothing	Utilities	\multicolumn{3}{c}{Shelter}
		i=0	13%	18%	0%	0%	0%	13%	18%
30	<1	122	108	103	33	64	122	108	103
31	1	150	117	108	33	66	126	99	90
32	2	150	104	91	42	68	130	90	79
33	3	150	92	77	42	69	131	80	68
34	4	187	102	82	42	70	133	72	58
35	5	187	90	69	42	73	129	62	48
36	6	187	79	59	70	67	124	53	39
37	7	222	83	59	70	68	125	47	33
38	8	222	74	50	70	68	125	42	28
39	9	222	65	42	70	68	125	37	24
40	10	258	67	42	70	67	124	32	20
41	11	258	60	35	70	68	126	29	17
42	12	258	53	30	101	96	144	29	17
43	13	282	51	28	101	96	144	26	14
44	14	282	45	24	101	99	148	24	12
45	15	282	40	20	101	102	192	27	14
46	16	314	39	19	121	102	192	24	12
47	17	314	35	16	121	102	192	21	10
TOTAL		4047	1304	954	1300	1413	2532	902	686

Basis: U.S.D.A.: economy, urban North Central   U.S.D.A.   Same basis as shelter.   Predicted values, App. D, divided by (1 + family size)

[355]

APPENDIX E

TABLE E-2 (cont.)

Child Costs and Net Work and Consumption Effects,
Third Child, "Low-income" Couple (three-year child spacing)

Commodity Inputs into the Child (c^N's)

Age of Couple	Age of Third Child	Medical Care 0%	13%	18%	Recreation 0%	Educ. 0%	All but food, shelter, med. care 0%	13%	18%
30	<1	434	384	368	3	2	102	90	86
31	1	34	27	24	7	2	108	85	78
32	2		24	15	7	2	119	82	72
33	3		21	11	9	2	122	75	63
34	4		18	15	9	2	123	67	54
35	5		16	13	8	2	125	60	46
36	6		14	11	13	4	154	65	48
37	7		13	9	14	4	156	59	41
38	8		11	8	13	4	155	52	35
39	9		10	6	13	4	155	46	30
40	10		9	6	12	4	153	40	25
41	11		8	5	14	4	156	36	21
42	12		7	4	21	3	221	45	26
43	13		6	3	21	3	221	40	22
44	14		5	3	26	4	230	37	19
45	15		5	2	27	12	242	34	17
46	16		4	2	27	12	262	33	16
47	17	34	4	2	27	12	262	29	13
TOTAL		1012	586	507	271	82	3066	975	712

Basis: U.S.D.A.   Predicted increment over childless couple, div. by no. of children in household, from App. D. Negative values replaced by 0's (recr., ages 0-5).   (Sum of clothing, recr., educ., util.)

APPENDIX E

TABLE E-2 (cont.)

Child Costs and Net Work and Consumption Effects,
Third Child, "Low-income" Couple (three-year child spacing)

Age of Couple	Age of Third Child	Net Effects of Child on Family Consumption of								
		Food			Shelter			Util.	Child's Clothing	Trans.
		i=0%	13%	18%	0%	13%	18%	0%	0%	0%
29	(preg.)	-200	-200	-200	-200	-200	-200	-73	-77	14
30	<1	85	75	72	-51	-45	-43	-19	13	-42
31	1	97	76	70	-46	-36	-33	-18	16	-38
32	2	112	78	68	-37	-26	-23	-13	21	-32
33	3	112	69	58	+32	20	17	+23	2	-36
34	4	68	37	30	38	21	17	28	4	-33
35	5	74	36	27	38	18	14	27	5	-29
36	6	164	70	51	-11	-5	-3	6	57	+13
37	7	165	62	44	-11	-4	-3	6	57	14
38	8	165	55	37	-11	-4	-2	6	57	14
39	9	207	61	40	+38	11	7	-70	7	30
40	10	51	13	8	38	10	6	-69	6	30
41	11	231	53	32	17	4	2	-82	7	13
42	12	111	23	13	-101	-21	-12	+80	-13	-145
43	13	111	20	11	-101	-18	-10	80	-13	-145
44	14	147	24	12	-82	-13	-7	95	-12	+4
45	15	248	35	18	31	4	2	12	198	-4
46	16	249	31	15	31	4	2	10	199	2
47	17	249	28	13	31	3	2	10	199	2
48	18	-7	-1	0	24	2	1	-4	0	-6
49	19	-7	-1	0	24	2	1	-4	0	-6
50	20	-7	-1	0	24	2	1	-4	0	-6
51	21	-7	-1	0	24	2	1	-4	0	-6
52	22	-7	-1	0	24	1	1	-4	0	-6
53	23	-7	-1	0	24	1	0	-4	0	-6
54	24	-7	-1	0	24	1	0	-4	0	-6
55-59	27	-40	-1	0	-25	-1	0	-20	0	-30
TOTAL		2357	638	419	-140	-267	-262	-9	733	-440

APPENDIX E

TABLE E-2 (cont.)

Child Costs and Net Work and Consumption Effects,
Third Child, "Low-Income" Couple (three-year child spacing)

Age of Couple	Age of Third Child	Medical Care 0%	13%	18%	Recreation 0%	Education 0%	Total Expenditures 0%	13%	18%
29	preg.	347	347	347	-13	0	117	117	117
30	<1	-4	-4	-3	-7	-1	-231	-204	-196
31	1	-1	-1	-1	-5	-1	-99	-78	-71
32	2	+2	1	1	-2	-1	-38	-26	-23
33	3	-15	-9	-8	-11	-9	-32	-20	-17
34	4	-13	-7	-6	-9	-9	+5	3	2
35	5	-14	-7	-5	-7	-9	15	7	6
36	6	-4	-2	-1	-7	-6	68	29	21
37	7	-4	-2	-1	-7	-6	68	26	18
38	8	-5	-2	-1	-8	-6	68	23	15
39	9	-35	-10	-7	-2	+6	9	3	2
40	10	-34	-9	-6	-2	6	9	2	1
41	11	-45	-10	-6	-12	6	-175	-40	-24
42	12	+33	7	4	-26	-7	-73	-15	-8
43	13	33	6	3	-26	-7	-73	-13	-7
44	14	42	7	4	-17	-7	+108	17	9
45	15	24	3	2	+61	+12	512	72	36
46	16	24	3	1	+60	12	513	64	31
47	17	24	3	1	+60	12	513	57	26
48		-2	0	0	-2	0	-42	-4	-2
49		-2	0	0	-2	0	-42	-4	-2
50		-2	0	0	-2	0	-42	-3	-1
51		-2	0	0	-2	0	-42	-3	-1
52		-2	0	0	-2	0	-42	-3	-1
53		-2	0	0	-2	0	-42	-2	-1
54		-2	0	0	-2	0	-42	-2	-1
55-59		-10	0	0	-5	0	-205	-7	-2
TOTAL		333	314	318	1	-15	785	-4	-73

Net Effects of Child on Family Consumption of:

APPENDIX E

TABLE E-3.

Child Costs and Net Work and Consumption Effects,
First Child, "High-Income" Couple

		Time Costs								
Age of Couple	Age of First Child	Total Child Care Time			Other Chore Increases for Wife		Child's Chore and Paid Work Contrib. (−)			
		hrs/yr	wife's wage	value of care time	hrs/yr	value	chore time	work time	total (hrs/yr)	value*
23	preg.	0	1.46	0	110.0	160.6	0	0	0	0
24	<1	1528.9	1.43	$2186.3	107.2	$153.3	0	0	0	0
25	1	1033.0	1.56	1611.5	175.7	274.1	0	0	0	0
26	2	695.4	1.63	1133.5	136.2	222.0	0	0	0	0
27	3	695.4	1.66	1154.4	136.2	226.1	0	0	0	0
28	4	695.4	1.68	1168.3	136.2	228.8	0	0	0	0
29	5	695.4	1.69	1175.2	136.2	230.2	0	0	0	0
30	6	356.5	1.71	609.6	93.5	159.9	−111.6	0	−111.6	−95.4
31	7	↑	1.71	609.6	↑	159.9	−111.6	0	−111.6	−95.4
32	8		1.71	609.6		159.9	−111.6	0	−111.6	−95.4
33	9		1.72	613.2		160.8	−111.6	0	−111.6	−95.9
34	10	↓	1.71	609.6	↓	159.9	−111.6	0	−111.6	−95.4
35	11	356.5	1.71	609.6	93.5	159.9	−111.6	0	−111.6	−95.4
36	12	124.0	1.70	210.8	31.1	52.9	−333.8	−72.2	−406.0	−517.6
37	13	↑	1.69	209.6	↑	52.6	−333.8	−72.2	↑	−514.6
38	14		1.70	210.8		52.9	−333.8	−72.2		−517.6
39	15		1.71	212.0		53.2	−333.8	−72.2		−520.7
40	16	↓	1.71	212.0	↓	53.2	−333.8	−72.2	↓	−520.7
41	17	124.0	1.71	212.0	31.1	53.2	−333.8	−72.2	−406.0	−520.7
42		0	1.70	0	0	0	0	0	0	0
43		↑	↑		↑	↑		↑	↑	↑
44										
45										
46										
.										
54		↓	↓		↓	↓		↓	↓	↓
55−59		0	1.70	0	0	0	0	0	0	0
TOTAL		8226.5		13,357.6	1685.3	2773.4	−2672.4	−433.2	−3105.6	3684.3

*Child's wage assumed = 1/2 of wife's for ages 6-11, 3/4 of wife's for ages 12-17.

[359]

APPENDIX E

TABLE E-3 (cont.)

Child Costs and Net Work and Consumption Effects, First Child, "High-Income" Couple

Age of Couple	Age of First Child	Total Value of net time cost 0%	8%	13%	Child's Impact on husband's paid work hrs/yr	value	Child's Impact on wife's paid work hrs/yr	value	Value of net work effect 0%	8%	13% =1*
23	preg.	$ 160.6	160.6	160.6	0	0	-220	-321.2	$ -321.2	-321.2	-321.2
24	<1	2339.6	2166.5	2068.2	50	112.5	-871.5	-1246.2	-1133.7	-1049.8	-1002.2
25	1	1855.6	1615.9	1476.4	↑	122.5	-734	-1145.0	-1023.0	-876.8	-801.0
26	2	1355.5	1076.3	939.4		131.5	-687.5	-1120.6	-989.1	-785.3	-685.4
27	3	1380.5	1014.7	846.2		140.5	-656.5	-1089.8	-949.3	-697.7	-581.9
28	4	1397.1	951.4	758.6		149.5	-589.5	-990.4	-840.9	-572.7	-456.6
29	5	1405.4	885.4	674.6		159.0	-574	-970.1	-811.1	-511.0	-389.3
30	6	674.1	393.0	286.5		168.0	-426	-728.5	-560.5	-326.8	-238.2
31	7	674.1	337.1	253.5		177.0	↑	-728.5	-551.5	-297.8	-207.4
32	8	674.1	314.0	224.5		186.0		-728.5	-542.5	-271.3	-180.7
33	9	678.1	289.2	200.0		192.5		-732.7	-540.2	-250.1	-159.4
34	10	674.1	289.2	175.9		199.0		-723.5	-529.5	-227.2	-138.2
35	11	674.1	267.6	155.7		205.5		-728.7	-523.2	-207.7	-120.9
36	12	-253.9	-93.4	-51.8		212.0	↓	-724.2	-512.2	-188.5	-104.5
37	13	-252.4	-85.8	-45.7		218.5	-426	-718.9	-501.4	-170.5	-90.8
38	14	-253.9	-80.0	-40.6		223.0	-96	-163.2	59.8	18.8	9.6
39	15	-255.5	-74.6	-36.0		227.5	-96	-164.2	63.3	18.5	8.9
40	16	-255.5	-69.0	-31.9	↓	231.5	-96	-164.2	67.3	18.2	8.4
41	17	-255.5	-63.9	-28.4	50	235.5	-96	-164.2	71.3	17.8	7.9
42		0	0	0	0	0	-43	-73.1	-73.1	-16.9	-7.2
43			↑	↑	↑	↑	↑	↑	↑	-15.6	-6.4
44										-14.5	-5.6
45										-13.5	-5.0
46										-12.4	-4.4
.										↑	↑
.			↓	↓	↓	↓	↓	↓	↓		
54		0	0	0	0	0	-43	-73.1	-73.1	-6.7	-1.7
55-59		0	0	0	0	0	-215	-365.5	-215	-15.7	-6.0
TOTAL		12446.2	9294.2	7985.7	900	329.0	-8899.0	-14674.4	-11232.9	-6841.1	-5289.7

*Discount Rate

[360]

APPENDIX E

TABLE E-3 (cont.)

Child Costs and Net Work and Consumption Effects,
First Child, "High-Income" Couple

Age of Couple	Age of First Child	Food i=0	Food 8%	Food 13%	Child's Clothing 0%	Utilities 0%	Shelter 0%	Shelter 8%	Shelter 13%
					Commodity Inputs into the Child (C^N's)				
24	<1	$183	169	162	44	116	199	184	176
25	1	225	193	176	53	129	213	183	167
26	2	225	179	156	56	144	223	177	155
27	3	225	165	138	59	150	221	162	135
28	4	289	197	157	63	156	242	165	131
29	5	289	182	139	66	173	250	158	120
30	6	289	168	123	271	178	261	152	111
31	7	343	185	129	281	183	268	145	101
32	8	343	172	114	291	188	274	137	91
33	9	343	159	101	298	191	279	129	82
34	10	411	176	107	305	195	284	122	74
35	11	411	163	95	306	215	276	110	64
36	12	411	151	84	435	191	260	96	53
37	13	458	156	83	444	194	264	90	48
38	14	458	144	73	470	202	275	87	44
39	15	458	134	65	477	204	278	81	39
40	16	531	143	66	483	206	280	76	35
41	17	531	133	59	489	208	283	71	31
TOTAL		6423	2969	2027	4891	3223	4630	2325	1657

Basis: U.S.D.A.: moderate cost, urban North Central   Predicted values, App. D.   Same basis as shelter.   Predicted values, App. D, divided by (1 + family size).

APPENDIX E

TABLE E-3 (cont.)

Child Costs and Net Work and Consumption Effects, First Child, "High-Income" Couple

Commodity Inputs into the Child (C^N's)

Age of Couple	Age of First Child	Medical Care 0%	8%	13%	Recreation 0%	Educ. 0%	All but food, Shelter, med. care 0%	8%	13%
24	<1	$465	431	411	0	0	160	148	141
25	1	64	55	50	0	0	182	156	143
26	2	64	51	44	0	0	200	159	1386
27	3	64	47	39	0	0	209	154	128
28	4	64	44	35	0	0	219	149	119
29	5	64	40	31	0	0	239	151	115
30	6	65	38	28	79	22	550	321	234
31	7	65	35	24	84	23	571	308	215
32	8	65	33	22	88	24	591	296	197
33	9	65	30	19	92	24	605	280	178
34	10	65	28	17	95	24	619	266	162
35	11	65	26	15	89	22	632	251	146
36	12	65	24	13	134	33	793	292	162
37	13	65	22	12	138	33	809	275	146
38	14	65	20	10	170	35	877	276	140
39	15	65	19	9	173	35	889	260	125
40	16	64	17	8	176	35	900	243	113
41	17	64	16	7	180	6536	7413	1853	823
TOTAL		1563	976	794	1498	6846	16458	5838	4673

Basis: U.S.D.A., plus $400 in obstetrical costs.   Predicted increment over childless couple, (App. D), divided by no. of children in household, plus 4 years' college.   (Sum of clothing, recr., educ., util.)

APPENDIX E

TABLE E-3 (cont.)

Child Costs and Net Work and Consumption Effects, First Child, "High-Income" Couple

		\multicolumn{9}{c}{Net Effects of Child on Family Consumption of}

Age of Couple	Age of First Child	Food i=0%	8%	13%	Shelter 0%	8%	13%	Child's Util. 0%	Clothing 0%	Trans. 0%
23	preg.	$ -27	-27	-27	14	14	14	-16	0	-54
24	<1	-27	-25	-24	35	32	31	-26	44	-192
25	1	+12	+10	+ 9	12	10	9	-47	53	-145
26	2	21	17	15	19	15	13	-15	56	-146
27	3	28	21	17	-19	-14	-12	-13	59	-148
28	4	42	29	23	38	26	21	- 7	63	-138
29	5	48	30	23	43	27	21	41	66	-140
30	6	134	78	57	62	36	26	40	271	-259
31	7	138	75	52	64	35	24	42	281	-270
32	8	143	72	48	66	33	22	43	291	-281
33	9	146	68	43	68	31	20	44	298	-291
34	10	148	63	39	73	31	19	46	305	-300
35	11	141	56	33	69	27	16	93	366	-282
36	12	260	96	53	-11	-4	-2	-16	435	-136
37	13	263	89	48	-11	-4	-2	-16	444	-139
38	14	316	100	51	+23	7	4	6	470	- 48
39	15	318	93	45	23	7	3	5	477	- 68
40	16	321	87	40	23	6	3	5	483	- 69
41	17	324	81	36	24	6	3	6	489	- 69
42		-35	-8	-3	-28	-6	-3	-20	0	- 70
43		-35	-7	-3	-28	-6	-2	-19	0	- 71
44		-35	-7	-3	-28	-6	-2	-20	0	- 72
45		-35	-6	-2	-26	-5	-2	-24	0	- 64
46		-35	-6	-2	-26	-5	-2	-25	0	- 66
.		.	.	.	.	.	.	.	.	.
54		-35	-3	-1	-26	-2	-1	-24	0	- 66
55-59		-180	-13	-3	-120	-9	-2	-120	0	-295
TOTAL		2116	933	555	152	259	212	-205	4891	-4,334

[363]

APPENDIX E

TABLE E-3 (cont.)

Child Costs and Net Work and Consumption Effects,
First Child, "High-Income" Couple

Age of Couple	Age of First Child	Medical Care 0%	8%	13%	Recr. 0%	Educ. 0%	Total Expenditures 0%	8%	13%
23	preg.	$390	390	390	10	0	+258	+258	+258
24	<1	-39	-36	-34	-25	0	-685	-634	-606
25	1	-37	-32	-29	-37	-1	-678	-581	-531
26	2	-36	-29	-25	-36	0	-661	-525	-458
27	3	-36	-26	-22	-37	0	-645	-474	-395
28	4	-33	-22	-18	-35	-1	-585	-398	-318
29	5	-33	-21	-16	-30	-1	-576	-363	-276
30	6	+33	19	14	79	22	84	49	36
31	7	35	19	13	84	23	96	52	36
32	8	37	19	12	88	24	109	54	36
33	9	39	18	12	92	24	117	54	35
34	10	40	17	10	95	24	119	51	31
35	11	43	17	10	89	22	131	52	30
36	12	20	7	4	134	33	174	64	35
37	13	21	7	4	138	33	183	62	33
38	14	43	14	7	170	35	236	74	38
39	15	43	13	6	173	35	559	163	79
40	16	44	12	6	176	35	585	158	73
41	17	45	11	5	180	36	594	149	66
42		-17	-4	-2	-17	1685	1356	313	133
43		-16	-3	-1	-17	1685	1315	281	114
44		-17	-3	-1	-17	1685	1308	259	101
45		-18	-3	-1	-14	1685	1375	253	94
46		-18	-3	-1	-14	0	-252	-43	-15
.		.	.	.	.	.	.	.	.
54		-18	-2	0	-14	0	-250	-23	-6
55-59		-115	-8	-2	-55	0	-1215	-89	-19
TOTAL		275	355	335	1066	6843	+1307	-995	-1462

(Predicted values from App. D plus $400 in obstetrical costs and a $1625-a-year college education.)

APPENDIX E

TABLE E-4.

Child Costs and Net Work and Consumption Effects,
Third Child, "High-Income" Couple (three-year child spacing)

Age of Couple	Age of Third Child	Total Child Care Time			Other Chore Increases for Wife		Child's Chore and Paid Work Contrib. (−)			
		hrs/yr	wife's wage	value of care time	hrs/yr	value	chore time	work time	total (hrs/yr)	value
29	preg.	0	1.66	0	46.3	76.9	0	0	0	0
30	<1	1186.6	1.59	1886.7	107.2	170.4	0	0	0	0
31	1	789.5	1.57	1239.5	175.7	275.8	0	0	0	0
32	2	455.4	1.55	705.9	136.2	211.1	0	0	0	0
33	3	442.0	1.54	650.7	136.2	209.7	0	0	0	0
34	4	442.0	1.52	671.8	136.2	207.0	0	0	0	0
35	5	442.0	1.51	667.4	136.2	205.7	0	0	0	0
36	6	221.9	1.50	332.9	93.5	140.3	−111.6	0	−111.6	−83.7
37	7	221.9	1.49	330.6	↑	139.3	−111.6	0	−111.6	−83.1
38	8	221.9	1.48	328.4		136.4	−111.6	0	−111.6	−52.6
39	9	246.7	1.46	360.2	↓	136.5	−111.6	0	−111.6	−51.5
40	10	246.7	1.45	357.7		135.6	−111.6	0	−111.6	−80.9
41	11	246.7	1.43	352.8	93.5	133.7	−111.6	0	−111.6	−79.5
42	12	110.7	1.41	156.1	31.1	43.9	−333.8	−72.2	−406.0	−429.3
43	13	110.7	1.39	153.9	↑	43.2	−333.8	−72.2	−406.0	−423.3
44	14	110.7	1.37	151.7		42.6	−333.8	−72.2	−406.0	−417.2
45	15	124.0		169.9	↓	42.6	−333.8	−72.2	−406.0	−417.2
46	16	124.0		169.9		42.6	−333.8	−72.2	−406.0	−417.2
47	17	124.0		169.9	31.1	42.6	−333.8	−72.2	−406.0	−417.2
48		0		0	0	0	0	0	0	0
49		↑		↑	↑	↑	↑	↑	↑	↑
50										
51										
52										
53										
54		↓		↓	↓	↓	↓	↓	↓	↓
55−59		0	1.37	0	0	0	0	0	0	0
TOTAL		5867.4		8886.0	1621.6	2437.6	−2672.4	−433.2	−3105.6	−3013.0

(mid-range estimate)

*Child's wage rate = 1/2 of wife's for ages 6−11.
3/4 of wife's for ages 12−17.

[365]

APPENDIX E

TABLE E-4 (cont.)

Child Costs and Net Work and Consumption Effects,
Third Child, "High-Income" Couple (three-year child spacing)

Age of Couple	Age of Third Child	Total value of net time cost			Child's Impact on husband's paid work		Child's Impact on wife's paid work		Value of net work effect		
		0%	8%	13%=i*	hrs/yr	value	hrs/yr	value	0%	8%	13%=i*
29	preg.	76.9	76.9	76.9	0	0	-92.5	-153.6	-153.6	-153.6	-153.6
30	<1	2057.1	1904.9	1818.5	0	0	-215	-341.9	-341.9	-316.6	-302.2
31	1	1515.3	1298.6	1186.5	↑	↑	-144.5	-226.9	-226.0	-194.4	-177.7
32	2	917.0	728.1	635.5			-113.5	-175.9	-175.9	-139.7	-121.9
33	3	890.4	654.4	545.8			-230.5	-354.9	-354.9	-260.9	-217.6
34	4	878.8	598.5	477.2			-163.5	-248.5	-248.5	-169.2	-134.9
35	5	873.1	550.1	419.1			-148	-223.5	-223.5	-140.8	-107.3
36	6	389.5	227.1	165.5			0	0	0	0	0
37	7	386.8	208.9	145.4			0	0	0	0	0
38	8	384.2	192.1	127.9			0	0	0	0	0
39	9	415.2	192.2	122.5			0	0	0	0	0
40	10	412.4	176.9	107.6			0	0	0	0	0
41	11	406.7	161.4	93.9			-330	-471.9	-471.9	-187.3	-109.0
42	12	-229.3	-84.4	-46.8			-330	-465.3	-465.3	-171.2	-94.9
43	13	-226.2	-76.9	-40.9	↓	↓	-330	-458.7	-458.7	-156.0	-83.0
44	14	-222.9	-70.2	-35.7	0	0	0	0	0	0	0
45	15	-204.7	-59.8	-28.9	50	248.0	-67	-91.8	156.2	45.6	22.0
46	16	-204.7	-55.3	-25.6	50	251.0	-67	-91.8	159.2	43.0	19.9
47	17	-204.7	-51.2	-22.7	50	253.3	-67	-91.8	161.7	40.4	17.9
48		0	0	0	0	0	-40	-54.8	-54.8	-12.7	-5.4
49		↑	↑	↑	↑	↑	↑	-54.8	-54.8	-11.7	-4.8
50								-54.8	-54.8	-10.9	-4.2
51								-54.8	-54.8	-10.1	-3.7
52								-54.8	-54.8	-9.3	-3.3
53							↓	-54.8	-54.8	-8.7	-2.9
54		↓	↓	↓	↓	↓	-40	-54.8	-54.8	-8.0	-2.6
55-59		0	0	0	0	0	-200	-274.0	-274.0	-34.5	-10.1
TOTAL		8310.9	6572.3	5721.7	150	752.5	-2778.5	-4054.1	-3301.6	-1866.6	-1479.3

*discount rate

[366]

APPENDIX E

TABLE E-4 (cont.)

Child Costs and Net Work and Consumption Effects,
Third Child, "High-Income" Couple (three-year child spacing)

		\multicolumn{3}{c}{Commodity Inputs into the Child (C^N's)}					
Age of Couple	Age of Third Child	\multicolumn{3}{c}{Food}	Child's Clothing	Utilities	\multicolumn{3}{c}{Shelter}
		*i=0%	8%	13%	0%	0%	0%	8%	13%
30	<1	173	160	153	61	97	155	144	137
31	1	214	183	168	61	120	162	139	127
32	2	214	170	148	98	126	167	133	116
33	3	214	157	131	98	130	170	125	104
34	4	273	186	148	98	133	174	118	94
35	5	273	172	131	98	136	170	107	82
36	6	274	160	116	144	144	164	96	70
37	7	325	176	122	144	133	167	90	63
38	8	325	163	108	144	135	169	85	56
39	9	325	150	96	144	136	170	79	50
40	10	390	167	102	144	138	172	74	45
41	11	390	155	90	144	139	173	69	40
42	12	391	144	80	210	168	198	73	40
43	13	436	148	79	210	199	199	68	36
44	14	436	137	70	210	200	205	65	33
45	15	436	127	61	210	258	268	78	38
46	16	482	130	60	281	222	269	73	34
47	17	482	121	54	281	223	271	68	30
TOTAL		6053	2806	1917	2780	2837	3423	1684	1195
Basis:		U.S.D.A.: moderate cost, urban North Central.			U.S.D.A.	Same as shelter.	Predicted values, App. D, divided by (1 + no. in household).		

*discount rate

[367]

APPENDIX E

TABLE E-4 (cont.)

Child Costs and Net Work and Consumption Effects,
Third Child, "High-Income" Couple (three-year child spacing)

Age of Couple	Age of Third Child	Medical Care 0%	8%	13%	Recreation 0%	Educ. 0%	All but food, shelter, med. care 0%	8%	13%
30	<1	458	424	405	9	4	171	158	151
31	1	58	50	45	13	5	199	171	156
32	2	59	47	41	16	5	245	195	170
33	3	59	43	36	17	5	250	184	153
34	4	59	40	32	20	5	256	174	139
35	5	59	37	28	19	4	257	162	123
36	6	61	36	26	31	12	331	193	141
37	7	61	33	23	32	12	321	173	121
38	8	61	31	20	33	12	324	162	108
39	9	61	28	18	33	12	325	150	96
40	10	61	26	16	34	13	329	141	86
41	11	61	24	14	34	13	330	131	76
42	12	61	22	12	54	10	442	163	90
43	13	61	21	11	54	10	473	161	86
44	14	61	19	10	66	10	486	153	78
45	15	61	18	9	138	34	640	187	90
46	16	61	16	8	140	34	677	183	85
47	17	61	15	7	142	6535	7181	1795	797
TOTAL		1084	930	761	885	6735	13237	4636	274

Basis: U.S.D.A., plus $400   Predicted increments   (Sum of clothing,
         in obstetrical costs. over childless   recr., educ.,
                                couple (App. D),   util.)
                                divided by no of
                                children in house-
                                hold, plus 4 years'
                                college.

[368]

APPENDIX E

TABLE E-4 (cont.)

Child Costs and Net Work and Consumption Effects,
Third Child, "High-Income" Couple (three-year child spacing)

Age of Couple	Age of Third Child	Food i=0%	8%	13%	Shelter 0%	8%	13%	Util. 0%	Child's Clothing 0%	Trans. 0%
29	preg.	-322	-322	-322	-171	-171	-171	-166	-127	-43
30	<1	+110	102	97	-66	-61	-58	-37	+20	-102
31	1	128	110	100	-60	-51	-47	-32	25	-95
32	2	138	110	96	-56	-44	-39	-29	28	-94
33	3	77	57	47	41	30	25	43	3	-93
34	4	89	61	48	48	33	26	49	7	-114
35	5	99	62	48	49	31	24	52	8	-78
36	6	223	130	95	-16	-9	-7	10	89	+32
37	7	226	122	85	-17	-9	-6	11	91	32
38	8	228	114	76	-16	-8	-5	7	92	34
39	9	288	133	85	+50	23	15	-144	178	82
40	10	291	125	76	51	22	13	-143	180	84
41	11	243	96	56	24	10	6	-174	165	36
42	12	160	59	33	-138	-51	-28	165	-38	-406
43	13	160	54	29	-139	-47	-25	167	-39	-411
44	14	204	64	33	-117	-37	-19	193	-25	-373
45	15	353	103	50	+41	12	6	20	342	-18
46	16	356	96	45	42	11	5	20	345	-17
47	17	357	89	40	42	11	5	20	348	-17
48		-13	-3	-1	-10	-2	-1	-9	0	-24
49		-14	-3	-1	-10	-2	-1	-10	0	-26
50		-14	-3	-1	-10	-2	-1	-9	0	-26
51		-14	-3	-1	-10	-2	-1	-9	0	-24
52		-14	-2	-1	-10	-2	-1	-11	0	-26
53		-14	-2	-1	-10	-2	-1	-11	0	-26
54		-14	-2	-1	-10	-1	0	-11	0	-26
55-59		-75	-9	-2	-50	-5	-2	-50	0	-120
TOTAL		3236	1338	808	-528	-323	-288	-88	1692	-1859

APPENDIX E

TABLE E-4 (cont.)

Child Costs and Net Work and Consumption Effects,
Third Child, "High-Income" Couple (three-year child spacing)

		\multicolumn{8}{c}{Net Effects of Child on Family Consumption of}								
Age of Couple	Age of Third Child	\multicolumn{3}{c}{Medical Care}			Recr.	Educ.	\multicolumn{3}{c}{Total Expenditures}		
		0%	8%	13%	0%	0%	0%	8%	13%
29	preg.	250	250	250	−52	0	−393	−393	−393
30	<1	−10	−9	−9	−17	−3	−234	−217	−207
31	1	−4	−3	−3	−13	−3	−163	−140	−128
32	2	−1	−1	−1	−10	−4	−129	−102	−89
33	3	−37	−27	−23	−24	−25	−64	−47	−39
34	4	−34	−23	−18	−20	−26	−2	−1	−1
35	5	−35	−22	−17	−17	−25	+14	9	7
36	6	−12	−7	−5	−17	−16	98	57	42
37	7	−12	−6	−5	−18	−15	94	51	35
38	8	−13	−7	−4	−18	−16	101	51	34
39	9	−94	−44	−28	−5	+19	3	1	1
40	10	−95	−41	−25	−4	19	9	4	2
41	11	−120	−48	−28	−30	19	−289	−115	−67
42	12	+90	33	18	−66	−17	−112	−41	−23
43	13	91	31	16	−67	−17	−112	−38	−20
44	14	112	35	18	−46	−17	+140	44	22
45	15	63	18	9	156	+34	857	250	121
46	16	64	17	8	158	34	870	235	109
47	17	64	16	7	159	35	875	219	97
48		−7	−2	−1	−6	1625	1529	353	150
49		−7	−1	−1	−5	1625	1524	326	133
50		−7	−1	−1	−6	1625	1523	302	117
51		−7	−1	0	−5	1625	1529	281	104
52		−8	−1	0	−5	0	−82	−14	−5
53		−8	−1	0	−5	0	−82	−13	−4
54		−8	−1	0	−5	0	−82	−12	−4
55−59		−50	−6	−2	−20	0	−495	−60	−15
TOTAL		165	148	155	−8	6476	6977	990	−21

(Predicted values from App. D plus $400 in obstetrical costs and a $1625-a-year college education.)

hunches about the commodity inputs are those figures given by the USDA for comparable income classes in the urban North Central region for 1960–61 in the cases of food and medical care. For these two commodity classes the USDA drew upon prior detailed studies of likely inputs into a child. For the other classes, I retained various suspicions about the techniques apparently used (and only partly explained) by the USDA. But my estimates, like theirs, are hunches.

Two details of the calculations embodied in Table E–1 through E–4 require elaboration here. The first relates to the savings lost by the couple with the extra child. When the child is in the household, the couple saves less or dissaves more. This reduction in saving continues at a lower level after the child has left the home, according to the regressions, because the child has interrupted the wife's career and lowered her earning power. What happens to the lost savings? It might be made up out of reduced consumption in the couple's later years or it might remain as a net reduction in the bequest left by the couple to their heirs. One way or the other, the lost savings represents part of the bundle of commodities (C^H's) involved in the extra activities (including one's bequest) that would have been pursued without the extra child. I shall assume that the extra savings without the child gets consumed when the couple is sixty years old.

The net savings effect thus needs to be allocated among commodities and added into the alternative bundle of inputs. This is done in Table E–5. The knotty problem relates to the rate of interest. The couple without the extra child could have accumulated more savings (or borrowed less) at the real rate of interest on their financial assets. Strictly, one should accumulate the savings effect for each year forward to age sixty at the real rate of interest. For 1960 the real rate of interest on long-term bonds was about 0.9 percent per annum, depending on the nominal rate and the recent rate of inflation chosen. To economize on dreary calculations, I simplified by having their savings accumulate at an interest rate of zero in Table E–5, allowing simple addition of the savings effects for each year. The total savings accumulated at age sixty by couples without the extra child was then allocated across commodity groups according to the budget shares shown for childless couples of that age and the appropriate income class in Appendix D.

The other detail to be explained is the treatment of the per-child income tax deduction in Table E–5. In 1960 each extra child entitled families like these to about an extra $100 a year for as long as the child was a dependent. For the "low-income" couple this added up to

APPENDIX E

Table E-5. Adjusting the Alternative Bundle (H Bundle) for Accumulated Savings and Foregone Income Tax Deductions Per Child.

	"Low-Income" Family		"High-Income" Family	
	1st child	3rd child	1st child	3rd child
(1) Total undiscounted change in income due to extra child (ignoring tax deduction):	- $12,656	- $2,710	- $37,057	- $7,202
(2) Total undiscounted change in consumption:	-2,727	785	1,307	6,977
(3) Total undiscounted change in saving = (1) - (2):	-9,929	-3,495	-38,364	-14,179
(4) Income tax reductions caused by per-child tax exemption:	+ $1,903	+ $1,903	+ $2,371	+ $2,371
(5) Net accumulation to be spent without the extra child at age 60 = -(3)-(4):	$8,026	$1,592	$35,993	$11,808
Amount in H-bundle spent at age 60 on: food	1,962	389	7,307	2,397
shelter	1,182	235	4,287	1,406
utilities	707	140	3,855	1,265
transportation	669	133	5,104	1,674
medical care	383	76	2,681	879
recreation	144	29	1,001	328
education	0	0	0	0
all other	2,979	590	11,758	3,859
Total	$8,026	$1,592	$35,993	$11,808

Note: the total to be spent in the H-bundle at age 60 was allocated across commodity groups according to the shares of each group in age-59 consumption for a childless couple in each income class, given in Table D-2 of Appendix D.

about $1,903 for the 18 years the child was in the home, and for the "high-income" couple the deduction added up to about $2,371 by the time the child finished college. Perhaps the most logical way to treat this extra disposable income is to add it into the original income profiles in Appendix A. Not having done so, I shall equivalently enter it now in Table E–5 as an offset to the savings losses associated with the extra child. Accordingly, the money accruing from the income tax deduction is a subtraction from the H-bundle, and is allocated across commodities in the same way as the other saving accumulation. The only effect of not entering the tax saving directly into the original income series is to substitute age-sixty subtractions from the H-bundle for commodity expenditures associated with raising the child at earlier ages. This does not affect any of the properties of the relative cost index.

APPENDIX F. The Index of Relative Child Costs, 1900–70

The shares of different commodity and time inputs in the cost of a child and the alternatives to that child can be used as the weights for an index of relative child cost. The 1960 cost shares for the first and third children of a low-income couple at a 13 percent discount rate, given in Table 4–6 and Table 4–7 in Chapter 4, have been selected as weights for indices of relative child costs covering the period 1900–70. This appendix elaborates on the calculations that combined these cost shares with wage, price, and tax data to produce the indices shown in Figure 4–3 in Chapter 4 and used in some of the fertility regressions of Chapter 5.

Table F–1 summarizes the cost shares to be used as weights for pricing the bundles of 1960 inputs into a first child, a third child, and the alternatives to each. These weights, as noted in Chapters 3 and 4, are not really appropriate for the years before World War I. Before that time children did not have any great effect on women's labor force participation, and the children themselves worked quite a bit, especially before the turn of the century. Thus, as argued in Chapters 3 and 4, the secular rise in real wages probably left the relative cost of children unchanged from about 1900 to about 1920, and one should probably extend the average index values given below for the 1920s back to the turn of the century.

Table F–1. 1960 Weights Used in Calculating an Index of Relative Child Cost.

	Net time inputs	Food	Shelter	All other commodities	Total
Inputs into a 1st child:	.470	.152	.144	.234	1.000
Inputs into the alternatives to a 1st child:	.202	.114	.141	.543	1.000
Inputs into a 3rd child:	.446	.192	.133	.229	1.000
Inputs into the alternatives to a 3rd child:	.377	.100	.174	.349	1.000

Source: Tables 4–6 and 4–7.

APPENDIX F

Before 1900 the upward drift of wage rates probably slightly lowered the relative cost of children.

Table F–2 gives the wage, price, and tax series to be combined with the weights in Table F–1. The number of input categories has been considerably reduced from the detail shown in Tables 4–6 and 4–7. Some of the available price indices showed such similar movements over this century that there was little point in keeping the categories separate. In

Table F-2. Wage, Price and Tax Indices Used in Calculating an Index of Relative Child Cost, 1900-1970. (Base = 1960.)

Year	(1) Wage rate index	× (2) Marginal tax rate adjustment	= (3) Tax- adjusted wage index	(4) Food price index	(5) Rent index	(6) Index of all other prices	(7) Tax-exemption adjustment 1st child	(8) Tax-exemption adjustment 3rd child
1970	150.3	.9693	145.69	130.6	120.1	135.5	1.0090	1.0157
1965	115.1	1.0087	116.10	107.3	105.7	106.8	1.0068	1.0119
1960	100.0	1.0000	100.00	100.0	100.0	100.0	1.0000	1.0000
1955	81.5	1.0219	83.28	92.7	91.9	88.2	1.0003	1.0005
1950	65.7	1.0620	69.77	84.7	76.8	79.0	1.0078	1.0137
1945	44.0	1.0082	44.36	57.6	64.1	59.9	.9788	.9613
1940	27.5	1.2189	33.48	40.0	61.3	47.3	1.0689	1.1208
1935	24.4	"	29.80	41.5	55.2	46.7	"	"
1933	19.0	"	23.16	34.8	59.0	45.1	"	"
1930	22.1	"	26.94	52.2	80.6	49.5	"	"
1925	21.8	"	26.52	55.0	89.2	48.9	"	"
1922	19.7	"	24.01	49.7	83.6	49.1	"	"
1920	20.3	"	24.68	69.9	70.8	48.7	"	"
1919	23.2	"	28.23	62.0	60.2	41.6	"	"
1914	8.7	"	10.57	33.9	54.1	24.9	"	"
1910	7.6	"	9.25	30.8	53.6	24.1	"	"
1900	6.0	"	7.26	24.0	46.0	22.4	"	"

Sources for Table F-2:

Col. (1): the wage rate index was derived by splicing together the following series chosen to reflect trends in the wage rates facing women: for 1900-1914, the hourly wage rate given for the textile industry in Albert Rees, Real Wages in Manufacturing, 1890-1914 (Princeton: Princeton University Press, 1961), p. 46; for 1914-48: the NICB series on average hourly earnings for women, given in U.S. Bureau of the Census, Historical Statistics of the United States, Colonial Times to 1957 (Washington: GPO, 1960), p. 94, Series D 660; and for 1948-1970: gross average hourly earnings, workers in all nondurable manufacturing industry, as cited in the Economic Report of the President, Feb. 1971, pp. 231, 233, and Jan. 1972, p. 231.

Cols. (4)-(6): For 1914-1970, I used the price series used by the Bureau of Labor Statistics in its Consumer Price Index, cited in various BLS Bulletins. To derive the "all other" index, it was necessary to consult the underlying commodity weights given in BLS, Consumer Prices in the United States, 1953-1958: Price Trends and Indexes (Washington: GPO, 1959), BLS Bulletin no. 1256, Table 2. For 1900-1914, I used the cost of living indices given in Rees, op. cit., p. 74.

Cols. (7)-(8): derived according to the procedure described in the text to this appendix.

[375]

APPENDIX F

other cases, the weights for an input were so similar between the inputs into a child and the inputs into the alternative to the child that little would have been gained by keeping separate account of that input's price trend. The result of all these considerations was that the inputs were aggregated into all time inputs, food, shelter, and all other commodities.

Movements in income tax rates play two roles in calculating the relative cost index. The wage-rate index must be multiplied by a term reflecting the marginal tax rate for each year, to derive the after-tax dollar price of an hour of a family member's time. This is done in Table F-2. The other role played by income taxes is the reduction in total child costs through the exemption for dependents. The greater the real value of this exemption, the lower the relative price of a child.

The marginal tax rate for our low-income couple in 1960 was 17.62 percent. To derive the marginal tax rates for couples in a comparative position in the national income distribution in other years, one could track down the tax schedules in effect for each year. The returns to such a tedious procedure seemed low when it is reasonable and simpler to tie movements in the marginal tax rate to movements in average tax rates for the nation as a whole. Accordingly, I have assumed a fixed ratio of the relevant marginal tax rate to the average tax rates[1] to get marginal tax rates for 1942–70.

Before about 1942 couples like the 1960 "low-income" couple paid no income taxes. This is true whether the phrase "couples like" the 1960 couple refers to couples at the same percentile of the income distribution for each year, as I intend, or couples with the same real income in 1960 consumer dollars. The data in Table F-3 show that World War II brought about half the population into the income-taxed ranks, while the postwar inflation has kept them there ever since. Thus for the years before World War II the marginal tax rate for the low-income couple is zero. This fact is reflected in the column in Table F-2 that shows the marginal tax adjustment (i.e., the share of disposable in total personal income) as an index based on 1960.

When low-income and median-income families became payers of income taxes during World War II, the personal exemptions in the income tax structure suddenly became relevant to them. Each child began to entitle them to exemptions, the value of which varied with the marginal

[1] See U.S. Department of Commerce, *Survey of Current Business* 49, no. 4 (April 1969), 22–25, for ratios of disposable to total personal income. Recent editions of the *Economic Report of the President* yielded the same ratio for 1970. One minus this ratio was used as the average-tax-rate proxy to which the marginal tax rate was indexed.

APPENDIX F

Table F-3. The Share of the Population Paying Income Tax, and the Current-Dollar Value of the Personal Income Tax Exemption for Each Dependent, Selected Years, 1913-1973.

	Percentage of total U.S. population covered by taxable returns	Yearly dollar value of income tax exemption per dependent
1913	n.a.	$ 0
1918	7.7%	$200
1921	5.7	400
1925	4.2	400
1930	3.3	400
1935	3.0	400
1939	5.0	400
1940	9.4	400
1941	24.7	400
1942	41.7	350
1944	74.3	500
1945	74.2	500
1946	55.8	500
1948	56.2	600
1949	54.3	600
1950	58.9	600
1955	69.7	600
1960	73.1	600
1965	76.6	600
1969	--	600
1970	--	650
1971	--	650
1972	--	700
1973	--	750

Source: Lawrence H. Seltzer, The Personal Exemptions in the Income Tax (New York: Columbia University Press, 1968), NBER Fiscal Studies no. 12, Tables 9 and 19; John T. Noonan and Cynthia Dunlap, "Unintended Consequences: Laws Indirectly Affecting Population Growth in the United States," in U.S. Commission on Population Growth and the American Future, Commission Research Reports, vol. VI, Aspects of Population Growth Policy (Washington: GPO, 1972), p. 123.

APPENDIX F

tax rate and the dollar value of the exemption. To calculate the percentage effect of this exemption on the absolute and relative cost of a child, I took the following steps for each year since 1942:

(a) Multiplied the dollar value of the exemption by the low-income couple's marginal tax rate to get the current-dollar yearly value of the exemption;
(b) Multiplied this figure by 18 to get the total undiscounted value of the exemption over the 18 years of hypothetical childhood;
(c) Divided this figure by the year's cost-of-living index, to convert it into 1960 dollars;
(d) Divided the 1960-dollar figure by the undiscounted value of the inputs into a first child, and a third child, in 1960.

This percentage effect on the relative and absolute cost of a child was then indexed on 1960 so that the overall index derived by multiplying the pre-exemption index by this exemption-effect index gave values to be compared to a 1960 = 1.000 base.

This procedure gives the more conservative of two similar estimates of how strongly taxes have affected relative child costs over the years. Note that real values of the income-tax exemption in various years were compared to a total child cost bill *for 1960*. One could adopt a different, and equally reasonable, procedure which would slightly magnify the sensitivity of the final relative cost index to changes in the value of the exemption. One could have argued that the total pre–tax-exemption costs of, say, a third child in 1945 would have been lower than those for the 1960 couple by the same percentage that median or average family income was lower in 1945 than in 1960. Taking this approach would involve dividing the real value of the income tax exemption by a lower total child cost before 1960 and a slightly higher total cost after 1960. Had this approach been taken, the index of relative child cost would have dropped more sharply during World War II, and would have risen more rapidly since then, than in the estimates presented here. The choice of approaches, however, affects the indices by less than one percent, even for 1945, when the choice matters most.

Table F–4 displays the indices of relative child cost calculated according to the procedures just described. The indices show the sudden subsidization of children by the income tax system during World War II. They also reveal a gradual upward drift caused by the fact that 1960 children are time-intensive, so that their relative cost has advanced with the rise in real wage rates.

Table F-4. Relative Child Cost Indices, 1900-1970.

First Child

Year	(1) Price of inputs into the child (P_N)	(2) Ditto, adjusted for income tax exemption (P'_N)	(3) Price of inputs into alternative activities (P_H)	(4) Relative Child Cost Index (P'_N/P_H)
1970	137.32	138.56	134.83	1.0276
1965	111.09	111.85	108.57	1.0302
1960	100.00	100.00	100.00	1.0000
1955	87.10	87.13	88.24	.9996
1950	75.21	75.80	77.48	.9783
1945	52.86	51.74	57.10	.9061
1940	41.72	44.59	45.64	.9771
1935	39.20	41.90	43.88	.9549
1933	35.23	37.66	41.46	.9083
1930	43.78	46.80	49.63	.9929
1925	45.10	48.21	50.76	.9844
1922	42.36	45.28	48.97	.9246
1920	43.82	46.84	49.38	.9485
1919	41.09	43.92	43.85	1.0016
1914	23.74	25.38	27.15	.935
1910	22.39	23.93	26.03	.919
1900	18.92	20.22	22.86	.885

Third Child

Year	(1)	(2)	(3)	(4)
1970	137.06	139.21	136.18	1.0223
1965	110.90	112.22	110.16	1.0187
1960	100.00	100.00	100.00	1.0000
1955	87.36	87.40	87.44	.9996
1950	75.68	76.72	75.70	1.0134
1945	53.09	51.04	54.54	.9357
1940	41.59	46.61	43.80	1.0643
1935	39.29	44.04	41.28	1.0668
1933	35.19	39.44	38.22	1.0319
1930	44.10	49.43	46.68	1.0589
1925	45.45	50.94	48.09	1.0593
1922	42.61	47.76	45.71	1.0448
1920	45.00	50.44	45.61	1.1058
1919	42.03	47.11	41.83	1.1262
1914	24.12	27.03	25.47	1.0612
1910	22.69	25.43	24.31	1.0461
1900	19.10	21.41	20.96	1.0215

Note: the figures used in Chapter 5's regressions for decadal rates of change in relative child cost are based on simple averages of the index for a third child above for each census year and the year five years earlier. Thus, for example, the rate of change in relative child cost across the 1940's is the percentage increase from the 1935+1940 average to the 1945+1950 average.

[379]

APPENDIX F

A further adjustment which was to be made in these estimates proved not to be feasible. Since the relative cost of children depends on the choice of discount rate, which is likely to respond somewhat to real (inflation-corrected) rates of interest, it seems reasonable to incorporate interest-rate movements into the index. Most of the direct costs of a child come in the first eighteen years, while the inputs into the activities foregone in having the child are spread over a longer period. It thus seems reasonable that the higher the real rate of interest, the higher the subjective rate of discount, and the higher the relative cost of children.

This reasoning offers an extra potential explanation of fertility movements. The one time in this century when real rates of interest were abnormally high was in the deflation and depression of 1929–33, an era in which fertility declined fairly rapidly. The one time when real rates of interest stayed abnormally low was the decade of the 1940s (including the year 1950), when one could buy a house with a mortgage bearing a negative real interest rate—and when the birth rate jumped. Taking account of interest-rate movements looks very convenient for an economic hypothesis.

The difficulty with the interest-rate adjustment is that the relative cost of a third child is not monotonically related to the rate of discount, as one would think. An inspection of the data in Tables 4–7 and 4–9 shows that as the discount rate progresses from 8 percent to 13 percent, and from 13 percent to 18 percent, the relative cost of a third child actually falls—even though the relative cost rises considerably from 0 percent to 8 percent. We have, in other words, a case of net present-value reversal. The reason for this is that in the earliest years of the third child's life the value of the inputs into him fall short of the value of the home time and commodities that would have been enjoyed in these early years if he had not been born. In the later years of his childhood, the opposite is true. Yet after the eighteenth year the pattern reverses again, with the existence of the child, now out of the home, still implicitly taking away from his parents the extra enjoyments they could have bought with the (mother's) earning power and savings he removed over eighteen years. This complexity of the time pattern for the third child destroys any simple link between the relative cost of a third child and rates of interest and discount. While the first-child index still conforms to intuition (cf. Tables 4–6 and 4–8), the least cryptic and most justified procedure was to leave all relative cost indices unadjusted for movements in interest rates.

APPENDIX G. Selected Data Used in Regressions on State Child-Woman Ratios, 1900–70

Most of the variables used in analyzing fertility patterns in Chapter 5 are based on the U.S. Census of population. The ways in which the raw census data have been reworked to get the regression variables are described in the list of variable definitions accompanying Table 5–1. The measures of present and prior income, however, have been calculated by a more time-consuming and complicated procedure than was necessary for the other variables. This appendix describes the derivation of the estimates of current income per person in the labor force (YWORKER) and of prior income per capita (YCAPORIG), and gives the estimates of both.

The variable YWORKER, current income per person in the labor force, was derived by adjusting figures on current-dollar personal income per capita for the share of the population in the labor force, the cost of living by region and census year, and the share of personal income lost in taxes. The basic figures on current-dollar personal income per capita are those estimates given for states by Easterlin (1900 and 1919–21) and by the Office of Business Economics (1930 on).[1] To get closer to income per earner, income per capita was divided by the share of the population that was in the labor force, or—for the censuses of 1900 through 1930—gainfully employed. No adjustment could be made for the average number of hours worked per person, though it would have been desirable on theoretical grounds. The adjustment for the share of personal income lost to taxes was not difficult, since such figures are given by the Office of Business Economics.[2]

---

[1] Richard A. Easterlin, "State Income Estimates," in Simon Kuznets, Dorothy Swaine Thomas et al., *Population Redistribution and Economic Growth in the United States, 1870–1950*, Philadelphia: American Philosophical Society, 1957, vol. I, Table Y–1; Charles F. Schwartz and Robert E. Graham, Jr., *Personal Income by States since 1929*, Washington: GPO, 1956, Table 2; and recent issues of the *Survey of Current Business*.

[2] The share of disposable income in total personal income is given for 1929–68 in *Survey of Current Business*, vol. 49, no. 4 (April 1969), pp. 22–25. The 1968 share was used for 1970. For the U.S. as a whole the share of income taken in net taxes in 1920 was 0.4 times as large as the share taken in 1929. It was assumed that this ratio of 0.4 applied to each state as well between 1920 and 1929. For 1900 taxes were assumed to be zero percent of personal income.

APPENDIX G

The most difficult adjustment to the raw figures on personal income per capita was the adjustment for differences in the cost of living. For the United States as a whole, there is the readily available urban Consumer Price Index published by the Bureau of Labor Statistics. More difficult is the task of determining how rural and regional urban cost-of-living indices differed from the national index. For the most part rural cost-of-living indices are lacking, and it must be assumed that regional differences in urban indices for any year are proportional to regional differences in weighted rural-plus-urban indices. A few studies have estimated separate cost-of-living indices for cities in benchmark years. By averaging these together into rough regional indices, one can estimate the ratios of regional to national costs of living. This was done for the benchmark years 1880, 1909, 1935, and 1967.[3] The next step taken was to interpolate these regional-to-national ratios between the benchmark years so as to get rough estimates of them for the decennial census years. These interpolated ratios were then applied to the national cost-of-living index to get a set of regional indices for each census year. The estimates resulting from this procedure are given in Table G-1. The estimates are rough, and may overstate the cost of living in regions with heavier than average shares employed in agriculture, such as the West North Central and East South Central divisions.

These adjustments yield a measure of real disposable income per worker that seems roughly satisfactory for present purposes. Further work is necessary, however, to develop estimates of the background, or prior, income per capita (YCAPORIG) experienced by the generation of young adults now resident in a given state at the time of census. As mentioned in the text to Chapter 5, it was arbitrarily decided that the prior income should be that experienced twenty years earlier in the

---

[3] The main sources used were: for 1880—Philip Coelho and James F. Shepherd, "Differences in Regional Prices: The United States, 1851–1880," *Journal of Economic History* 34, no. 3 (September 1974), Table 2 (I am indebted to Philip Coelho for an advanced copy of their data); for 1909—Great Britain, Board of Trade, *Cost of Living in American Towns*, London: HMSO, 1911, Cd.5609; for 1935—Margaret Loomis Stecker, *Intercity Differences in Costs of Living in March, 1935—59 Cities*, New York: DeCapo Press reprint of 1937 edition, 1971, Works Progress Administration Research Monograph XII; for 1967—U.S. Department of Labor, Bureau of Labor Statistics, *Handbook of Labor Statistics—1970*, Washington: GPO, 1970, BLS Bulletin 1666, p. 326; and for extending the 1935 ratios of Mountain (Denver) and Pacific to national indices back to 1920—U.S. Department of Labor, *Handbook of Labor Statistics—1947*, Washington: GPO, 1947, BLS Bulletin 916, p. 108, and idem, *Retail Prices, 1890–1928* (1929), Bulletin 495, p. 31.

APPENDIX G

Table G-1. Regional Cost-of-Living Indices, Census Years, 1880-1970.

(New England, 1960 = 1.000)

	New England	Middle Atlant.	E.N. Cent.	W.N. Cent.	South Atlan.	E.S. Cent.	W.S. Cent.	Moun- tain	Pacific
1970	1.347	1.281	1.275	1.280	1.187	1.166	1.150	1.267	1.303
1960	1.000	.951	.947	.950	.881	.865	.854	.941	.967
1950	.803	.785	.779	.777	.731	.713	.711	.774	.789
1940	.482	.484	.480	.475	.453	.440	.443	.476	.482
1930	.584	.595	.582	.585	.572	.557	.557	.547	.588
1919-21	.626	.635	.606	.629	.638	.626	.607	.748	.650
1910	.337	.340	.316	.340	.358	.353	.332	--	--
1900	.298	.297	.275	.300	.313	.299	.289	--	--
1890	.323	.318	.294	.322	.336	.311	.308	--	--
1880	.363	.353	.325	.358	.373	.335	.340	--	--

Notes: Both in the construction of regional relatives and in the use of the estimates in deriving real incomes, certain states have been put in divisions other than those to which they are officially assigned: Kentucky has been included in the East North Central division rather than the East South Central, and Delaware, Maryland, and the District of Columbia have been shifted from the South Atlantic to the Middle Atlantic division. These shifts seemed in order in view of the similarity of the cost-of-living indices of cities in these states to those of cities in the regions to which they were re-assigned. Alaska and Hawaii were excluded from all calculations.

[383]

APPENDIX G

places in which the current state residents were born. This is obviously a rough way of tracking the income experience of young adults. Young adults' tastes are presumably affected by income experiences more recent than twenty years back, and including current income per worker along with incomes per capita twenty years earlier may not do full justice to the income history affecting tastes. Nor is the share of a state's current population coming from a given place of origin necessarily equal to the share of young adults born there. In addition, the migrating families' prior incomes may not have been in constant ratio to the average incomes in the places of birth, as the use of these averages implies. Yet the use of data on states and nations of birth and incomes per capita twenty years earlier seems to offer a reasonable proxy for aggregate prior income experience.

The derivation of prior income per capita (YCAPORIG) is a time-consuming procedure. One must first allocate the current population of young females (15–49) to different places of birth, both regions of the U.S. and foreign countries. Each place-of-origin share is then multiplied by the real income per capita in that place of origin twenty years earlier. The products are then summed to arrive at a measure of prior income per capita. The illustration in Table G–2, which is referred to in Footnote 10 to Chapter 5, should clarify the calculation of YCAPORIG. Note that the value of YCAPORIG turns out to be slightly less than the 1920 value of income per capita in Minnesota itself. This was the average outcome, though YCAPORIG was sometimes far below, and sometimes above, the prior income per capita in the state of current residence. YCAPORIG and the in-state prior income were strongly, but certainly not perfectly, correlated.

To calculate YCAPORIG with a twenty-year lag, it was necessary to add two sets of income estimates not needed for YWORKER. One was a set of estimates of personal income per capita by states for 1910, to be used in computing the prior income variable for the 1930 observations. The Easterlin estimates were not able to cover 1910. It was therefore necessary to interpolate between 1900 and 1920 incomes per capita on the basis of an aggregate resembling income originating in the state for 1900, 1910, and 1920. The interpolating procedure and the resulting estimates are given in Table G–3. These estimates are probably not very reliable, and any scholars requiring greater precision of 1910 income estimates than was needed here are advised to take greater care and make up their own interpolations.

The other set of extra income estimates needed for deriving YCAPO-

APPENDIX G

Table G-2. Illustrative Calculation of the Value of Prior Income per Capita (YCAPORIG): The Case of Minnesota, 1940.

(1) Place of birth	(2) Share of 1940 Minnesotans born there	(3) 1920 personal income per capita there (in 1960 $)	(4) = (2) × (3)
Other countries	.106	$ 465	$ 49
New England	.0029	1288	1
Mid. Atlantic	.0087	1372	12
E.N. Central	.0747	1159	87
S. Atlantic	.0020	601	1
E.S. Central	.0021	540	1
W.S. Central	.0026	771	2
Mountain	.0042	869	4
Pacific	.0026	1350	4
Minnesota and all other*	.7942	902 (Minnesota)	716
Total	1.0000		$876 = prior income per capita (YCAPORIG)

*All other = all other states within the same region plus a small miscellaneous share from U.S. overseas possessions, etc.

[385]

APPENDIX G

Table G-3. Interpolated Estimates of 1910 Personal Income Per Capita, Non-Western States.

(current dollars per person)

Alabama	$137	Nebraska	296
Arkansas	139	New Hampshire	272
Connecticut	318	New Jersey	335
Delaware	252	New York	396
Florida	217	North Carolina	117
Georgia	154	North Dakota	309
Illinois	382	Ohio	287
Indiana	262	Oklahoma	195
Iowa	287	Pennsylvania	282
Kansas	276	Rhode Island	325
Kentucky	190	South Carolina	128
Louisiana	173	South Dakota	280
Maine	251	Tennessee	157
Maryland	249	Texas	192
Massachusetts	358	Vermont	264
Michigan	279	Virginia	166
Minnesota	277	West Virginia	176
Mississippi	123	Wisconsin	251
Missouri	278	Contiguous U.S.	277

Method of interpolation: (1) Compute a proxy for state income originating in non-service industries: value of product in manufacturing minus costs of materials in manufacturing, plus value of products in agriculture, plus 0.86 times the value of the production of mining. Repeat this calculation for each state for the censuses of 1900, 1910, 1920. (The mining coefficient of 0.86, or one minus 14 percent, is based on Gallman's observation that the cost of materials was usually somewhere between 12 and 16 percent of the value of mining output in the nineteenth century: Robert Gallman, "Commodity Output, 1839-1899," in William N. Parker (ed.), Trends in the American Economy in the Nineteenth Century (Princeton: Princeton University Press, 1960), NBER Studies in Income and Wealth no. 24, p. 53).
(2) Divide by the state's population for each of the three censuses.
(3) Compute the share of the 1900-1920 movement of this proxy for income originating per capita that occurred in the decade 1900-1910.
(4) Multiply one plus this share by the Easterlin estimate of personal income per capita in 1900 to arrive at the proxy for state personal income per capita in 1910.

APPENDIX G

RIG is a set of incomes per capita in 1960 dollars for the various foreign countries sending large numbers of immigrants to the United States. Scholars have made some attempts to calculate international ratios of GNP per capita for the last 100 years. These ratios are obviously very crude impressions and are beset by unresolvable index number problems. Nevertheless the available estimates do correspond to what one would have felt were the ratios of the foreign background incomes of immigrants to the average background incomes of native-born Americans. To capture the changing relationship of foreign to domestic income levels, I averaged rough estimates of four foreign areas' income positions relative to the U.S. The averaging used the shares of immigrants from each of the four areas as weights. Table G-4 reports the final average ratios of foreign to U.S. prior income. These ratios were multiplied by the average personal income per capita in the U.S. to get the background incomes of immigrants. Some accuracy was presumably lost in the aggregation of countries of origin into only four groups, and in the use of the same ratio for all states of immigrants' residence at the time of the census. The ratios in Table G-4 nonetheless seem like a more efficient device for capturing the changing mix of socioeconomic backgrounds of U.S. immigrants than the use of a whole set of immigration variables specific to countries of origin.

With these side-calculations of background income, and with several hours at the calculator, it proved possible to calculate the constant-dollar background incomes for each state for each of the seven censuses used in the fertility analysis of Chapter 5. The estimates of prior income per capita (YCAPORIG) are presented in Table G-5, for the benefit of scholars seeking to rework the analysis of fertility or the determinants of support for education. For a wider group of scholars, the underlying data on each state's real per capita income since 1880 are presented in Table G-6.

APPENDIX G

Table G-4. Average Ratios of Foreign to U.S. Income Per Capita Since the Mid-Nineteenth Century.

Census year for child/woman ratio (C.f. Ch.5)	Year of hypothesized experience of foreign income per capita for immigrants	Period used for immigration share weights	Great Britain	Northwestern Europe other than Great Britain and Ireland	All other	Canada	Immigration-weighted average ratio of foreign to U.S. income per capita
1970	1950	1956-57	.5435	.3533	.2283	.6902	.3278
1960	1940	1946-50	.7752	.6357	.3721	.6667	.5577
1950	1930	1936-40	.7874	.5591	.3976	.6732	.5117
1940	1920	1926-30	.6536	.4706	.3464	.6797	.4438
1930	1910	1916-20	.7936	.5794	.3333	.8016	.4438
1920	1900	1906-10	.8621	.5862	.3276	.7672	.4213
1910	1890	1896-1900	.9716	.6329	.4327	.8051	.5207
1900	1880	1886-1890	1.0811	.6795	.5378	.8430	.7116
1890	1870	1876-80	1.1905	.7262	.6429	.8810	.7992
1880	1860	1866-70	"	"	"	"	.8327
1870	1850	1856-60	"	"	"	"	.8127
1860	1840	1846-50	"	"	"	"	.7613

Procedure: (1) Divide the rest of the world into the four areas listed above. (2) For each year of hypothesized foreign income experience from 1840 through 1950, guess roughly at the ratio of GNP per capita in each area to GNP in the U.S. Use the available ratio of GNP per capita comparing Great Britain to the U.S.; for the other Northwestern Europe category use the ratio of German to U.S. GNP/cap.; for all other use the ratio of Italian to U.S. GNP/cap.; and for Canada use the available Canada/U.S. ratio. (Sources for interpolated census-year relatives: (a) "Economic Growth: The Last Hundred Years," National Institute Economic Review, no. 16 (July 1961), p. 37; and (b) E. H. Phelps Brown and Margaret H. Browne, A Century of Pay (New York: St. Martin's Press, 1968), Chs. 1A, 2A, 3A.) (3) Multiply each area's income relative by the share of immigrants coming into the U.S. from that area in each period. For Canada, use only the share of the Canadian-born population residing in the U.S. in the census year used for child-woman ratios. Allocate the remaining reported immigrants from Canada to the other three areas in proportion to the direct immigrants to the U.S. from each. (4) Sum these products of income relative times immigration shares to get the average ratios reported in the right-hand column. These ratios are graphed in Figure 7-5, and were multiplied by the level of personal income per capita for the contiguous U.S. to get the foreign levels of average background income, like the figure of $465 in Table G-2 above, used to calculate YCAPORIG.

[388]

APPENDIX G

Table G-5. Estimated Prior Personal Income per Capita, States, 1900-1970. (1960 consumer dollars)

Current census:	1900	1920	1930	1940	1950	1960	1970
Prior income yr.:	1880	1900	1910	1919-21	1930	1940	1950
State							
Alabama	244	301	400	510	491	665	1191
Arizona	--	--	--	885	901	1076	1611
Arkansas	266	347	457	569	450	717	1150
California	--	--	--	1119	1108	1343	1813
Colorado	--	--	--	925	959	1093	1677
Connecticut	628	749	804	1094	1345	1616	1933
Delaware	563	724	748	1082	1287	1642	2068
Florida	241	385	628	740	850	1113	1590
Georgia	236	283	437	551	550	765	1325
Idaho	--	--	--	856	909	1031	1638
Illinois	567	786	1004	1173	1193	1377	1934
Indiana	452	654	782	896	853	1079	1717
Iowa	498	651	821	890	859	1040	1714
Kansas	428	612	786	919	796	913	1619
Kentucky	372	447	613	676	584	707	1223
Louisiana	401	438	523	692	638	808	1423
Maine	406	590	700	921	933	1043	1378
Maryland	484	672	729	1110	1163	1382	1773
Massachusetts	659	804	881	1224	1245	1442	1749
Michigan	509	610	775	1042	1001	1263	1804
Minnesota	480	624	760	876	910	1115	1633
Mississippi	249	288	360	464	375	532	1023
Missouri	454	605	784	903	926	1066	1672
Montana	--	--	--	825	896	1145	1833
Nebraska	480	664	829	874	876	928	1688
Nevada	--	--	--	1105	1051	1427	1975
New Hampshire	507	633	731	967	1034	1137	1490
New Jersey	624	760	829	1087	1242	1489	1899
New Mexico	--	--	--	693	672	887	1460
New York	668	851	930	1308	1408	1515	1913
North Carolina	174	236	334	558	519	730	1318
North Dakota	487	624	827	719	553	759	1515
Ohio	527	719	817	999	1047	1248	1780
Oklahoma	338	463	632	832	699	877	1505
Oregon	--	--	--	1001	865	1173	1738
Pennsylvania	579	732	754	1064	1185	1239	1755
Rhode Island	915	773	812	1162	1181	1384	1741
South Carolina	194	242	364	530	433	697	1167
South Dakota	477	594	792	773	643	784	1481
Tennessee	261	346	458	650	611	790	1346
Texas	308	464	572	859	736	965	1673
Utah	--	--	--	745	875	1015	1556
Vermont	463	559	746	903	952	1033	1398
Virginia	236	366	478	676	704	1031	1565
Washington	--	--	--	1003	1005	1210	1790
West Virginia	273	389	522	812	746	909	1420
Wisconsin	458	593	740	939	953	1088	1668
Wyoming	--	--	--	1036	957	1176	1835
District of Columbia	--	--	--	1167	1345	1190	2100

Table G-6. Real Personal Income per Capita after Taxes, States, 1880 and 1900-1970. (1960 consumer dollars)

State	1880	1900	1910	1919-21	1930	1940	1950	1960	1970
Alabama	224	294	388	496	468	626	1136	1548	2181
Arizona	--	--	--	927	914	1011	1536	1900	2499
Arkansas	232	308	419	537	392	563	1067	1466	2228
California	--	--	--	1518	1470	1686	2109˙	2425	2931
Colorado	--	--	--	963	1032	1106	1687	2082	2601
Connecticut	738	933	944	1247	1544	1832	2119	2404	3047
Delaware	534	741	741	1082	1320	1778	2193	2366	2576
Florida	212	358	606	676	783	1080	1613	1956	2709
Georgia	231	275	430	542	529	730	1297	1654	2417
Idaho	--	--	--	790	884	950	1538	1733	2246
Illinois	640	945	1209	1351	1358	1520	2117	2431	3022
Indiana	462	662	829	953	874	1125	1795	2047	2527
Iowa	469	673	844	888	846	1025	1725	1846	2574
Kansas	335	623	812	927	782	876	1624	2013	2628
Kentucky	329	436	601	655	547	651	1147	1483	2106
Louisiana	412	443	521	696	629	793	1422	1725	2350
Maine	410	628	745	966	960	1056	1380	1638	2152
Maryland	484	687	732	1132	1180	1422	1804	2114	2731
Massachusetts	804	1020	1062	1428	1394	1567	1866	2104	2765
Michigan	538	673	883	1170	1094	1372	1953	2160	2749
Minnesota	489	690	815	902	916	1073	1639	1939	2568
Mississippi	245	281	348	446	346	485	970	1268	1977
Missouri	439	627	818	920	850	1073	1699	1951	2523
Montana	--	--	--	831	899	1171	1913	1924	2398
Nebraska	436	707	871	879	868	902	1746	1973	2575
Nevada	--	--	--	1242	1472	1767	2213	2615	2999
New Hampshire	545	718	807	1040	1086	1159	1604	1873	2401
New Jersey	716	933	985	1262	1397	1645	2080	2494	3119
New Mexico	--	--	--	632	595	764	1378	1793	2165
New York	793	1088	1167	1608	1663	1710	2138	2447	3046
North Carolina	172	230	327	550	500	701	1290	1580	2357
North Dakota	553	697	909	721	509	717	1520	1633	2175
Ohio	545	807	908	1154	1122	1346	1888	2157	2685
Oklahoma	238	394	587	824	648	819	1462	1940	2545
Oregon	--	--	--	1130	1022	1256	1862	1981	2419
Pennsylvania	629	842	829	1159	1172	1293	1817	2068	2640
Rhode Island	769	983	964	1339	1305	1487	1846	1937	2510
South Carolina	193	236	358	523	414	663	1120	1404	2187
South Dakota	486	610	824	849	597	736	1471	1715	2208
Tennessee	242	338	445	572	572	751	1298	1431	2313
Texas	288	478	578	881	724	951	1708	2000	2707
Utah	--	--	--	737	904	996	1545	1858	2227
Vermont	463	638	783	918	953	1018	1361	1623	2108
Virginia	228	351	464	653	657	1000	1539	1826	2624
Washington	--	--	--	1173	1104	1335	1937	2130	2672
West Virginia	239	374	492	799	708	876	1387	1622	2225
Wisconsin	480	651	794	991	992	1111	1708	1980	2516
Wyoming	--	--	--	1196	1039	1244	1931	2110	2579
District of Columbia	--	--	--	1862	2080	2363	2520	2704	3523
United States	501	693	827	1047	1045	1219	1761	2056	2661

Index

agriculture: demand shift in, 183, 249; depression of 1920s, 174; in fertility patterns, 164–66; growth of, 253; income shift away from, 248–50; labor employment in, 183, 248; population shift away from, 218, 230, 231; and urbanization, 164–66. *See also* farm women; farms

baby boom: after World War II, 12–13, 21–23, 34, 135, 138–40, 169–73, 209–15; and education, 209–15; in 1950s and 1960s, 22–23, 138–39
Becker, Gary S., 38, 44n
birth control: Catholic attitudes toward, 23, 67–68, 167; education related to, 39–40, 207–15, *tables, 210, 212–13*; in higher-status families, 19–20; imperfect contraception and birth probabilities, 61–66; and income inequality, 8–9, 181–82; pill and IUD, 23; Place's propaganda for, 10; socioeconomic factors in, 64–66
birth rate: decline from 1800 to middle of 1930s, 137–38; decline from 1860 to 1935, 174–76. *See also* baby boom; fertility patterns
blacks: birth rate, 138; effect of children on father's work time, 276; fertility patterns, 168–69
boarders and lodgers, 115n, 279, 281
Bowen, William, 111, 263, 267, 274, 346

Cain, Glen G., 110
capital accumulation, rate of, 253–56
Carter, Anne P., 257
Cartter, Allan, 215
Catholics: attitudes toward birth control, 23, 67–68, 167; education related to family size, 39, 40; fertility patterns and marriage, 166–67
child care time, 98-99, 102; chore effects, 319–21, *table, 320*, class differences in, 304–07; and education, 26–27, 102; and sibling position, 26–27, 197–203, *table, 202*, 285–87, 316–19; of working mothers, 27, 199, 307–16, *table, 310–15. See also* time inputs
child costs, 13, 64; in baby boom and bust, 22; discount rate, 96–97; education related to, 41–43; and modernization, 20–21; rural and urban, 84, 132–33; and savings, 96; and status, 20; and taxes, 17, 135, 376, 378; total, and child inputs, 346–73, *tables, 347–70, 372*; and wages, 16, 20–21
child costs, relative, 83–136, 163–64, 170; class differences, 132–33; and commodity inputs, 85, 89–93, 102–10, *table, 104–08*, 121, 124–25; definition of concept, 84–87; economic influences, model of, 14–18; for first and third children, by income level, *tables, 126–31*; formula, 89–97; index, 98–136, 374–80, *tables, 374, 375, 377, 379*; and job-interruption effect on wage rates, 261–73; movements over time, 133–36; and time inputs, 98–99, *table, 100–02*; and work time, 15–16, 42, 100–21, *tables, 112, 116*
child labor, 16; wage rates, 21
child-woman ratio, 144, *tables, 149–53, 158–59*, 381–90, *tables, 383, 385, 386, 388–90*
children: earnings, 21, 90–91, 120–24, *table, 122*, 282–84; effects on consumption patterns, 322–73, *tables, 324–45, 347–72*; family inputs related to, 66–77, 85–86, 89–95, 98–99, 102–03, 109–10; on farms, 16, 42, 119–21, 133; in home, effects on work time of family, 274–84, *tables, 278, 280–81*; investments in, and fertility, 181–217; labor-intensive, 42, 95, 110, 113, 132; time-intensive, 16, 132; unplanned or unwanted, 63–66; work at home, 16, 42, 90–91
chore effects, 319–21, *table, 320*
climate, population growth affecting, 6

[391]

INDEX

Coale, Ansley, 139–40, 173
Cohen, Malcolm S., 277
commodity inputs, 44–49; and child costs, 85, 89–93, 102–10, *table, 104–08*, 121, 124–25; and sibling position, 201, 204–05
consumption patterns: and child costs, 16–17, 92, 121, 124–25; effects of children on, 322–73, *tables, 324–45, 347–72*; and modernization, 20–21
costs, family, analysis of, 45–58. *See also* child costs

demand shift: in agriculture, 183, 249; and child costs, 16–17; and fertility reduction, 11; government influence on, 256–57
Duncan, Beverly, 206

Easterlin, Richard A., 22, 38, 82, 139, 140, 170
education: and baby boom, 209–15; birth control related to, 39–40, 207–15, *tables, 210, 212–13*; and child care time, 26–27, 102; child costs related to, 41–43; expenditures for, 27–29, 209–15; family inputs related to, 68–69, 209–15; fertility related to, 23, 38–42, 65–66, 140, 167–68, 170–73, 209–15; and GNP, 211; and labor force, 239–42, *table, 241*; of mother, 207–09; school support and fertility, 9, 24, 27–29, 182; sibling position and school achievement, 25–26, 184–207; tastes and aspirations related to, 41
Engel, Ernst, 102
Engel's Law, 248–49
environmental quality and population growth, 5–6

family: fertility analysis of, 37–82; intergenerational influences on behavior, 72–74; siblings, *see* sibling position
family inputs, 66–74; child-related, 66–77, 85–86, 89–95, 98–99, 102–03, 109–10; and education, 68–69, 209–15; prior, in fertility pattern, 18–20, 141; tastes related to, 68–74, 162; total, and child costs, 346–73, *tables, 347–70, 372. See also* commodity inputs; time inputs
family planning: and family input preferences, 66–74; imperfect contraception and birth probabilities, 61–66; models, analytical, 43–61; timing of births, 59–61
family size: education related to, 23, 38–42, 207–09; and income inequality, 8–9, 25–27, 181–82; optimal number of births, 57–61; and sibling achievement, 184–207, *tables, 191–94, 196–97*; and total-expenditure elasticities, 124–27
farm women: child care time, 99; work at home and in farming, 117–19; work loss in pregnancy, 114
farms: children on, 119–21; 133; children's work on, 16, 21. *See also* agriculture
fathers, effects of children on work time, 110–11, 274–78, *table, 278*
fertility: aggregate, and school inputs, 209–15; class differences in, 79–81; economic aspects of, 12–13; economic influences, model of, 14–18; education related to, 23, 38–42, 65–66, 140, 167–68, 170–73, 209–15; historical data on, 80–81, 137–77; income inequality related to, 6–11, 24–34, 174, 181–84; income related to, 138, 140–43; and investments in children, 181–217; and labor force, 10–11, 24, 182–83, 216, 258–59; and modernization, 20–21, 74–81, 138; and race, 168–69; and socioeconomic mobility, 81–82
fertility analysis of households, 37–82
fertility patterns: cross-sectional, 18–20, 145–69, *tables, 146–61*; decline, 1800 to middle of 1930s, 137–38; decline, 1860–1935, 174–76; in 1920s, 173–74; 1965 and later, 139; postwar boom and bust, 21–23, 169–73. *See also* baby boom; since Civil War, 137–77
fertility reduction: and demand shift, 11; economic aspects of, 12–13; and educational achievement, 185; and income inequality, 8–9; and labor force, 10–11; and modernization, 12, 20–21

[392]

fertility-status relationship: in baby boom, 23; negative, in cross-sectional pattern, 18–20
Finegan, T. Aldrich, 111, 263, 267, 274, 346
food prices: and child costs, 16–17, 95; and modernization, 20
foreign-born population, 230–31

Gallman, Robert, 225
Garfinkel, Irving, 275, 276
government, influence on income, 256–57
Greenberg, David H., 275, 276
Guilbert, M., 305

Haines, Michael R., 282
Hall, Robert, 276, 277
Hermalin, Albert I., 25
Hill, C. Russell, 304–06

immigration, 30, 230–31, 239–44
income: baby boom related to, 22; current, and prior outputs per person, 22; estimates, data on, 142–43; fertility related to, 138, 140–45, 162–64; population growth reduces, 3–5; prior income experience, 145, 162–63
income inequality: aggregate, measurement of, 217–19; and agriculture, 248–50; before Civil War, drift to concentrated wealth, 219–32; and capital accumulation, 253–56; and family size, 8–9, 25–27, 181–82; fertility related to, 6–11, 24–34, 174, 181–84; government influence on, 256–57; historical trends in, 217–35; and inflation, 244–46; and labor supply, 30–31, 216–59; measures of, 220–21; in 1920s, 174; and sibling position, 25–27; and technological progress, 250–53; and wages, 30, 33–34, 232–33
inflation, income and wages affected by, 244–46
inputs, see commodity inputs; family inputs; time inputs
interest rates, 380

Japan, fertility increase recommended, 10

Jencks, Christopher, 181
Jews, education related to family size, 39, 40
job-interruption effect, 92, 93, 113, 114, 261–73, *table, 268–72*
Jones, Alice Hanson, 225

Keller, Robert, 252
Kelley, Allen C., 282
Kendrick, John W., 252
Kosters, Marvin, 275, 276
Kuznets, Simon, 234, 249

labor force: and education, 239–42, *table, 241*; fertility increase and reduction affecting, 10–11, 24, 182–83, 216, 258–59; growth of, 235–44, 258–59; and immigration, 30, 230–31, 239–44; and income inequality, 30–31, 216–59; quality growth, 236–44, *table, 238–39*. See also wages; working mothers
labor-saving and labor-using bias, 250–53
labor unions, 246–48
land: availability of, 248; collapse of values in 1920s, 174
Lazear, Edward, 261
Leibowitz, Arleen J., 304, 306
Lerman, Robert I., 277
Lewis, H. Gregg, 247

McIntosh, Susan, 110
macroeconomic theories on fertility and income inequality, 9–11, 24, 29, 182–83, 216, 259
Main, Jackson T., 225
Malthus, Thomas Robert, 9
Markus, Gregory, 206–07
marriage: agriculture related to, 165; of Catholics, 166–67; education related to, 167–68; in fertility patterns, 137, 165–68; late, and fertility, 39; and working women, 42n
Michael, Robert T., 261
microeconomic theories on fertility and income inequality, 8–11, 24, 181–82, 216
Mincer, Jacob, 264–67
modernization: and consumption, 20–21; and fertility, 20–21, 74–81, 138

INDEX

mothers, working, *see* working mothers

Namboodiri, N. K., 38

Olson, E., 214

parents: living with grown children, 109; support by children in old age, 109–10
Paul VI, Pope, 167
Pius XI, Pope, 167
Place, Francis, 10
Polachek, Solomon W., 264–67
pollution, population growth increases, 5–6
population growth: environmental quality lowered by, 5–6; income inequality affected by, 6–9, 32–34; income per capita reduced by, 3–5; wages related to, 9–11
postwar baby boom, *see* baby boom
price index, relative, and child costs, 93–95
productivity, growth of, 252–53, 257–58

race and fertility, 168–69
Rea, Samuel A., Jr., 277
Reed, Ritchie, 110
Rees, Albert, 263–64
relative child costs, *see* child costs, relative
rent, expenditures for, 125
Ricardo, David, 4

Sato, Eisaku, 10
Shultz, George W., 264
sibling position: and achievement, 184–207, *tables, 191–94, 196–97*; and commodity inputs, 201, 204–05; and family inputs, 198–201; and inequality, 25–27; and time inputs, 26–27, 198–203, *table, 202*, 205–07, 285–321, *tables, 290–303, 310–15, 320*
Simon, Julian L., 275
Social Security, 109
socioeconomic mobility and fertility, 81–82
Soltow, Lee, 225, 229, 231
Stafford, Frank P., 304–06
status in fertility patterns, 18–20, 23
Sweet, James A., 114, 119

sweet old mother effect, 114
Sweezy, Alan, 140, 173
Szalai, Alexander, 304, 305

tastes: education related to, 41; family inputs related to, 68–74, 162
taxes and child costs, 17, 135, 376, 378
technological progress, 250–53
time inputs, 44–49; and child care time, 202–03, *table, 202*; and child costs, 98–99, *table, 100–02*; and sibling position, 26–27, 198–203, *table, 202*, 205–07, 285–321, *tables, 290–303, 310–15, 320*
Tolley, G. S., 214
Turchi, Boone A., 274–77

unions, 246–48
urbanization and agriculture, 164–66

Vanek, Joanne, 304

wages: before Civil War, 232–33; and child costs, 16, 20–21, 89–90n, 120–21, 135; 1860–1929, 233; fertility increase and decrease affecting, 182–83; and income inequality, 30, 33–34, 222–33, 244–46; and inflation, 244–46; job-interruption effect, 92, 93, 113, 114, 261–73, *table, 268–72*; and labor force growth, 236; occupational pay ratios, 222–24; population growth related to, 9–11, 24, 33–34; rate of change in skilled-wage ratio, 237, 240
wealth: concentration of, before Civil War, 219–32; shares of, held by top wealth-holders, 226–28
Williamson, Jeffrey G., 218, 252
Wilson, Maud, 98, 119
woman-child ratio, *see* child-woman ratio
women: child care time, *see* child care time; ever-married or single, *tables, 154–57, 160–61*; on farms, *see* farm women; late marriage and fertility, 39; work and age of marriage, 42n; work in home, late nineteenth century, 115
work time: and child costs, 15–16, 42, 110–21, *tables, 112, 116*, 278–82,

[394]

table, 280–81; of fathers, effects of children in home, 110–11, 274–78, *table, 278*

working mothers, 16, 21, 42; age-wage profiles, 266–67; child care time, 27, 199, 307–16, *table, 310–15*; and grown-up children, 113–14; job-interruption effect, 92, 93, 113, 114, 261–73, *table, 268–72*; work loss during pregnancy, 113, 114; work time and child costs, 110–21, *tables, 112, 116*, 278–82, *table, 280–81*

World War I and income distribution, 29, 30, 233

World War II: and child costs, 134–35, 170; and income, 140, 234; and population increase, *see* baby boom; and wages, 246

Zajonc, R. B., 206–07

Library of Congress Cataloging in Publication Data

Lindert, Peter H
Fertility and scarcity in America.

Includes index.

1. Family size—Economic aspects—United States.
2. Fertility, Human—Economic aspects—United States.
3. Income distribution—United States.   I. Title.

HB915.L56   301.32′1′0973   77–71992
ISBN 0–691–04217–9

DATE DUE